# MIGHTY
# EIGHTH

# ACES
# OF THE
# MIGHTY
# EIGHTH

## Jerry Scutts &
## John Stanaway

First published in Great Britain in 2002 by Osprey Publishing,
Elms Court, Chapel Way, Botley, Oxford OX2 9LP, United Kingdom.
Email: info@ospreypublishing.com

Previously published as Aircraft of the Aces 1 *Mustang Aces of the Eighth Air Force*, Aircraft of the Aces 19 *P-38 Lightning Aces of the ETO/MTO*, Aircraft of the Aces 24 *P-47 Thunderbolt Aces of the Eighth Air Force*

ISBN 1 84176 619 4

Editor: Sally Rawlings
Series editor: Tony Holmes
Aircraft profiles by Chris Davey, Keith Fretwell, Tom Tullis,
 John Weal & Iain Wyllie
Figure Artwork by Mike Chappell
Scale drawings by Mark Styling
Index by Alan Thatcher
Design by Tony Truscott

Origination by Grasmere Digital Imaging, Leeds & Magnet Harlequin
 Uxbridge, UK
Printed in China through Bookbuilders

02 03 04 05 06   10 9 8 7 6 5 4 3 2 1

**Note: Part one of this title also includes aces from the Ninth AF and the MTO due to the paucity of Eighth AF-only Lightning aces.**

Cover photograph: 2nd Lt Arthur C Cundy of the 352nd FS, 353rd FG in a propaganda shot taken in 1944. (© United States Air Force)

Back cover photograph: Bob Johnson and fellow 56th FG aces.

For a catalogue of all Osprey Publishing titles please contact us at:

**Osprey Direct UK, PO Box 140,
Wellingborough, Northants, NN8 2FA, UK**
E-mail: **info@ospreydirect.co.uk**

**Osprey Direct USA, c/o MBI Publishing,
729 Prospect Ave, PO Box 1,
Osceola, WI 54020, USA**
E-mail: **info@ospreydirectusa.com**

Or visit our website: **www.ospreypublishing.com**

# CONTENTS

Sometime during the course of the war in Europe, German aircrew prisoners of war were surveyed as to the fighter types that they would most and least least prefer to meet in combat. Not surprisingly, the majority chose the Spitfire as the type they would least like to encounter, whilst the P-38 Lightning was selected as the fighter they would prefer to engage.

Unfortunately the reason for this preference was not recorded, but the fact that the P-38 was identifiable at a greater distance (meaning that it was easier to both stalk and avoid), and the natural tendency of pilots flying single-engined fighters to feel a sense of superiority over multi-engined aircraft, must have been deciding factors in the view of German pilots. Moreover, the P-38 was often encountered in inferior numbers, thus ensuring the enemy an advantage during the engagement – indeed, by the time more Lightnings became available in June 1944, the decision had already been made to transfer the type out of the Eighth Air Force.

That the P-38 often flew operations at a disadvantage is a fact not unknown to either side of the conflict. That there were fewer Lightnings than any other American fighter was a fact mitigated by the worldwide demand for the P-38. Also, the Lightning was the only USAAF fighter type committed to operations over northern Europe powered by the Allison V-1710 engine, which proved so unreliable in the cold and damp conditions that the already modest force was further reduced in number.

For all its disadvantages, both real and psychological, the P-38 *did* spread a great deal of apprehension amongst Axis airmen and soldiers, especially in North Africa and the Mediterranean. Throughout the duration of the war, all sane Axis soldiers and aircrew expressed a healthy respect for the armament of the Lightning, which lived up to the fighter's popular name at least thanks to the murderous concentration of fire emanating from the battery of four .50-calibre machine guns and single 20 mm cannon fitted in the nose of the aircraft. German pilots also expressed surprise at the way the P-38 could pull into a zoom climb without the aid of a dive or full power application. Some opponents even learned to be wary of the Lightning's ability to turn almost within its own track and reverse positions with a pursuing fighter at altitudes below 25,000 ft.

Whatever the relative merits of the P-38 in combat against the Axis air forces over Europe and the Mediterranean, the fighter's pilots and groundcrews felt fervent affection for the twin-engined Lockheed design. The dedication of those men who first took the P-38 into combat in North Africa finally blossomed into a fighting record that boasted 37 aces by the end of 1943 – a figure higher than for any other USAAF fighter type in the desert war. Indeed, so successful was the P-38 in-theatre that the 82nd Fighter Group (serving with the Fifteenth Air Force over Italy and southern Europe) held the USAAF scoring record with more than 500 aerial victories for a number of months before ultimately being overtaken by the more numerous Mustang groups in March 1945.

USAAF pilots who flew the P-38 against the European Axis exhibited a combination of eagerness, dedication, skill and impudence in the face of a remorseless enemy. From the pioneers of *Torch* to the scrapping youngsters who relentlessly hunted the Luftwaffe in the air and on the ground in the spring of 1945, the P-38 aces played their part in the Allied victory.

# PIONEER P-38 ACES

The P-38 was involved in the first successful aerial engagement between an American unit and the Luftwaffe when, on 14 August 1942, fighters of the 33rd Fighter Squadron (FS) encountered a four-engined Focke-Wulf Fw 200 Condor on patrol off the coast of Iceland and succeeded in damaging the aircraft. According to the official version (disputed by several eye-witnesses), Lt Elza E Shahan of the 27th FS observed the combat from above and swooped down in his P-38 to finish off the stricken German reconnaissance bomber. Whichever squadron delivered the mortal blow, Shahan was credited with a half-kill and the P-38 secured its place in history as having achieved the USAAC's first aerial victory against the Luftwaffe in World War 2.

During June/July 1942 the 1st FG deployed to England using the long-range capabilities of the P-38F to cross the Atlantic. In August another batch of Lightnings was flown along the same route via Labrador, Greenland and Iceland. Of the 186 aircraft that set out 179 successfully made the trip, and the first operational sorties from England were subsequently flown between 28 August and the weeks immediately prior to the November invasion of North Africa (Operation *Torch*). The P-38 would enjoy its first successes, and betray its faults, while generating its first aces over the deserts of Algeria and Tunisia.

The two squadrons of the 14th FG (the 37th and 48th FSs, which left the 50th FS in Iceland) were the first to become operational on 11

**A quartet of anonymous P-38Fs fly in tight line astern formation for the camera over southern California in July 1942. Early-build Lightnings were heavily utilised in the training role by newly-equipped fighter groups prior to embarking overseas for the conflict in far-off North Africa**

November 1942. On that day the group flew its premier mission and, according to group records, encountered enemy aircraft for the first time. The first opportunity for heavy scoring came 13 days later when the 49th FS accounted for approximately 11 aerial victories and several ground claims. Lts Virgil Lusk and James Butler were each credited with four Savoia-Marchetti SM 81 Pipistrello transports, the former pilot having almost achieved the highly coveted 'ace in a day' status when he was awarded a fifth .SM 81 as probably destroyed – intriguingly, the squadron's Daily Intelligence Report actually credits Lusk (who was subsequently killed in a flying accident near NAS San Diego in P-38G-13 43-2307 on 9 March 1943) with the fifth kill!

On 28 November another 14th FG pilot almost became an 'ace in a day'. Lt Ervin Ethell of the 48th FS was on a reconnaissance mission over Tunisia when his flight bounced an escorted group of German transport aircraft. Flying on Ethell's wing that day was Lt Carl Skinner, while Lts James Butler and Redmond Evans of the 49th FS completed the flight that encountered the Ju 52/3ms, and their quartet of escorting Bf 109s, over Lake Bizerte.

Exploiting their height advantage, the American pilots dived into the enemy formation and Ethell swiftly downed four Ju 52/3ms and probably destroyed a Bf 109 that was after Skinner. The latter pilot was actually attacked by two Messerschmitts (later confirmed as Bf 109Gs from II./JG 53), one of which was shot up so badly by Ethell that it was last seen smoking and shedding pieces as it disappeared behind a hill. Despite the efforts

The associated caption for this superb Lockheed official photograph, released in July 1942, read as follows;

'DESIGN FOR VICTORY — Resembling winged monsters from Mars, these warplanes of revolutionary design are very much part of today's war in the clouds. They are Lockheed "Lightning" P-38's and rest on one of many Lockheed assembly lines awaiting final touches before joining other "Lightnings" in the fight for freedom. The P-38, super-streamlined and super-charged, is the world's fastest airplane, designed specially to intercept and destroy high-flying enemy bombers before they can unload their bombs on vital objectives. The nacelle in the middle of the center-section carries the pilot-gunner of this speedy fighter. It is a one-place machine, powered by two Allison engines. The "Lightning's" twin booms and twin rudders give it greater stability and streamlining.'

These E-models have been adorned with the old pre-12 May 1942 national marking (*via Aeroplane*)

of his squadronmate, Carl Skinner was shot down by the remaining German fighter, and James Butler also failed to return. Postwar research tends to suggest that they were the victims of Leutnant Gunther Seeger and Oberfeldwebel Stefan Litjens.

Three Lightning pilots had now scored a quartet of kills, but officially at least, none of them would go and achieve that all important fifth victory. However, another 14th FG pilot scored a signal kill (a Ju 88) on 28 November 1942, and he *would* subsequently go on to attain ace status – Lt Virgil Smith of the 48th FS was credited with a further four kills and one damaged by 12 December, thus becoming the first P-38 ace in the process.

Meanwhile, the 1st FG had flown out to Algeria from England, initially with just the 27th and 94th FSs, although the group eventually returned to full strength when the 71st FS eventually arrived in North Africa. Twenty-four hours after Lt Ethell had led his flight on its successful

Premier P-38 ace Lt Virgil Smith of the 48th FS/14th FG is seen posing in front of his P-38F-1 *"KNIPTION"* in England during the autumn of 1942. Within weeks of this photo being taken, Smith, and the rest of the 14th FG, were embroiled in the battle for North Africa (*Ilfrey*)

reconnaissance mission into Tunisia, both the 1st and 14th FGs encountered German aircraft once again, the groups' pilots being credited with two Bf 110s and two Ju 88s destroyed. Future aces Lt Jack Ilfrey and Capt Newell Roberts made their first claims on this mission, whilst Virgil Smith claimed to have damaged a *Zerstörer*.

A certain amount of confusion attends this mission in the light of Twelfth Air Force rethinking of victory claims. Jack Ilfrey remembers firing and getting hits on both Bf 110s engaged that day, and can also recall seeing Virgil Smith damage at least one of the German twin-engined fighters. However, sometime later in the war some authority within the USAAF decided to drop fraction credits for Twelfth Air Force victories and duly granted full credit for the 48th FS claim to another pilot, thus denying Smith any victory claim at all. The 94th FS claim, on the other hand, has remained divided between Roberts and Ilfrey in spite of the policy change.

The 1st and 14th FGs saw much action in the final weeks of 1942, and whilst the American pilots enjoyed numerous successes in battle, they also learned painful lessons at the hands of their battle-seasoned German and Italian opponents. Losses were suffered on the ground as well as in the air, for the 14th FG had nine of its precious P-38Gs destroyed in raids by Ju 87s and Ju 88s on its Maison Blanche base, in Algeria, on 16 and 20 November.

Both groups continued to suffer mounting casualties into 1943, for not only were inexperienced P-38 pilots having to face combat-hardened foes, they were being forced to do so from a numerically inferior position due to the paucity of Lightnings in North Africa. The Allies were committed to a broad front in-theatre, and the four (later five) P-38 squadrons were expected to not only patrol the area but also provide tactical ground attack support and, eventually, fighter escort for heavy bombers that were beginning to strike at strategic targets. North Africa was given a priority in allocation of the P-38, but even with almost total commitment of the fighter, there were simply not enough aircraft available to complete the various mission requirements.

Nevertheless, operations did continue, and the P-38 pilots slowly began to make their presence felt. For example, on 30 November 1942 single Bf 109 kills were claimed by Virgil Smith (his second confirmed victory) and Capt Joel A Owens, who also damaged another Messerschmitt fighter to register the first victories for the 27th FS – this was also the latter pilot's first encounter with the enemy.

On this historic occasion 16 P-38s of the 27th FS had escorted B-17s (of the 97th Bomb Group) sent to attack a naval base at Bizerte, in Tunisia. The bombers had already turned for home when Owens noticed a Bf 109 coming up fast through a hole in the cloud. Somehow the Lightning pilot collected himself after the excitement of seeing his first enemy fighter, and diving to close range scored telling hits around the wingroot and cockpit which sent the German aircraft rolling out of sight into the clouds below.

While he was climbing back to rejoin the bombers another Bf 109 was observed by Owens off to his left. The enemy fighter was just positioning itself for an attack on the Flying Fortresses when the 27th FS pilot slipped in directly behind it and shot the Messerschmitt down.

**Cadet Virgil Smith is seen apparently ready and eager for operational life whilst undertaking his flying training in 1941. He was finally rated a pilot at Luke Field, in Arizona, just five days after the Pearl Harbor raid had plunged America into World War 2 (*Ilfrey*)**

Capt Owens had followed the 1st FG out to North Africa 15 days prior to scoring his first kill, having flown at low level from RAF Chivenor, in Devon, across the Bay of Biscay and down into North-West Africa during the long flight.

On 2 December a flight of 94th FS P-38Gs flew a fighter sweep to Gabes, in Tunisia, which netted six kills, four of which were split evenly between future aces Jack Ilfrey and Newell Roberts. The latter pilot had led the sweep, with Ilfrey heading up the second element and Lts William Lovell and Richard McWherter flying as wingmen for the respective element leaders. The four P-38s thoroughly strafed the Faid Pass before continuing 'on the deck' to the port town of Sfax, where everything looked peaceful and a warship was spotted anchored in the harbour.

Pressing on on to Gabes from the north, the P-38 pilots saw a number of Bf 109s in the throes of scrambling from the airstrip as they arrived overhead. Roberts called out the enemy fighters to Ilfrey over the radio and the P-38s swiftly climbed to 1000 ft in what seemed like seconds, before plunging down into the enemy formation. Taking full advantage of their superior speed and height, each of the P-38 pilots claim a German fighter destroyed on the initial pass.

Roberts 'bagged' his first victim with a burst from dead astern at close range, describing the result of his fire in the following extract from his Form D – 'I hit the third one, giving it a long burst, and saw it blow up in the air'. Parts of the fighter scattered in all directions and some pieces hit Roberts's P-38, but he nevertheless made a hard turn to the left and shot down a second Messerschmitt ('I hit another Me 109 at about 200 ft and saw heavy black smoke pouring from it – Lt McWherter saw this plane crash to the ground') that he had managed to get into his sights.

After shooting down his first Bf 109, Jack Ilfrey made the mistake of turning through 180°, which duly brought him face to face with a second Messerschmitt fighter in the process of taking off. Rapidly taking aim, the Lightning pilot managed to shoot the German fighter down, but not before his opponent had shot up the P-38's left engine. Two more Bf 109s then latched onto Ilfrey's tail after the intrepid pilot had managed to out-turn another Messerschmitt despite the damage to his left engine. The American pilot somehow avoided the enemy gunfire long enough (his comment afterward was 'Nothing in life is so exhilarating as to be shot at and missed!') for Bill Lovell to come around and shoot the two German fighters off his comrade's tail. Jack Ilfrey became understandably enthusiastic about Bill Lovell at that point, and although he tried to confirm at least one of the Messerschmitts for his rescuer, the official record of the day only granted him one destroyed and a second Bf 109 damaged.

Joel Owens scored his second victory whilst escorting 301st Bomb Group (BG) B-17s on a raid to Bizerte just two days later. Flying 20 miles southwest of the target at 19,000 ft, the 27th FS pilot spotted a battle-damaged Flying Fortress being set upon by enemy fighters.

With his wingman, Lt Lee Mendenall, following behind, Owens rapidly closed on a Bf 109 that had just completed its run on the bomber and was turning into the attacking P-38s. Firing five bursts from head-on, the Lightning pilot saw strikes from 500 yards until he broke off at about 100 yards. Owens could not, however, confirm his kill as his attention was immediately diverted by other Messerschmitt that had arrived on the

**Although Virgil Smith is officially recognised as being the premier P-38 ace, this man came mighty close to achieving the coveted accolade in a single sortie on 28 November 1942. Ervin Ethell of the 48th FS/14th FG claimed four confirmed aerial victories and one probable on that date, and later wenton to unofficially destroy a further ten aircraft on the ground. He is seen here in his cadet days (*Jeff Ethell*)**

scene. All was not lost though for former 27th FS CO, Maj John Welt-man, saw the stricken fighter go down in flames just as he attacked yet another Bf 109. Owens' kill was doubly confirmed some weeks later when one of the grateful B-17 gunners made a delayed report that he saw the enemy fighter hit the ground and burst into flames.

## FIRST P-38 ACE

Sometime after the North African campaign had been completed the Twelfth Air Force inexplicably changed its policy concerning the award-ing of shared aerial victories. In the general shuffle of credits, the totals for 1942 were modified to affect the dates that certain P-38 pilots achieved their fifth victories. As mentioned earlier, Newell Roberts participated in the shooting down of six enemy aircraft between 29 November 1942 and 9 February 1943, and despite the policy change, he retains half-credit for the Bf 110 he shared with Jack Ilfrey on 29 November and an Italian Cant Z 1007 he helped destroy with another 94th FS pilot on 12 December. Thus, he is officially credited with five aerial victories.

Jack Ilfrey has always maintained that he scored his fifth and sixth vic-tories – a pair of Fw 190s – during a bomber escort mission on 26 Decem-ber 1942 (thus making him the premier P-38 ace), although officially these count as only his third and fourth *full* kills. Virgil Smith was origi-nally listed with two Bf 109s, a Ju 88 and a one-third credit for a Ju 52 that he attacked with two other pilots on 7 December 1942 before he claimed a Fw 190 five days later. Even with the half-credit for the Bf 110 on 29 November, he would have been credited with 4.83 victories under the old policy. He also claimed another Bf 109 on 28 December to give him ace status under any form of accounting.

However, the revised crediting gave him a full kill for the Ju 52 claimed on 7 December, thus making him an ace when he scored his Fw 190 vic-tory on the 12th. Far from being bitter about this revision of scores, Jack Ilfrey enthusiastically endorsed the status of his old aviation cadet class-mate, and fellow Texan, Virgil Smith as the first P-38 ace of the war. Since both of these pilots were pioneers in the deployment of the P-38 fighter against the European Axis powers, it is fitting that they should be the first to be recognised as successful fighter aces. What follows is a brief bio-graphical appraisal of their careers.

Virgil H Smith grew up in McAllen, Texas, and was enrolled in the first Civilian Pilot Training Program whilst still at college. He was selected for the Army Air Corps (later Army Air Forces) Cadet Program in April 1941, and graduated in the class of 41-1 at Luke Field, Arizona, on 12 December 1941. Smith joined the 14th FG's 48th FS in time to fly across the Atlantic to England with the group during the summer of 1942. After completing a handful of missions in western Europe, he moved with the 48th to North Africa in support of the *Torch* landings. After gaining his final victory on 28 December, Smith was involved in yet another combat 48 hours later near Gabes in which his P-38F was severely damaged. Whilst attempting to crash-land the stricken fighter, Smith struck a ditch and his aircraft exploded, killing him instantly. The USAAF's first P-38 ace was buried on New Year's Day 1943 in the European cemetery at Constantine, and then later reinterred in McAllen, Texas.

Virgil Smith's fellow Texan, Jack Ilfrey, was perhaps the paradigm

American fighter pilot, being both brave and unruly, and yet affable and skilled at the same time. Many of his commanders reported being happy to have a pilot of his calibre under their direction, yet at the same time felt uneasy at the daredevil risks he took in the air, or the lack of discipline he showed on the ground. After Jack had been demoted for some wild indiscretion with the 20th FG in England later in the war, his commander wrote a letter on his behalf requesting that his rank be reinstated lest an operational squadron be led into combat by a second lieutenant!

Ilfrey almost spent the war in internment when he and several other P-38 pilots were forced down in neutral Portugal whilst enroute to North Africa from south-west England. A malfunctioning fuel system had resulted in a hasty landing in Portugal during the flight to North Africa in November 1942. Following his unexpected arrival, Ilfrey was prevailed upon by his 'hosts' to demonstrate the controls of the then top secret P-38 that he flew – an armed soldier trained his weapon on the pilot in the cockpit to discourage any attempt to fly the P-38 away.

Ilfrey, however, was just reckless enough to depend on what he knew about his Lightning's sudden acceleration as soon as the throttles were advanced for taxying. He pointed out each feature of the fighter's behaviour as he started the engines and worked them up to the point of moving the aircraft. Without any warning, Ilfrey advanced the throttles and swept the observers off the wings when the aircraft lurched forward. Ignoring the standard take-off protocol, he hastily urged his P-38 into the air while the excited Portuguese made futile gestures at the impertinent American as he roared into the air, and back into the war.

Having survived 142 combat missions, Jack Ilfrey returned to civilian life after the war and worked quietly for many years as a banker in his

The irrepressible Jack Ilfrey stands by one of his P-38s in North Africa. At any moment his impish smile would cross his face, and German pilots or American commanding officers alike would be wise to take care! Despite perhaps being the unwitting victim of revisions to the Twelfth Air Force's kill credit policy post-North Africa, Ilfrey freely acknowledges that his old friend Virgil Smith was the first P-38 ace of World War 2 (*Ilfrey*)

Capt Newell Roberts of the 94th FS/1st FG was one of the first aces of the North African campaign, having scored five kills by 9 February 1943. Capt Roberts became Dr Roberts after the war, following the completion of courses at the University of California, the University of Liverpool and finally Baylor University in Texas (Roberts)

native Texas. He later moved into in real estate, and in 1979 wrote of his wartime experiences in his autobiography, titled after the P-38 that he used later with the 20th Fighter Group in England, the aptly named *Happy Jack's Go Buggy*.

Interestingly enough, all of the North African aces used the same P-38s that they brought down with them from England throughout their initial combat period. All were P-38F-1 models, and they that stood up surprisingly well to the Bf 109F/Gs and Fw 190s they encountered. P-38Gs began to appear at the beginning of 1943, and they eventually equipped all three Mediterranean Lightning groups until about the middle of the year when H-models arrived in-theatre.

It was an ironic feature of the Mediterranean air war that priorities forced P-38 units to use older variants well after other theatres had adopted advanced types – some new pilots in the 1st, 14th and 82nd FGs were more than a little surprised to find that they had been assigned older G- and H-models upon their arrival in the Mediterranean when they had left brand new P-38J/Ls behind in stateside training units!

Another pioneer P-38 pilot to attain Lightning ace status in North Africa was Capt Newell Orville Roberts, who was also a Texan, albeit transplanted from Indiana where he attended Purdue University. As mentioned earlier in this chapter, according to available records Roberts shared the Bf 110 with Jack Ilfrey on 29 November 1942, and got two Bf 109s three days later before he shared in the destruction of a Z 1007 with former 94th FS CO, Maj Glenn E Hubbard, on 12 December to give him more than three confirmed victories by the end of the year. He was credited with a further two aerial victories (both Bf 109s) on 7 and 9 February 1943 to make him a full-fledged ace, and claimed two more Messerschmitt fighters as probably destroyed and damaged. Roberts also participated in ground strafing raids against a large airfield discovered southwest of Tripoli on 8 January 1943 – he actually led two follow-up missions on this target which resulted in the destruction of a number of aircraft on the ground. Newell Roberts won the Distinguished Flying Cross with four Oak Leaf Clusters as a result of his successes.

The last of the pioneer P-38 aces to score five kills was Joel Owens, who, after securing early scores for the 27th FS in November/December 1942, failed to achieve his next victory until the last day of January 1943 – by

**This unique shot, taken in May 1943 following the 14th FG's return to combat after a three-month reorganisation period, shows, from left to right, Lt Col Troy Keith (Group Commander), leading American World War 1 ace Eddie Rickenbacker, C L Tinker and early P-38 ace Maj Joel Owens (Deputy Group Commander)** (*Owens*)

which time he had been made commander of the squadron. Having escorted a large formation of 17th BG B-26 Marauders on an uneventful raid on the town of Gabes, Owens was just about to break off the mission and return to base when a flight of Bf 109s bounced the Lightnings before a warning call could be given.

As the fighters split up an a wild manoeuvring battle ensued over several thousand feet, Owens saw his chance to attack two of the Messerschmitts. Instructing his element leader to take the fighter on the left while he took the one on the right, he dived down and lined up his intended victim in his gunsight. However, his fire flew wildly past the skidding target, leaving Owens to surmise that his foe had had plenty of experience duelling with Tomahawks, Kittyhawks and Hurricanes of the Desert Air Force, for his evasive manoeuvre was to pull straight up into a zoom climb. Rather than leaving the P-38 behind, this tactic only saw the Lightning close even more rapidly, which must have horrified the German pilot. Owens got off a few shots before the enemy fighter stalled out and went into a dive. Recovering several thousand feet closer to the desert floor, the Bf 109 pilot once again tried to outclimb the Owens, but this time the American centred his fire on the fuselage of the fighter and the *Jagdflieger* was obliged to jettison his canopy and take to his parachute.

Owens later transferred to the 14th FG to serve as its Deputy CO, and whilst fulfiling this role he scored his final victories – two more Bf 109s – on 10 May 1943. Following his tour of duty in North Africa, Owens went on to complete a further spell in the frontline flying P-38s in the European theatre with the Ninth Air Force's 370th FG. Even though he scored the requisite fifth victory late in the North African campaign, he is still counted as one of those pioneer P-38 aces of the initial operational period.

15

# DESERT WAR

By the end of January 1943 the 14th FG had been worn down by the heavy demands of its arduous mission schedule. Used primarily in the ground attack/support role, the group had lost 32 of its original complement of 54 pilots, and had just seven operational P-38s to its name when relieved on 28 January by the Lightning-equipped 82nd FG. The 14th FG was pulled out of the frontline and eventually allocated an additional unit, the 37th FS (formerly with the 55th FG). By the time the group returned to action in May, the North African campaign was over, and it turned its attentions instead to operations over the Mediterranean.

Despite suffering appalling losses, the combat record of the 14th FG was nevertheless impressive when the heavy odds against which it flew are taken into account – 62 Axis aircraft were claimed between 21 November and 23 January. On the latter date 16 14th FG P-38s bounced a number of German aircraft taking off from an airfield near Mendenine, shooting down a solitary Bf 109 before a general mêlée ensued in which six of the Lightnings and a number of other Axis aircraft were lost. Due to the feroc-

Seen flying over the southern Pacific in early 1942, a four-ship of heavily-weathered 82nd FG P-38Es formates beneath the open bomb-bay of a Hudson bomber for Lockheed photographer Eric Miller. The group undertook a rigorous training programme prior to being sent firstly to England in the autumn, and then on to North Africa in the New Year

The mangled wreckage of Lt Irvin Ethell's P-38F-1 *TANGERINE* is examined by Luftwaffe personnel soon after it was shot down whilst being flown by another a pilot from the 48th FS. Note the right gun bay panel which carries the aircraft's nickname (*Jeff Ethell*)

ity of the engagement, the American pilots were understandably too occupied to witness their victims crashing. Despite the 14th FG enduring near-crippling losses in both men and machinery, in the final analysis the determination of the group's crews justified its presence in the desperate struggle of the early desert war.

The shortage of serviceable P-38s in-theatre had been felt as soon as late December 1942, when the call went out for all available Lightnings in England to be rushed to the area. The 82nd FG responded to the call, being posted from St Eval, in Cornwall, to Tafaroui, in Algeria, just prior to Christmas. Flying their P-38s via the Bay of Biscay, a number of pilots engaged the enemy for the first time on 23 December whilst en route to North Africa. Four Ju 88s bounced the 95th FS, and its A-20 navigation leader, from the rear, quickly shooting down the Havoc and the trailing P-38 of Lt Earl Green – the latter pilot survived the incident and subsequently evaded both capture and internment.

Reacting quickly to the carnage occurring behind him, formation leader Maj Bob Kirtley wheeled around and turned head on into the German attackers. His wingman stayed with him as he followed the Ju 88s after they had broken off the engagement and dived into the clouds below. When the major came out of the undercast he found himself directly behind one of the fleeing fighter-bombers, so he closed to within

Premier P-38 ace Lt Virgil Smith is seen posing beside his P-38 on 14 December 1942 – just two days after scoring his all important fifth victory. As detailed in chapter one, Smith's final tally of six was not confirmed until years after the war when he was controversially given full credit for shared victories scored early on in his brief frontline career (USAF)

Factory-fresh P-38Gs have their engines run after being re-assembled following a precarious Atlantic crossing by freighter. This photograph was taken at Lockheed's British Reassembly Division, sited at Liverpool's Speke Airport, on 16 January 1943, each fighter spending between six and eight hours on the line having their engines checked at various rpm to ensure that they had withstood the sea voyage. Once passed fit for service, these Lightnings were rushed south to North Africa in order to relieve the chronic P-38 shortage at the front

100 yards of his target in order to make the most of the meagre 50 rounds per .50-calibre gun that he had been allotted for the flight – ammunition had been kept to a minimum in order to allow the Lightnings to carry more fuel for the long transit. As it turned out, the solitary burst that Kirtley managed to get off before his guns hissed empty was enough to start a fire in the left engine of the Ju 88, and the major duly watched his target glide into the sea. Lt Arthur Brodhead, who had followed Kirtley down, accounted for a second Junkers fighter-bomber.

Once safely ensconced in Algeria, elements of the 82nd FG commenced patrols over the eastern part of the North African battleground during the last days of 1942 – the group finally reassembled at Tafaroui in the first week of 1943. Fittingly enough, the first aerial victory to fall to an 82nd FG pilot in North African skies was scored by the man who would later become the group's top ace flying its most celebrated P-38. Lt William 'Dixie' Sloan of the 96th FS was part of an escort of 319th BG B-26s on what would become known as 'The Gabes Meat-run' on 7 January when he claimed one of six Bf 109s attempting an interception.

Sloan was self-effacing about his first victory, recounting in an inter-

This view, taken by a *Flight* staff photographer in December 1942, shows to good advantage the potent armament fit of the Lightning – four .50-calibre machine guns and a solitary 20 mm cannon. The armourer is seen here adjusting the belt feed of one of the machine guns (*Aeroplane*)

Another photo in the *Flight* sequence reveals the weather to be less than ideal for flying – winter mist would hardly be a problem once this Lightning arrived at its final destination – Algeria (*Aeroplane*)

view conducted many years after the war that the only reason he downed the enemy fighter was that it got in the way between him and his base at Tafaroui! On this mission Sloan used P-38F-15 43-2112 (nicknamed *"SAD SACK"*), which was the regular mount of future Lightning ace Capt Ernest Osher of the 95th FS. The latter pilot, who would go on to command this unit between 1 May and 26 July 1943, scored virtually all of his five victories in 43-2112. *"SAD SACK"* remained in the frontline until early 1944, during which time it was used by various pilots to destroy as many as 16 aircraft – a phenomenal success rate which earned it a reputation for being one of the best examples of the P-38 ever manufactured.

It seems highly likely that Capt Osher was using *"SAD SACK"* when he claimed his first victory (a Bf 109) during a bomber escort to Tunis on 29 January. Fellow 82nd FG pilot, and future ace, Lt Claude Kinsey also got a Bf 109 that had attempted to intercept the American formation – by the time the 96th FS pilot had been shot down over Cap Bon on 5 April, he had become the top P-38 ace in North Africa with seven confirmed aerial victories, two probables and one damaged.

On 30 January the Gabes area was visited once again by the 82nd FG's 96th FS, with a further eight victories being tallied. One confirmed and one probable (both Bf 109s) fell to Kinsey, an Fw 190 was claimed by 96th CO, and future seven-kill ace, Maj Harley Vaughn (his second victory) and yet another Bf 109 was credited to 'Dixie' Sloan.

In spite of these successes, the 82nd FG still had to contend with the same hardships which had all but destroyed the 14th FG. The Axis air forces continued to enjoy both numerical superiority and an edge in experience that resulted in the P-38 units suffering grievous losses and crippling battle damage. To make matters worse, the 82nd was also forced to sustain aircraft losses incurred by other Lightning operators within the Twelfth Air Force from its own limited stocks, resulting in the demand for P-38s reaching acute levels once again during the 'dark period' of January-February 1943. Spares were also in short supply, making necessary the unseemly sight of groundcrews swarming over damaged P-38s to cannibalise parts for their own worn, and near to unserviceable, aircraft.

Flying in the face of such adversities, the 96th FS opened its February scoring with an impressive seven victories for just one loss on the second day of the month. Sixteen P-38s were once again escorting B-26s of the 319th BG on an anti-shipping strike off Cape Bon when a swarm of German and Italian aircraft were encountered. The Lightnings were forced to take a defensive stand in a great Lufbery circle, with each P-38 following another for mutual protection.

Like Jack Ilfrey, 'Dixie' Sloan has been accused over the years of occasionally disrupting the strict 96th FS tactical discipline, but during this sortie all he did was simply shift his sights ever so slightly when a Bf 109 foolishly decided to enter the circle. The German fighter exploded under the concentrated weight of Sloan's fire, and every member of the circle witnessed the wreckage crash into the Mediterranean. When the Lufbery later broke up and the P-38s dashed for home, Sloan was bounced by another fighter which severely damaged his Lightning prior to being shaken off. Feeling rather vulnerable in his shot up fighter, the redoubtable young P-38 pilot was able to find cover with the very B-26 formation that he had earlier been protecting. So secure was Sloan with

A beaming Lt William 'Dixie' Sloan of the 96th FS/82nd FG poses by P-38F-15 43-2064 sometime between 2 and 15 February 1943. Sloan was surprised a few years ago by a telephone call from the leader a B-26 formation who renewed their wartime friendship by thanking him for his escort on 2 February 1943, and then jokingly chided him for stealing the Marauder pilot's victory while accepting the protection of the B-26's guns! (*USAF*)

his Marauder 'fighter cover' that he managed to shoot down an attacking Do 217 as the bombers left the target area – an event again witnessed by virtually the entire American formation.

Thirteen days later, during yet another B-26 escort, Sloan claimed his fourth Bf 109 to become the 82nd's first ace. He had been a relative 'wild-cat' within the highly disciplined 96th FS, whose strict adherence to radio procedures had led to many surprise bounces of the enemy by the group's P-38s – even German veterans of the campaign remarked favourably on this aspect of the squadron's fighting prowess postwar. However, like most other high scoring fighter pilots, Sloan often went beyond the bounds of discipline in the air, resulting in him scoring victories nearly every time he met the enemy. Indeed, not only did 'Dixie' Sloan enjoy more success than his comrades in the group, he also became the top-scoring ace of the Twelfth Air Force with 12 victories and 5 damaged.

The effect of air discipline on the 82nd FG is evinced by the fact that its credited victories were divided between more than 200 pilots. Aside from Sloan's haul, only the 96th FS's Flt Off Frank Hurlbut (nine destroyed, one probable and four damaged by 2 September 1943) and Lt Charles Zubarik (eight destroyed, and one damaged by the time he was shot down and captured on 24 May 1943) scored anywhere near double figures in the Mediterranean. The 82nd FG remained the top-scoring American fighter unit in the Mediterranean (with 553 victories) for almost two years before finally being surpassed by Mustang groups in 1945.

## 1ST FG

January 1943 brought more strategic missions on top of the tactical runs to Gabes, Sfax and Bizerte. Whilst participating in the former, the 71st FS of the 1st FG downed two fighters over Tripoli on the 12th of the month, one of these being credited to Lt Meldrum Sears (his second kill). Squadronmate Lt Lee Wiseman claimed his first victory on 4 February, and both pilots would enjoy more success during April.

Capt Ernest K Osher and his groundcrew stand by the famed P-38F-15 43-2112/ "SAD SACK", which the former used to claim most of his five victories. The veteran fighter had been credited with as many as 16 kills by the spring of 1944 (USAF)

Another man who would score heavily during early 1943 was Lt John Wolford of the 27th FS/1st FG, who had actually claimed his first victory (an 'Me 109E') on 3 December 1942 near Bizerte airfield whilst flying a P-38F. He lodged the following combat report for this action;

'Lt SULLIVAN and I turned left into two ME-109, which were diving from about 4 to 5000 ft above us. Lt SULLIVAN had completed his turn and I was about 100 yards behind him still turning. One ME-109 made a quick turn from his altitude, at this time about 1 to 2000 ft above us, to Lt SULLIVAN'S right and behind, and cut between Lt SULLIVAN and myself. I saw the E/A give Lt SULLIVAN one burst before I could bring my sights into line When I had turned sharply enough to bring my sights to bear, I gave the E/A a wild burst to try to turn him from Lt SULLI-VAN. Time did not permit me to line my sight carefully, because of the short distance between the E/A and Lt SULLIVAN, now about 50 yards. As I fired my cannon ran out of ammunition and two mg's jammed. Tightening my turn as much as I could, I slipped over the E/A to the right side, from which I took another shot with the two good guns. As I shot, Lt SULLIVAN started a turn to the right and the E/A followed. I observed the tracers entering the cockpit of the E/A. After the tracers entered the cockpit the E/A shook slightly and continued a gentle turn to the right, nosing down gradually. No evasive action was taken by the E/A, and the last time I saw him, he was headed straight down through the clouds, the clouds being about 3000 ft level. I could not follow him down because of the crippled condition of Lt SULLIVAN'S ship, behind which I weaved to keep off any further attack. No further attack was experienced. During my attack on the first E/A the second E/A evidently got a shot at me as I had a hole in my right wing tip, severing the navigation light wire, a glancing shot off the left wheel door, and a clean hole through one blade of the left propeller. I claim this E/A as destroyed.'

Wolford went on to add two more Bf 109s, a Fw 190 (plus a second Focke-Wulf damaged) and a Macchi MC 200 to his tally during March 1943, achieving ace status on the 23rd of the month. He was finally posted Missing In Action near Trapani on 19 May, having taken his score to five destroyed and two damaged.

Capt Darrell Welch (five kills and three damaged) was another veteran pilot of the 27th FS who claimed a Bf 109 (his second) on 23 March, and who go on to attain more victories during April. Similarly, Lt John Mackay (six kills and one probable) also downed a Bf 109 for his first score on 23 March as a precursor to more successes in April/May.

From the final days of March until the Axis surrender in North Africa on 13 May, the shrinking perimeter around Cap Bon, forced Luftwaffe transports to fly a hazardous route between Sicily and Tunisia. During April this narrow corridor offered long-ranging P-38s the opportunity to destroy 100+ aircraft – mostly Ju 52/3ms.

In the weeks prior to the 'slaughter', future Lightning aces began to score more freely. One such pilot was the 27th FS's Lt Daniel Kennedy in his colourful P-38G *THE BEANTOWN BOYS*, which he used to shoot down his first confirmed kill (an Fw 190) on 8 March. The 96th FS enjoyed great success 12 days later when it claimed 11 aircraft during an anti-shipping strike. Future seven-kill ace Lt Ward Kuentzel claimed his first two victories (Bf 109s) in P-38F-15 43-2153, whilst Claude Kinsey

Lt Gerald Rounds of the 97th FS/82nd FG flew a number of exciting missions from North Africa during the opening days of the Italian invasion. All five destroyed, one probable and two damaged claims credited to Rounds comprised Bf 109s. He particularly remembers his third victory on 24 May 1943 over Alghero airfield, on Sardinia, when he enticed a pursuing Messerschmitt to under-shoot his P-38, thus instantly switching from being victor to victim (*Gerald Rounds*)

97th FS/62nd FG pilot Lt Thomas Ace White scored a Bf 109 on 28 February 1943 for his fifth victory and an Me 210 on 11 March for his final claim. Both were scored in P-38G-10 42-12943 (*Blake*)

'made ace' in P-38G-10 42-12871 when he downed a 'single-engined two-seat Italian fighter'. Harley Vaughn also tasted success flying P-38G-5 42-12827 by downing a Ju 88, and Charles Zubarik claimed a pair of Bf 109s in his usual G-10, 42-13054.

The nature of air combat drastically changed during the first week of April as the Twelfth Air Force set about the wholesale destruction of the Luftwaffe's air transport fleet in the Mediterranean. Codenamed Operation *Flax* by the Allies, fighter patrols were set up to sever the Axis air bridge from Sicily to Tunisia. This was effectively achieved in just three days of fighting, the first combat taking place on the 5th when 50-70 transports, escorted by 30 fighters, were sighted heading for Cap Bon. The 1st FG's 27th FS waded into the formation and exacted a toll of roughly 16 aircraft for the loss of two P-38s.

Between them, John MacKay and Darrell Welch scored a good portion of the 27th's claims when they each accounted for three aircraft apiece. The latter pilot's trio of victories, comprising three Ju 52/3ms, earned him ace status, whilst MacKay claimed two Junkers transports followed by an Fw 189 twin-boom reconnaissance aircraft, which he chased inland before shooting it down – these successes took for his tally to four.

Elsewhere, the 82nd FG engaged a mixed formation of roughly 20 Bf 109s and Ju 52/3ms whilst escorting B-25 Mitchells of the 321st BG on an anti-shipping sweep. Once again the P-38 pilots seized the initiative and claimed nine transports and eight escort aircraft destroyed, but at a price – four Lightnings failed to return to base.

One of the P-38 pilots lost was Claude Kinsey, who had swiftly downed two Junkers transports in flames to raise his tally to seven victories when he felt a heavy blow to his body which he attributed to fire from the enemy escort. Even though he was badly injured and forced to fly at 350 mph low over the water to effect his escape, Kinsey managed to bale out of his stricken fighter near the Tunisian shoreline and struggle ashore. His legs were injured, he had burns on his face and he found out later that his ribs were crushed, all of which ruled out the chance of evading capture. Five Arabs quickly appeared on the beach where Kinsey was huddled and carried the wounded American to an Italian camp.

Five days later the 71st FS made its contribution to *Flax* when its pilots claimed roughly half of the 40+ Axis aircraft destroyed. During the morning patrol the squadron ran into a formation of Italian Savoia-Marchetti transports, escorted by Macchi MC 200 fighters, and by the time the P-38s were done, at least 20 transports and two fighters had been downed.

Meldrum Sears added four transports to the Ju 52/3m and Fi 156 that he had claimed in January to become the latest ace of the 1st FG, whilst Lee Wiseman 'bagged' two more Junkers tri-motors and a MC 200 to add to the Fw 190 he had claimed two months earlier. Forty-eight hours after his triple success he claimed his fifth, and last, victory (another Fw 190).

Soon after midday on the 10th the 82nd FG ran into yet another formation of 25 Ju 52/3ms, escorted by Bf 110s and Ju 88s, whilst escorting B-25s sent to bomb Cap Bon. The Lightnings claimed ten transports and three of the escorts while the B-25s also accounted for ten Ju 52/3ms.

One 97th FS pilot who achieved 'acedom' during this engagement was Lt Ray Crawford, who tore into the Junkers transports and swiftly claimed two of them to register his fourth and fifth victories. Lt Bill

Lt Jack Ilfrey and one of his groundcrew pose by various parts of *TEXAS TERROR*, alias P-38F-1 41-7587. Note that the sixth victory swastika in the top photograph has been hastily taped out, indicating that the Twelfth Air Force's policy change in crediting shared victories had already been acted upon by the 1st FG – this marking referred to a Bf 110 kill Ilfrey had split with the late Virgil Smith on 29 November 1942, the latter individual being posthumously credited with the whole victory (*both Ilfrey*)

Schildt of the 95th FS also got a Bf 109 to augment a Bf 110 kill scored on 31 January. Less than 24 hours later he too would be an ace.

Schildt's 95th FS took the scoring honours on the 11th. No fewer than 19 P-38s were on a *Flax* sweep when 20 transports, escorted by fighters, were sighted halfway between Sicily and Cap Bon. Two flights of P-38s tackled the escorts while the others tore into the Ju 52/3ms.

Schildt led his flight into the heart of the transports' formation and sent three of them flaming down into the sea. The scene quickly turned into one of carnage as the water seemed to be on fire with burning debris, pieces of Ju 52/3m jutting out of the water at varying angles. One transport landed intact on the surface and several crewmen were spotted clinging to the wings hoping to be rescued. Officially, the 95th downed all 20 Ju 52/3ms and seven of the escorts, including three Bf 109s, two Bf 110s (from III./ZG 26) and a solitary Ju 88, for the loss of three pilots. Schildt's trio of kills victories made him the 82nd's fifth ace.

Later that same morning the 96th FS flew a similar mission and ran into another formation of transports low over the water, duly dispatching five of them for the loss of a single P-38. One of the Ju 52/3ms was claimed by former Flt Off Frank Hurlbut, participating in his first mission since arriving from England – the young 20-year-old from Salt Lake City would eventually become the second-ranking ace of the 82nd FG. The 82nd was now the dominant USAAF fighter unit in the Mediterranean with 170+ aerial victories, and since the beginning of April P-38 pilots had claimed in excess of 100 transports, plus escorting fighters.

However, the crowning *Flax* mission was flown on 18 April when American P-40s and RAF Spitfires claimed 59 transports destroyed in a record operation. The Curtiss fighter stole further glory from the P-38 in North Africa by producing the top USAAF ace of the period in Capt Levi

Chase of the 33rd FG, who ended the campaign with ten victories. His P-38 equivalents were Claude Kinsey of the 96th FS and Meldrum Sears of the 71st FS, both of whom scored seven kills.

## THE END IN MAY

By the end of the fighting in North Africa the enlarged 14th FG had returned to the action once again, this time with a full group complement comprising three units – the 37th, 48th and 49th FSs. And although the surrender of the 250,000 Axis troops trapped on Cap Bon on 13 May had signalled the end of the Desert War, P-38 units were already ranging across the Mediterranean into southern Europe in search of the enemy.

Indeed, the 82nd FG's 95th FS claimed six Italian transports and three escort fighters south-west of Marettimo Island a full eight days prior to the Axis capitulation in Tunisia, Ernest Osher (flying *SAD SACK*) downing an SM 82 transport and a Macchi MC 200 fighter. He followed up this double success on 11 May with the destruction of a Bf 109 over Marsala, on the island of Sicily, achieving ace status in the process.

Two days prior to Osher's Bf 109 kill, the 14th FG had scored its first victories of the renewed tour when four aircraft were claimed. Amongst the successful pilots on this day was future seven-kill ace Capt Herbert Ross of the 48th FS, who was credited with the destruction of an MC 202. Twenty-four hours later it was the turn of Deputy Group CO, Maj Joel Owens, to at last 'make ace' when he added to the 14th FG's tally with a pair of Bf 109s – his first kill had been scored as long ago as 30 November 1942. He submitted the following combat report upon returning to base;

'1. While acting as leader of Big Ben (37th) Squadron escorting B-17s to Bo Rizzo A/D on 10 May 1943, the following engagements took place:

'2. I was leading a flight of six P-38s attempting to cover the withdrawal of the last group of bombers at 26,000 ft, then a red smoke shell burst and about 20 E/As appeared. One made an attack on White section and I turned into the attack. I stalled my ship and dropped about 2000 ft. I was immediately surrounded by four E/A, one of which made an attack from six o'clock. I waited until he started firing, then I broke sharply to the right then made a diving turn left and the E/A was about 150 yards in front of me. I fired two bursts and the E/A went down with a large volume of black smoke coming out underneath his engine. I did not watch the E/A, but instead turned into a new attack. I made a steep spiral dive to about 15,000 ft and levelled out, then two more E/A attacked, one from six o'clock and the other from four o'clock. I again broke to the right and followed with a vertical reversement. One of the E/A overshot me and was about a hundred yards in front of me, climbing to the left. I got on his tail and fired a long burst from 100 yards; he fell off into a spin and after about four turns of the spin he broke into flames and went into the sea. While I was watching him the other E/A made an attack and scored hits on my left rudder and radiator. I immediately went into a spin to about 4000 ft, went into some clouds and came home. The E/A did not follow.

'3. I learned when I returned to base that Lt Hendrix had seen both E/A burst into flames and fall into the sea. Claim: 2 ME 109s destroyed.'

Another pilot to secure 'acedom' in early May was Charles Zubarik of the 96th FS, whose controversial kills scored on the morning of the 5th

Lt Claude Kinsey had become the top P-38 ace in North Africa by the time he was shot down on 5 April after scoring his sixth and seventh victories – two Ju 52/3ms – off Cap Bon. Kinsey remained a PoW until escaping on 29 October 1943 and walking over a hundred miles back to Allied lines. He was subsequently posted back to the USA and saw out the remainder of the war as an instructor (*Blake*)

were achieved in rather unusual fashion . Whilst escorting B-25s north of Cap Serrat, Zubarik noticed that one of his engines was showing the early signs of trouble, so he reluctantly broke of the mission and turned back for home. He had no sooner reversed his course and set off for the 82nd FG's base at Berteaux when his engine started running normally again, so he decided to try and find his flight once more. However, rather than encountering P-38s, Zubarik ran straight into a formation of five Me 210Cs, and while he tried to get above the enemy to commence a diving attack, the Lightning pilot noticed two of the wildly manoeuvring Messerschmitts collide and fall into the sea!

He managed to stay above the remaining fighters, but wisely decided to make for home in view of their superior number, and the suspect nature of one of his engines. The troublesome Allison did eventually run away later in the flight, and Zubarik was forced to make an emergency landing in a wheat field. When he did finally coax his P-38 back into the air and affect a recover at Berteaux early in the evening, he was frustrated in his

71st FS/1st FG pilots who did well during the 10 April 1943 sweep of the transports re-live the action off Cap Bon for the camera – left to right, Lts Walter J Rivers (final total of 4 destroyed, 2 probables and 2 damaged), John L Moutier (final total of 4.5 destroyed and 2 damaged), Meldrum Sears (final total of 7 destroyed, including four Ju 52/3ms on this date) and Lee V Wiseman (final total of 5 destroyed, including two Ju 52/3ms and an MC 200 this date) (*USAF*)

Lt Charles J Zubarik officially gained his fifth victory on 13 May 1943 when he claimed an MC200 south-west of Cagliari, Sardinia. The two question marks at the right of his scoreboard signify a pair of Me 210s that he had forced to collide exactly a week prior to his Macchi kill. As these could not be confirmed by independent witnesses, the Twelfth Air Force refused to credit Zubarik with them, hence the question marks. The 96th FS/82nd FG's third-ranking ace was shot down and taken prisoner on 24 May 1943 (*James Crow via Steve Blake*)

attempts to get credit for the two colliding German aircraft. In the end he was denied these 'kills' by the USAAF, and had to settle for a pair of question marks as victory symbols on the side of his P-38 instead.

Zubarik officially confirmed his 'ace status' on 13 May when he destroyed an MC 200 south-west of Sardinia, and went on to score his sixth, and final, recognised victory on eight days later – his Bf 109 was just one of seven kills credited to the 82nd on this day. On 24 May he was shot down south of Vanafiorita airfield, fellow ace, and squadronmate, 'Dixie' Sloan violating official policy by refuelling and going back to look for Zubarik. Sadly, all he discovered was the burning wreck of a P-38G in the Sardinian scrub. When he returned home, a dejected Sloan found 'hot words and cold shoulders' for a welcome, but he was later overjoyed to hear that Zubarik was alive and a prisoner of war.

Other future aces enjoyed more luck during May, however, the 95th FS's Lt Louis Curdes adding two Bf 109s on the 19th to the trio of Messerschmitts he had claimed on only his second mission on 29 April. Frank Hurlbut got his second kill (an Fw 190) on the 20th, John MacKay of the 27th FS his fifth and sixth (and last) victories – two Bf 109s – on the 25th, future five-kill man Lt Sidney Weatherford of the 14th FG's 48th FS opened his account on the 28th (with a Bf 109), and finally Daniel Kennedy of the 27th FS finished the month with a Bf 109 on the 31st.

By the end of May 1943 P-38s were roaming all over in the western Mediterranean in search of the enemy, and within a few days they would be constantly engaging Axis aircraft over southern Europe proper.

# MEDITERRANEAN WAR

The first real victories beyond the North African campaign were the seizures of the islands of Pantelleria and Lampedusa, which were surrendered by the Axis without invasion on 11 and 12 June 1943 respectively. This followed in the wake of a severe pounding by aerial forces beginning 31 May, the wavering Italian garrisons deciding to capitulate to the inevitable.

P-38s were in the forefront of the action because of their longer range, and some fruitful engagements were fought. On 18 June the 96th FS engaged the enemy whilst escorting B-25s to Sardinia, the Lightning pilots being positioned low over the water when the first six enemy fighters appeared, followed by many until the battle turned into a general mêlée. The P-38s individually climbed into the action at about 10,000 ft, claiming 16 interceptors for the loss of a single fighter and no bombers.

Amongst the successful pilots was Lt Larry Liebers, who shot down two MC 202s and a single MC 205 to become the latest ace of the 82nd FG. Frank Hurlbut claimed a Bf 109 and an Re 2001 to take his tally to four, as did Lt Edward Waters courtesy of a Bf 109, whilst Ward Kuentzel claimed a MC 202 for his third victory. Finally, 'Dixie' Sloan also got an MC 200 to raise his tally to eight.

The 82nd FG enjoyed further success during the opening phase of the invasion of Sicily, five enemy fighters falling to unit during a ground attack mission on the Gerbini airfields on 5 July. A number of German and Italian interceptors had scrambled to engage the P-38s as they left the target and reached the Sicilian coast. 'Dixie' Sloan claimed a Bf 109 and a Re 2001 to break into double figures, whilst Lt Gerald Rounds of the 97th FS claimed another Bf 109 for his fourth kill.

Once the invasion had commenced, the 82nd temporarily flew sorties from Libya under the direc-

This photo was taken around 19 May 1943, soon after Lt Louis Curdes (centre) had claimed two Bf 109s for his fourth and fifth victories. Curdes and Lts J G Oliver (left) and R Embrey (right), accounted for four Bf 109s on the 19th. The former pilot later spent time as a PoW after being downed in August 1943, but went on to fly P-51s in the Pacific following his release, and score a solitary Japanese kill – plus a USAAF C-47 that was attempting to land at an enemy airfield in error. Curdes disabled the transport, forcing it to ditch offshore and allowing its crew to be rescued by friendly forces (*USAF*)

tion of the RAF's No 320 Wing. On the day of the actual landings (10 July) the 96th FS put up another sterling display by claiming seven *Schlacht* (ground attack) Fw 190s and solitary examples of the Ju 88, Bf 109 and MC 200. 'Dixie' Sloan 'bagged' the Italian fighter to become the leading ace of the Twelfth Air Force with 11 confirmed victories, whilst Frank Hurlbut got three of the Focke-Wulfs to become an ace with seven kills. Larry Liebers also confirmed one Fw 190 and damaged two others for his sixth victory. Ward Kuentzel claimed the Ju 88 and yet another Fw 190 for victories number five and six, and Edward Waters claimed the Bf 109 for his seventh, and final, score.

It was the turn of the 14th FG to get amongst the transports once again on 18 July, P-38s of the 37th and 48th FSs chancing upon 15 Ju 52/3ms heading for Sardinia whilst they were escorting a Sunderland flying boat on a rescue mission. The Lightning pilots jumped the hapless Junkers transports and shot them all down, four falling to Lt Lloyd Hendrix (his only victories) and two to future five-kill ace Lt Paul Wilkins. Pilots of the 48th FS shared the remaining nine transports, two apiece going to future aces Sidney Weatherford (taking his overall score to four) and Capt Herbert Ross (his second and third victories).

'Dixie' Sloan got his final kill on 22 July – the day Allied troops entered Palermo – during whilst escorting B-25s sent to bomb a railroad junction at Battopaglia, on the Italian mainland. Just after the Mitchells had left the target and set their noses down for more speed, a trio of enemy fighters attempted to intercept the fleeing bombers but were quickly driven off by the 26 escorting P-38s. Two more Bf 109s quickly joined in the fray towards the rear of the bomber formation, but they too were intercepted in time by Sloan's and Kuentzel's flights – both aces closed so tightly on their targets that they could see the pilots' yellow cloth helmets. The Lightning pilots fired their guns almost simultaneously, sending both enemy fighters down in flames.

Sixteen days later ten Bf 109Gs of II./JG 77 were on a *freie jagd* (fighter sweep) just off the south-west coast of Italy when they bounced 30 Lightnings from above. Sixteen of the P-38s were from the 96th FS, and they responded so quickly that they shot down the fighter flown by Leutnant Egon Graf and damaged Unteroffizier Philipp's Messerschmitt so badly it he had to force-land at Vibo Valentia. Frank Hurlbut claimed an 'Fw 190' during this operation as his eighth victory, and is likely that his victim was Leutnant Graf.

## INVASION OF ITALY

The end of August and beginning of September 1943 saw the Mediterranean-based P-38 units play an instrumental part in the return of the Allies to the European mainland via the Italian peninsula. For example, on 25 August the 1st and 82nd FGs were part of the surprise strafing mission on the airfields of the Foggia plain which resulted in over 100 claims for aircraft destroyed on the ground – Lt Joe Miller and now Maj Herbert Ross of the 48th FS also claimed an MC 202 apiece in the air. For Ross it would be his fifth (of seven) victory, while Miller would claim four with the 48th and a fifth with the British-based 474th FG in March 1945.

During the same period Lt Clarence Johnson of the 96th FS downed two Fw 190s on 20 August and two more Bf 109s on 2 September. He

Lt Clarence Johnson of the 96th FS claimed four enemy aircraft (MC 202 on 21 May 1943, two Fw 190s on 20 August 1943 and a Bf 109 on 2 September) before being posted to the 436th FS in England. He achieved 'ace status' with his new unit when he downed an Fi 156 on 22 June 1944, this victory also being the 436th's premier score. Johnson was later shot down and killed on 25 September whilst flying a P-51D-10 (*Blake*)

Lt Richard J Lee is seen wearing the DFC (the medal to the left) that he won for attacking several Italian fighters while one of his engines was disabled. He was credited with one MC 202 during the 21 August 1943 mission, later adding four more during his time with the 94th FS/1st FG (*R J Lee*)

Lt James Hollingsworth of the 37th FS (in British Guinea Base t-shirt) poses informally with his groundcrew sometime in mid-1943. Although only officially credited with three confirmed aerial kills and seven ground victories with the 479th FG, many historians believe that Hollingsworth enjoyed considerably more success. However, he loathed filing combat reports, and duly missed out on being officially recognised as an ace (*Tom Hollingsworth*)

48th FS pilots Bill Broome, Herbert Ross, Fred Haupt and John Lindstrom pose with Bob Hope in front of Ross's *2nd LITTLE KARL* at Saint Marie du Zit in July 1943. Hope was on one of his famed USO trips entertaining the troops, whilst the 48th FS was just beginning to build its incredible scoring record of 159 confirmed kills – the highest tally in the 14th FG. Herbert Ross was later nicknamed 'Herbie the Boat Sinker' following his precision attack on the famous pre-war Italian ocean liner *Rex*, which saw him put a bomb down one of the vessel's funnels (*Weatherford*)

would also later achieve 'ace status' flying P-38s in England, this time with the P-38J-equipped (later exchanged for P-51Ds, a type Johnson used to claim his sixth and seventh victories on 11 September, and in which he was later shot down and killed on the 23rd of the same month) 479th FG – indeed his fifth kill, scored on 22 June 1944, was also his unit's first confirmed victory. Fellow 82nd FG pilot Louis Curdes got his final two victories (Bf 109s) on 27 August in P-38G-10 42-13150, thus raising his tally to eight. The pilot then suffered mechanical trouble which forced him down near Benevento, where he was duly captured. Curdes remained in captivity for a only a matter of days, however, as he and several other P-38 pilots managed to effect an escape and subsequently survive behind enemy lines until crossing into Allied territory on

P-38F-1 41-7649 *"WALLY"* was used by 48th FS CO, Maj W C Walles, in late 1942. It is seen here just moments after take-off from Youks-les-Bains airfield, in Algeria (*Jerry Scutts*)

Lt Sidney Weatherford of the 48th FS admires the markings on his P-38G. The phrase *TOMMIE'S LUCKY PENNY* was a promise the pilot had made to his wife that he would turn up again after his combat days had ended – he scored five victories before he made good his promise. Sadly, flame-haired Sidney Weatherford was killed in action near Wonson, Korea, on 11 August 1952 whilst at the controls of an F-84D from the 58th Fighter-Bomber Group (*Weatherford*)

27 May 1944. Curdes later added a ninth kill to his tally on 7 February 1945 whilst flying P-51Ds with the 3rd FG in the Pacific.

On 2 September Clarence Johnson 'bagged' a Bf 109 destroyed and two probables in what was later described as one of the most intense operations flown by P-38s in the Mediterranean. Charged with escorting B-25s sent to bomb a marshalling yard near Naples, the Lightning pilots encountered a host of enemy fighters as they approached the Italian coast – 23 Messerschmitts were subsequently reported to have been destroyed for the loss of 10 P-38s. Bf 109Gs from JGs 77, 53 and 3 all participated in the engagement, and the *Jagdwaffe* admitted the loss of seven pilots, including 67-kill *Experten* Oberleutnant Franz Schiess, whilst claiming the destruction of 13 P-38s. All the B-25s survived the mission.

One of the most successful operations flown by P-38s in the latter part of 1943 was undertaken by the 37th FS on 9 October. Newly-promoted squadron commander Maj Bill Leverette was leading his unit on a fighter sweep of the Aegean Sea in support of British naval ships when a formation of Ju 87 dive-bombers was sighted about to commence an attack on the vessels. Leverette immediately dove after the diving Stukas in an attempt to intercept them before they could inflict serious damage to the ships below.

During the uneven fight that followed, 16 Ju 87s were claimed destroyed and five classified as damaged or probably destroyed. Bill Leverette was credited with the destruction of no less than seven of the Stukas, and he recounted this stunning action to Eric Hammel for inclusion in the latter's excellent volume, *Aces Against Germany - The American Aces Speak, Volume II* (Presidio Press, 1993);

'Until nearly the end of the first week of October 1943, the 14th FG was mostly flying in support of our troops in Italy. At the time, however, British Prime Minister Winston Churchill had committed a squadron of Royal Navy surface ships and a small contingent of RAF fighters and bombers to harass the large Italian and German force that was occupying

Lt Richard Campbell of Ferriday, Louisiana, saw action with the 37th FS from the end of the North African campaign to the invasion of Italy. He got his first two victories (Bf 109s) on 18 May 1943 whilst escorting B-17s on a raid against the Trapani Milo airfield on Sicily. An MC 202 and a third Bf 109 followed on 15 June and 9 July respectively. Campbell participated in one of the first B-26 raids to Rome ten days later, and 'made ace' with a brace of Bf 109s (plus one damaged) on 28 August. P-38G-15 *EARTHQUAKE McGOON* was his assigned Lightning throughout his tour. Campbell later served on the China-Burma-India front in 1945 (*USAF*)

the Dodecanese Islands, which are in the Aegean Sea off the south-west coast of Turkey. It was Churchill's plan to invade the islands and somehow bring Turkey into the war on our side. Churchill pestered Gen Dwight Eisenhower into providing a force of American fighters for this side-show operation, and the 1st and 14th FGs were selected. On 4 October, we suddenly moved from our more-or-less permanent base at Sainte-Marie-du-Zit, Tunisia – 30 miles south of Tunis – to a crude RAF satellite field known as Gambut-2, near Tobruk, Libya, about eight miles west of the Egyptian border.

'On 9 October, at 1030 hours, I took off with nine P-38s from the 37th FS. We were to cover a force of one Royal Navy cruiser and four Royal Navy destroyers that were bombarding the German and Italian garrison on the Isle of Rhodes. Shortly after take-off, two planes were forced to return to Gambut-2 because of engine trouble. This left me with Red Flight, which consisted of three P-38s. I was leading Red Flight and Lt Wayne Blue was leading White Flight.

This 27th FS/1st FG P-38G was forced to belly-land at the group's Gerbini base, on Sicily, on 6 September 1943 after sustaining combat damage. Two ubiquitous GMC trucks have been rapidly rigged up with lifting hoists in order to remove the forlorn fighter from the middle of the airfield (*Howard Levy via Aeroplane*)

Lts Hattendorf, Walker and Schoenberg of the 97th FS pose beneath squadron 'war horse' P-38F-15 43-2112, nicknamed *"SAD SACK"*. Frustratingly for Jack Walker, he finished his combat tour with four victories and a probable – although comments made by a German ace touring the USA years later tend to indicate that *he* may have been Walker's fifth confirmed victim, as he casually requested to see the P-38 man's flight plan to set the record straight! (*Blake*)

'We flew all the way on the deck to stay beneath the German radar coverage from Crete. We sighted the British warships at almost exactly noon, 15 minutes before we were scheduled to arrive. The ships were approximately 15 miles east of Cape Valoca, on the Isle of Scarpanto (Kárpathos). I contacted them on their radio-control frequency and was told they had *been* attacked. I misunderstood, however, and thought the controller had

The 96th FS's Lt William J 'Dixie' Sloan is seen in front of his P-38G-5 42-12830 *Snooks IV1/2* at the end of his combat tour on 9 August 1943, having accounted for eight German and four Italian aircraft between 7 January and 22 July. He remained the top American ace in the Mediterranean until 1944, and later flew over 50 missions with the redesignated USAF during the Berlin Airlift of 1948 (*National Archives*)

said that the ships were *being* attacked. I could see that the cruiser was smoking from the stern.

'I led my P-38s up to 6000 ft and began a counter-clockwise circle around the ships just out of range of nervous anti-aircraft gunners. As I reached 8000 ft and was about halfway through the first circuit, Lt Homer Sprinkle, the number four man in my flight, called out, "Bogies at one o'clock!" There was a cloud of them in the distance. They were slightly higher and approaching the ships from the north-west.

'I immediately added power to speed up the climb, and I changed course to pass slightly behind the bogies, in order to make a positive identification as to the type of enemy aircraft. It quickly became clear that they

**Looking rather pleased with himself at the end of a successful mission, Flt Off Frank Hurlbut of the 96th FS poses in the cockpit of his P-38G in mid-1943. Note the Lightning's unique (at least for a fighter) 'spectacle grip' cantilevered control wheel in the the pilot's right hand** (*Blake*)

**Wearing distinctive 'BA' unit codes on its radiator housing, this 96th FS P-38G is seen at Lecce, Italy, in late 1943** (*Fred Selle*)

were Junkers Ju 87 gull-winged dive-bombers, probably out of Crete or the airfield at Scarpanto. There were 25 or 30 of them, in three flights.

'Before we could get within firing range of the Stukas several of them made dive-bombing runs on the British warships. At least one hit was scored on a destroyer, which broke in two and sank immediately.

'As we closed on the Stukas – it was about 1215 – I told Lt Blue to hold up his flight momentarily in case there were more enemy aircraft, possibly fighters, following the Stukas. With my flight, I immediately closed on the left rear quarter of the Stuka formation. The obvious plan of attack was to get in close to the Stukas and clobber them with short, accurate bursts from our .50-calibre machine guns.

'Before the Germans knew we were there, I attacked the nearest enemy aeroplane ahead of me. I fired a short burst with the .50s from about 20°. Smoke poured from the left side of the Stuka's engine.

'The Stuka pilots who still had bombs aboard jettisoned them as soon as the shooting started. Several of my pilots also reported later that a number of the Stukas jettisoned their fixed main landing gear as well.

'As soon as I saw the smoke coming from the first Stuka, I broke to my left and attacked a second Stuka from its rear and slightly below. After I fired a short burst from about 200 yards, this aeroplane rolled over and spiralled steeply downward.

'I broke away to the left again and turned back toward the formation of Stukas. As I did, I saw both Stukas that I had already fired on strike the water. Even though each Stuka had a rear gunner armed with twin 7.92 mm machine guns on a flexible mount, I'm sure that neither of the rear gunners had fired at me.

'I attacked a third Stuka from a slight angle off its left rear. I opened fire at this aeroplane just as the rear gunner fired at me. The gunner immediately ceased fire, and I saw the pilot jump out of the aeroplane, although I did not see his parachute open. The gunner did not get out.

'I continued on into the enemy formation and attacked another Stuka – my fourth – from an angle of 30°. I observed cannon and machine-gun fire hit the Stuka's engine, and I saw large pieces of cowling and other parts fly off. The engine immediately began smoking profusely, and the Stuka nosed down.

'I broke away upward and to my left, and then I re-entered the enemy formation. Another Stuka was nearly dead ahead. I opened fire again with my cannon and machine guns from an angle of about 15°. The canopy and various parts of this Stuka flew off, and a large flame shot out of the engine and from along the left wing

Leading USAAF 'ace-in-a-day' Bill Leverette is seen here whilst still a flying cadet in early 1940 (*USAF*)

Now a fully-fledged fighter ace, Bill Leverette poses with fellow 37th FS pilot Bob Margison. The latter was credited with one of the Ju 87s downed during the epic 9 October 1943 mission, and also observed many of the splashes left by Leverette's seven victims after they had hit the sea (*Ethell*)

root. The gunner jumped out of the aeroplane as I passed it.

'Continuing into the formation, I approached a sixth Stuka from below and to his left rear, but on a crossing course that would take me over to the right rear, heading slightly away from it. I was closing so fast that the only way to bring my guns to bear was to roll the P-38 tightly left, to an almost inverted attitude. As my guns lined up on the Stuka momentarily, I opened fire at very close range and observed concentrated strikes on the upper right side of the engine. The engine immediately began to smoke, and I broke away slightly to my left. My element leader, Lt Troy Hanna (who claimed five and one damaged during this engagement, Ed.), saw this aeroplane strike the water.

'I attacked the seventh Stuka from straight behind and slightly below. The rear gunner fired at me briefly, but he stopped as soon as as I fired a short burst of my own. As the Stuka nosed slightly down, I closed to minimum range and fired a short burst into the bottom of the engine and fuselage. Some Stukas were known to have wooden propellers, and this one acted as though its prop had been shattered and completely shot away. The Stuka abruptly and uncontrollably pitched downward, and I was instantly looking broadside at a nearly vertical Stuka directly in front of me. I was already committed to passing underneath him, so I intuitively jammed the control yoke forward as hard as I could. I heard and felt a large *thump* as I went past him. Looking back, I saw a falling object that I at first feared was my left tail. But the tail was still in place. The

Lt Harry Hanna was credited with having destroyed five Stukas (and damaged a sixth) during the 9 October mission – these were his only successes in a 50-mission tour. He is seen here after having just been awarded the DFC for his part in the operation. Bill Leverette received the Distinguished Service Cross, the second-highest American military decoration (*USAF*)

Fitted with 360 US gal drop tanks, P-38Gs of the 96th FS undertake bomber escort duty (Blake)

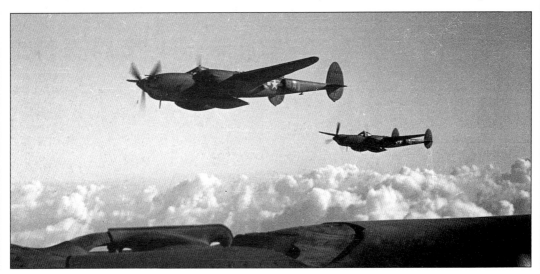

falling object was probably the Stuka pilot or rear gunner, who had been catapulted out of his cockpit by the negative G forces that were exerted on the plunging Stuka.

'After we landed, it became obvious that the jolt I had felt was from my left propeller cutting into the Stuka with almost two feet of all three blades. The damage to the leading edge of the blades was surprisingly light. We later reasoned, in view of the minor damage, that the prop most likely sliced through a light structure, probably the rudder and fin. This indicated that instead of passing underneath the Stuka, as I intended, I had actually grazed across the uppermost section of the steeply diving German aeroplane. Fortunately for me, the Stuka went down faster than my P-38, or I would have ploughed headlong into it.

'By this time, the surviving Stukas were approaching the south coast of the Isle of Rhodes, and all of my pilots had declared themselves out of ammunition. My own guns had all stopped firing – out of ammo – during my last pass. At about 1230, we made a 180° right turn around a lighthouse on a big rock off the southern tip of Rhodes and headed south.

'In addition to my seven kills, Lt Troy Hanna was credited with five Stukas destroyed, Lt Wayne Blue got one aeroplane (a lone Ju 88 twin-engined type that had closely followed the Stukas), Lt Homer Sprinkle (Hanna's wingman) got three Stukas and a Stuka probable, and Lt Robert Margison (Blue's wingman) got one Stuka. That's 16 Stukas and 1 Ju 88.'

German records admit to the loss of eight dive-bombers, but Leverette believes that the total of sixteen is accurate as one of the P-38 pilots descended to the surface of the water to count the splashes left by the downed German aircraft and confirmed that the number was definitely in double digits. Whatever the truth of the matter, Leverette claimed a record number of confirmed kills for a single P-38 flight in the ETO/MTO, and was duly awarded a Distinguished Service Cross.

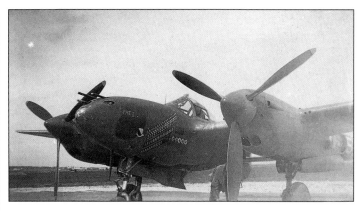

Although of poor quality, this rare scrapbook photo shows 14th FG CO Col Oliver Taylor's P-38G *PAT II*. The colonel's impressive combat record has been meticulously recorded on the fuselage just forward of the wing root (*Taylor*)

Maj Warner Gardner (wearing a personalised A-2 jacket adorned with 95th FS patches) is seen conversing with his groundcrew in front of P-38J *"LITTLE BUTCH V"*. Gardner, who gained all five of his victories in June/July 1944, later died on 9 September 1968 as a result of injuries he had suffered in a hyrdoplane accident during a race on Lake Michigan 24 hours earlier (*Blake*)

Lt Franklin Lathrope and Cecil Quesseth are seen in southern Italy in 1944. Lathrope became one of the last aces of the 94th FS when on 10 May 1944 he claimed two Bf 109s to add to his previous trio of Messerschmitt fighters destroyed (*Cook*)

With his P-38J streaming oil (note the black coating beneath the right engine and lower tailpane, and the feathered propeller), the pilot of this 27th FS/1st FG Lightning has decided to formate closely with the 2nd BG B-17Gs below him in order to rely on them for protection in an impromptu exchange of roles (*IWM*)

## 15TH AIR FORCE

At the beginning of November 1943 all P-38 units were transferred to the newly-organised, and strategic-optimised, Fifteenth Air Force. The record of the P-38 with the Twelfth Air Force was impressive, for in the year of operations from the commencement of the North African campaign to the transfer to the Fifteenth, the P-38 had generated 37 aces who had claimed more enemy aircraft than any other fighter type serving in the USAAF. By comparison, American-flown Spitfire squadrons had generated 12 aces and P-40 units just 10.

Veteran P-38 aces continued to accrue victories with the new Fifteenth too, Bill Leverette, for example, scoring a further four kills starting with a Bf 109 during an escort mission to Athens on 14 December. Paul Wilkins also claimed victories for the 37th FS, downing a Bf 109 on 16 December, an Fw 190 on 10 January 1944 and another Bf 109 three days later.

For 94th FS aces Lts Richard Lee and Donald Kienholz, their tallies straddled the change over. The former pilot added an Fw 190 on 11 November and two Bf 109s on 11 March 1944 to his successes in August and September, whilst Kienholz, having scored in August and October, claimed his fourth (an Fw 190) on 20 December, his fifth (another Fw 190) on 21 January 1944 and his last (a Bf 109) nine days later.

During April 1944 four Fifteenth Air Force groups converted to the P-51B/C, this change marking the start of the gradual decline of the P-38 as the Mustang took the lion's share of the escort missions – and consequently the majority of kills. By March 1945 the 82nd FG's long-standing victory record had been bettered by two Mustang groups, but the P-38 still held a slight advantage in the overall number of accredited kills.

Aerial engagements involving the P-38 had steadily tailed off during the summer of 1944, and in September no contact reports were filed at all. However, up to that point Lightning pilots had still been undertaking some remarkable missions, producing further aces.

The first of these missions came on 2 April when the 1st, and 82nd FGs escorted B-17s and B-24s sent to bomb the notoriously difficult target of Steyr, in Austria. Eleven victories were recorded for no losses by the pilots of these groups, but the 'star performers' of the day were the men of the 14th FG, who arrived to perform their target support role just in time to intercept 75 Axis fighters hell-bent on attacking the bomber formation. In a savage

action that lasted for 20 minutes, the P-38 pilots beat off repeated attacks and downed 18 enemy fighters without loss in the process. Lt John McGuyrt claimed a Bf 110 and an Re 2001 to add to the two Bf 109s destroyed, and two probables, he had claimed earlier in his tour. He would destroy another Bf 109 18 days later for his final victory.

Twenty-four hours after the epic Steyr mission, Lt Roland Leeman (four destroyed and four damaged) used the 95th FS's venerable P-38F-15 "SAD SACK" to claim a Bf 109 kill during an escort to the Budapest area. This was reckoned to be at least the 12th victory attributed to the Lockheed fighter, which had scored its first success as long ago as 7 January 1943! Further victories would follow until the distinguished fighter was retired after suffering flak damage during a bomber escort mission in late May 1944 – 17 months in action was surely a record for any P-38.

Lightning aces continued to score throughout April, the 49th FS's Lt Warren Jones claiming two Bf 109s (out of eight credited to the unit) for his second and third victories during an escort mission to Italian marshalling yards on the 7th, squadronmate, and future ace, Lt Louis Benne also getting a pair of Messerschmitts for his first kills. Bill Leverette scored his 11th victory – a Bf 110 – whilst performing the role of bomber escort five days later, and Lt Tom Maloney went one better with two Bf 110s confirmed protecting bombers sent to Wiener-Neustadt on 23 April. These were his second and third victories. Lt Franklin Lathrope, meanwhile, got his second (of five) Bf 109 during the same 1st FG escort.

May saw some of the 14th FG's wildest ever dogfights, which resulted in several of the group's pilots becoming aces. Lt Jack Lenox had damaged two Bf 109s and probably destroyed another before he finally scored his first confirmed Messerschmitt victory during a 23 May escort to an Italian marshalling yard. Twenty-four hours later Lenox was on another escort – this time to an Austrian airfield – when he shot down an 'Me 210' (most likely an Me 410) and then found himself on the tail of a second enemy fighter whose pilot was trying to abandon his disintegrating aircraft. Fascinated by the scene unfolding in front of him, Lenox stopped

Described as a 'hot and aggressive' pilot by his contemporaries in the 14th FG, Lt Phil Goldstein accounted for eight German aircraft – split evenly between air and ground kills. His strafing successes were never confirmed, however, hence the swastikas *without* circles on his provocatively named P-38. He and fellow Jew Lt Bob Seidman enjoyed taunting the 'master race' with their impudently marked fighters

Lt Seidman claimed three Bf 109s destroyed and another damaged on his first combat in December 1943. Although he later 'made ace' with two more Messerschmitt victories in 1944, Seidman was shot down and killed by flak on 14 May whilst flying P-38J 42-104259 (*Huff*)

'Ace-in-a-day' and Ploesti survivor Lt Herbert 'Stub' Hatch points to the swastikas that denote his victories on the nose of his P-38H *Mon Amy*. After the war it was discovered that the Fw 190s he thought he had shot down on 10 June were in fact Romanian I.A.R.80s (*USAF*)

firing and turned on his gunsight camera. However, a second foe used the P-38 pilot's fixation with his target to slip in and heavily damage the Lightning.

Lenox quickly took evasive action and checked himself, and his aircraft, out once the enemy had been shaken from his tail. His left engine was shot out, but even more serious was the shattered canopy and spatter of blood around the left arm that he could no longer move. Lenox took a pain-killing shot from the hypodermic needle in his emergency pack and set an anxious course for home. Fortunately, the P-38 was still in good flying shape and his paralysed arm had been merely caught on a throttle lock. The blood had come from the smallest scratch, and Lenox was disgusted with himself for the mild panic that had seen him use the hypodermic needle.

Two days later Lenox was flying on the wing of 14th FG Commander, Col O B Taylor, during an escort to French airfields when the latter went into a terminal velocity dive in his P-38J in order to confirm the crash of an Fw 190 for his fifth kill – indeed, this manoeuvre had been so ferocious that the experienced 'Obie' Taylor had difficulty recovering from it. With certain relief he looked around after pulling out of the dive and was surprised to find that Lenox was still alongside him in formation!

Lenox went on to score his final victories on yet another spectacular mission to Petfurdo, Hungary, on 14 June. Although the 49th FS arrived on station late, it nevertheless caught tardy defending fighters scrambling to attack the bombers in a brisk dogfight. Lenox despatched two Bf 109s in flames and sent another down trailing dark smoke – he was later credited with having destroyed all three. Louis Benne also got amongst the enemy whilst leading a flight of relatively inexperienced pilots, 'bagging' two Bf 109s before both the engines in his P-38J-15 (42-104229) were shot out and he was forced to take to his parachute. Later, whilst in a nearby hospital recovering from his wounds, now PoW Benne had the unusual experience of meeting the pilot who had shot him down!

May 1944 was also a notable month for the 14th FG for other reasons too, for the eventual top scoring P-38 ace of the group (and the entire Fifteenth Air Force for that matter) joined the 48th FS on the 17th. Lt Michael Brezas would go on to score 12 kills in seven weeks between 8 July and 25 August – those who knew him claim that his tally was much higher, but the modest Brezas scorned personal glory. Despite his nor-

mally mild manner, Brezas had nothing but scorn for the Soviet forces who treated him so 'uncomradely' after he had been shot down and spent time in their care. He later claimed that his treatment was so bad that he would search the skies for Russian as well as German aircraft!

Two other 49th FS pilots showed a similar disdain for the anti-semitic policies of the Nazi regime. Lt Bob Seidman had a Star of David painted on the nose of his P-38 to challenge thus-minded German pilots, whilst Lt Phil Goldstein went a step further by naming his P-38J-15 *JEWBOY* in both English and German. Seidman got five Bf 109s in the air before being lost to flak during a strafing mission on Udine in P-38J 42-104259 on 14 May. Goldstein claimed an Fw 190 on 25 May for his third, and last, kill, and is also unofficially credited with four ground victories.

## PLOESTI

One of the most daring – if not entirely successful – missions flown by P-38s during the Mediterranean war was the Ploesti raid of 10 June 1944, the 1st and 82nd FGs sending no less than 94 Lightnings to dive-bomb the Romano-Americano refinery with 46 1000-lb bombs. The 1st FG was tasked with providing fighter cover for the operation, which saw the P-38s go in low under enemy radar before climbing to bombing altitude.

Somewhere along the line the 71st FS erred from the flight plan and strayed directly over an enemy airfield. In one fateful moment the Lightning formation divided and shot down a transport aircraft and several fighters, before being bounced by a large formation of Romanian

P-38J-15 43-28258 *PAT III* is seen being taxied into the 14th FG dispersal at Triolo, Italy, by Col Oliver B 'Obie' Taylor sometime during early June 1944. The colonel contracted polio soon after this shot was taken and he was invalided home (*Taylor*)

'Obie' Taylor and his faithful ground-crew pose for the camera (*Taylor*)

I.A.R.80 fighters. Lt Herbert 'Stub' Hatch was about to turn to the left with his flight when one of the I.A.R.80s closed on him from the right, allowing the P-38 pilot to simply manoeuvre into the Romanian fighter and shoot it down. As the I.A.R.80 dived earthwards, Hatch now found himself facing at least five more enemy fighters.

Totally outnumbered, Hatch watched the lead element of his flight decimated before he could actually do anything about it. His wingman, Lt Joe Morrison, stayed on Hatch's wing long enough to watch him shoot down two more I.A.R.80s, and probably destroy or damage several others fastened to the tails of other 71st FS P-38s. After claiming two more enemy fighters destroyed and three damaged or destroyed, Hatch ran out of ammunition. The entire combat had taken place at little more than a few hundred feet over a plain between mountains.

Emmit Wilson and Lt Michael Brezas flank the 48th FS's victory scoreboard at Triolo in early August 1944. A quick examination of the latter reveals that Brezas was clearly the most productive pilot in the unit when it came to destroying the enemy – a further two swastikas would have to be squeezed in alongside his name before the month was out (*Collins*)

95th FS squadronmates Maj Warner Gardner and Lt Charles Adams exchange mutual congratulations in the wake of a one-sided action fought over Austria on 8 July 1944. Adams destroyed three Me 410s and Gardner claimed a fourth during the mission, raising the former pilot's tally to six and the latter's to four. Gardner 'made ace' 18 days later when he downed a by now rare He 111 over Manesti airfield (*Blake*)

Charles Adams points to the six swastikas that decorated the nose of his P-38J-15 *Judy Ann* (43-28796). He only used this machine to down one of his victims (a Bf 110 on 26 June) however. The tactical situation on 8 July so favoured the 82nd FG that Adams felt a twinge of conscience in the wake of his trio of victories (*Adams via Blake*)

Most of the 71st FS were shot down (22 P-38s were lost in total) before Hatch's flight could react, and the 'ace-in-a-day' was the only squadron member to reach home after the mission. Several pilots landed at Allied bases, or were forced down between the target and home, whilst a number became PoWs and others (including Joe Morrison) found their way back on foot. Verifying evidence (ciné film and eyewitness accounts) saw Hatch credited with five confirmed, one probable and one damaged.

Everett Miller of the 94th FS also scored his final three kills during the Ploesti mission to be credited with five victories overall. At around mid-day he had encountered an Fi 156 observation aircraft and two Romanian-operated CR 42 biplanes and duly dispatched them all.

A Fifteenth Air Force P-38 slips in close to offer personal protection to a lone B-17 returning from a raid. Bomber crews regularly expressed their appreciation to escorting P-38 pilots, as often the mere sight of the twin-boom fighter was enought to persuade Luftwaffe interceptors to search for unguarded targets instead (*IWM*)

## FINAL MTO P-38 ACES

The 27th FS put up an impressive display from the end of May until the middle of August 1944, claiming 40+ aircraft shot down and producing its final two aces. Tom Maloney claimed a Bf 109 on 31 May as did Lt Phil Tovrea, these successes being the former pilot's fifth victory and the

latter's first. Tovrea quickly caught up with Maloney, however, for he claimed an Fw 190 on 2 July for his fifth victory. Sixteen days later, whilst escorting a raid on the Friedrichschafen jet assembly plant, he downed two Fw 190s and a Bf 109 to take his finsl score to eight.

Tom Maloney was leading a 1st FG formation of 12 P-38s on a dive-bombing mission in support of the invasion of southern France on 15 August when eight Bf 109s jumped the American formation. In the wild fight that ensued, Maloney claimed two fighters to take his score to eight. Four days later he was forced down off the invasion shore during another mission, and whilst walking along the beach to find help he set off a land mine. Badly wounded, Maloney painfully made his way through the marshes that thrive in the area for the next few days until he contacted some French civilians, and finally a Canadian soldier. It took Tom Maloney a full three-and-a-half years of hospital treatment to recover.

The last of the 82nd FG aces can trace their early successes back to the ill-fated Ploesti raids. Lt Walter Carroll of the 96th FS claimed an Me 210 as the first of his eight victories on 10 June, whilst Lt Charles Adams was flying P-38J-15 43-28654 with the 95th FS six days later on an escort mission for B-24s sent to bomb Vienna when he and Lt James Holloway (six kills) were forced to steeply dive after a pair of Fw 190s that had latched onto the tails of other P-38s. Each pilot claimed a fighter, Adams as his second victory and Holloway as his first.

On 26 June the 82nd FG ran into another determined fight when twin-engined Messerschmitt fighters doggedly attacked their bomber formation, losing 12 to the P-38s. Charles Adams, flying his usual P-38J-15 (43-28796), destroyed a Bf 110, James Holloway claimed another

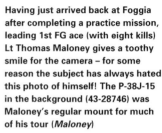

**Having just arrived back at Foggia after completing a practice mission, leading 1st FG ace (with eight kills) Lt Thomas Maloney gives a toothy smile for the camera – for some reason the subject has always hated this photo of himself! The P-38J-15 in the background (43-28746) was Maloney's regular mount for much of his tour (*Maloney*)**

**This P-38L-1 was christened *Maloney's Pony* in September 1944 in the absence of the well-liked ace, who had been grievously wounded on 19 August when he trod on a mine after crash-landing his battle-damaged Lightning north-west of Marseille. Maloney never actually saw this P-38 'in the flesh', but was nevertheless heartened to know that his loyal groundcrew ensured that at least some of his spirit remained in the 27th FS in his absence**

*Zerstörer*, Maj Warner Gardner (soon commander of the 95th FS) downed two others for the first of his five victories and Lt Robert Griffith of the 97th FS added an Me 410 to score the second of his five.

8 July also proved to be a 'stellar' day for the 82nd FG, as its pilots claimed yet more twin-engined fighters. Just the day before the group had begun building on its new record of 500 confirmed aircraft shot down – the first group in Fifteenth Air Force to achieve such a tally – by 'bagging' five Bf 109s. Walter Carroll had claimed one of for his fourth victory, followed by three Me 410s on 8 July. Charles Adams also claimed three Messerschmitt 'twins' on this day to take his tally to six. Years later Adams remembered the mission with a touch of bitter irony – 'I shot them all from behind', he would shrug with a laconic voice. 'Was that fair?'

Whether it was fair or not, the 82nd claimed all 16 fighters encountered in a classic interception. The Me 410s were spotted in clear skies, and the Lightning pilots were duly able to position themselves to cut off any escape. After the mission the interrogating officers had to cut the debriefing short when they received more claims than there were Me 410s in the formation! Sixteen were claimed, with an added three Bf 109s, one Fw 190 and a trainer, for a total of 21 aircraft shot down for no losses. Robert Griffith was credited with one of the Bf 109s for his fifth victory.

On 26 July the 82nd escorted B-24s to the Vienna area in a mission which culminated with the last victories for its aces. Warner Gardner got a He 111 for his fifth kill, Walter Carroll an Fw 190 for his eighth and Maj Claud Ford, CO of the the 97th FS, a Bf 109 for his fifth.

Fittingly, Michael Brezas gained the last confirmed victories for the P-38 aces when he downed two Fw 190s and damaged another during a mission to Czechoslovakia on 25 August 1944. It was appropriate that the last victories scored by a P-38 ace should be credited to the Fifteenth's ranking Lightning pilot, who had gained 12 kills in such a short time. Even though P-38 groups continued to collect odd victories until late April 1945, the days of the aggressive fighter aces were over.

**Thomas Maloney shared top scorer status in the 1st FG with fellow 27th FS pilot Lt Phil Tovrea, who claimed a trio of kills to take his tally to eight on 18 July 1944 – Maloney confirmed his eighth on 15 August. The two pilots (who occasionally flew together) shared a mutual respect for each other both as fighter pilots and individuals (*Maloney*)**

**P-38Js of the 95th FS/82nd FG are seen on a long range sweep of the Italian-Austrian border (*McMonegal via Blake*)**

# EIGHTH AND NINTH AIR FORCE ACES

When the P-38 returned to combat in England in mid-1943 it was *the* American fighter type of the period – the Thunderbolt still had range, reliability and 'combatability' problems, the Warhawk had proven unsuitable for the ETO and the Merlin Mustang was at least sixth months away from frontline use. Every USAAF fighter group commander wanted the type for his squadrons, but the Lightning was being produced in smaller numbers than any other America fighter, making it the rarest machine of its type on a worldwide scale.

Added to its paucity in numbers was the persistent unreliability of its powerplant – the Allison V-1710 engine – in the cold and damp conditions typically found in north-west Europe. This resulted in large numbers of Lightnings being grounded, thus leaving too few serviceable aircraft available to adequately escort heavy bombers headed for continental Europe on the outward leg of their mission. However, despite being few in number, the P-38's unique planform often alerted enemy interceptors to the fighter's presence, and German pilots would consequently avoid even engaging a single flight of four in accordance with a Luftwaffe high command directive. Consequently, fewer American bombers were attacked and losses became supportable despite the relatively small number of P-38s available.

The Lightning had been introduced to the Eighth Air Force in the late summer of 1943, seasoned stateside operators of the P-38 in the shape of the 20th and 55th FGs commencing their work-ups to operational flying in the middle of September. The number of aircraft made available to the newly arrived groups was barely sufficient to allow operations to commence, the 55th FG having to actually commandeer a number of P-38H-5s from the 20th FG when it flew its first combat sorties on 15 October 1943.

Operations kicked off with a

Lt (later Captain) Robert Buttke of the 343rd FS/55th FG claimed two Bf 109Gs during his first combat on 3 November 1943, a pair of Me 210s and a damaged Bf 110 on 10 February 1944 and another Bf 109G confirmed and a second damaged on 22 April. His final score comprised a half-share in a Ju 88 achieved on 27 February 1945 whilst flying a P-51D (*IWM*)

38th FS pilot Lt Jerry Brown became the 55th FG's premier ace when he claimed a Fw 190 and He 111 on 15 April 1944. he had earlier scored his first victory, on January 31, shooting down a Bf 109G at high altitude (between 28,000 and 33,000 ft) over Venlo, in Holland

sweep over the Dutch coast just 24 hours after the disastrous Schweinfurt Raid, which had seen 60 out of 291 unescorted B-17s shot down and the USAAF's daylight bombing campaign temporarily halted. Stilling themselves for the bombers' return, the Luftwaffe's fighter force left the 55th FG alone as it found its feet in further incursions over occupied Europe. Even the weather was kind to the Lightning pilots, who made the most of clear skies and little opposition to find their feet in the ETO. By November the group was ready to meet the enemy.

On the 3rd of the month the daylight bombing campaign resumed with a raid on Wilhelmshaven, the 'heavies' forming up at about 30,000 ft and being duly escorted for the very first time by P-38s of the 55th FG on the final leg of the route.

Naturally, the Luftwaffe was unaware that the USAAF possessed a fighter that could reach this far into occupied Europe (the P-38 had a range of 850 km, compared with 600 km for the P-51A and 450 km for the P-47C without external tanks), and reacted to the bomber force as it had done in the past. JG 1 sent up a mixed force of Fw 190As and Bf

Capt Chet Patterson of the 338th FS/55th FG was a daring and cunning flight leader who claimed four German aircraft destroyed before being posted home on rotation, having just failed to secure that elusive fifth kill. He was one of the first pilots in the ETO to appreciate the positive fighting points of the P-38 – firepower, range and manoeuvrability (*Patterson*)

49

# COLOUR PLATES

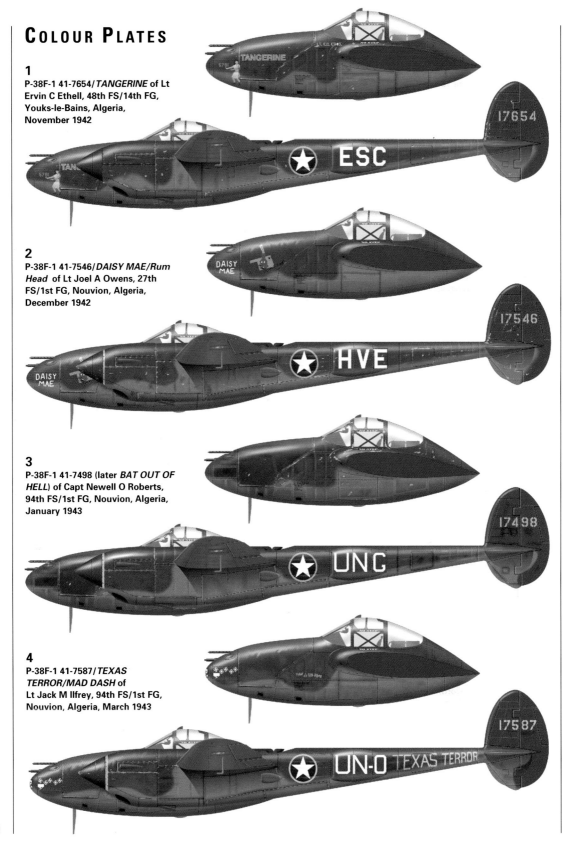

**1**
P-38F-1 41-7654/*TANGERINE* of Lt
Ervin C Ethell, 48th FS/14th FG,
Youks-le-Bains, Algeria,
November 1942

**2**
P-38F-1 41-7546/*DAISY MAE/Rum
Head* of Lt Joel A Owens, 27th
FS/1st FG, Nouvion, Algeria,
December 1942

**3**
P-38F-1 41-7498 (later *BAT OUT OF
HELL*) of Capt Newell O Roberts,
94th FS/1st FG, Nouvion, Algeria,
January 1943

**4**
P-38F-1 41-7587/*TEXAS
TERROR/MAD DASH* of
Lt Jack M Ilfrey, 94th FS/1st FG,
Nouvion, Algeria, March 1943

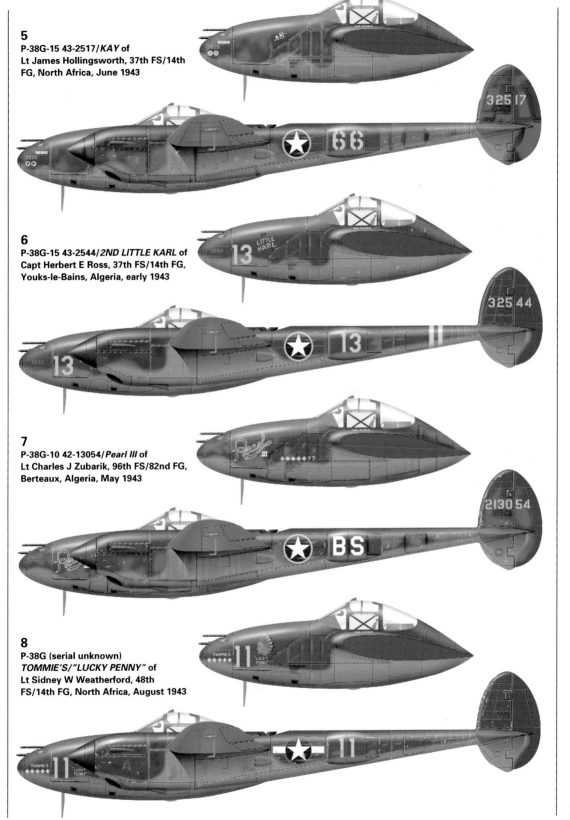

**5**
P-38G-15 43-2517/*KAY* of
Lt James Hollingsworth, 37th FS/14th
FG, North Africa, June 1943

**6**
P-38G-15 43-2544/*2ND LITTLE KARL* of
Capt Herbert E Ross, 37th FS/14th FG,
Youks-le-Bains, Algeria, early 1943

**7**
P-38G-10 42-13054/*Pearl III* of
Lt Charles J Zubarik, 96th FS/82nd FG,
Berteaux, Algeria, May 1943

**8**
P-38G (serial unknown)
*TOMMIE'S/"LUCKY PENNY"* of
Lt Sidney W Weatherford, 48th
FS/14th FG, North Africa, August 1943

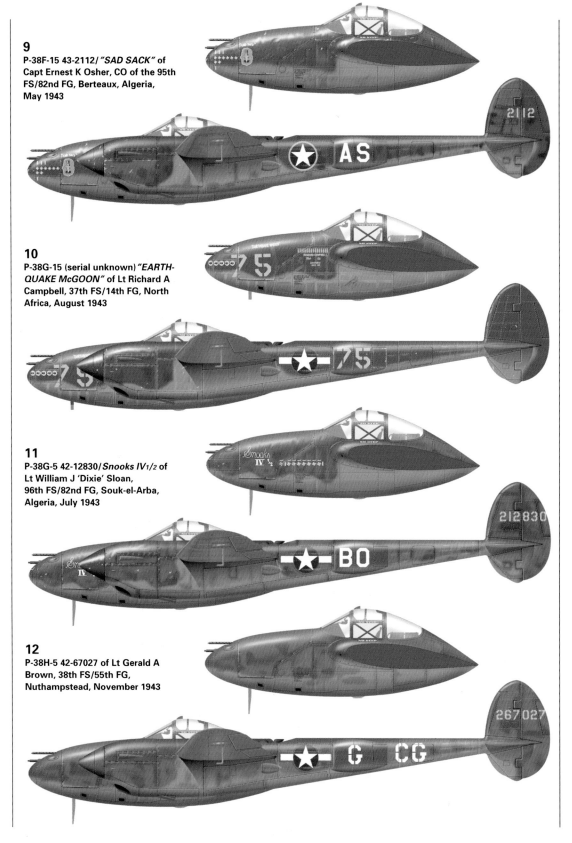

**9**
P-38F-15 43-2112/*"SAD SACK"* of
Capt Ernest K Osher, CO of the 95th
FS/82nd FG, Berteaux, Algeria,
May 1943

**10**
P-38G-15 (serial unknown) *"EARTH-QUAKE McGOON"* of Lt Richard A
Campbell, 37th FS/14th FG, North
Africa, August 1943

**11**
P-38G-5 42-12830/*Snooks IV₁/₂* of
Lt William J 'Dixie' Sloan,
96th FS/82nd FG, Souk-el-Arba,
Algeria, July 1943

**12**
P-38H-5 42-67027 of Lt Gerald A
Brown, 38th FS/55th FG,
Nuthampstead, November 1943

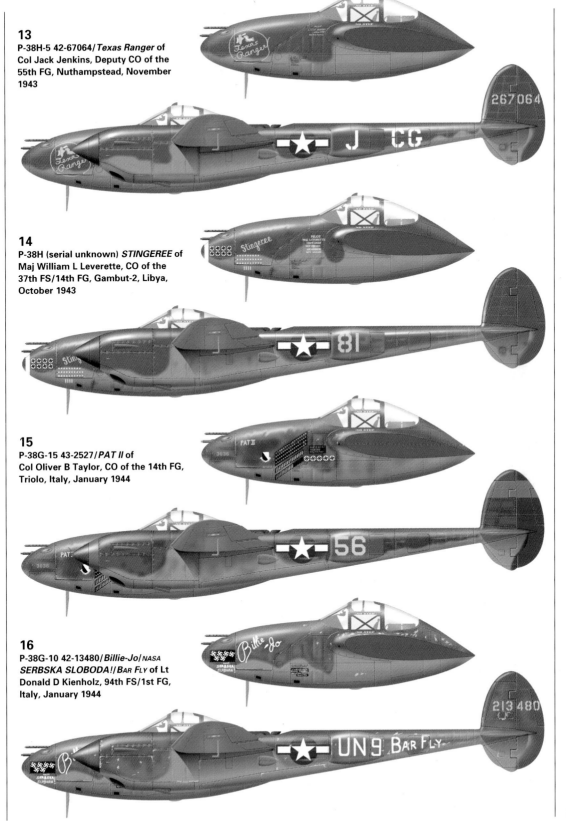

**13**
P-38H-5 42-67064/ *Texas Ranger* of
Col Jack Jenkins, Deputy CO of the
55th FG, Nuthampstead, November
1943

**14**
P-38H (serial unknown) *STINGEREE* of
Maj William L Leverette, CO of the
37th FS/14th FG, Gambut-2, Libya,
October 1943

**15**
P-38G-15 43-2527/ *PAT II* of
Col Oliver B Taylor, CO of the 14th FG,
Triolo, Italy, January 1944

**16**
P-38G-10 42-13480/ *Billie-Jo*/ NASA
*SERBSKA SLOBODA!*/ *BAR FLY* of Lt
Donald D Kienholz, 94th FS/1st FG,
Italy, January 1944

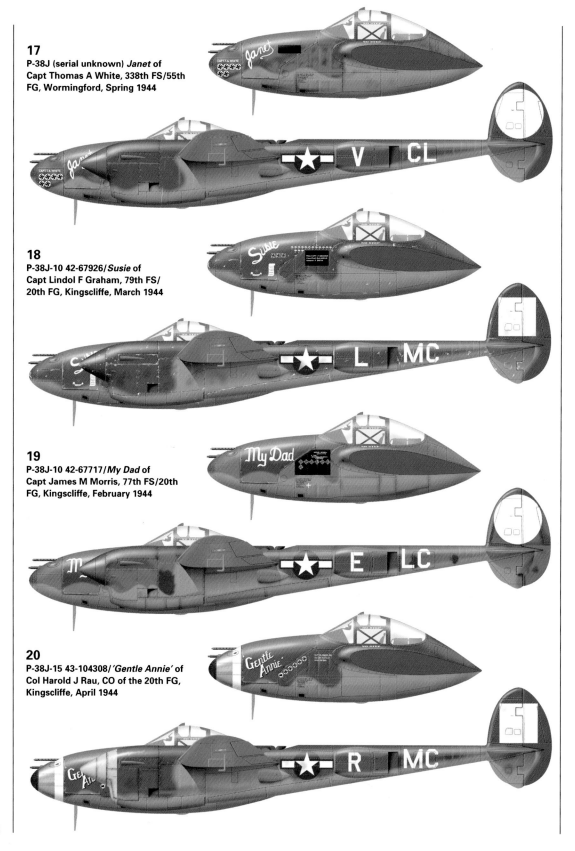

**17**
P-38J (serial unknown) *Janet* of
Capt Thomas A White, 338th FS/55th
FG, Wormingford, Spring 1944

**18**
P-38J-10 42-67926/*Susie* of
Capt Lindol F Graham, 79th FS/
20th FG, Kingscliffe, March 1944

**19**
P-38J-10 42-67717/*My Dad* of
Capt James M Morris, 77th FS/20th
FG, Kingscliffe, February 1944

**20**
P-38J-15 43-104308/*'Gentle Annie'* of
Col Harold J Rau, CO of the 20th FG,
Kingscliffe, April 1944

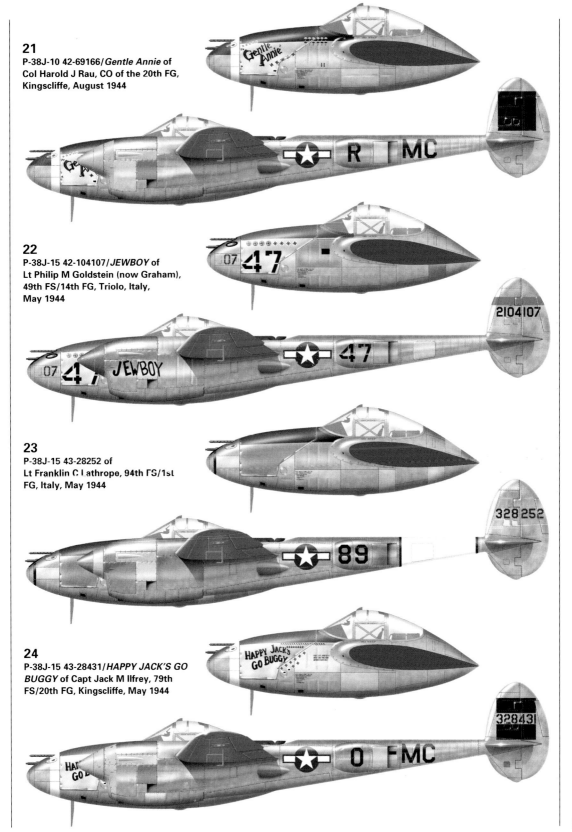

**21**
P-38J-10 42-69166/*Gentle Annie* of
Col Harold J Rau, CO of the 20th FG,
Kingscliffe, August 1944

**22**
P-38J-15 42-104107/*JEWBOY* of
Lt Philip M Goldstein (now Graham),
49th FS/14th FG, Triolo, Italy,
May 1944

**23**
P-38J-15 43-28252 of
Lt Franklin C Lathrope, 94th FS/1st
FG, Italy, May 1944

**24**
P-38J-15 43-28431/*HAPPY JACK'S GO
BUGGY* of Capt Jack M Ilfrey, 79th
FS/20th FG, Kingscliffe, May 1944

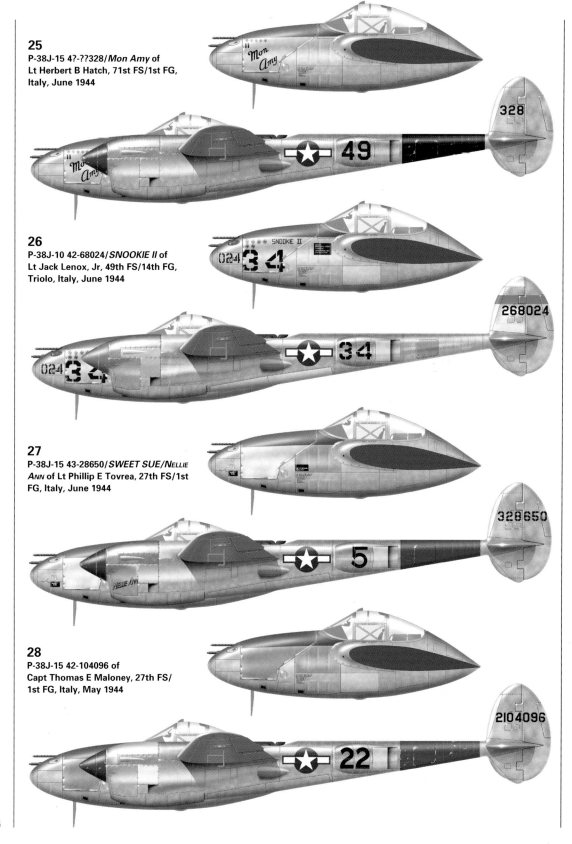

**25**
P-38J-15 4?-??328/*Mon Amy* of
Lt Herbert B Hatch, 71st FS/1st FG,
Italy, June 1944

**26**
P-38J-10 42-68024/*SNOOKIE II* of
Lt Jack Lenox, Jr, 49th FS/14th FG,
Triolo, Italy, June 1944

**27**
P-38J-15 43-28650/*SWEET SUE*/*NELLIE
ANN* of Lt Phillip E Tovrea, 27th FS/1st
FG, Italy, June 1944

**28**
P-38J-15 42-104096 of
Capt Thomas E Maloney, 27th FS/
1st FG, Italy, May 1944

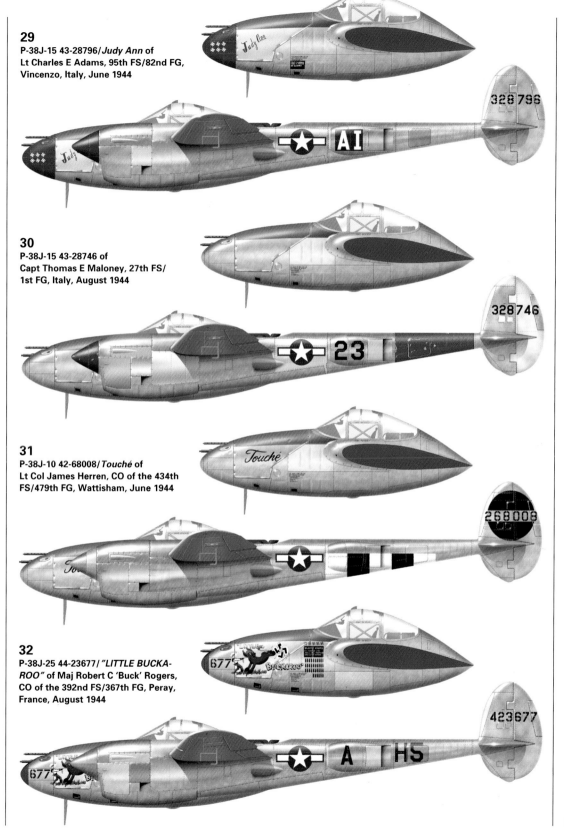

**29**
P-38J-15 43-28796/*Judy Ann* of
Lt Charles E Adams, 95th FS/82nd FG,
Vincenzo, Italy, June 1944

**30**
P-38J-15 43-28746 of
Capt Thomas E Maloney, 27th FS/
1st FG, Italy, August 1944

**31**
P-38J-10 42-68008/*Touché* of
Lt Col James Herren, CO of the 434th
FS/479th FG, Wattisham, June 1944

**32**
P-38J-25 44-23677/*"LITTLE BUCKA-
ROO"* of Maj Robert C 'Buck' Rogers,
CO of the 392nd FS/367th FG, Peray,
France, August 1944

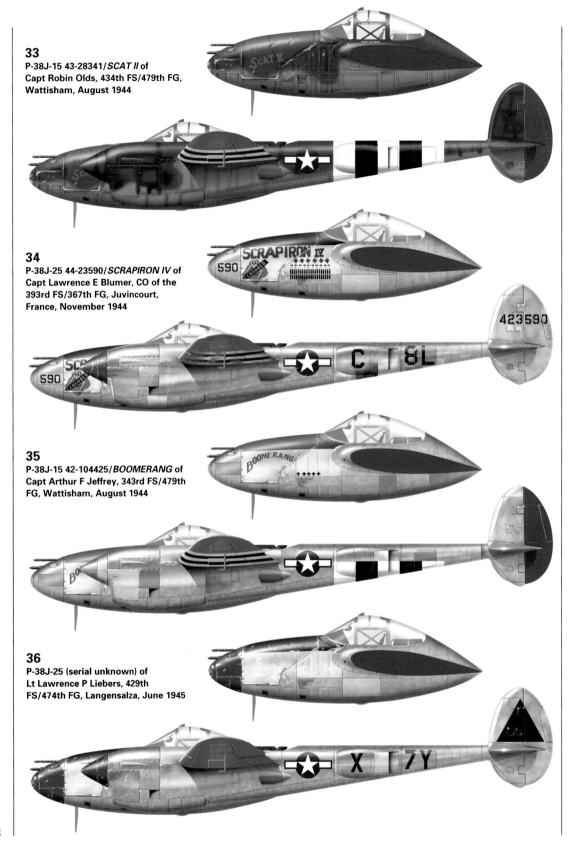

**33**
P-38J-15 43-28341/*SCAT II* of
Capt Robin Olds, 434th FS/479th FG,
Wattisham, August 1944

**34**
P-38J-25 44-23590/*SCRAPIRON IV* of
Capt Lawrence E Blumer, CO of the
393rd FS/367th FG, Juvincourt,
France, November 1944

**35**
P-38J-15 42-104425/*BOOMERANG* of
Capt Arthur F Jeffrey, 343rd FS/479th
FG, Wattisham, August 1944

**36**
P-38J-25 (serial unknown) of
Lt Lawrence P Liebers, 429th
FS/474th FG, Langensalza, June 1945

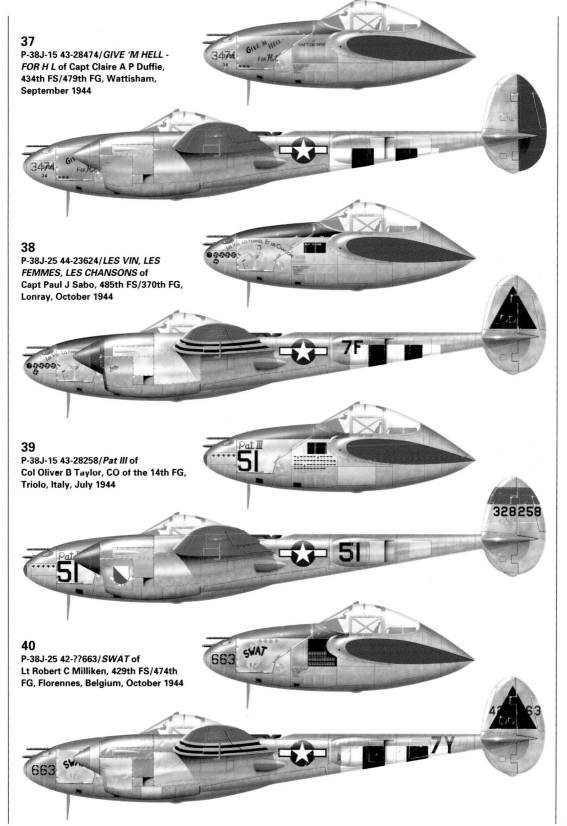

**37**
P-38J-15 43-28474/*GIVE 'M HELL -
FOR H L* of Capt Claire A P Duffie,
434th FS/479th FG, Wattisham,
September 1944

**38**
P-38J-25 44-23624/*LES VIN, LES
FEMMES, LES CHANSONS* of
Capt Paul J Sabo, 485th FS/370th FG,
Lonray, October 1944

**39**
P-38J-15 43-28258/*Pat III* of
Col Oliver B Taylor, CO of the 14th FG,
Triolo, Italy, July 1944

**40**
P-38J-25 42-??663/*SWAT* of
Lt Robert C Milliken, 429th FS/474th
FG, Florennes, Belgium, October 1944

**1**
Col Oliver Taylor, CO of the
14th FG, Triolo, Italy, Spring
1944

**3**
Lt William 'Dixie' Sloan, 96th
FS/82nd FG, Grombalia,
Tunisia, September 1943

**2**
Lt Richard Campbell, 37th
FS/14th FG, North Africa,
January 1944

**6**
Lt James Morris, 77th
FS/20th FG, Kingscliffe,
February 1944

**4**
Lt Claude Kinsey, 96th
FS/82nd FG, North Africa,
March 1943

**5**
Capt Lindol Graham, 79th
FS/20th FG Kingscliffe,
September 1943

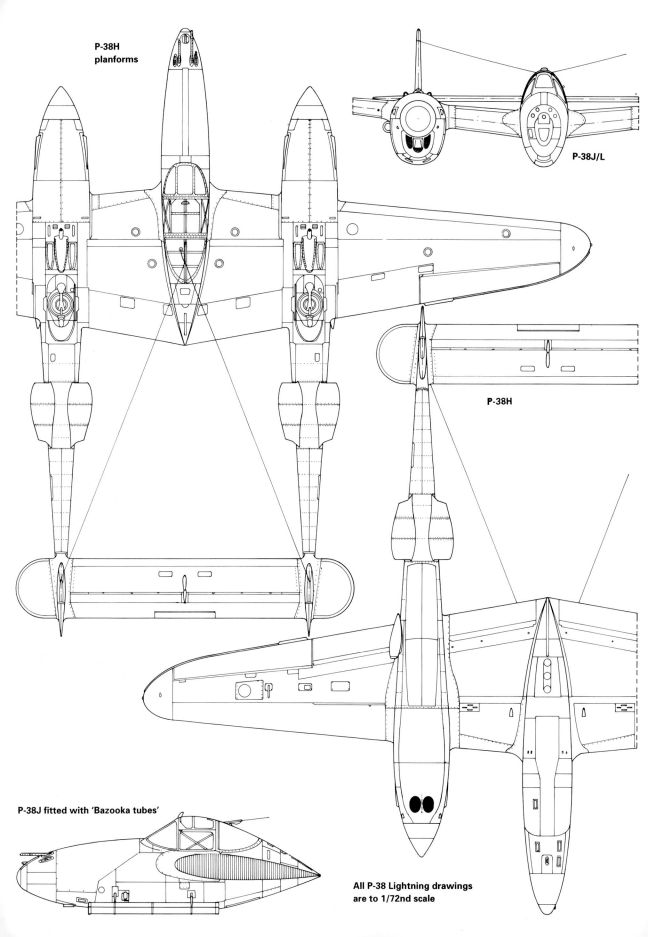

P-38H
planforms

P-38J/L

P-38H

P-38J fitted with 'Bazooka tubes'

All P-38 Lightning drawings
are to 1/72nd scale

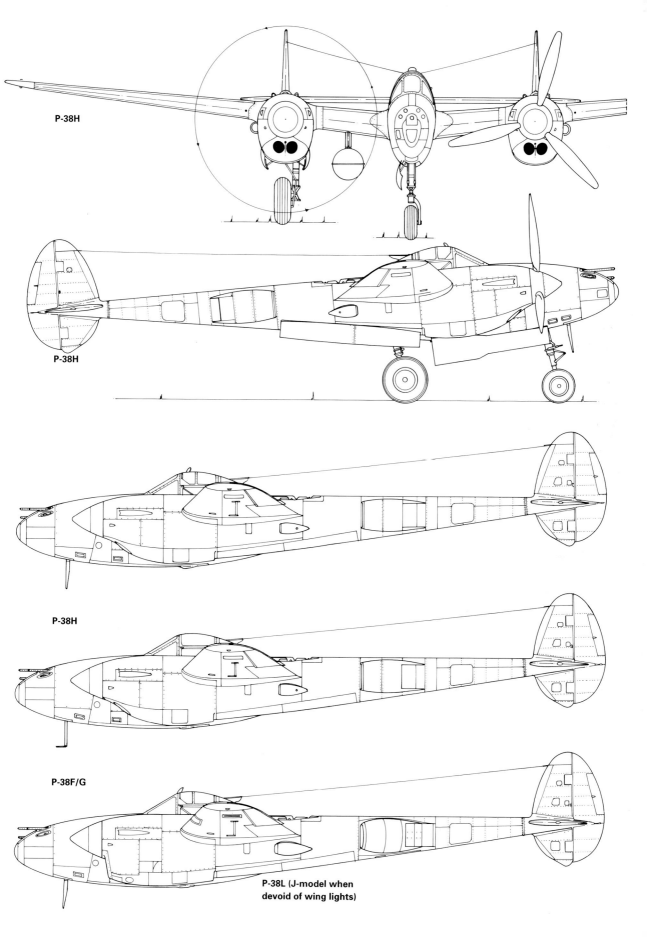

P-38H

P-38H

P-38H

P-38F/G

P-38L (J-model when
devoid of wing lights)

# COLOUR PLATES

## 1

**P-38F-1 41-7654/*TANGERINE* of Lt Ervin C Ethell, 48th FS/14th FG, Youks-le-Bains, Algeria, November 1942**

The 14th FG was allocated one of the first blocks of P-38Fs built by Lockheed during the summer of 1942, Lt Ethell flying this example from England to North Africa with the 48th FS in time to play an active part in Operation *Torch*, which commenced at the beginning of November 1942. It did not take the 14th FG long to score its first kills either in the air or on the ground, with several pilots managing to run up combined air and ground tallies before the end of the month. Ethell almost became the first P-38 ace in a single mission when he downed four Ju-52/3ms and a probable Bf 109 on 28 November whilst flying this fighter. He also came close to achieving a record number of ground victories in the P-38, being unofficially credited with ten Axis aircraft destroyed. Unfortunately for Ethell, the Twelfth Air Force only recognised aerial victories, thus leaving him twice deprived of unique records in the P-38. *TANGERINE* was later shot down in action whilst being flown by another 48th FS pilot.

## 2

**P-38F-1 41-7546/*DAISY MAE/Rum Head* of Lt Joel A Owens, 27th FS/1st FG, Nouvion, Algeria, December 1942**

Like Ervin Ethell, Joel Owens also flew his P-38F-1 down to North Africa from England and had begun his scoring run by the end of November. Indeed, he achieved the first kill for the 27th FS, and had scored five confirmed, one probable and a damaged claim by the end of the campaign. The *DAISY MAE* part of the aircraft's nickname was not a reference to the famous cartoon character, but to the girlfriend of Owens's crewchief – the rest of the pilot's flight were not aware of this, and mistakenly adopted names of other characters in the comic strip for their aircraft! *RUMHEAD* is a humourous reference to the state of Oklahoma, the home of several flight members, including Owens. He actually had a star placed on the geographical location of his hometown, Skiatook, on the stylised green map of Oklahoma that adorned the port gun access panel.

## 3

**P-38F-1 41-7498 (later *BAT OUT OF HELL*) of Capt Newell O Roberts, 94th FS/1st FG, Nouvion, Algeria, January 1943**

Roberts used this plain F-1 from the beginning of the North Africa landings, flying it on 29 November when he shared in the destruction of Bf 110 with future ace Jack Ilfrey. Because of the severe shortage of Lightnings, and associated spare parts, in-theatre, some F-1s remained in the frontline long after the North African campaign had ended in May 1943. Indeed, Roberts's P-38 lasted long after he had rotated

home in March 1943, having completed his prerequisite 50 (actually 52 in his case) combat missions. A Lt Hagenback duly inherited the by now well-worn 'UN - G' soon after Roberts left, adding the evocative name *BAT OUT OF HELL*, with appropriately horrific nose art, during the Sicilian campaign in July-August 1943.

## 4

**P-38F-1 41-7587/*TEXAS TERROR/MAD DASH* of Lt Jack M Ilfrey, 94th FS/1st FG, Nouvion, Algeria, March 1943**

Like his contemporaries, Ilfrey flew this fighter from England to north-west Africa, via a temporary stop-over in Portugal due to an engine malfunction. He boldly named the fighter *TEXAS TERROR* on the port boom in order to indicate his predisposition to any Axis airmen he encountered, and *THE MAD DASH* on the starboard boom to commemorate the long overwater flight undertaken by the P-38s to North Africa. This Lightning was damaged beyond repair sometime in late 1942 or early 1943, and was apparently cannibalised to keep other 94th FS P-38s flying.

## 5

**P-38G-15 43-2517/*KAY* of Lt James Hollingsworth, 37th FS/14th FG, North Africa, June 1943**

Hollingsworth was already part of the 37th FS (originally part of the then US-based 55th FG) when it joined the 14th FG in time for the group's second combat tour in May 1943. Although a very successful pilot in combat, Hollingsworth was reputedly so disdainful of combat records that he had to be coaxed on occasion to even mention his exploits. Officially, he is credited with three confirmed aerial victories (Do 217 on 25 May and Bf 109s on 24 June and 19 August 19), one unconfirmed kill (MC 202 on 15 June) and a damaged (Bf 109 on 18 May) during his 1943 combat tour. Hollingsworth later flew with the 434th FS/479th FG, claiming a further seven ground victories.

## 6

**P-38G-15 43-2544/*2ND LITTLE KARL* of Capt Herbert E Ross, 37th FS/14th FG, Youks-le-Bains, Algeria, early 1943**

Herbert Ross scored seven confirmed aerial kills, as well as one probable and a damaged claim, between 9 May and 6 September 1943. There were no traces of victory marks to be found on the photos of *2ND LITTLE KARL* taken during this period, and it is possible that Ross chose not to adorn his aircraft accordingly. The two yellow bands on the aft booms were flight leader's stripes, which suggest that this is how the P-38 appeared during the early stages of Ross's combat tour. The aircraft's nickname referred to the pilot's son.

## 7

**P-38G-10 42-13054/*Pearl III* of Lt Charles J Zubarik,**

## 96th FS/82nd FG, Berteaux, Algeria, May 1943

'Shorty' Zubarik was element, and sometimes flight, leader of the 96th FS until he was shot down and captured on 24 May 1943 near Vanafiorita airfield. He and fellow squadron ace 'Dixie' Sloan were both element mates and firm friends up until Zubarik's death in September 1979. His official victories included a Ju 52/3m and an Fw 190 on 21 January 1943, a damaged Fw 190 on 29 January 29, two Bf 109s on 20 March, an MC 200 on 13 May and another Bf 109 on eight days later. The two question marks at the right of his scoreboard refer to a pair of Me 210s that collided and crashed when the German formation of five Messerschmitt 'twins' was attacked by Zubarik on 6 May 1943. The pilot was actually heading back to base alone with a malfunctioning engine when he came across the enemy formation, and because there were no other witnesses to the crash, Zubarik was never officially given credit for them.

## 8
### P-38G (serial unknown) TOMMIE'S/"LUCKY PENNY" of Lt Sidney W Weatherford, 48th FS/14th FG, North Africa, August 1943

This P-38G was named after Weatherford's wife as a promise to her that he would turn up again after his tour. His aerial victories were all scored over a three-month period from 28 May to 26 August 1943, and included a Bf 109 on 28 May 28, an MC 202 on 12 July, two Ju 52/3ms on 18 July and another Bf 109 on 26 August. Weatherford was one of the first pilots to 'make ace' with the newly-committed 48th FS following the 14th FG's return to the fray in early May 1943 after a fourth-month period of rest and rebuilding.

## 9
### P-38F-15 43-2112/ "SAD SACK" of Capt Ernest K Osher, CO of the 95th FS/82nd FG, Berteaux, Algeria, May 1943

Pilots of the 82nd FG claim that this P-38 was made 'absolutely right' by Lockheed, duly giving them something of an edge in combat. As many as 16 confirmed victories, plus several probable and damaged claims, were attributed to "SAD SACK" during its long career in the frontline. Although 'Dixie' Sloan scored his first aerial victory in the aircraft on 7 January 1943 (a Bf 109), it was then adopted by Maj Robert Kirtley, and later Maj Ernest Osher, both of whom commanded of the 95th FS for a time during their respective combat tours of North Africa. Kirtley got a Ju 88 and an Ar 196 floatplane in "SAD SACK" on 21 February 1943, whilst Lt John Cappo used the fighter to good effect during the rout of Axis transport aircraft on 11 April 1943, claiming two Ju 52/3ms – he also 'bagged' a Bf 109 with the Lightning 18 days later. Five-kill ace Ernest Osher is recorded as having downed his third and fourth victories with "SAD SACK" on 5 May 1943, the aircraft subsequently enjoying its final success in the air as late as 13 April 1944 with Flt Off Roland Leeman at the controls – "SAD SACK" was damaged by flak and taken out of service soon afterwards.

## 10
### P-38G-15 (serial unknown) "EARTHQUAKE McGOON" of Lt Richard A Campbell, 37th FS/14th FG, North Africa, August 1943

Flying with the 37th FS, Campbell was also amongst the elite band of 14th FG pilots to achieve 'acedom' early on in the group's second tour of duty. He scored his first two Bf 109s destroyed (and a third damaged) on 18 May 1943, followed by another Bf 109 as a probable ten days later – the latter score was achieved flying "EARTHQUAKE McGOON". Campbell's third confirmed kill took the form of a MC 202 on 15 June, followed by yet another Bf 109 destroyed on 9 July. He made sure of his ace status with a double Bf 109 score (plus a third fighter damaged) on 28 August 1943. Richard Campbell later completed a second tour in the China-Burma-India (CBI) theatre in 1945, but he failed to add to his tally.

## 11
### P-38G-5 42-12830/ Snooks IV1/2 of Lt William J 'Dixie' Sloan, 96th FS/82nd FG, Souk-el-Arba, Algeria, July 1943

Sloan became the leading ace of not only the 96th FS/82nd FG, but also the entire Twelfth Air Force, when on 22 July 1943 when he downed a Bf 109 for his 12th victory. This tally would secure him top spot amongst USAAF fighter pilots in the Mediterranean for the next nine months until Mustang pilot Maj Herschel 'Herky' Green claimed his 13th victory for the 325th FG on 7 April 1944 (see Aircraft of the Aces 7 - Mustang Aces of the Ninth & Fifteenth Air Forces and the RAF for further details). The nickname Snooks IV1/2 refers to the fact that so much of this P-38 was made up of spare parts from cannibalised Lightnings that only about half of the aircraft was original! It would seem likely that Sloan used this fighter when he gained his victories during the Sicily invasion period – namely a Bf 109 and a Re 2001 on 5 July and an MC 200 on 10 July 1943.

## 12
### P-38H-5 42-67027 of Lt Gerald A Brown, 38th FS/55th FG, Nuthampstead, November 1943

On 13 November 1943 Jerry Brown (flying this aircraft) and Capt Joe Myers comprised one of the elements put up by the 55th FG to escort bombers on a particularly rough mission to Bremen. The former pilot had already succeeded in damaging an attacking Bf 109 short of the bomber stream when another fighter latched onto his tail and pumped cannon and machine-gun fire into the hapless P-38. Seeing Brown's predicament, Myers managed to shoot the determined German off his colleague's tail, allowing Brown to somehow coax his gravely damaged P-38 home. Once back at Nuthampstead, the bullet-riddled Lightning was the source of much amazement for Lockheed and USAAF technical experts alike, who counted in excess of 100 bullet and cannon hits on the aircraft's fuselage. Flying J-10 model P-38s, Jerry Brown went on to destroy a Bf 109 at high altitude on 31 January 1944, an Fw 190 on 18 March, another Bf 109 on 8 April and a He 111 and a second Fw 190 exactly a week later.

## 13
### P-38H-5 42-67064/*Texas Ranger* of Col Jack Jenkins, Deputy CO 55th FG, Nuthampstead, November 1943

The first victories to fall to the P-38 in north-west Europe were scored by the 55th FG on 3 November 1943, future group commander Jack Jenkins claiming a Bf 109 shot down and an Fw 190 probably destroyed. It would seem from a postwar examination of JG 1's records that Jenkins could actually have claimed both fighters destroyed, as the *Jagdgeschwader* admitted the loss of two fighters in action with P-38s on this day. The colonel tasted success in *Texas Ranger* just once more, using the Lightning to destroy an Fw 190 22 days after his 'double' haul. Jenkins led the first American fighters over Berlin on 3 March 1944 when the 55th FG ranged over the German capitol – his P-38 on this occasion was *Texas Ranger IV*.

## 14
### P-38H (serial unknown) *Stingeree* of Maj William L Leverette, CO 37th FS/14th FG, Gambut-2, Libya, October 1943

Named after a southern American variation of the stingray, this P-38H was used by William Leverette (a native of Florida, hence the 'fishy' nickname) to claim most, if not all, of his 11 aerial victories. The seven Ju 87s that he claimed on 9 October 1943 constituted a record for American pilots in Europe. This astounding tally has often been questioned by ex-pilots and historians alike, but Leverette recently assured the author that one of the P-38 pilots in his formation descended to low altitude over the becalmed sea in order to confirm numerous splashes in the water made by the crashing Stukas. Once the latter individual had returned to base, the number of splashes he reported was consistent with the tally of kills claimed by the successful P-38 pilots. Leverette later destroyed a Bf 109 on 14 December 1943, a Bf 110 on 24 February 1944, another Bf 109 on 18 March and a final Bf 110 on 12 April.

## 15
### P-38G-15 43-2527/*PAT II* of Col Oliver B Taylor, CO of the 14th FG, Triolo, Italy, January 1944

Taylor scored one confirmed kill, one probable and one damaged in this Lightning on 20 December 1943, all three of his foes being Bf 109s encountered during a sweep over Eleusis airfield, in Greece. He gave up *PAT II* towards the end of the following month, receiving a later specification Lightning in its place. The supply problem was always critical in the MTO due to the theatre's distance from the main air depots in Britain. Squadrons were therefore forced use early-build P-38Fs, Gs and Hs for far longer periods than other Lightning outfits in the ETO and Pacific/CBI. After scoring his first successes in December, Col Taylor added a second Bf 109 destroyed to his tally on 10 January and

another Messerschmitt fighter damaged 17 days later. It seems likely that the five scores represented by the victory marks on the side of the fighter's gondola reflect his haul from December and January, for Taylor did not finally achieve 'ace status' until 27 May 1944 whilst flying a P-38J.

## 16
### P-38G-10 42-13480/*Billie-Jo*/NASA *SERBSKA SLO-BODA!*/*BAR FLY* of Lt Donald D Kienholz, 94th FS/1st FG, Italy, January 1944

By the end of January 1944 Kienholz had achieved six confirmed kills and one damaged claim, and like a number of his contemporaries, he used his early-model P-38G for a relatively long time. His first victory was a Bf 109 scored on 13 August 1943 and his last score was also a Messerschmitt fighter, downed on 30 January 1944. Most of his victories were scored during the initial stages of the invasion of Italy, although his last kill in 1943 was an Fw 190 shot down on the same Eleusis airfield sweep on 20 December that Col Oliver Taylor had enjoyed his first combat success. During one strafing mission he had the unnerving experience of being turned upside-down with one flak burst and righted again with the next!

## 17
### P-38J (serial unknown) *Janet* of Capt Thomas A White, 338th FS/55th FG, Wormingford, Spring 1944

White placed the six swastikas on the nose of this 338th FS P-38J even though he had scored all six of his victories with the 97th FS/82nd FG in North Africa between January and March 1943. The aircraft was named after the daughter of the squadron's Intelligence Officer, Wally Ryerson, with whom White maintained a correspondence. Sometime after the captain had left the 338th, the nose of the fighter was painted red (in the same shade as the spinners) through the first two letters of the name. No photos have been found of the P-38 wearing invasion stripes, so it seems likely that the aircraft had been taken out of service before 6 June 1944.

## 18
### P-38J-10 42-67926/*Susie* of Capt Lindol F Graham, 79th FS/20th FG, Kingscliffe, March 1944

The 79th FS was blessed with a number of skilled Lightning pilots, but Capt 'Lindy' Graham was considered to be the 'pick of the bunch'. Rookie pilots looked up to him as the example to follow, for he had been with the unit since its arrival in the frontline, and had scored 5.5 victories in under three months. Thus, when Graham was killed in *Susie* on 18 March 1944, the unit felt it as a body blow. Graham's 'big day' in combat was 29 January, when he downed three Fw 190s in two separate engagements on the same bomber escort mission whilst flying J-10 42-67497. He went on to 'make ace' in the fighter depicted in this profile during a confused aerial clash involving several P-38s and a formation of Bf 110s on 20 February south-west of Brunswick – he claimed two Messerschmitt 'twins' destroyed. The red star painted beneath the fighter's nickname (and the attendant white scroll to its immediate right) was worn in honour of a former Lockheed employee killed in action during World War 2 – these markings were to be found on a number of P-38s, having been carefully applied at the factory immediately prior to the aircraft being delivered to the USAAF. The white Eighth Air Force group recognition symbol on the tail was not added to the P-38 until early March 1944.

## 19

### P-38J-10 42-67717/*My Dad* of Capt James M Morris, 77th FS/20th FG, Kingscliffe, February 1944

Although P-38J-10 42-67717 was the aircraft adorned with 'Slick' Morris's impressive tally, he only claimed one of his 7.333 victories with it – an Me 110 downed over Schweinfurt on 24 February 1944. Morris was the Eighth Air Force's first P-38 ace, and he scored 5.333 of his kills in J-10 42-67871. Four of these came in a single sortie on 8 February 1944, the two Fw 190s and two Bf 109Gs he downed on this mission setting a scoring record at the time for the P-38 in the ETO. Morris got his final kill (an Me 410) in P-38J-15 43-28397 on 7 July 1944, but was in turn so badly shot up by the stricken fighter's remote-controlled waist guns that he too was forced to bale out – he spent the rest of the war as a PoW.

## 20

### P-38J-15 43-104308/ *'Gentle Annie'* of Col Harold J Rau, CO of the 20th FG, Kingscliffe, April 1944

Although this machine wears Col Rau's full kill tally, it was not the P-38 he used on 8 April 1944 to lead a last-minute fighter sweep over Germany during which he scored all his victories – and his group won a Distinguished Unit Citation. He managed to down one Bf 109, as well as confirm four unidentified twin-engined aircraft destroyed on the ground during the course of the legendary mission. 20th FG aces Morris and Fiebelkorn also claimed ground victories on this mission. 43-104308 was lost during a strafing mission when hit by flak at Le Treport on 16 June 1944, its pilot, Lt Earl O Smith, managing to evade capture.

## 21

### P-38J-10 42-69166/*Gentle Annie* of Col Harold J Rau, CO of the 20th FG, Kingscliffe, August 1944

Following the loss of the original *Annie*, Rau made use of this P-38J-10 for a brief period, despite the fact the fighter was an older J-10 variant. The aircraft shows signs of having been relieved of its original olive drab (OD) paint scheme – note the OD panel surrounding the gun troughs. It was a highly unusual move for a group commander to choose anything but the latest specification machine operated by the trio of squadrons under his charge for his personal mount, and Rau's decision to fly this veteran J-10 was probably influenced by the fact he was due to become tour-expired in August. In any event, the second *Gentle*

*Annie* was in service for less than a month before the 20th FG converted to the P-51D Mustang.

## 22

### P-38J-15 42-104107/*JEWBOY* of Lt Philip M Goldstein (now Graham), 49th FS/14th FG, Triolo, Italy, May 1944

Two Jewish pilots within the 49th FS displayed the admirable impudence in decorating their P-38s in defiance of Nazi-oriented Luftwaffe pilots. Lt Robert Seidman placed a large Star of David on the side of his P-38, and duly shot down five German fighters with it before he succumbed to flak during a strafing raid on the airfield at Udine on 14 May 1944. Squadronmate Goldstein (Graham) painted the name *JEWBOY* on the left engine cowling and repeated the taunt in German on the right. He scored his first victory over a Bf 109 on 2 April 1944, and subsequently claimed a Fiat G 50 on 9 May and a Fw 190 16 days later. He also damaged two Bf 109s and destroyed four more aircraft on the ground.

## 23

### P-38J-15 43-28252 of Lt Franklin C Lathrope, 94th FS/1st FG, Italy, May 1944

There was very little in the way of personal identification markings applied to the P-38s of the 1st FG in 1944, five-kill ace Franklin Lathrope's J-15 being typical of the Lightnings flown by the trio of squadrons within the group. Like other aces of the 1st, Lathrope simply accepted any fighter assigned to him for the day, and got on with flying the mission. Number 89 was the aircraft assigned to him on 10 May 1944 when he scored his fourth and fifth victories – two Bf 109s – south of Weiner Neustadt. In point of fact all his victories were Bf 109s, the first being claimed on 11 March 1944, followed by a damaged claim 18 days later, his second confirmed destroyed on 23 April and his fourth on the 29th of the same month.

## 24

### P-38J-15 43-28431/*HAPPY JACK'S GO BUGGY* of Capt Jack M Ilfrey, 79th FS/20th FG, Kingscliffe, May 1944

Although a brilliant pilot, Jack Ilfrey also had a reputation for recklessness both on the ground and in the air. Despite a spell in America after the completion of his first tour in May 1943, his 'history' followed him from the MTO to the ETO when he started his second tour in England with the 79th FS/20th FG in April 1944. Ilfrey tried to live up to his colourful reputation as often as possible, finding his various escapades (and the subsequent punishments) the best release for the tension of daily air combat. His two aerial victories with the 79th FS came whilst flying this J-15 on 24 May 1944 during a bomber escort to Berlin. Ilfrey climbed into the Bf 109 top cover and shot one down at 30,000 ft before inadvertently ramming a second, losing about four feet of wing and sending the German fighter down in flames. Although he survived this mission, Ilfrey went down in this same fighter on 13 June 1944 when it was hit by fire during an a strafing mission on the airfield at Angers, in France. He managed to evade capture and returned to Kingscliffe, where he served firstly as Operations Officer and then CO of the 79th FS from 27 September to 9 December 1944.

## 25
### P-38J-15 4?-??328/*Mon Amy* of Lt Herbert B Hatch, 71st FS/1st FG, Italy, June 1944

Despite having accrued little combat experience during the first two months of his tour with the 1st FG, Lt 'Stub' Hatch showed just how effective the stateside training for fighter pilots was when he downed five Romanian I.A.R.80s (misidentified as Fw 190s at the time) during the ill-fated Ploesti mission of 10 June 1944. His only previous taste of aerial combat had come on 6 May when had shared in the probable destruction of a Bf 109 with another 71st FS pilot. Hatch's official tally for the 10 June mission was five aircraft downed, one probably destroyed and another damaged. His first three victories were captured by his gun camera before the film broke, whilst the others were confirmed by downed 71st FS pilots (Hatch was the only pilot to make it back to base with his P-38) who later turned up.

## 26
### P-38J-10 42-68024/*SNOOKIE II* of Lt Jack Lenox, 49th FS/14th FG, Triolo, Italy, June 1944

Lenox was a firebrand who confirmed five enemy aircraft destroyed and a probable, plus three additional damaged claims, within a six-month span. His first confirmed victory was a Bf 109 scored on 23 May 1944, which was followed up less than 24 hours later by a Me 210, and then a damaged Bf 109 on the 25th. Lenox 'made ace' during a big battle involving the 14th FG over Petfurdo, in Hungary, on 14 June 1944, the P-38 pilot claiming three Bf 109s shot down.

## 27
### P-38J-15 43-28650/*SWEET SUE*/*NELLIE ANN* of Lt Phillip E Tovrea, 27th FS/1st FG, Italy, June 1944

Tovrea was the scion of a wealthy family who decided to do his bit for his country by becoming an ace with the 27th FS in 1944! He used 43-28650 very rarely, scoring kills in at least four other P-38Js, although he managed to claim two Bf 109s in this fighter on 16 June 1944. Tovrea's most productive day came on 18 July 1944 when he downed two Fw 190s and a Bf 109, and damaged a further two Focke-Wulfs, while flying P-38J-15 43-28734. His final score was eight confirmed, one probable and three damaged.

## 28
### P-38J-15 42-104096 of Capt Thomas E Maloney, 27th FS/1st FG, Italy, May 1944

Being squadronmates, Maloney and Tovrea often flew on the same missions, and apparently enjoyed a mutual respect for one another. Much like Tovrea, Tom Maloney flew whatever fighter was available on the day, but remembers J-15 43-28746 #23 as his usual

mount. He used the P-38 featured here in profile on 28 May 1944 to down a Do 217 over Buxim, in Yugoslavia, and a Bf 109 over Ploesti three days later. Maloney's final tally of eight kills was comprised of four Bf 109s, two Bf 110s, an Fw 190 and a Do 217.

## 29
### P-38J-15 43-28796/*Judy Ann* of Lt Charles E Adams, 95th FS/82nd FG, Vincenzo, Italy, June 1944

Although Adams used this P-38 as his own mount, all bar one of his six victories were scored in other aircraft. *Judy Ann*'s sole success took the form of a Bf 110 downed east of Vienna on 26 June 1944, the pilot's remaining scores being achieved in P-38G-10 42-13199 (Me 210) on 13 April, P-38J-15 43-28654 (Fw 190) on 16 June and P-38J-15 44-23188 (three Me 410s) on 8 July – the 95th FS claimed six Messerschmitt 'twins', plus five other types, on this mission over Vienna. So one-sided was the action that the squadron debriefing officers had to stop the pilots' claims when more they exceeded the entire total of the enemy formation! Judy Ann was the name Adams's daughter.

## 30
### P-38J-15 43-28746 of Capt Thomas E Maloney, 27th FS/1st FG, Italy, August 1944

Maloney scored his final two kills (both Bf 109s) in this P-38 on 15 August 1944. Having met Tom Maloney on several occasions, the author finds it hard to imagine this exceptionally agreeable person finding enough aggression within him to destroy or damage a dozen enemy in aerial combat. The truth of the matter is that he was tough enough to tangle with Luftwaffe veterans on a more than equal footing, plus make a full recovery from horrendous injuries suffered when he trod on a land mine on the coast of southern France after being shot down on 19 August 1944. Despite his wounds, Maloney managed to evade the enemy for a number of days before finally being rescued.

## 31
### P-38J-10 42-68008/*Touché* of Lt Col James Herren, CO of the 434th FS/479th FG, Wattisham, June 1944

A popular commander, Herren led the 434th FS during its first months with the Eighth Air Force from May through to September 1944. This unit provided three of the 479th FG's four aces, all of whom had been led with deftness and determination by Herren during their first crucial combat sorties. He scored all his P-38 aerial victories on 26 September 1944 when the 479th garnered 29 confirmed claims for just a single loss. Herren also claimed a Ju 52/3m on the ground and shared a stationary He 111 with another pilot when the group destroyed a number of aircraft during a series of strafing runs on 18 August 1944. He was finally killed in action in a P-51D during yet another ground attack mission in October 1944. P-38J-10 *Touché* was unusual in sporting a black ID disc on its twin tails, for the 434th FS had previously used a white triangle on its OD

Lightnings and the 435th the circle marking – perhaps this aircraft had been 'acquired' from the latter unit at some point. The squadron painter hated the tedium of accurately masking off the tail symbols, and he was quite pleased when the 434th adopted to the simple all-red rudder marking in August 1944.

## 32
**P-38J-25 44-23677/ "LITTLE BUCKAROO" of Maj Robert C 'Buck' Rogers, CO of the 392nd FS/367th FG, Peray, France, August 1944**

As mentioned in chapter six, the J-25 model of the P-38, with its hydraulically-boosted ailerons and underwing divebrakes, arrived in the ETO too late to see service with the Eighth 8th Air Force, but *was* extensively employed by the three P-38 groups of the Ninth Air Force towards the end of 1944. The J-25 was not only the fastest version of the P-38, but also the most manoeuvrable. Maj 'Buck' Rogers was another popular commander, who led the 392nd FS with fairness and competence according to those who served with him. All his victories were scored on the ground during a single mission on 25 August 1944, Rogers being credited with five Ju 52/3ms destroyed on an airfield near Dijon, in France. As previously mentioned, the Ninth Air Force did not grant individual credits for aircraft destroyed on the ground, thus Rogers is an unofficial ace.

## 33
**P-38J-15 43-28341/SCAT II of Capt Robin Olds, 434th FS/479th FG, Wattisham, August 1944**

This P-38 was one of the few in the 434th FS that retained an olive drab camouflage scheme right up until the type was replaced by the P-51D in late September 1944. Fred Hayner began the squadron practice of painting the rudder red in place of the geometric symbol on the tail, and aside from this marking, and the aircraft's nickname, there is no photographic evidence of any other personal or official embellishments to Olds's P-38 except in the memory of the former individual. Olds himself remembers nothing of his Lightning, other than the general squadron codes ('L2-W') and the name SCAT on the nose. Hayner fortunately used standard markings throughout the squadron, 'his' aircraft being the most distinctively marked of all 479th FG P-38s.

## 34
**P-38J-25 44-23590/SCRAPIRON IV of Capt Lawrence E Blumer, CO of the 393rd FS/367th FG, Juvincourt, France, November 1944**

Blumer was one of the more 'enthusiastic' fighter pilots within the 394th FS/367th FG, his aircraft being given the nickname SCRAPIRON in view of the condition that he often brought them back to base in. He managed to claim five Fw 190 fighters shot down on 25 August 1944 while coming to the rescue of his comrades during a strafing mission (it is uncertain whether he was flying this aircraft at the time). The Fw 190 unit involved in the action was the relatively new JG 6,

which admitted the loss of 16 fighters in its daily records, while the P-38 group claimed 20 victories. Blumer scored one more Fw 190 kill in November, but marked his final P-38 with a row of seven swastikas, possibly indicating a sixth aged Fw 190 that he damaged during the course of his record haul on 25 August. He finished his tour as CO of the 393rd FS, having led the unit from November 1944 to January 1945.

## 35
**P-38J-15 42-104425/BOOMERANG of Capt Arthur F Jeffrey, 343rd FS/479th FG, Wattisham, August 1944**

Another 434th FS ace who started his scoring in the P-38 and finished it with the P-51D/K, Jeffrey claimed his first four kills between 5 July (a rare Fw 200 Condor, downed over Cognac/Chateaubernard airfield) and 28 August 1944 (a Ju 52/3m, claimed over Sedan/Douzy airfield). The reason for the fifth cross, applied slightly to the left of the remaining four victory symbols, remains unexplained, unless Jeffrey anticipated confirmation of a victory which subsequently did not become recorded in any way (confirmed, probable or damaged). The second of Jeffrey's confirmed Lightning haul took the form of an Me 163 rocket interceptor, engaged over Wilhelmshaven on 29 July 1944 in this very P-38. It is interesting to speculate just how the combat would have gone if he had been using a J-25 model, for although Jeffrey was given a destroyed credit, it is now believed that his foe managed to land with substantial battle damage. Having risen to command the 434th FS by the end of his tour, Jeffrey scored a further ten kills in the Mustang to make him the group's leading wartime ace.

## 36
**P-38J-25 (serial unknown) of Lt Lawrence P Liebers, 429th FS/474th FG, Langensalza, June 1945**

Liebers was assigned to the 474th FG soon after VE-Day and received this 'clean' P-38. With hostilities over, he thus ended the war with seven confirmations gained with the 96th FS/82nd FG in North Africa in 1943 – five of these were Italian aircraft, this tally being the highest scored by a USAAF pilot. No markings other than unit or national were apparent on photos of this aircraft, suggesting that the fighter was extremely clean at least when Liebers began using it in the late spring of 1945. With no more action to be seen, Liebers, and many other P-38 pilots for the group, transferred out in July an ended up flying C-47s instead. Having survived so much action in World War 2, Larry Liebers was killed in an AT-7C Navigator accident in California on 21 August 1946.

## 37
**P-38J-15 43-28474/GIVE 'M HELL - FOR H L of Capt Claire A P Duffie, 434th FS/479th FG, Wattisham, September 1944**

Another 'combined' ace from the 434th FS, Duffie

claimed three Bf 109s in the air and two other ground victories mostly in this P-38. The reason for the distinctive inscription on the nose is known only to Duffie. This P-38 was finally retired from service, still with the remnants of its D-Day stripes intact, around 28 September 1944 when the 479th FG completed its transition to the P-51D.

## 38
**P-38J-25 44-23624/*LES VIN, LES FEMMES, LES CHANSONS* of Capt Paul J Sabo, 485th FS/370th FG, Lonray, October 1944**
The French phrase that comprises the name of this P-38 indicates the mentality of most young American pilots – 'wine, women and song'. Paul Sabo accounted for 1/3 of a Fw 200 with the 77th FS/20th FG on 5 February 1944 and an Fw 190 with the 485th FS/370th FG on 20 October 1944. The tally on the nose of the P-38 indicates that Sabo was sure of more than his official victories, being credited with four other aircraft destroyed or damaged.

## 39
**P-38J-15 43-28258/*Pat III* of Col Oliver B Taylor, CO of the 14th FG, Triolo, Italy, July 1944**
Col Taylor kept his P-38J-15 with the 49th FS during his time as CO of the 14th FG. There is no record that he scored any victories in this particular fighter, although Wilson H Oldhouse claimed an Fw 190 while flying it on 11 June 1944. Taylor was struck down with polio at about this time and eventually transferred out of the group on 17 July, command having since transferred to Col Daniel Campbell.

## 40
**P-38J-25 42-??663/*SWAT* of Lt Robert C Milliken, 429th FS/474th FG, Florennes, Belgium, October 1944**
Milliken became one of the last P-38 aces in the ETO when he claimed a Bf 109 on 18 December 1944 near Köln. His first victories in this P-38J-25 were probably the two Fw 190s that he claimed on 12 September 1944 near Aachen – a further three remained unconfirmed damaged. All the P-38J-25s illustrated in invasion markings must have been early examples that operated from airfields just inland from the Normandy beaches, since there was little chance that the sub-type could have reached any operational areas by 6 June 1944. *SWAT* was Milliken nickname.

# FIGURE PLATES

## 1
Col Oliver Taylor, CO of the 14th FG at Triolo, in Italy, in the spring of 1944, is seen wearing regulation cotton-khaki pants (shade 1), or 'Chinos', with an open-necked matching shirt, over which he has donned an A-2 jacket, minus rank tabs. His life preserver is a small and snug B-3, whilst his helmet is an RAF-issue Type D – the British helmet was renowned for not only giving

better ear protection than its American equivalent, but also improved radio clarity due both to its deeper ear cups and better sealing around the ears themselves. The mask attached to the highly-prized helmet is a USAAF standard issue A-10, as are the B-7 goggles. Finally, Taylor has A-6A single-strap boots on his feet.

## 2
Lt Richard A Campbell flew with the 37th FS/14th FG in North Africa in 1943, and he is seen wearing typically improvised flying gear synonymous with the theatre. His trousers are khaki paratrooper issue (note combat webbing), whilst his shirt is standard USAAF rig, with sleeves permanently rolled up – these cotton shirts were comfortable to wear, although they stayed permanently creased once worn due to the combination of sweat and heat. His life preserver is again a B-3, to which he has attached a map board, which is also tied around his right thigh. Campbell's helmet is a standard issue USAAF AN-H-15 summer helmet – the goggles are B-7s. He is holding a full B-8 parachute pack.

## 3
Lt William 'Dixie' Sloan of the 96th FS/82nd FG, as he appeared at Grombalia, Tunisia, in September 1943. He is attired in standard-issue khaki shirt and trousers, with a heavily-stained B-3 life preserver worn over his chest. Sloan carries a Colt .45 in a shoulder holster, with an associated magazine pouch clipped to his waist belt – note too the sunglasses case just above it.

## 4
Lt Claude Kinsey of the 96th FS/82nd FG in North Africa in March 1943. Again he is wearing summer-issue 'khakis', although these are tucked into RAF 1940 Pattern boots. Kinsey's sheepskin-lined jacket is a heavy B-3, pirated from a bomber crewman, whilst his cap is very much '50 mission crushed'.

## 5
Capt 'Lindy' Graham of the 79th FS/20th FG at Kingscliffe in September 1943. The future ace is wearing woollen OD trousers (turned up rather than tucked into his Russet GI issue boots) and a regulation army issue Jacket, Combat, Winter, known as a 'Tanker's jacket'. Graham has on an OD wool shirt, the former complete with pin-on metal collar insignia. tabs. His helmet is again ex-RAF, although this time it's an earlier Type C – the attached goggles are USAAF B-7s, as are the pilot's horsehide riding gloves. Finally, his parachute pack is a B-8.

## 6
Lt James Morris of the 77th FS/20th FG at Kingscliffe in February 1944. He is wearing a 'Tanker's jacket' and bib overalls (second pattern), over which a ubiquitous B-3 life preserver has been donned. His gloves are fur-lined gauntlet style RAF Type Ds his helmet/goggles combination identical to Lindol Graham's and his mask an A-14. Finally, his uniform is completed by a pair of heavy A-2A double-strap flying boots and a neck scarf.

**Morale remained high in spite of early difficulties with the P-38. These 338th FS pilots watch a colleague demonstrate his rather unorthodox method for combating one of the Lightning's most notorious (and enduring) features in north-west Europe – the icy cold cockpit temperature (*Patterson*)**

109Gs to intercept the Americans over Holland. They received a rude surprise.

According to JG 1's records, the P-38 pilots managed to ambush a formation of its fighters and break it up completely. By the time the action had finished, the German fighters had not only failed to inflict significant damage on the bombers, but had themselves been badly mauled instead.

Thirteen fighters were reported lost by JG 1 during this engagement (four Fw 190A-6s and nine Bf 109Gs). P-47 pilots of the 56th, 78th and 4th FGs had accounted for six German fighters, leaving the remaining seven to the 55th. The P-38 pilots claimed to have downed six aircraft, but this number was later reduced to three by the conservative rules of the time. In one of those all too rare moments in aerial combat, it would seem that the 55th FG had actually performed better than it was officially given credit for.

One of the pilots who did receive confirmation for two Bf 109Gs destroyed during this mission later went on to become the first ace of the 343rd FS/55th FG in April 1944. Lt Bob Buttke was a native of California who rose to the rank of captain in the 55th FG, completing two tours (the first in Lightnings and the second in Mustangs) and gaining five victories in P-38s and a ¹/₂-victory in P-51s. The remaining Messerschmitt downed on 3 November fell to P-38 leader (and future 55th FG CO) Lt Col Jack Jenkins, who also claimed one of the Fw 190s as a probable.

Two days later the 55th FG's 38th FS was escorting B-24s to Munster in rough weather at 17,000 ft when a force of Do 217 bombers, protected by Bf 109Gs (again from JG 1), was intercepted. Once again German unit records indicate that three Messerschmitt fighters were lost in the exchange, whilst all the P-38s subsequently returned to base unscathed.

This level of success was not to last, however, for things started to go wrong as early as the mission to Bremen on 13 November. A savage battle was fought in the thinning air at ceilings in excess of 25,000 ft, which saw the P-38 force reduced to 36 aircraft following the onset of mechanical problems triggered by the cold and damp conditions synonymous with these higher altitudes. Seven P-38s were lost and 16 others badly damaged, with only seven German interceptors being claimed in return. The bomber force took light losses 'on a supportable level'.

One of the damaged Lightnings that returned to its base at Nuthampstead in the wake of the mission attracted both considerable technical interest and sheer wonderment that it had actually returned at all. P-38H-5 42-67027 of the 38th FS (coded 'CG-G') boasted in excess of 100 bullet holes and five cannon shell rips, yet it held together long enough to allow Lt Gerald A Brown – who was to subsequently become the first P-38 ace of the 55th FG on 15 April 1944 – to return to his Hertfordshire base. Much of the damage had been inflicted by a tenacious Bf 109G pilot who had attached himself to Brown's tail and refused to be shaken by the

American's wild evasive manoeuvres. Brown's flight leader, Capt Joe Myers, eventually came to the rescue just as the German delivered a stunning blow that drew plumes of brown smoke from one engine. Fortunately Myers was able to shoot the determined foe down, and thus claim the first of his four-and-a-half aerial victories.

The mission of 25 November was marginally more successful, despite elements of the 55th FG being bounced at 15,000 ft by Fw 190As of II./JG 26 over Lille-Hazebrouck. Capt Chet Patterson of the 338th FS swiftly led his middle flight up to 17,000 ft before diving down to aid another P-38 he had spotted duelling with two Fw 190s. Patterson set his combat flaps for manoeuvre and opened fire at one of the Focke-Wulfs at 300 yards – his wingman saw the fighter catch fire and the pilot bale out.

Four Fw 190s were claimed during the action for the loss of Lt Manuel Aldecoa. After the war it was determined that Knight's Cross holder, and *Gruppenkommandeur* of II./JG 26, Major Johannes Seifert (an *Experten* with 57 kills – see *Aircraft of the Aces 9 - Focke-Wulf Fw 190 Aces of the Western Front* for more details) was killed after his starboard wing had struck Aldecoa's Lightning. The American pilot was seen to bale out, but he apparently died during the descent.

Members of the 20th FG also began flying missions in November in preparation for their operational debut the following month. One such individual was future seven-kill ace Lt James 'Slick' Morris of the 77th FS, who saw his first action on the 29th when he led the second element of a four-ship flight that was operating with another identical formation to create an eight-aircraft squadron.

About 15 miles west of Bremen two Bf 109Gs made a feigning attack from the front that forced the eight P-38s to drop their external fuel tanks.

Capt Lindol Graham and his crew pose in front of his P-38J-10 in late February/early March 1944. Graham named each of his Lightnings *Susie*, and usually flew with the code letters 'MC-L' applied to the fighter's twin booms. His first aircraft was paid for by Lockheed employees and was dedicated to a former worker who had been killed in action. When Graham confirmed his fifth victory his P-38J-10 (42-67926) was decorated with an ace of spades marking, which is just visible immediately above the nose-gear leg in this photograph (*Cook*)

Lt James Morris and his crew chief pose by P-38J *Black Barney* of 20th FG CO, Col B M Russell, soon after the former's record mission of 8 February 1944. Morris claimed two Fw 190s and two Bf 109Gs during sortie in question (*IWM*)

Carrying near-mandatory belly tanks on their inner wing pylons, a flight of 20th FG P-38Hs taxy out from their dispersal at Kingscliffe, Northamptonshire, at the start of another long escort mission in late 1943

The leader of Morris's flight then took off after the lead Messerschmitt, and Morris followed behind to take his turn at the enemy. Under orders to maintain contact with the bombers, Morris stayed with the Bf 109 long enough to fire a burst at the retreating German, but the Luftwaffe had won the skirmish by persuading the P-38 pilots to lose their drop tanks.

Fortunes for the rest of the Lightning escort were not much better, Chet Patterson describing the action as '. . . an all-out, wild, movie style combat spectacular'. He managed to claim another Bf 109 that was on the tail of a P-38, and gave the unorthodox order for his flight to break up and fight individually. That daring command must have worked for all four Lightnings returned home.

The other flights of P-38s were not so lucky, however, as once again seven fighters were posted as missing and still others returned with serious battle damage. Only three Luftwaffe fighters were claimed, but the P-38s had again sufficiently divided the attention of the German interceptors to keep bomber losses down. The month of November came to a close with the P-38 groups having lost 17 of their number, while officially claiming 23 enemy aircraft destroyed.

P-38J-10 42-67757 of the 38th FS/55th FG was the subject of an extensive recognition photo-shoot soon after its arrival in the UK at the end of 1943. The results of the flight were widely circulated throughout Allied air and ground forces in order to familiarise 'the troops' (particularly bomber gunners and AA battery crews) with the shape of the Lightning from all possible angles (*AWM*)

# 20th FG

By late December 1943 the 20th FG at last achieved operational status. Enough P-38s (including a few brand new J-models) had been received, and a number of pilots had completed missions with the 55th FG. Independent group operations commenced on 28 December with a sweep of Holland by 38 Lightnings, followed two days later by a bomber escort mission to Ludwigshafen, with the 20th providing withdrawal support.

Future 5.5-kill ace Lt Lindol Graham received his baptism of fire on the last day of 1943 when the 20th FG flew a target umbrella mission to the Bordeaux area. Flying P-38J-10 42-67497, he was leading the 79th FS contingent in 'White Flight' as it orbited at 22,000 ft when two Fw 190s were sighted below. He immediately went to 'punch off' his drop tanks in order to configure the fighter for combat, but these would not release for some reason – he was still able to dive after one of the enemy fighters using his combat flaps, however. Before the Fw 190 was able to reach the safety of cloud cover, Graham fired a long burst from 350 yards that produced visible strikes on the fighter's right wing. Although later only credited with having damaged the Fw 190, he had nevertheless commenced his short, but effective, career against the Luftwaffe.

January and February 1944 were good months for the 20th FG. Even though losses continued to be high, the group scored its first victory on 7 January when Lt Willis Taylor claimed a Bf 109 that was about to fire rockets into a bomber formation. The 20th had one of its best days with

20th FG CO Col Harold J Rau is seen with his crew, TSgt James A Douglas, Sgt Grant L Beach and SSgt Luther W Ghent, in front of their P-38J-15 43-104308 *'Gentle Annie'* at Kingscliffe in April 1944. Sitting obediently at Col Rau's feet is his dog Honey (*Ilfrey*)

Jerry Brown and the 55th FG's intelligence officer pose for a publicity shot soon after the former was credited with scoring his fifth victory on 15 April 1944. The P-38J in background was a new arrival for the 38th FS, the fighter being delivered in protective brown camouflage – the 55th FG was by this time flying natural metal P-38s only (*Brown*)

On 21 May 1944 338th FS pilot Lt Peter Dempsey was flying P-38J-10 42-67440 'CL-J' on a bomber escort mission when he went down with his flight to strafe a German airfield on his way home. Spotting telegraph wires in his path a split second before he hit them, the pilot frantically attempted to dive *underneath* them, but only succeeded in getting steel cabling wrapped tight around the right rudder, and chopping the top off the left one! Despite having effectively locked up both rudders, suffered serious flak and machine gun damage and had an engine all but knocked out (which had deposited oil all over his windscreen), Dempsey managed to nurse his ailing fighter back to his Wormingford base (*Patterson*)

the P-38 13 days later when 10 Luftwaffe fighters were claimed during a target support mission for the largest bomber operation flown to date.

Lindol Graham was the star of the day, getting one Fw 190 on the way in, and a further two on the way out. All three aircraft had been zeroing in on the tail box of bombers when Graham had successfully latched onto their tails and caused them to explode. Equally as remarkable as the triple haul itself was the fact that Graham had used just a miserly 583 rounds of .50-calibre ammunition and 36 rounds of 20 mm cannon shell.

Further success came the way of the 20 th FG on 8 February when the group escorted B-17s to the Frankfurt area, although the mission did not get off to a good start when no fewer than 14 P-38s had to abort due to mechanical difficulties. James 'Slick' Morris (in P-38J-10 42-67871) was covering one of the ailing P-38s when he sighted a Bf 109 at 12,000 ft. He

Inevitably housed in a Nissin hut, the operations room of the 383rd FS/364th FG at Honington is seen after the mission brief on 20 April 1944. The chalkboard at the extreme right of the photo makes the sobering announcement concerning the day's target (*USAF*)

closed in and fired from 100 yards, and the pilot was observed to bale out.

A few minutes later he spotted two Fw 190s taking off from an airfield in Sedan and he duly used his speed and height advantage to quickly despatch both. Morris's flight had by now disappeared, so he wisely decided to set a safe course for home. However, no sooner had he turned west when he came across yet another Bf 109 near the French town of Denain. Quickly latching onto the fighter's tail, Morris scored strikes on the enemy's canopy, but local flak batteries had by now got a track on the Lightning and the American had to be content with leaving his victim heading for the ground pouring smoke at less than 300 ft. Four victories in a single mission was a record for VIIIth Fighter Command in February 1944.

The New Year brought the 55th FG mixed success. There were no great missions in terms of aircraft destroyed, and their loss rate tended to be the highest for any American type during the first part of 1944. The two most destructive elements for the P-38 in northern Europe were enemy fighter action and the weather, the latter not only inducing mechanical failure but also sapping pilot morale with its numbing cold and damp conditions.

However, there were victories to be had in the cold, thin, atmosphere for determined 55th FG pilots. The 38th FS's Lt Jerry Brown overcame these obstacles on 31 January to down his first confirmed victory (he had damaged a *Gustav* near Bremen in P-38H-5 42-67028 on 13 November 1943) near Venlo. He had intercepted a Bf 109G at 28,000 ft and fired at it with his guns until the fighter disintegrated, as his combat report recounts;

'I was flying Swindle Yellow Three on a sweep to protect dive-bombing by another group when, near the vicinity of Venlo, we were bounced by 15

This 77th FS/20th FG P-38J-10 came to grief at the 364th FG's Honington base on 4 May 1944, the fighter appearing to have suffered a collapsed right undercarriage leg whilst taxying for to take-off. The base's fire tenders have liberally sprayed the ground around the rather embarrassed looking Lightning in order to disperse the spilled fuel from the ruptured right drop tank (*Scutts*)

to 20 enemy aircraft from 5000 ft above. We immediately turned into them and started climbing. The enemy aircraft retained their altitude all the time, and would not let us get above them. My flight, led by Capt (Joseph) Myers (4.5 destroyed and 2 damaged), climbed to 33,000 ft trying to get above, and, although we were holding our own, we could not get above owing to their initial advantage in altitude. Because of this, we broke off and started down to rejoin the rest of the squadron. The enemy aircraft half-rolled and came after us. My wingman, Lt Patterson, was bounced and I called for him to break left. The enemy aircraft followed him and got strikes on his right wing. Calling Capt Myers to cover me, I broke down and got on the tail of the '109. My first burst from 100 yards at 28,000 ft hit him on the right side of the canopy. He immediately half rolled and started down, but I half rolled also and closed to 50 yards and

Maj John Lowell of the 384th FS/364 th FG is seen receiving his DFC from group CO, Lt Col Ray Osborn, at Honnington. Lowell destroyed or damaged four enemy fighters on his first two missions – 6/8 March 1944. By the time the 364th converted to P-51Ds in late July 1944, he had three confirmed aerial victories and two ground kills. Lowell added a further 3.5 aerial kills to his tally flying the Mustang (*USAF*)

The 55th FG's Lt Marvin Glasgow (extreme left) scored a probable kill and a damaged while flying this P-38J. He is seen here on 11 May 1944 with his groundcrew at the group's Wormingford base (*USAF*)

observed strikes all over the plane. His empennage blew off, as did his right wing tip. After breaking away, I saw the Me 109 going down and out of control. As a result, I claim one Me 109G destroyed.'

On 10 February the 343rd FS's Bob Buttke teamed up with Capt Paul Hoeper when German twin-engined fighters attempted to threaten the bombers on the way to Brunswick. Hoeper was credited with one Me 210 while Buttke got two others (flying P-38H-5 42-67047) and damaged a Bf 110, although he was obliged to come home on one engine.

Following his quartet of kills on 8 February, Jim Morris had to wait just 72 hours to score that all important fifth victory (again flying 42-67871), and thus become the the Eighth Air Force's first P-38 ace. His combat report detailing this historic action read as follows;

'I was leading Blue Flight (77th) Squadron. Rendezvoused with bombers and took up rear position with Yellow Flight on starboard side of bombers . . . Four (4) Me 109s bounced Yellow flight. (We dropped our) tanks and turned with combat flaps into (the enemy). Fired (at the enemy) as Me 109s closed on Yellow Four . . . fired approximately 400 rounds at 60° deflection . . . Saw strikes on E/A and smoke and flame. I then saw it go into an inverted spin. I watched it spin into (the undercast) still in flames at 16,000 ft.'

Although Morris had achieved personal success, it had come at a high price – eight P-38s failed to return to base at the end of the sortie, the 20th FG having claimed just three German aircraft shot down in return during the fierce engagement. These raw statistics prove that the Luftwaffe's favoured tactic of continually battering larger P-38 formations with small, highly mobile, flights of interceptors was proving most effective.

Lindol Graham joined Jim Morris as an ace 12 days later when he claimed two Bf 110s over the Brunswick/Gotha area. This time the 20th FG had a more favourable return, downing five Fw 190s and a Bf 109G, in addition to Graham's pair, for just one loss. On 24 February 'Slick' Morris once again regained ranking P-38 ace status when he downed a Bf 110 over Schweinfurt for his sixth victory.

## 364th FG

Eighth Air Force bombers began to appear over Berlin in daylight during early March 1944 just as the third P-38 group in the command was declared operational The 364th FG flew its first sorties on the 3rd, and scored its premier victories over the following few days.

Capt George Ceullers of the 383rd FS/364th FG is seen with his men in front of P-38J 42-68017 *Connie & Butch Jnr.* in the late spring of 1944. The pilot used this machine to score 1.5 kills and one damaged in March/April 1944, before going on to claim a further nine aerial victories flying the P-51D (*Scutts*)

On 6/8 March P-38s were credited with just 10 confirmed destroyed out of a total haul of roughly 160 enemy fighters claimed by USAAF fighter escorts. Despite the poor return, three of the victories were nevertheless scored by future 364th FG ace Capt John Lowell. Having previously served as a project officer on the P-38 programme at Wright-Patterson Field prior to his frontline posting, Lowell enjoyed an intimate understanding of the Lightning's capabilities. He first proved his prowess on the 6th when he claimed two Bf 109s destroyed west of Hannover, although one of these was reduced to a probable due to the blurred nature of his gun camera footage – the device had vibrated badly when the quartet of .50-calibre guns housed just above it had been fired.

Two days later Lowell did indeed manage to get two Bf 109Gs confirmed as destroyed north-east of the German capitol. By 9 April Lowell's three aerial victories had been combined with an Fw 190 and Ju 52/3m destroyed on the ground to earn him five credits (and ace status) according to the rules then observed by the Eighth Air Force.

Capt George Ceullers of the 383nd FS also scored his first victories in a Lightning on the 8th, downing an Fw 190 and damaging a second over Berlin – he would later accrue a further nine kills whilst flying the P-51D.

Luftwaffe awareness of the growing escort menace during the first months of 1944 urged more desperation on their part in combating the daylight missions. During the March-April period USAAF pilots noted that German opposition had became notably more determined, and as a consequence greater claims were made by both sides. Record numbers of

Maj Joseph B McManus served as CO of the 383rd FS during the spring and summer of 1944, during which time he completed a large number of bomber escort sorties – just look at the impressive mission tally which adorns the side of his P-38J, christened *Marie*. This photograph was taken at Honington on 15 June 1944 (*USAF*)

Tension or relief shows on Capt Jack Ilfrey's face, depending on whether the mission is beginning or ending. A veteran ace of Operation *Torch* with the 94th FS/1st FG in 1942/43, Illfrey was posted to England for his second tour in April 1944, joining the 79th FS/20th FG. He served as Operations Officer with the unit from June to September, before assuming command of the 79th FS – a position he held until December, when his tour expired. Illfrey had arrived in the ETO with 5.5 kills to his name, and he added a further two to this tally on 24 May 1944 when he downed a pair of Bf 109Gs over Eberswalde whilst flying this very P-38J-15 (43-28431) (*Ilfrey*)

This official photograph shows the first P-38J to land in France following Operation *Overlord*, the aircraft hailing from the 367th FG. This group moved from its base at Ibsley to Beuzeville on 22 July 1944, becoming the first Ninth Air Force P-38 outfit to do so – the 370th FG followed two days later, and the 474th FG on 6 August (*Scutts*)

victories were registered almost weekly by Eighth Air Force fighters as the Luftwaffe lost irreplaceable fighter veterans.

One such desperate mission was flown on 18 March when a mammoth force of more than 700 B-17s and B-24s met savage resistance on their way out of the target area. The standard Luftwaffe policy of avoiding escort fighters was forgotten as the Bf 109Gs and Fw 190s attacked at every opportunity. The 38th FS's Jerry Brown was heavily involved in driving the enemy away from the bombers when he noticed an Fw 190 fastened to the tail of another P-38. He managed to draw a firing pass on the apparently preoccupied German fighter and swiftly shot it down.

Meanwhile North African P-40 veteran Lt Col Mark Hubbard was leading the 20th FG over another part of the continent when he drove his P-38s in too close to the enemy and ultimately paid the price. Although he colonel was not a P-38 enthusiast by any means, he nevertheless wanted the 20th FG to exercise extreme aggression no matter what type aircraft they were using. Leading the group into attack a gaggle of Bf 109Gs, Hubbard had claimed two-and-a-half fighters shot down (with another probably destroyed) before he himself went down in P-38J-10 42-67708 and was taken prisoner. Ironically, in view of his dislike of the Lightning, Hubbard had became an ace during the course of this mission as he had previously scored four kills in P-40.

The 77th FS ran into Bf 110s on 18 March and shot down three of them. These victories were not without cost, however, as P-38 ace Capt Lindol Graham was killed in action. He and his wingman, Lt Art Heiden, were hard on the tail of an evading *Zerstörer* when the pilot put his twin-engined fighter down in the snow. Heiden then watched in disbelief as Graham made a pass at the fleeing German crew, misjudged his altitude and clipped the snow-covered ground, before turning over and crashing.

During the spring of 1944 the Luftwaffe lost all parity with the Allied air forces. Following the 'Big Week' raids on the German aircraft industry, and the Berlin missions in March, the Luftwaffe found itself hard-pressed to counter the aerial threat. With fewer targets to shoot down, the Eighth Air Force accelerated its offensive by attacking aircraft on the ground. Results were initially modest, but by war's end USAAF fighters were claiming more victories on the ground than in the air.

Following the loss of Mark Hubbard on the 18th, command of the 20th FG passed to Lt Col Harold Rau, who led the group with more affection for the P-38, whilst still showing determination to get at the enemy.

On 8 April the 20th FG was scrubbed from an escort mission to Germany because of poor weather blanketing Kingscliffe, but by noon the sky had cleared sufficiently enough for Lt Col Rau to obtain permission for a free sweep to the Salzwedel area. Leading the group at the head of the 79th FS, Rau took his flight through four passes at an airfield north of Salzwedel and claimed 13 single- and twin-engined types destroyed and one 'twin' damaged. Rau himself had got four multi-engined aircraft before seven Bf 109Gs bounced the squadron and shot down a single P-38. Spotting a second Lightning in grave trouble with a Messerschmitt closing in from behind, Rau swiftly centred the German fighter in his

Jack Ilfrey's P-38J-15 (43-28431) draws a crowd upon its recovery back at Kingscliffe following the ace's double Bf 109G haul on 24 May 1944. A close examination of the aircraft's starboard wingtip reveals collision damage sustained during Ilfrey's ramming attack on one of the Messerschmitt fighters during the engagement. This P-38 was later lost on 13 June when Ilfrey was shot down by flak during a strafing run near Angers (*Ilfrey*)

Jack Ilfrey and a groundcrewman make a close examination of the damage for the camera on the afternoon of 24 May 1944. Spares for Lightnings were no longer in short supply by the spring of 1944, and this aircraft would have been quickly patched up with a replacement outer wing section in just a matter of days (Ilfrey)

sights and struck it a mortal blow for his fifth combined victory of the day. Unfortunately the Bf 109G continued on its course long enough to collide with its intended victim, and both aircraft crashed.

Jim Morris added three twin-engined aircraft on the ground (partly shared with two others) to his tally to maintain his position as top P-38 ace of the Eighth, whilst Lt Ernest Fiebelkorn also claimed an unidentified twin-engined machine on the ground to begin a scoring run that would include 9.5 air victories (9 with the P-51D) and two ground kills.

Newly-promoted Capt Jerry Brown also scored on the 8th when he downed a Bf 109G for his third victory. Exactly a week later he destroyed a Fw 190 and a He 111 to 'make ace'. On 22 April Robert Buttke was credited with a Bf 109G shot down and another damaged to also become a P-38 ace – the sole pilot to do so with the Lightning in the 343rd FS.

Despite the fact that the 55th FG would score more than 50 aerial victories during the next few months prior to converting onto Mustang in July, no other P-38 pilot would register his fifth kill.

## SUMMER FORTUNES

It was rather ironic that just as the P-38 was about to enter a period much more favourable to securing aerial successes, a decision was made to ter-

One of the USAAF's great fighter aces, Maj J D 'Whispering John' Landers had already 'made ace' on P-40Es in the Pacific as long ago as Boxing Day 1942 when he joined the 38th FS/55th FG in April 1944. He added a further four kills (a Bf 109G on 25 June and three Me 410s on 7 July) and a damaged (another Bf 109G) to his tally whilst flying the P-38J-15, rising to command the 38th FS in early July 1944. Landers' final 4.5 kills were scored with the P-51D whilst on his third combat tour (as CO of the 78th FG) in March 1945 (*Tabatt*)

minate its service with the Eighth Air Force. Warm weather usually brought out the best features in the fighter's mechanical components, and the new J-25 model, fitted with power controls and dive flaps, would largely miss flying with Eighth Air Force groups altogether – although the type served the three Lightning groups within the Ninth Air Force well.

20th FG CO Lt Col Cy Wilson (ex-boss of the 55th FS) was perhaps the only Eighth Air Force pilot to experience success with the modified J-model when he claimed a Bf 109G on 25 June. 20th FG veterans sometimes claim that Wilson was flying a late J- or L-model on this sortie, but he was in fact using P-38J-15 43-28393, with 55th FS codes 'KI-W' – this aircraft was one of about a dozen P-38s that had been modified with kits hurriedly shipped to England. On the engagement in question, the colonel was escorting B-24s out of France when 15 Messerschmitts were sighted below. Wilson gave chase, and his fighter was indicating 450 mph in a near-vertical dive at 17,000 ft when he caught up to one of the Bf 109s and shot it down at 9000 ft.

Eighth Air Force P-38s had one of their best days a few weeks before

Lt George Gleason of the 434th FS/479th FG is seen at Wattisham flanked by his groundcrew early on in his tour in mid-1944. He downed three Bf 109Gs (and damaged a fourth) near Munster on 26 September and also claimed two ground victories with the P-38 – he thought the fighter was ideal for ground attack work, but much preferred the P-51D for aerial combat. Indeed, he scored seven kills with the Mustang after the 479th had traded in its Lightnings in late September (*Gleason*)

converting to Mustangs. On 7 July the 20th and 55th FGs escorted the bombers to oil refineries in Halle, Germany, claiming 25 of the 77 aircraft shot down by USAAF aircraft that day – the 55th 'bagged' 18 of this total for no losses. Incidentally, the group accounted for its 100th aerial success on this date, having commenced operations just nine months earlier. The crack 56th FG (flying P-47s) was the first Eighth Air Force group to break the 100 barrier, doing so in seven months.

The seven remaining victories scored on 7 July fell to the 20th FG, although they lost a single P-38. That latter happened to be none other than the ranking Lightning ace in northern Europe, Capt Jim Morris, who was in the process of shooting down an Me 410 when the fuselage-mounted rear guns of the mortally damaged German aircraft hit his P-38 (J-15 43-28397) and forced the ace to bale out. He spent the rest of the war in a PoW camp, his final tally totalling 7.3 aerial kills and three ground victories.

August was a banner month for all USAAF fighters over the continent, including the P-38s that remained on strength with the new 479th FG (the only Lightnings left within the Eighth Air Force) and the three Lightning units of the Ninth Air Force. There were 27 successful days during the month for fighters of the two air forces, with P-38 pilots not only making claims on eight of those days, but actually dominating the scoring on at least three dates.

One of the most successful Lightning exponents during this period was newly-promoted Capt Robin Olds, who had been flying in the ETO with the 434th FS/479th FG since the group's arrival in-theatre in April/May 1944. A talented and aggressive pilot, whose remarkable leadership skills would see him promoted to command his unit before the end of his tour, Olds finally scored his first kills on the morning of 14 August near Mont-mirail, in France. This successful engagement is recounted in his Form D;

'I was flying Newcross Red Two on a Fighter Rhubarb mission under VIIIth Fighter Command Field Order Number 513. I was alone on the deck heading approximately 330°, when I saw two unidentified aircraft one or two miles away at one o'clock in a turn heading 70° at an altitude of approximately 200 ft. I cut across below them and pulled up behind and identified them positively at Fw 190s. Then I opened fire on the trailing E/A from dead astern, at about 400 yards, and fired a five- to eight-

Lt Arnold Helding of the 434th FS/474th FG poses with his P-38J, christened *LUCKY LADY*, in mid-1944

The irrepressible Robin Olds of the 434th FS/479th FG is seen (with the rank of major) squatting on the wing root of his P-51K 44-72922 *SCAT VI* in April 1945. Eight months earlier he had become the last fighter pilot in the Eighth Air Force to claim five aerial victories with the P-38, adding three Bf 109Gs (downed near Rostock) on 25 August 1944 to a pair of Fw 190s he had claimed 11 days earlier (*Gleason*)

second burst. I observed many strikes on the left wing and the left side of the fuselage, so I changed point of aim slightly to the right and put a concentrated burst into the fuselage. I observed big pieces flying off the German aircraft and wisps of flame and heavy black smoke poured out of it. The E/A then went into (an) uncontrolled half roll going down to the right. At this time we were both just above the trees at an altitude of not more than 100 ft.

'The second E/A broke left in a violent evasive skid right on the deck and I followed, so I did not observe the first German hit the ground because my right wing blanketed him. I was turning inside the second German, so I fired in short bursts at a range of approximately 350 to 200 yards, observing a few strikes. The E/A did a complete 360° turn and pulled out straight and level, still on the deck. Then I fired again, approximately a five second burst from dead astern, and observed many strikes. Large pieces of the German ship flew off. He then zoomed and I followed, continuing to fire, still more strikes and pieces occurring. At the top of the zoom the German pilot parachuted, his 'chute opened almost at once, so that I had to cock up on a wing to keep from hitting him. I saw this second German ship hit the ground and explode.'

Olds became the Eighth Air Force's last P-38 ace 11 days later when he claimed a trio of Bf 109Gs over the Baltic coast near the city of Rostock. He would go on to claim a further eight kills flying P-51Ks (see *Aircraft of the Aces 1 - P-51 Mustang Aces of the Eighth Air Force* for more details) by May 1945, before adding a further four MiG victories over Vietnam some 22 years later to raise his tally to 17 destroyed and 1 damaged.

Only one other 479th FG pilot achieved ace status during the group's

P-38 period, Capt Clarence Johnson of the 436th FS scoring his fifth (and the group's first) kill during a strafing mission in the Reims area on 22 June. Having pulled up over a hill in P-38J-15 43-28697 ('9B-R'), the pilot was surprised to see a Fi 156 Storch looming rapidly in his sights. Reacting quickly, Johnson set the defenceless communications aircraft alight with a burst of fire and watched it crash, with the rest of his flight as witnesses. He had previously scored four kills, one probable and one damaged flying with the 96th FS/82nd FG (see chapter three for details) over the Mediterranean during a combat tour completed in late 1943.

The 479th earned a Distinguished Unit Citation for strafing missions in August and September, these sweeps seeing a large number of aircraft destroyed on the ground and at least 25 in the air – a sizeable quantity of ground claims were lodged on 18 August and 5 September, whilst roughly 25 aerial kills were credited to the pilots on 26 and 28 September.

Returning to the 18 August strafing run, passes were made on the airfields at Nancy and Essey which resulted in 434th FS CO Lt Col J M Herren being credited with a Ju 52 and He 111 destroyed, and Robin Olds also claiming a Heinkel bomber and two Ju 88s. Future 12-kill ace (three with the P-38 and nine with the P-51D) Lt George Gleason claimed an Fw 190 and shares in two other machines, whilst Lt Thomas Olson was credited with four aircraft – he followed this success up with two more ground kills on 5 September.

## NINTH AIR FORCE P-38s

Three fighter groups within the Ninth Air Force flew the P-38 in the tactical role, the units concerned commencing operations in late April and early May as a precursor for the D-Day invasion on 6 June 1944. Despite relatively few aerial victories being scored by the squadrons within these groups, the 367th and 474th FGs nevertheless managed to generate four aces, plus at least one that completed his scoring in the P-38 after gaining three kills with the P-40 in China – Maj Joseph Griffin shot down a Bf 109 on 17 June and two Fw 190s on 14 August to attain ace status.

Despite having flown operational missions from 25 April onwards, the 474th FG's first aerial kills were not achieved until the afternoon of 6 July when three Fw 190s were downed and a further four recorded as probables. The 429th FS's Lt Robert 'Swat' Milliken was flying P-38J-10 42-67495 during the sortie when he noticed an Fw 190 strafing 428th FS pilot Lt James Frederick as he descended in a parachute. So enraged at the thought of his defenceless comrade being attacked in his 'chute, Milliken dived after the German fighter at full throttle.

The Lightning pilot later recounted how the resulting action was the only classic turning fight he ever experienced in combat. After a few minutes of chasing around the countryside, the Fw 190 was damaged enough to persuade the pilot to take to his own parachute. Curiously enough, the battle had taken place in a wide circle over the same territory, affording the previously defeated Frederick a grandstand view of the action. Once rescued, the downed P-38 pilot could not thank Milliken enough.

25 August was also a day of accelerated aerial combat for the P-38 pilots of the Ninth Air Force, who continued to perform their perilous ground

Robin Olds' squadronmate Capt James M Hollingsworth was as enthusiastic about the P-38 as George Gleason was about the P-51D. Indeed, he used the fighter to claim no fewer than six ground kills in a single sortie on 5 September 1944, which was almost certainly an Eighth Air Force record for the Lightning (*Hollingsworth*)

Capt Lawrence Blumer is presented with the DSC by none other than Maj-Gen Carl A Spaatz, Commander of the USAAF in Great Britain, for his performance on 25 August 1944, when he led the 393rd FS to the rescue of another 367th FG unit that was under attack. Blumer's squadron claimed 14 Fw 190s in the subsequent engagement, five of which fell to the DSC winner himself (*USAF*)

The groundcrewman perched on the wing root of this P-38J seems to be staring at the fighter's complex nose-art rather quizzically. This could be because the aircraft's pilot, Capt Paul J Sabo of the 485th FS/379th FG, was himself unsure as to the number of aircraft he had actually destroyed – hence the question mark on one of the kill symbols instead of a swastika. Sabo, who flew with both the 20th FG and the 370th, claimed a total of 5.333 aircraft damaged or destroyed between 5 February and 20 October 1944 (*Crow*)

attack duties. Undoubtedly the 'star of the day' was the 393rd FS's Capt Larry 'Scrappy' Blumer, who led his flight down behind a gaggle of Fw 190s that were devasting P-38s from another 367th FG unit. Blumer swiftly downed five Focke-Wulf fighters and damaged a sixth, which managed to clear the battle area. Later in the day the 392nd FS made a strafing run on an airfield at Dijon and claimed 16 Ju 52/3ms destroyed, five of these being attributed to squadron CO, Maj Robert 'Buck' Rogers.

The 474th FG also tasted success on the 25th when its trio of squadrons downed 21 aircraft during a large battle in the Laon area – this took the

On 25 August 1944, Maj Robert 'Buck' Rogers led the 392nd FS on an attack on a French airfield in this P-38J-25 (44-23677), destroying five Ju 52/3ms during myriad strafing passes. Unfortunately for Rogers, the Ninth Air Force did not grant credits for ground victories, so the swastikas painted beneath the cockpit of the fighter failed to technically qualify him as an ace (*Crow*)

overall Ninth Air Force P-38 group haul to 41 aerial and 16 ground victories. These impressive tallies came at a price, however, for the 474th lost eleven P-38s and the 367th FG eight. Five-kill ace Lt Lenton Kirkland of the 429th FS accounted for his first two victories – Bf 109Gs – in P-38J-25 44-23565 (coded '7Y-E') on this date.

It was determined after the war that relatively new *Geschwader* JG 6 had lost 16 of its Fw 190s to P-38s on 25 August, thus giving one of the P-38 groups (probably the 367th) a reasonably accurate victory tally.

Ninth Air Force P-38s enjoyed good 'hunting' for the rest of 1944, the 474th, for example, running into German fighters during a strafing mission on 13 October and duly downing 11 of them, with Bob Milliken getting his fourth Fw 190. His 429th FS was in action again eight days later when Lenton Kirkland got an Fw 190 for his third confirmed kill.

November and December were crucial months in the final destruction of the once potent Luftwaffe. Contacts between German fighters and the heavy bombers were sporadic at best, and were in no way threatening the burgeoning daylight campaign. Even the tactical bombing and strafing missions of the Ninth Air Force were now finding more resistance from anti-aircraft fire than from fighter interception.

Not all Luftwaffe fighters had been wiped from the skies, however, as the 367th FG found out on 19 November whilst escorting bomb-laden P-47s of the 368th FG to the Duren area on a ground attack mission – no fewer than 25 Fw 190s were engaged en route to the target. Larry Blumer, who was leading the 393rd FS element of the escort, reacted swiftly to the attack by attempting to drop his tanks but they would not budge. Never-

theless, he still went after the enemy and shot down one of the Fw 190s. He was now one of the elite P-38 pilots to down more than five Focke-Wulf fighters. Other 367th FG pilots claimed six Fw 190s for no losses.

December saw the waning presence of the P-38 in northern Europe, most group commanders within the Ninth Air Force preferring the more rugged P-47 for ground attack missions than the rather delicate (by comparison) P-38. However, Lightning pilots still got in some strikes between the end of the year and spring of 1945, one such December mission seeing the P-38 take a heavy toll of German aircraft when units claimed 19 destroyed in the air on the 17th (on the same day P-47 pilots claimed 55 and P-51D pilots six.) On Christmas Eve Spitfires and Lightnings engaged Fw 190Ds of II./JG 26, and the P-38s claimed two enemy aircraft destroyed and the Spitfires at least one other.

The last P-38 aces to gain all their victories on-type were Bob Milliken and Lenton Kirkland of the 429th FS/474th FG on 18 December. The group encountered about a dozen Bf 109Gs in combat with P-47s northwest of Köln at 12,000 ft, and after shedding their bombs, the Lightning pilots entered the fray. Kirkland got two Messerschmitt fighters and Milliken another to each register their fifth aerial victories.

That was not quite the end of the P-38 aces in Europe, however, for Capt Joseph E Miller, who had scored a quartet of kills with the 48th FS/14th FG over Italy in mid-1943, was transferred to the 429th FS/474th FG in early 1945 to commence a second tour. He duly accounted for a single Fw 190 on 13 March whilst supporting troops pushing into Germany, Miller's victory creating the last P-38 ace in Europe. The Lightning's war in the ETO/MTO had begun in August 1942 with tentative sweeps over France, and did not finally come to end until a 429th FS pilot shot down an Si 204 transport on the last day of the war, 8 May 1945.

Lt Robert Milliken of the 429th FS/474th FG was one of just a handful of P-38 pilots to 'make ace' with the Ninth Air Force. Credited with four Fw 190s and a single Bf 109G between 6 July and 18 December 1944, Milliken also has the distinction of being the last pilot to achieve ace status with the Lightning in northern Europe (*Milliken*)

# GROUND CLAIMS

The question of ground claims by USAAF fighter pilots is a troubling one in light of the fact that much of the Luftwaffe was destroyed on the ground during the final phase of the war, with large numbers of enemy aircraft often being rendered useless in a single pass. To make matters worse, the Eighth Air Force was the only organisation to accord ground claims equality with aerial victories in respect to acknowledging the achievements of aces. Recognising that they could no longer compete on an equal footing in the skies during the last months of the war, but still hoping to distract attacks on vital targets, the Luftwaffe lined up large numbers of aircraft at heavily-defended airfields across Germany as a lure for marauding Allied fighters. Although this desperate tactic often saw skilled pilots trained in the art of aerial combat sacrificed in an attempt to destroy mostly non-operational aircraft, American fighter groups took a heavy toll of German aircraft, often claiming hundreds in single sorties.

Heading the strafing tally were the P-51D groups, who claimed over 4000 aircraft destroyed, followed by the P-47 units with 3000+ and finally the P-38 with 749. The paucity of this latter figure reflects the fact that P-38s flew fewer sorties than either the P-51D or the P-47.

Perhaps the first occasion on which the Lightning claimed ground victories was in north-western Africa when the 14th FG destroyed approximately six transports and bombers on the ground (plus a number of others that had succeeded in taking off) on 24 November 1942. The action resulted in several of the participating pilots being credited with at least five combined air and ground victories.

The greatest strafing mission involving P-38s in the MTO was flown on 25 August 1943 when two groups of Lightnings came in 'under the

*CRAZY MAIZIE* was a P-38H flown by the 96th FS/82nd FG in the Mediterranean in late 1943. Note the mission tally on the extreme nose of the fighter (*Blake*)

**Again adorned with a log of completed missions on its nacelle, veteran P-38G *Little Willie* of the 96th FS is seen on a featureless airfield in North Africa in mid-1943 (*Blake*)**

radar' and shot up a large percentage of the enemy aircraft found on the various fields scattered across the Foggia plain. Lt Joe Solko of the 82nd FG was flying the unit's celebrated P-38F-15 *"SAD SACK"* on this occasion, and he duly claimed damaging no fewer than nine Ju 88s when he returned to base. Solko had used the P-38's combat flaps to slow the fighter down during his gunnery passes, dropping its nose to a highly advantageous attitude. He later recounted how he practically looked down into the cockpits of the bombers '. . . dancing on their landing gear . . .' as the bullets and shells struck.

In later months, as the Allied armies slowly advance up the Italian peninsula, most enemy aircraft were withdrawn beyond the range of tactical fighters, and fewer claims were subsequently made – far more aerial victories were confirmed on deep penetration missions over defended enemy cities. Fewer claims in general were available to the Fifteenth Air Force, while more ground kills fell to the Eighth and Ninth Air Forces.

Reinforcing the latter statistic, two Eighth Air Force P-38 groups actually earned Distinguished Unit Citations partly because of strafing success. The first citation was won by the 20th FG for a sweep of the Salzwedel area, about 80 miles north-west of Berlin, on 8 April 1944, the group claiming seven aircraft in the air and 21 on the ground.

This mission had only been flown because group CO, Col Harold Rau, had hastily organised a replacement sweep following the scrubbing of a scheduled escort mission due to bad weather. Conditions rapidly improved as the day wore on, and the colonel succeeded in getting permission from Eighth Air Force Headquarters to make the sweep. Forty-four P-38s from the three squadrons duly took off from Kingscliffe at about 1400 hours and arrived over the target a few minutes before 1600.

The Lightnings descended from 7000 ft and generally 'beat up' anything of military value. Rau had already claimed three unidentified twin-engined aircraft and a Ju 52/3m on the ground when he broke off his strafing runs and took his flight back up to 10,000 ft in order to perform

the role of top cover. Although the flak was intense by this time, seven Bf 109Gs made a slashing attack on the P-38s still strafing and succeeded in shooting one down. Rau then attempted to come to the rescue of a second P-38 under attack, and although he succeeded in mortally damaging the Messerschmitt fighter, the German pilot nevertheless collided with the P-38 he was pursuing and both aircraft crashed.

Despite the 20th FG enjoying great success on this day, top honours went to the 479th FG for claiming more than 60 aircraft on the ground (as well as another 29 in the air) during the period 18 August to 28 September 1944. Robin Olds, George Gleason, James Herren and Thomas Olson raised their combined air and ground totals to five or more during this period, whilst James Hollingsworth scored six aircraft (two Do 217s and four Me 410s) on the ground at Ettingshausen, Germany, on 5 September for what is perhaps a record for the P-38 in Europe.

Maj Robert 'Buck' Rogers, CO of the 392nd FS, had his day of strafing aircraft on 25 August 1944, when he led the squadron to an airfield south of Dijon and found it packed with Ju 52/3ms all neatly lined up – USAAF intelligence later concluded that the transports had been assembled to fly important German personnel out of France. All 16 aircraft were destroyed on the ground, and it was determined later by eyewitness account that Rogers had destroyed five aircraft in two passes. Unfortunately for him, there was no provision in Ninth Air Force policy to officially recognise ground claims, so Rogers has only the personal satisfaction of knowing that he destroyed five enemy aircraft.

The matter of official accreditation for aircraft destroyed on the ground is a thorny one. Some pilots of the Eighth Air Force are credited with as many as 10 aircraft destroyed in a single attack, lending credence to the suggestion that destroying grounded machines was a simpler matter than outmanoeuvring an operational aircraft in the air. There is no doubt that special dangers attended attacks on grounded aircraft, but victories were also less complicated by definition of the target(s) being immovable.

P-38Js of the 38th FS/55th FG are seen on a bomber escort mission during May 1944. This month saw Lightnings flying both escort and ground attack missions in preparation for D-Day. Late spring 1944 was also a period of transition for fighters in the ETO, as new aircraft began to be taken on strength in a natural metal finish, rather the traditional olive drab and grey (*USAF*)

# EARLY DAYS

By the early spring of 1943, three USAAF fighter groups – the 4th, 56th and 78th – were flying the P-47 Thunderbolt from bases in England. Having American rather than British fighters (the 4th had flown Spitfires from September 1942) in the hands of Army Air Force units undoubtedly gave the planners of the Eighth Air Force's bomber offensive a little more confidence. The P-47 was capable of escorting heavy bombers further than was previously possible with Spitfires, although the operational doctrine of using fighters in this role had hardly been addressed. How best fighters could protect the B-17 and B-24 formations on their daylight heavy bombing missions would remain a matter for discussion throughout much of 1943.

But at least with the re-equipment of the in-theatre 4th Fighter Group (FG) at Debden and the arrival in the UK of the 56th and 78th FGs, bomber escort would be handled by fighters with similar capability and slightly more range than Spitfire Mk IXs. The latter aircraft still escorted the Eighth's 'heavies' to targets in the vicinity of Paris, however, and the RAF would continue to offer short-range penetration and withdrawal support to American heavy and medium bomber crews, who were more than welcome comrades in the Allied struggle to defeat Germany.

Of these three US fighter groups, only the 4th had combat experience, its component units tracing their lineage back to the volunteer 'Eagle' squadrons of the RAF. Inevitably comparing the newcomer with the Spitfire, the 'Debden Eagles' looked askance at the huge and portly Thunderbolt, with some pilots seriously doubting its ability to fight on equal terms with the Luftwaffe's small, highly agile and deadly Bf 109s and Fw 190s. RAF pilots were equally sceptical of its potential.

As early as December 1942 the 4th FG got the word that it would receive the P-47 for heavy bomber escort missions. There were some

pilots who felt great relief at being released from the endless convoy patrols they had been flying in Spitfires, although the 'Rhubarbs' and medium bomber escort sorties had occasionally brought excitement. In the event, there was little contact with the P-47 until enough aircraft had been delivered and conversion training had been completed in April 1943.

Before any of the Thunderbolt groups got into combat, the question of minimising risks to pilots as result of faulty recognition had to be addressed. The RAF liaison personnel attached to the Eighth Air Force thought that the P-47's superficial resemblance to the Focke-Wulf Fw 190 should be offset by painting white nose and tail bands on all operational Thunderbolts. This work, initiated at depots as early as 6 February 1943, was to serve P-47 groups well, particularly on bomber escort missions where gunners usually adopted the rule of shoot first and ask questions later. The highly visible recognition markings saved numerous pilots from being shot down by accident.

As the original group to equip with the type in the USA, the 56th was much more sold on the capabilities of the P-47 than the units comprising the 4th FG. Having extensively flown the Republic fighter, the group had materially assisted the manufacturer in developing the early production models into something that (unlike previous US fighters) was estimated to have an even chance when the time came to take on the Luftwaffe.

The last of the original Thunderbolt groups to form up was the 78th FG. Having trained on P-38s in America, its component units came to England without aircraft, and they soon found themselves flight testing its first P-47s. Initial impressions of the aircraft were mixed, with a number of pilots drawing unfavourable comparisons between the Thunderbolt and the Lockheed twin – such reaction was not uncommon at the time, and it soon passed. In any case, there were simply not enough P-38s available at the time to equip the 78th, this situation causing much consternation amongst certain individuals in higher echelons, who viewed the Lightning as a better aircraft for escort missions in the European Theatre of Operations (ETO) – see *Aircraft of the Aces 19 - P-38 Lightning Aces of the ETO/MTO* for further details.

Training flights occupied the groups during the early part of the year, 50 hours being specified before a man could be considered proficient on the P-47. Pilots had to come to terms both with numerous technical malfunctions suffered by the early 'combat worthy' P-47Cs and the huge challenge to navigation and formation flying posed by England's weather. Few Americans had ever seen anything like the solid cloud cover, freezing rain and fog that prevailed over this part of the world, and that the weather could be just as lethal to single-seat fighters as the Luftwaffe was grimly proven on numerous occasions. Training flight accidents, often to weather-related causes, inflicted a steady toll right through to VE-Day.

**Once the groups had finished painting their early P-47Cs with full three-letter codes, each aircraft was allocated to a pilot – who, judging by the nose art visible on these Thunderbolts, clearly lost no time in personalising their aircraft. This formation shot was one of a number taken for publicity purposes depicting Thunderbolts of the 62nd FS/56th FG. Flying P-47C-5 LM-O (41-6347) is Capt Eugene 'Gene' O'Neill, who had joined the then 62nd Pursuit Squadron within the 56th Pursuit Group in December 1941. During his tour of duty in the ETO – which lasted until 20 February 1944, and saw him tally 200 combat hours – O'Neill claimed 4.5 kills (he has often been erroneously credited with five). All bar one of these victories was claimed in the aircraft featured in this photograph**

Affiliation flights with the bombers they were primarily in England to escort was an important part of each fighter group's non-operational flying. It was vital that the bomber gunners recognised the P-47 to prevent accidental 'victories' over 'enemy' fighters. The white bands helped, as they were visible over a considerable distance. Formating on a B-24 in this view is P-47C-5 (41-6342) of the 62nd FS, this shot being yet another of those taken in the sequence which featured the photograph seen on the previous page (*via M Bowman*)

It was not until late February 1943 that the radio and engine problems that had dogged the early P-47s were rectified to the extent that combat missions could at last be flown. Although no operational sorties had been completed up to this point, groundcrews had nevertheless remained busy during the period as more aircraft arrived in England. Technical problems would persist well into 1943, but pilots soon learned to live with them, and thus not become overly distracted from the job in hand. They schooled themselves not to be unnerved by the crackling and buzzing that emitted from their R/T headsets, the odd behaviour of Pratt & Whitney engines under certain flight conditions or the less than sparkling performance of their aircraft at lower altitudes. They also applied themselves to heeding warnings about the reputedly dangerous flight condition known as 'compressibility' that the P-47 could get into in a high speed dive.

Behind the scenes, the Eighth Air Force and Republic technical troubleshooters made an intensive effort to better tailor the P-47 to European conditions. To their credit, they largely overcame the not inconsiderable problems this posed, and duly provided the fighter groups with an aircraft that would soon prove its potential.

Potential to destroy other aircraft in combat the P-47C had in abundance, for its eight .50-cal Browning machine guns firing up to 425 rounds per gun were equal in terms of firepower to most fighters armed with cannon. Some American pilots even thought that eight guns was excessive, with comments voiced to this effect by doubters probably bearing the weight factor in mind, for the P-47 was, at 14, 925 lbs fully loaded, certainly no lightweight. On the other hand, they might have been slightly chagrined at the implication that Republic thought they needed all those guns because they couldn't shoot straight!

Whether or not a pilot had a favourable attitude towards the P-47 often depended on what he had flown before. The 4th FG's combat experience on Spitfires had bred a widespread attitude that the British fighter was an almost impossible act to follow. Nobody could deny that the two aircraft were very different indeed, but comparisons did not really mean much.

On the face of it, one could cite the fact that it took a P-47C twenty minutes to reach 30,000 ft and a Spitfire Mk IX less than seven-and-a-half as being a strong indicator that the Thunderbolt would be useless if it had to climb fast in the battle area, but this turned out not to be too much of a drawback. The P-47 did indeed have a poor rate of climb which had to be allowed for, but virtually all combat aircraft have their weak points.

The situation vis-a-vis the P-47 was not helped by a vague operational plan outlined by VIII Fighter Command that failed to appreciate the important role to be played by the escort fighter in the American daylight bomber offensive. At this stage in the war some bomber commanders still

reckoned that they could cope without fighter help by adopting tight, self-defensive, formations. VIII Fighter Command leader Gen Frank O'Dell Hunter (who had little fighter experience himself) could hardly counter this school of thought at the time for his early-model P-47Cs could not fly much further than Paris on escort duty. It was consequently left to the group commanders, and their flight leaders, to more or less develop their own tactics and deploy their forces to the best advantage.

Fortunately all the groups in England had commanders who would shoulder this responsibility as if they had been pre-ordained for it. Individuals such as Hubert Zemke, Don Blakeslee and Chesley Peterson helped write the book on early escort operations from the UK, creating a solid foundation for future American fighter force missions.

For the ordinary USAAF fighter pilot in the UK in the early months of 1943, the prospect of combat with the Germans was both exciting and daunting. Many had heard stories of how good the *Jagdflieger* were, but when they came to England and learned more about how the RAF had managed to keep them at bay during the Battle of Britain, these details were well noted. Clearly, the Germans were not invincible, and although the Americans had last fought them in European skies in 1918 (notwithstanding the handful who had fought for the Republicans in the Spanish civil war), these combats had become somewhat obscure by 1943.

That first world conflict nevertheless brought to mind the possibility that someone in VIII Fighter Command could equal or better the score of the famous World War 1 ace Eddie Rickenbacker. He had knocked down 26 enemy aircraft, which sounded a lot to novice USAAF fighter pilots in

Artistic imagination ran riot on USAAF aircraft during the war, and in some cases the 'nose art' tended to dominate the standard markings. Lt W J O'Connor of the 63rd FS/56th FG at Horsham St Faith shows off the artwork on his P-47C, along with his canine mascot 'Slipstream'

the spring of 1943. As with the 1914-18 conflict, five aerial victories was the minimum required to take the title of ace, but as to how they would fare, these modern counterparts of the Spad and Nieuport pilots of the last war, only time would tell.

## LUFTWAFFE STRENGTH

Ranged against Allied bomber incursions over the European continent in the early spring of 1943 was a substantial part of the Luftwaffe day fighter force at almost its peak wartime strength. With JGs 1, 2 and 26 as the cornerstone *Jagdgeschwader* able to oppose the USAAF fighter force, VIII Fighter Command was initially outnumbered – on 31 March the enemy could call on 513 single-engined fighters based in the West and 185 based within the borders of the Reich. A substantial number of twin-engined *Zerstörers* and nightfighters (some 460 at this stage of the war) could also be called upon, the Bf 110 equipping most of the component units, although the *Nachtjagd* also included Ju 88s, Do 17s and Do 217s.

The twin-engined force was supported from May 1943 by the Me 410, although American fighter pilots consistently reported encounters with the Me 210 during this period, although this is extremely doubtful as most of these were stationed in the Middle East. The type's misidentification was almost certainly down to Allied Intelligence failing to appreciate that the Me 410 was a virtually new aircraft, although it bore a very close resemblance to its unsuccessful forerunner. But the fact that the later

**It took time for the USAAF to appreciate that the 'finger four' was the most practical fighter formation ever devised, the RAF being strongly in favour of more outmoded formations. The Americans initially followed their advice, but soon found that they had to work out their own formations if they were to meet the Luftwaffe on equal terms. A basic leader-wingman grouping was found to be vital in combat**

Messerschmitt twin-engined fighters had a single tail unit rather than the twin fins and rudders of the Bf 110 leads one to wonder if on some occasions at least the aircraft being shot down were not in fact Ju 88s – enemy aircraft recognition was never a strong point of USAAF fighter pilots.

The Ju 88 was certainly used for bomber interceptions, although the significant difference in size between this and the Messerschmitt 'twins' would surely have been appreciated, if not through visual observation then by film from the gun cameras of the P-47s. Although combat footage often cleared up doubts, the film exposed was not always of the best quality as 'fogging' often obliterated any image(s) captured on celluloid. Despite all the checks into victory claims, anomalies regarding the aircraft type involved in some combats were perpetuated.

## April 1943

Debden airfield in Essex witnessed a buzz of excitement on 8 April as the 4th FG took off for 'Circus 280', as this was the first time that all three squadrons had been able to fly the P-47 operationally. Little of note occurred during the sortie, however, the 'Eagles' instead 'taking in the sights' of Dunkirk before heading home. Four Thunderbolts from the 56th and 78th FGs also went along for the experience, sweeping inland for about 15 miles to the St Omer area.

On the afternoon of 13 April the war finally began for the 56th FG, based at Horsham St Faith in Norfolk. Each component squadron – the 61st, 62nd and 63rd FSs – contributed four P-47s apiece for a twelve-ship probe across the Channel. More familiar with the Thunderbolt's flying characteristics than any other unit within the Army Air Forces, the 56th could concentrate on the fundamental details of deploying the aircraft in combat, rather than the physical flying of it. At first the group adopted the standard RAF 'javelin' formation, as had been recommended. Although the American pilots duly complied with this advice given by seasoned combat veterans, few of them felt that the stepped-down formations actually gave them enough flexibility should the enemy be encountered.

The 56th's pilots instead worked out their own formations, and on subsequent missions the German 'finger four' spread was adopted,

The early 'short' cowling flaps that identified the widely used P-47C are shown above 'Mac' McCollom's personal aircraft in the 4th FG (*via M Bowman*)

although familiarity with this formation did not come immediately. Various positions were flown in order to find the best ones for combat manoeuvrability, mutual leader/wingman cover and ease of changeover.

The Duxford-based 78th FG also marked 13 April as its true combat debut date, for the 2nd and 83rd FSs laid on morning and afternoon sweeps along the French coast, accompanied by 4th FG aircraft. Pilots from the former group noted in their diaries that the Germans ignored them completely! Not much would happen for the rest of the month, despite the 78th flying more sweeps along the coast of France.

These early sorties were more a source of annoyance than anything else for some pilots, as the radio reception problems with the P-47 persisted. Also giving some trouble at this early stage were the turbo superchargers and the R-2800-59 Double Wasp engines in general. 'Across the pond' work on improving the P-47C model Thunderbolts continued.

On 15 April Maj Don Blakeslee's victory over an Fw 190 near Knocke marked the start of the P-47's combat career proper in the ETO. Part of 'Rodeo 204', the 4th FG was led by Operations Officer Lt Col Chesley 'Pete' Peterson on a sweep which took in an area stretching from Furnes, in Belgium, to Cassel, in France. Just after 1700, Blakeslee (leading the 335th FS, with two squadrons of the 56th following) spotted three Fw 190s at 23,000 ft – some 5000 ft below the Thunderbolts. Blakeslee led the bounce, and brief combats ensued while he dived after a single Focke-Wulf. Firing short bursts, the American pilot pulled out at 500 ft as the German pilot unsuccessfully attempted to bail out over Ostend. For Don, who had been given command of the 335th in November 1942 and received promotion to major rank on 1 January 1943, this Fw 190 was only his fourth confirmed kill in almost two years of frontline flying, the

**Although the risk of the Luftwaffe attacking US fighter stations in England was much reduced by early 1943, units usually dispersed aircraft, and some airfields already had revetments designed to minimise damage if the enemy did appear. At Duxford the 78th FG utilised dispersals complete with air raid shelters (the entrance to which is visible immediately forward of the aircraft's fin), as this fine view of a P-47C-5 of the 82nd FS shows (*via W Bodie*)**

Some 56th FG pilots brought 'a little bit of Americana' to England in the form of the 'Lil Abner' characters from Al Capp's 'Dogpatch' cartoons. As shown in this June 1943 view, 'Abner 'himself adorns the nose of Capt 'Gene' O'Neill's LM-O. Indeed, the cartoons became so popular with the pilots of the 62nd that the unit even had a 'Dogpatch Flight' for a time

gun camera having otherwise denied him better than two probables and seven damaged claims on the Spitfire Mk Vb whilst serving with the RCAF's No 401 Sqn and the RAF's No 133 'Eagle' Sqn

Withdrawing, the rest of the 4th encountered five Fw 190s five miles off Ostend and Peterson attacked. Two aircraft were downed (one by Peterson for his seventh, and last, kill) for the loss of two P-47s, with Peterson himself bailing out into the Channel after his aircraft suffered engine problems. This was not an encouraging start, and some pilots blamed the P-47, which they compared unfavourably with the Spitfire.

Surprisingly, given his success during the sortie, one of those still not totally convinced by the new fighter was Don Blakeslee, as the following quote from future 4th FG P-47 ace James 'Goody' Goodson reveals;

'I checked Capt Don Blakeslee out on the P-47. Of course he didn't like it. It was daunting to haul seven tons of plane around the sky after the finger-tip touch needed for the Spit. I tried to sell Blakeslee on the opportunities this plane could open for us. "For one thing", I said, "they'll never be able to dive away from us again". He must have been listening. On 15 April 1943, Blakeslee was leading us over Belgium when we spotted a couple of Fw 190s. We attacked – as usual they dived away, and we followed. Admittedly it took a while. We jumped them at a little over 20,000 ft and Blakeslee was at 500 ft before he finally blew his victim out of the sky and into a suburb of Ostend. It was the first victory for the P-47. Back at Debden, I caught up with Blakeslee at debriefing. "I told you the "Jug" could out-dive them!" Grudgingly he conceded, "Well it damn well ought to be able to dive – it sure as hell can't climb!"'

By 29 April the 78th was able to send out 36 P-47s, with the aim being to eventually have 48 available for operations. New aircraft arrived regularly and were issued to the squadrons as soon as they had been checked and passed fit for combat. This usually meant a complete overhaul and change of radio set to comply with British emergency procedures.

## MAY 1943

On 3 May the 56th flew a 'Rodeo' led by CO, Lt Col 'Hub' Zemke, but bad weather resulted in a recall. This aborted sweep *was* significant in another way, however, for it was numbered Field Order 8 rather than 'Rodeo 212', denoting that the USAAF mission numbering system had been instigated by VIII Fighter Command. Such a change made more sense for the Americans as the former system was only really understood by the 4th FG, and was in any case getting unwieldy – under the RAF system, new USAAF pilots might have wondered why they appeared to be flying their 200th mission instead of their first! British mission descriptions such as 'Ramrod', 'Rodeo' and 'Circus' remained in place, however.

Putting up 48 P-47s for a 'Ramrod' for the first time on 4 May, the 78th FG had to wait a further ten days before meeting the Luftwaffe in strength. Making contact with B-17s over Belgium (which would quickly become a familiar rendezvous area), the pilots waded into Fw 190s attacking the bombers. They claimed three shot down, 83rd FS CO (and future boss of the 78th FG) Maj James J Stone gaining the distinction of 'bagging' the 78th's first kill. Future five-kill ace Capt Charles London of the 83rd FS was also credited with a probable on this sweep, having fired at an Fw 190 (in P-47C-5 41-6335/HL-B) he had caught up with northwest of Antwerp. The price for these successes was high – three P-47s were lost.

Of the 117 Thunderbolts that crossed into enemy airspace on 14 May, the 56th contributed 37. Led by recently promoted Col Zemke, the 62nd FS was away first to offer withdrawal support for 1st Bomb Wing B-17s,

Leading that same 62nd flight in June 1943 was P-47D-1 42-7870 LM-R. The cameraman used the open waist gun position of a B-24 to capture the 56th's fighters on film (*via P Jarrett*)

Pilots of the 4th FG at Debden viewed their mighty new steeds with awe. Comparing a P-47 to a Spitfire was bound to be an exercise in futility, as the two fighters were so different. This line up shows that some pilots were able to make the transition smoothly enough, as it includes 1Lt Don Gentile's *Donny Boy* (coded VF-T) parked second from the right. A veteran No 133 'Eagle' Sqn pilot, Gentile had his groundcrew adorn his new P-47 with two kill markings to denote his double score with the Spitfire Mk Vb during the Dieppe invasion on 19 August 1942. He later went on to claim four and one shared kills with the Thunderbolt, before enjoying even greater success with the P-51B (*IWM CH 21338*)

but the day was marred by problems with radios, engines and, in one instance, guns that refused to fire. Zemke himself was obliged to return before he had crossed the Dutch coast, although not before he thought he had claimed his first kill (an Fw 190). However, his gun camera film could not support the claim back at base, and it became a probable, then a damaged. Pilots from the 61st and 63rd FS fared no better, although shots were exchanged with enemy fighters.

All groups experienced unproductive sweeps and bomber escort sorties during this period – perhaps fortunately, considering the limited experience of many of the pilots – when very little of note occurred, and the 78th did not see action with the Luftwaffe again until 16 May.

On the 16th it all came at once – over 100 Fw 190s were found. Units divided up to take on separate swarms of fighters, and the 84th scored kills two and three for the group for the loss of Flg Off Charles R Brown.

A Bf 109 kill credited to the 334th FS's Lt Duane 'Bee' Beeson (flying P-47C 41-6212/QP-I) near Ostend on 18 May was the start of a string of victories this pilot would score while the 4th FG still flew the P-47. 'Bee' became an ace (12 kills) during the 'Eagles'' Thunderbolt period, a feat few of his fellow pilots emulated. Some pilots found it hard to come to terms with Republic's mighty fighter after flying the totally different Spitfire, but not Beeson. He had joined the 'Eagles' *after* the Spitfire period and had not flown it in combat, so was unaware of any comparison.

By the end of May the Duxford group had flown another 11 missions with little action to report, this situation being much the same for the 56th FG 'Wolfpack'. Many enemy fighters were seen on missions and pilots opened fire on a few occasions, but had to break off to evade hostile action or withdraw because of technical malfunction or low fuel state.

Although pilots may have personally felt some frustration at this point, the P-47s were nevertheless seen by the bomber crews to be 'in their part of the sky' just in case. The mere presence of American fighters often broke up the large-sized German gaggles, which could be lethal for the bombers if multiple fighters were free to make their attack runs. En masse, the US 'heavies' were not generally easy to shoot down, and it took a great deal of concentration for the *Jagdflieger* to do so. Having to worry about being jumped by escort fighters made a difficult task that much worse, so for the men in the Fortresses and Liberators, a successful escort did not always mean that dozens of enemy fighters had to be shot down. The mere presence of 'little friends' was enough.

## JUNE 1943

Early June was also quiet for the 56th. Capt Francis 'Gabby' Gabreski took over leadership of the 61st FS on the 9th, and three days later future six-kill ace Capt Walter Cook (flying P-47C-5 41-6343/LM-W) opened the 'Wolfpack's' score when his 'Red Flight' jumped Fw 190s near Ypres, in Belgium. There was little doubt as to the fate of Cook's target, as his fire exploded ammunition in its left wing and sheared part of it off.

On the morning of 22 June 1st Lt Jim Goodson (flying P-47D-2 42-7959/VF-W) of the 4th FG's 336th FS found himself behind an Fw 190 ten miles northwest of Hulst, and he quickly sent it earthwards. He was on the road to becoming another of the 4th's early aces.

As a pilot and commanding officer eager 'lead from the front', 'Hub' Zemke had the dual responsibility of placing the best qualified men in leadership slots at the head of the 56th FG's squadrons and to generally ensure that the unit functioned as efficiently on the ground as in the air. It took a vast organisation, from clerks and latrine orderlies to armourers and cooks, to keep a fighter group at a high level of efficiency, and in mid 1943, Zemke had little time away from the office when he was not flying.

Not a man to stifle initiative, he listened patiently to any sound ideas as to how his P-47s could improve their performance, offer better protection to the bombers and challenge the Luftwaffe fighter force. It was hard going at times, as there were very few operational guidelines to follow.

Some pilots needed to appreciate that they were part of a team. Lone heroes were not likely to survive for long, but some men would completely forget the sound principles of the well-disciplined unit and go charging into the German fighters the minute they were spotted. Zemke, and other fighter commanders, had to admonish such individualists, although they did not wish to stifle an aggressive spirit. And 'hot rock' fighter pilots were not alone in failing to grasp the significance of teamwork, for Zemke also faced considerable apathy from various quarters including Eighth Air Force bomb group commanders, some of whom had little idea of how vital fighter protection was to the success of daylight precision bombing. In the air, Zemke's first two confirmed kills came on 13 June when he destroyed a pair of Fw 190s in rapid succession in the vicinity of Cassel. A third Focke-Wulf was claimed as damaged.

It was 22 June before Charles London was able to confirm his first kill – an Fw 190 that went into the sea off Walcheren Island. On the 29th London made it three, destroying two Bf 109s near Gournay.

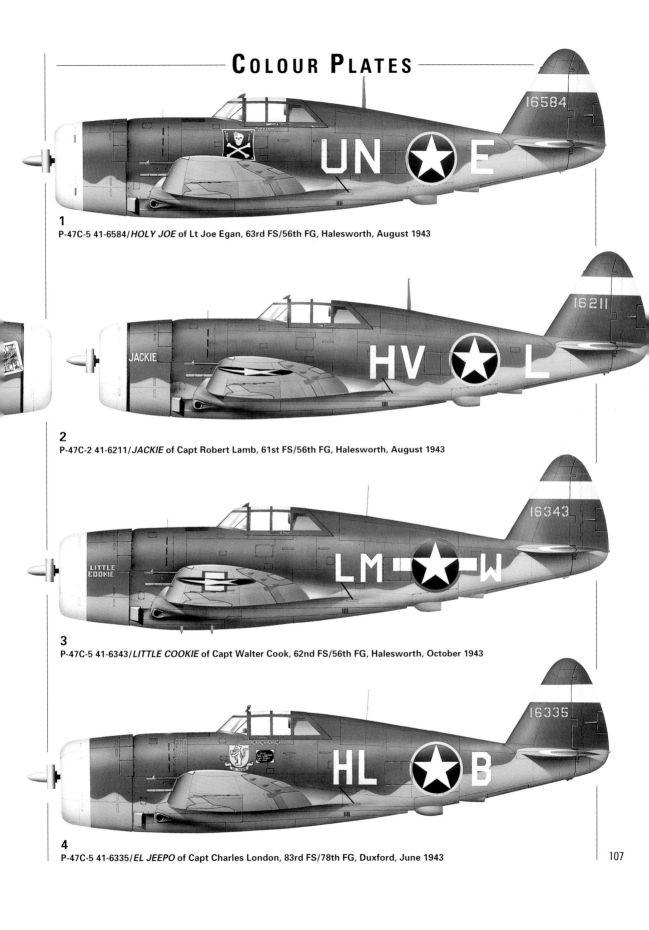

**1**
P-47C-5 41-6584/*HOLY JOE* of Lt Joe Egan, 63rd FS/56th FG, Halesworth, August 1943

**2**
P-47C-2 41-6211/*JACKIE* of Capt Robert Lamb, 61st FS/56th FG, Halesworth, August 1943

**3**
P-47C-5 41-6343/*LITTLE COOKIE* of Capt Walter Cook, 62nd FS/56th FG, Halesworth, October 1943

**4**
P-47C-5 41-6335/*EL JEEPO* of Capt Charles London, 83rd FS/78th FG, Duxford, June 1943

**5**
P-47C-5 41-6330/*"MOY TAVARISH"* of Col Hubert Zemke, CO of the 56th FG, Horsham St Faith, June 1943

**6**
P-47C-5 41-6630/*Spokane Chief* of Maj Eugene Roberts, CO of the 84th FS/78th FG, Duxford, August 1943

**7**
P-47D-6 42-74641/*Feather Merchant II* of Maj Jack Price, CO of the 84th FS/78th FG, Duxford, November 1943

**8**
P-47D-15 42-76179/*Little Chief* of Lt Frank Klibbe, 61st FS/56th FG, Halesworth, March 1944

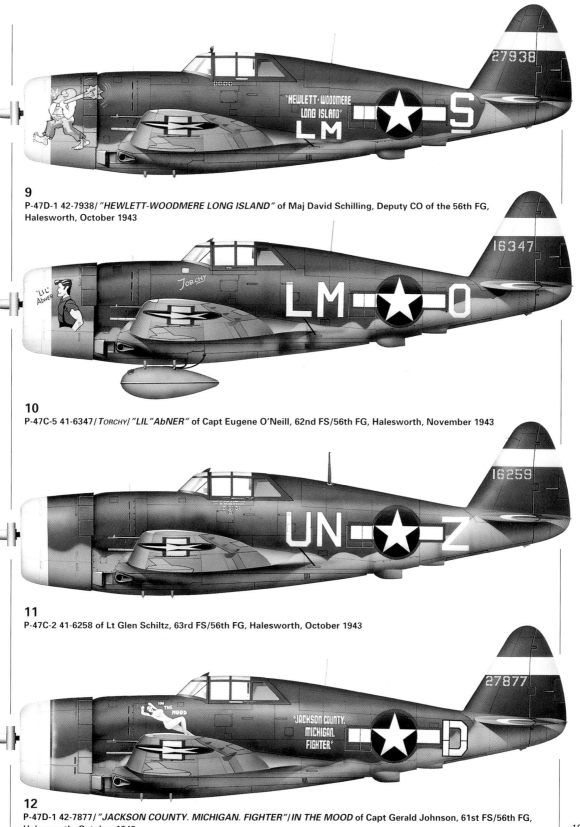

**9**
P-47D-1 42-7938/*"HEWLETT-WOODMERE LONG ISLAND"* of Maj David Schilling, Deputy CO of the 56th FG,
Halesworth, October 1943

**10**
P-47C-5 41-6347/*TORCHY*/*"LIL"AbNER"* of Capt Eugene O'Neill, 62nd FS/56th FG, Halesworth, November 1943

**11**
P-47C-2 41-6258 of Lt Glen Schiltz, 63rd FS/56th FG, Halesworth, October 1943

**12**
P-47D-1 42-7877/*"JACKSON COUNTY. MICHIGAN. FIGHTER"*/*IN THE MOOD* of Capt Gerald Johnson, 61st FS/56th FG,
Halesworth, October 1943

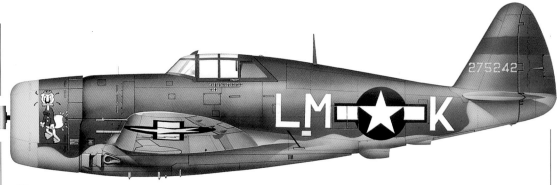

**13**
P-47D-11 42-75242 of Capt Michael Quirk, 62nd FS/56th FG, Halesworth, February 1944

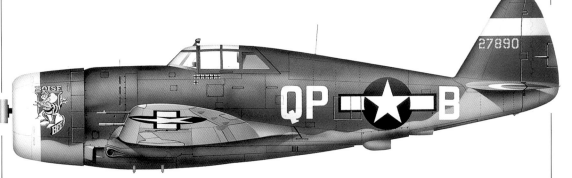

**14**
P-47D-1 42-7890 *BOISE BEE* of Lt Duane Beeson, 334th FS/4th FG, Debden, January 1944

**15**
P-47D-5 42-8473 *Sweet LOUISE/Mrs Josephine/Hedy* of Capt Virgil Meroney, 487th FS/352nd FG, Bodney, March 1944

**16**
P-47D-10 42-75068 of Lt Raymond Wetmore, 370th FS/359th FG, East Wretham, April 1944

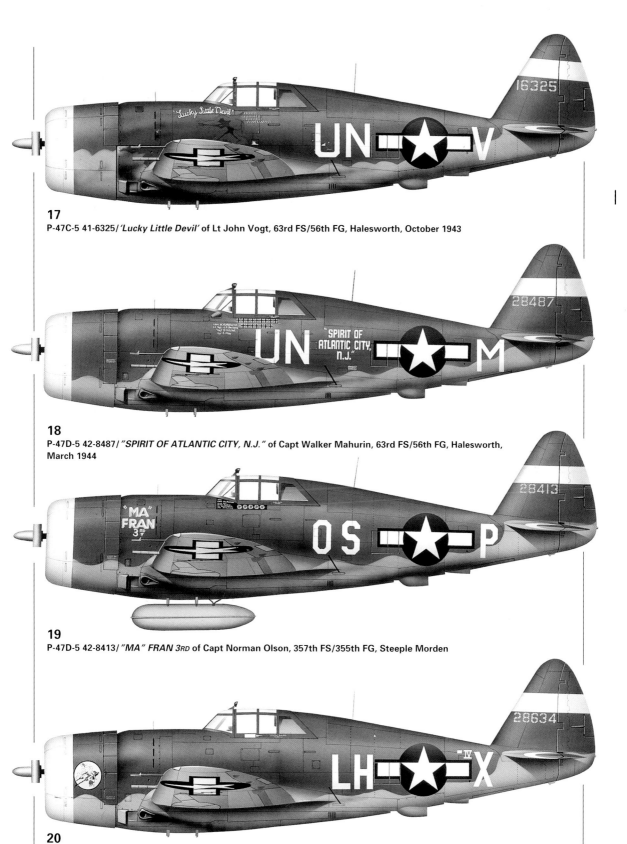

**17**
P-47C-5 41-6325/'*Lucky Little Devil*' of Lt John Vogt, 63rd FS/56th FG, Halesworth, October 1943

**18**
P-47D-5 42-8487/*"SPIRIT OF ATLANTIC CITY, N.J."* of Capt Walker Mahurin, 63rd FS/56th FG, Halesworth, March 1944

**19**
P-47D-5 42-8413/*"MA" FRAN 3RD* of Capt Norman Olson, 357th FS/355th FG, Steeple Morden

**20**
P-47D-5 42-8634/*Dove of Peace IV* of Lt Col Glenn Duncan, CO of the 353rd FG, Metfield, December 1943

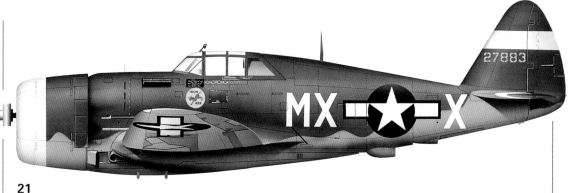

**21**
P-47D-1 42-7883/*IRON ASS* of Maj Jack Oberhansly, CO of the 82nd FS/78th FG, Duxford, December 1943

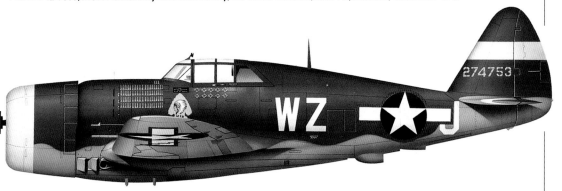

**22**
P-47D-6 42-74753/*OKIE* of Lt Quince Brown, 84th FS/78th FG, Duxford, March 1944

**23**
P-47D-6 42-74750/*Lady Jane* of Lt John Truluck, 63rd FS/56th FG, Halesworth, March 1944

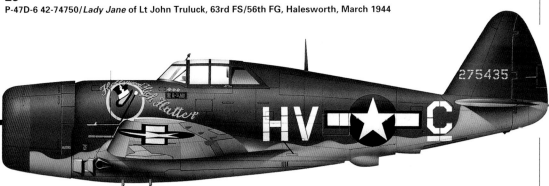

**24**
P-47D-11 42-75435/*Hollywood High Hatter* of Lt Paul Conger, 61st FS/56th, Halesworth, December 1943

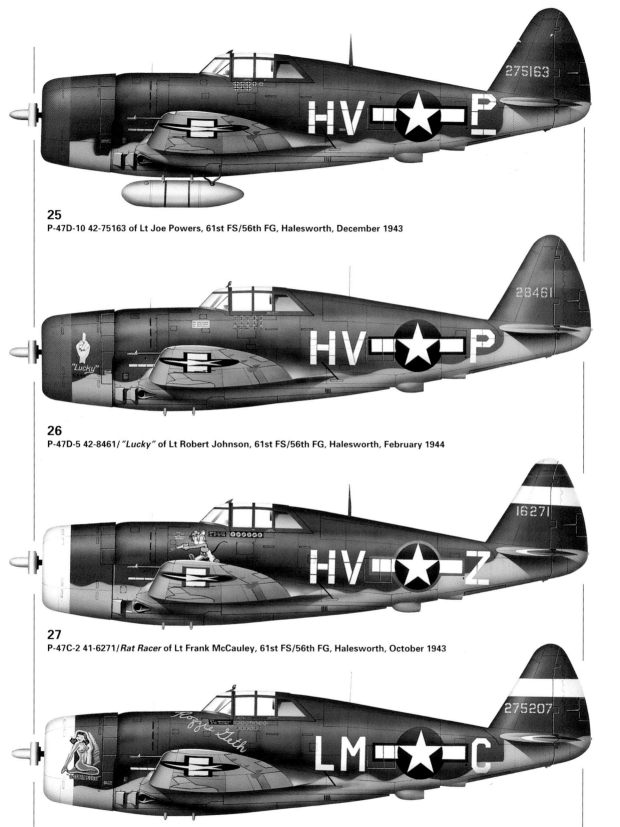

**25**
P-47D-10 42-75163 of Lt Joe Powers, 61st FS/56th FG, Halesworth, December 1943

**26**
P-47D-5 42-8461/*"Lucky"* of Lt Robert Johnson, 61st FS/56th FG, Halesworth, February 1944

**27**
P-47C-2 41-6271/*Rat Racer* of Lt Frank McCauley, 61st FS/56th FG, Halesworth, October 1943

**28**
P-47D-10 42-75207/*Rozzie Geth*/ *"BOCHE BUSTER"* of Lt Fred Christensen, 62nd FS/56th FG, Halesworth, March 1944

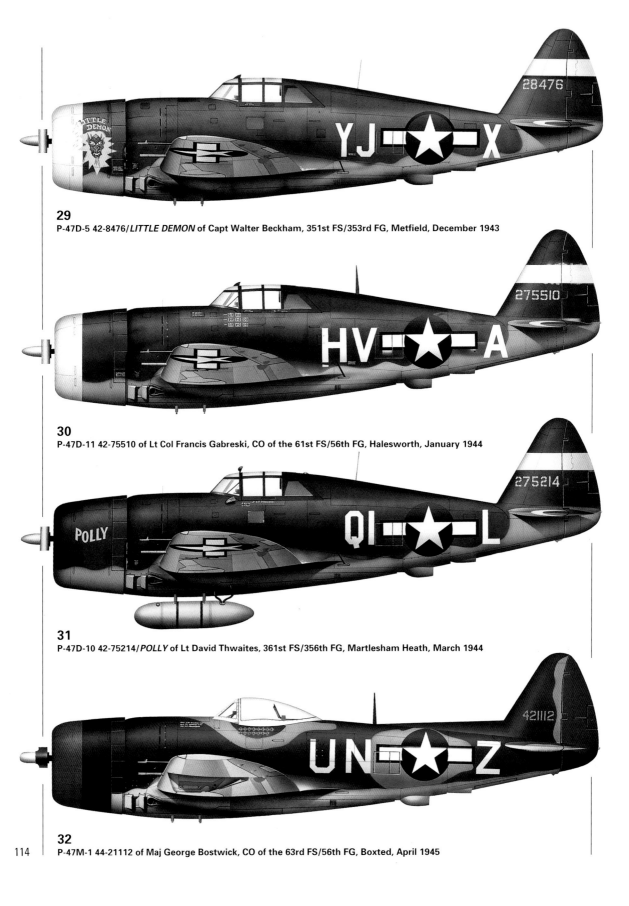

**29**
P-47D-5 42-8476/*LITTLE DEMON* of Capt Walter Beckham, 351st FS/353rd FG, Metfield, December 1943

**30**
P-47D-11 42-75510 of Lt Col Francis Gabreski, CO of the 61st FS/56th FG, Halesworth, January 1944

**31**
P-47D-10 42-75214/*POLLY* of Lt David Thwaites, 361st FS/356th FG, Martlesham Heath, March 1944

**32**
P-47M-1 44-21112 of Maj George Bostwick, CO of the 63rd FS/56th FG, Boxted, April 1945

**33**
P-47D-22 42-26299 of Capt Cameron Hart, 63rd FS/56th FG, Boxted, December 1944

**34**
P-47D-25 42-26641 of Col David Schilling,CO of the 56th FG, Boxted, December 1944

**35**
P-47D-21 42-25698/*Okie* of Maj Quince Brown, 84th FS/78th FG, Duxford, September 1944

**36**
P-47M-1 44-21108 of Capt Witold Lanowski, 61st FS/56th FG, Boxted, November 1944

**37**
P-47D-22 42-26044/*Silver Lady* of Maj Leslie Smith, 61st FS/56th FG, Boxted, May 1944

**38**
P-47D-21 42-25512/*Penrod and Sam* of Capt Robert Johnson, 62nd FS/56th FG, Boxted, April 1944

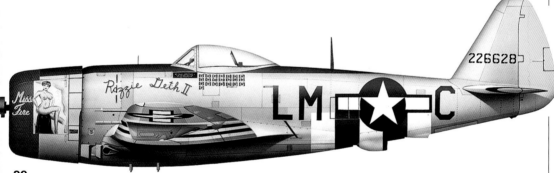

**39**
P-47D-25 42-26628/*Rozzie Geth II*/*Miss FIre* of Capt Frederick Christensen, 62nd FS/56th FG, Boxted, July 1944

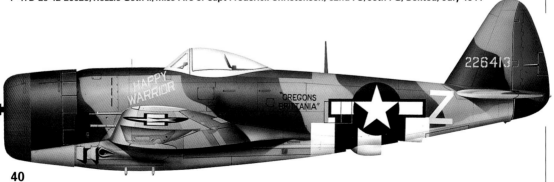

**40**
P-47D-25 42-26413/*"OREGONS BRITANNIA"*/*HAPPY WARRIOR* of Col Hubert Zemke, CO of the 56th FG, Boxted, June 1944

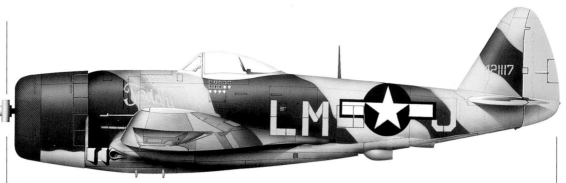

**41**
P-47M-1 44-21117/*Teddy* of Maj Michael Jackson, 62nd FS/56th FG, Boxted, January 1945

**42**
P-47D-26 42-28382/*"OLE COCK III"* of Capt Donavon Smith, 61st FS/56th FG, June 1944

**1**
Lt Col Dave Schilling, Deputy CO of the 56th FG at Halesworth in March 1944

**2**
Col 'Hub' Zemke, CO of the 56th FG at Halesworth in December 1943

**3**
Lt Robert Johnson of the 61st FS/56th FG at Halesworth in October 1943

**4**
Maj Gerry Johnson of the 360th
FS/356th FG at Martlesham Heath in
January 1944

**5**
Capt 'Gabby' Gabreski, CO of the 61st
FS/56th FG at Horsham St Faith in
June 1943

**6**
Lt Col Eugene Roberts, Deputy CO of
the 78th FG at Duxford in October
1943

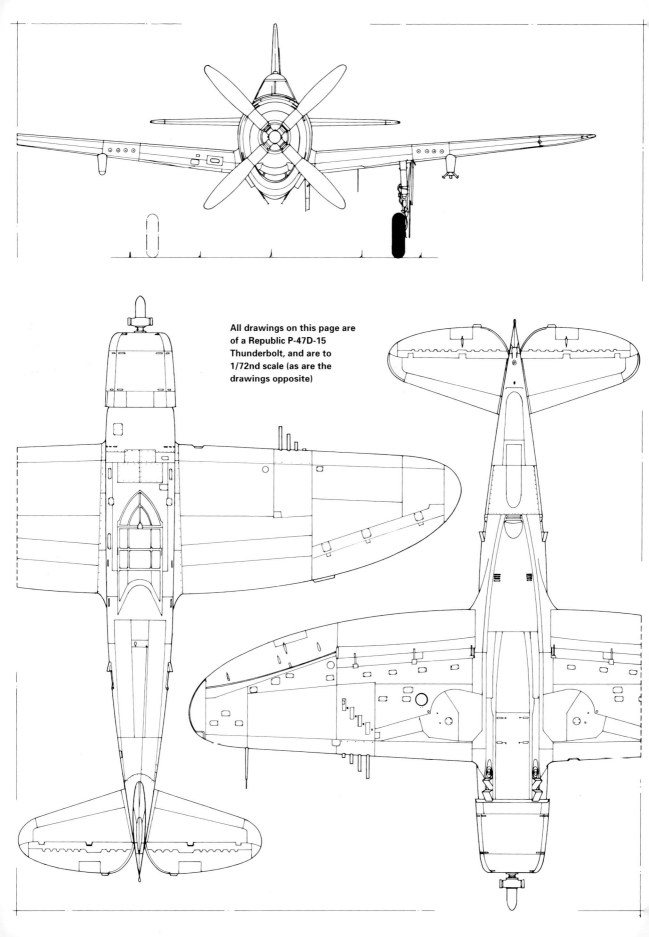

All drawings on this page are
of a Republic P-47D-15
Thunderbolt, and are to
1/72nd scale (as are the
drawings opposite)

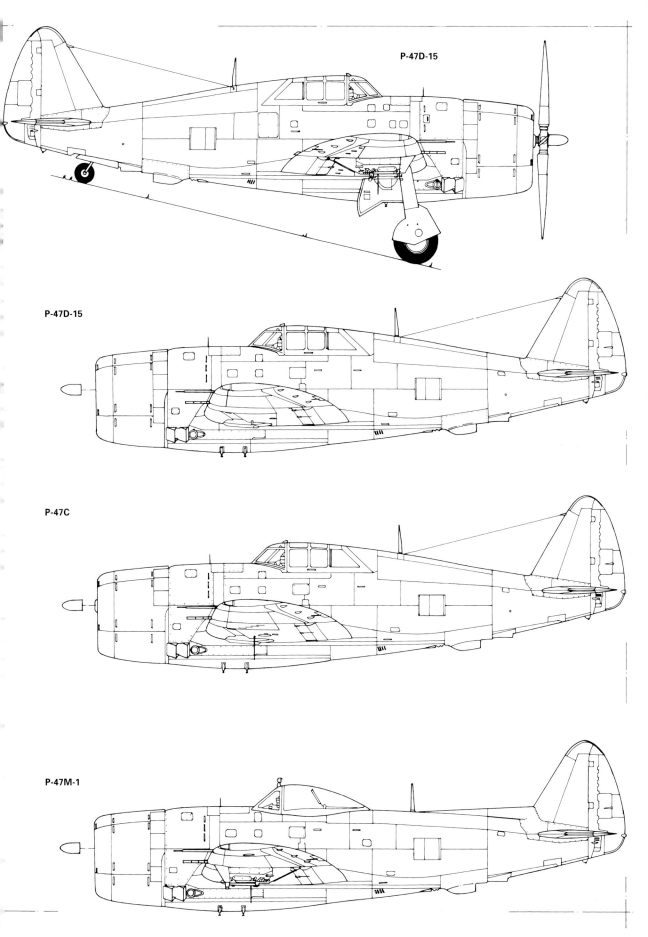

P-47D-15

P-47D-15

P-47C

P-47M-1

# COLOUR PLATES

## 1

**P-47C-41-6584/*HOLY JOE* of Lt Joe Egan, 63rd FS/56th FG, Halesworth, August 1943**

Seen in standard P-47 camouflage and early ETO markings, this aircraft was used by five-victory ace Lt Joe Egan to down his first kill (an Fw 190) on 19 August 1943. his remaining kills were scored in P-47D-10 42-75069/UN-E and P-47D-15 42-75855/UN-E. Some sources indicate that this aircraft survived long enough to have the red bordered national insignia applied.

## 2

**P-47C-2 41-6211/*JACKIE* of Capt Robert Lamb, 61st FS/56th FG, Halesworth, August 1943**

Like Joe Egan, future seven-kill ace Capt Robert Lamb used this aircraft to claim his first victory on 19 August (again an Fw 190). He was still flying it in mid-October when he claimed an 'Me 210' damaged on the 18th. The scrap view shows the starboard side of the fighter's nose cowling, which had been adorned with a rendition of a queen of hearts playing card

## 3

**P-47C-5 41-6343/*LITTLE COOKIE* of Capt Walter Cook, 62nd FS/56th FG, Halesworth, October 1943**

Capt Walter Cook scored four of his six victories in this P-47C-5, which was his assigned aircraft – it bore the name *LITTLE COOKIE* on both sides of the cowling. His remaining two kills (a pair of Fw 190s) were achieved on 11 November 1943 in P-47C-2 41-6193/LM-B, which he had been forced to use after *LITTLE COOKIE* suffered a flat tyre and subsequent propeller damage when landing on 20 October 1943. Cook completed 66 missions before returning to the USA in February 1944.

## 4

**P-47C-5 41-6335/*EL JEEPO* of Capt Charles London, 83rd FS/78th FG, Duxford, June 1943**

This famous aircraft is depicted in artwork based on the photograph seen on page 32, the P-47 having been used by VIII FC's premier ace, Capt Charles London, to score all five of his kills, one probable and two damaged between 14 May and 30 July 1943 – a fifth swastika was added to the tally seen here following his 'ace making' double haul on the 30th. *EL JEEPO* experienced no paint changes in the few months that London flew it.

## 5

**P-47C-5 41-6330/*"MOY TAVARISH"* of Col Hubert Zemke, CO of the 56th FG, Horsham St Faith, June 1943**

Flown by Col 'Hub' Zemke on many of his early missions at the head of the 56th FG, this Thunderbolt bore the legend *"MOY TAVARISH"* (*"MY COMRADE"*) from May 1943 – there is some evidence to suggest that the name was also repeated on the starboard side too, with the letters painted in a half circle. The big fighter also carried the ID letter code 'Z', which reflected the surname of the pilot, and was a privilege of rank afforded to flight, squadron and group commanders only. Zemke, who felt uneasy about commanders displaying such individualism, had the name and the 'spoked wheel' (both a play on his nickname, 'Hub', and a symbol of him being the commander of the 56th) insignia removed at an unknown date

– the personal embellishment had certainly been removed by September 1943 when, as UN-S, it was noted with red-bordered national insignia . Zemke used this aircraft to register his first trio of kills between 14 May and 19 August. It was finally written off in a crash landing with Lt Adam Wisniewski at the controls on Christmas Eve, 1944.

## 6

**P-47C-5 41-6630/*Spokane Chief* of Maj Eugene Roberts, CO of the 84th FS/78th FG, Duxford, August 1943**

Maj Roberts was able to use this aircraft to achieve six of his nine confirmed kills, plus the solitary probable that he kicked off his tally with on 1 July 1943. The ace's opening trio of kills were then scored in P-47C-2 41-6240/WZ-E, before returning to his *Spokane Chief* for – as far as is known – the aircraft's first confirmed victory on 17 August. CO of the 84th FS for much of his frontline tour, Eugene Roberts was promoted to lieutenant-colonel in October 1943 and given the position of Deputy Group CO. By the time he was posted to a desk job in VIII FC HQ, he had flown 89 missions.

## 7

**P-47D-6 42-74641/*Feather Merchant II* of Maj Jack Price, CO of the 84th FS/78th FG, Duxford, November 1943**

Capt Jack Price was assigned this P-47 in the spring of 1943, and he was able to gain the last two of his five victories whilst flying it. He had earlier used three different Thunderbolts to gain his first three kills – C-2s 41-6270/WZ-A and 41-6228/WZ-N, and C-5 41-6333/WZ-V. At some stage in the fall of 1943 reports suggest that the individual code letter of this aircraft changed from 'Z' to 'A', although this remains unconfirmed.

## 8

**P-47D-15 42-76179/*Little Chief* of Lt Frank Klibbe, 61st FS/56th FG, Halesworth, March 1944**

Lt Frank Klibbe decorated at least two of his P-47s with a Red Indian head motif, complete with war bonnet and the wording *Little Chief*. This was the third Thunderbolt assigned to him, and he is believed to have scored four of his seven kills in it. Klibbe's missions with the 56th FG's 61st FS totalled 63.

## 9

**P-47D-1 42-7938/*"HEWLETT-WOODMERE LONG ISLAND"* of Maj David Schilling, Deputy CO of the 56th FG, Halesworth, October 1943**

This early-build D-model was the first of its type assigned to then Maj Dave Schilling, who was one of just four 56th FG aces to break the 20-kill mark. Not just a great fighter pilot, Schilling was also one of the best group leaders produced by VIII FC, having been a member of the 56th FG from 2 June 1941. CO of the 62nd FS until August 1943, he failed to score any kills until becoming Deputy Group CO of the 56th. Schilling was assigned this P-47 War Bond subscription aircraft after his switch the group HQ flight, although he scored his first three victories using two other Thunderbolts (C-5s 41-6343/LM-W and 41-6347/LM-O). He enjoyed his first success with this aircraft on 8 October 1943 (an Fw 190), shortly after which Schilling was forced to crash-land in it. The P-47 was duly repaired and used by Schilling to add a further 2.5 kills to his tally up to 29 November when, for reasons unknown, he switched to another Thunderbolt.

## 10

**P-47C-5 41-6347/ *TORCHY/ "LIL "AbNER"* of Capt Eugene O'Neill, 62nd FS/56th FG, Halesworth, November 1943**

Capt Gene O'Neill used this P-47C-5 to score his first 3.5 victories in November/December 1943 – the fraction was a Bf 110 he jointly shot down on 26 November 1943. The aircraft also carried a third name – *Jessie O* – on the starboard side adjacent to the cockpit. Having joined the 62nd FS in 23 December 1941 (it was still designated a pursuit squadron then), O'Neill used P-47 D-10 42-75125/LM-E- to score his final kill on 6 February 1944. Although listed as an ace in numerous publications, both USAF Historical Study 85 and VIII FC Final Assessment credit him with 4.5 kills, having failed to find any record of that elusive fifth victory that would have made him an ace.

## 11

**P-47C-2 41-6258 of Lt Glen Schiltz, 63rd FS/56th FG, Halesworth, October 1943**

One of a number of Thunderbolts used by Lt Glenn Schiltz to record his final tally of 8-0-3, this was the P-47 in which its pilot 'made ace' on 11 December 1943 by downing an 'Me 210' (his only kill in the aircraft) near Emden.

## 12

**P-47D-1 42-7877/ *"JACKSON COUNTY. MICHIGAN. FIGHTER"/IN THE MOOD* of Capt Gerald Johnson, 61st FS/56th FG, Halesworth, October 1943**

A captain by the time he used this particular Thunderbolt to score 5.5 aerial victories, Gerald W Johnson was one of the 'Wolfpack's' most outstanding pilots. The machine shown in profile was photographed in colour (in three-quarter front view), although just one poor snapshot exists to show the War Bond inscription. It was assigned to and flown by Gerry Johnson for his first confirmed victory on 26 June 1943 (an Fw 190), and he continued to use it until the end of 1943, although his final kill with the aircraft was scored on 14 October (another Fw 190). All Johnson's P-47s were 'razorbacks', and he achieved kills in at least five different aircraft.

## 13

**P-47D-11 42-75242 of Capt Michael Quirk, 62nd FS/56th FG, Halesworth, February 1944**

Mike Quirk had used two P-47C-2s (41-6215/LM-K and 41-6295/LM-K) and a D-2 (42-22481/LM-S) to score his first three kills before being assigned this P-47D-11. He went on to score 6.5-1-1 in this aircraft, the last of which was claimed on 25 February 1944 (an Fw 190). The Thunderbolt's overpainted tail band indicates a transition to coloured tactical markings, which this aircraft duly received while Quirk was still its regular pilot. He rose in rank to major on 17 September 1944 , but by that time he had already been a PoW for a week after being downed by flak over Seligenstadt airfield on the 10th of the month. Quirk's final tally was 11-1-1.

## 14

**P-47D-1 42-7890 *BOISE BEE* of Lt Duane Beeson, 334th FS/4th FG, Debden, January 1944**

This aircraft was responsible for the destruction of no fewer than 11 enemy fighters whilst flown by Lt (later Capt) Duane 'Bee' Beeson, who finished the war as one of the highest scoring VIII pilots, with 17.333 kills by April 1944. The 334th FS

pilot transitioned onto the P-51 in late February 1944, taking a tally of 12 kills scored on P-47s with him – Beeson was easily the ranking Thunderbolt ace within the 4th FG, and also the leading ETO ace when lost to flak on 5 April 1944.

## 15

**P-47D-5 42-8473 *Sweet LOUISE/Mrs Josephine/Hedy* of Capt Virgil Meroney, 487th FS/352nd FG, Bodney, March 1944**

Virgil Meroney was the first, and only, pilot to 'make ace' while the Bodney group flew the P-47, his score being an impressive nine kills and one damaged over a period of some three-and-a-half months between 1 December 1943 and 16 March 1944 – all of these victories were scored in this P-47. The above quoted names were, in order, Meroney's wife, Crewchief Giesting's wife and Sgt Gillenwater's wife. The last name appeared on the starboard cowling, while *Mrs Josephine* was painted on a slant in approximately the same place as *Sweet LOUISE*. Yet another ace downed by flak, Meroney was lost whilst flying one of his first sorties in a P-51B on 8 April 1944.

## 16

**P-47D-10 42-75068 of Lt Raymond Wetmore, 370th FS/359th FG, East Wretham, April 1944**

Although Lt Ray Wetmore of the 359th FG fell just short of being a full P-47 ace with a total score of 4.25, his aircraft is included here to represent the group. The highest scoring Thunderbolt pilot in the group, his closest rival was Lt Robert Booth of the 369th FS, who got four kills. Two of Wetmore's haul (Fw 190s) were scored on 16 March 1944 in this aircraft, and he used two other P-47s (D-5 42-8663/CR-G and C-2 41-6282/CS-O) to claim his remaining successes. The eight-kill tally marked on the fighter is something of a mystery, as even by counting all Wetmore's reported contacts with enemy aircraft (six in all P-47s flown) as confirmed kills, this still does not match up with the symbols shown. The explanation must surely be that another pilot enjoyed success while flying this P-47.

## 17

**P-47C-5 41-6325/ *'Lucky Little Devil'* of Lt John Vogt, 63rd FS/56th FG, Halesworth, October 1943**

John Vogt was one of a number of VIII FC pilots who downed enemy aircraft while flying the same type of aircraft with more than one group – in his case the 56th and 356th FGs. The P-47C-5 depicted was his first assigned aircraft in the 56th, and he used it to score his first three victories, before moving on to P-47D-10 42-75109/UN-W. He also flew a P-47D-20 and finally a D-25 'bubbletop' after transferring to the 360th FS/356th FG, with whom he scored his last three kills for a final tally of 8-0-1.

## 18

**P-47D-5 42-8487/ *"SPIRIT OF ATLANTIC CITY, N.J."* of Capt Walker Mahurin, 63rd FS/56th FG, Halesworth, March 1944**

Capt 'Bud' Mahurin shot down a total of 19.75 aircraft, ranging from Fw 190s to a Ju 88, during his lengthy career with the 56th. This War Bond presentation aircraft (the second assigned to Mahurin) was used for all but three of these victories – the first two (Fw 190s) were achieved in C-2 41-6259/UN-V on 17 August, and he claimed a Bf 109 (and a second damaged) in D-11 42-75278/UN-B on 29 November. Unusual in that it retained its full squadron code letters (the inscription tended to replace the two letters on other subscriber-purchased P-47s), this machine is not known to have had any other form of personal marking on the starboard side. Mahurin was eventually shot down in this machine on 27 March 1944 by the rear gunner of Do 217 that he helped destroy south of Chartres.

## 19

### P-47D-5 42-8413/ "MA" FRAN 3RD of Capt Norman Olson, 357th FS/355th FG, Steeple Morden

Once again a sole group representative as an 'all-P-47' ace, Capt Norman Olson scored 6-0-2 during the 355th FG's brief seven-month association with the Republic fighter in the ETO. Although not definitely confirmed, it is presumed that this particular D-5 was the only P-47 assigned to the ace, although he also used a D-2 and a D-6 to achieve his full score. Having transitioned to the P-51B in late March, Olson was killed on 8 April 1944 when his Mustang was shot down by flak near Celle Hofer.

## 20

### P-47D-5 42-8634/ Dove of Peace IV of Lt Col Glenn Duncan, CO of the 353rd FG, Metfield, December 1943

Maj (later Lt Col/Col) Glenn Duncan had an outstanding career with the 353rd FG, and he flew at least four P-47s to score a total of 19.5 victories. The D-5 depicted here was apparently named Dove of Peace IV, although the exact location of the name (on the starboard side) has been impossible to trace. The fact that this aircraft was number four assumes that there were three others, although they were not necessarily P-47s. Duncan had served briefly with the 361st FG before transferring to the 353rd on 14 March 1943, which suggests that the other 'Doves' may have been aircraft flown in the USA prior to his move overseas.

## 21

### P-47D-1 42-7883/ IRON ASS of Maj Jack Oberhansly, CO of the 82nd FS/78th FG, Duxford, December 1943

The second P-47 assigned to Jack Oberhansly, this aircraft bears the modified form of his personal insignia. Previously, Oberhansly had flown C-5 41-6542/MX-W, which carried the same name on the port side, but in a square. The aircraft depicted was used by Oberhansly to score two kills and a probable on 27 September and 30 November 1943, the pilot then using P-47D-11 42-75406/MX-Z to achieve his next four successes. Oberhansly's sixth, and last, kill came in 'bubbletop' D-28 44-19566//MX-X on 28 August 1944.

## 22

### P-47D-6 42-74753/ OKIE of Lt Quince Brown, 84th FS/78th FG, Duxford, March 1944

Quince Brown's final tally of 12.333 kills were obtained in just under a year of combat operations between 27 September 1943 and 1 September 1944. This aircraft is his originally-assigned Thunderbolt, which he used to score 7.333 of his kills, including his first six successes – Brown also destroyed enemy aircraft in three other Thunderbolts; D-6 42-74723/WZ-X, D-5 42-8574/WZ-D- and D-25 42-26567/WZ-V. OKIE (the nickname perpetuated Brown's Oklahoma background) reverted to another pilot with the ID code 'V' following Brown's assignment of natural-metal 'razorback' D-5 42-8574/WZ-D.

## 23

### P-47D-6 42-74750/ Lady Jane of Lt John Truluck, 63rd FS/56th FG, Halesworth, March 1944

John 'Lucky' Truluck scored his first kill in his assigned P-47D-1 42-7853/UN-R before using the aircraft depicted here to score his second and third victories. He then enjoyed success with D-5 42-8488/UN-A on 26 November (an Fw 190 destroyed and a Bf 110 damaged) before reverting back to Lady Jane to 'make ace' on 24 February 1944 with an Fw 190 kill. Truluck claimed his sixth kill in D-10 42-75206/UN-G, although he went back to Lady Jane again to score his seventh, and final, victory (an Fw 190), plus a damaged (a Bf 109),on 15 March 1944.

## 24

### P-47D-11 42-75435/ Hollywood High Hatter of Lt Paul Conger, 61st FS/56th, Halesworth, December 1943

This grandly-named Thunderbolt was the first aircraft assigned to Paul Conger, who was almost certainly responsible for the three kills marked under the cockpit. He was subsequently assigned War Bond subscription P-47D-1 42-7880/HV-N "REDONDO BEACH, CALIFORNIA" and finally P-47M-1 44-21134/UN-P-. Like many other aces, Conger used at least three P-47s not assigned to him to reach his final tally of 11.5 kills.

## 25

### P-47D-10 42-75163 of Lt Joe Powers, 61st FS/56th FG, Halesworth, December 1943

Although Lt Joe Powers was assigned this particular aircraft in the autumn of 1943, he failed to score any kills in it until 11 December – by which time he had already claimed two victories (both Bf 109s) in C-2 41-6267/HV-V and C-5 41-6337/HV-S. His first victories in the D-10, which he named Powers Girl, came on 11 December when he destroyed a Bf 109 and a Bf 110, and damaged a second Zerstörer. Powers subsequently flew a number of missions mostly in other P-47s (including 41-6267 again), although he scored kills in Powers Girl in January, February and March 1944. A captain by the time his tour ended in May 1944, Joe Powers' final tally was 14.5-0-5.

## 26

### P-47D-5 42-8461/ "Lucky" of Lt Robert Johnson, 61st FS/56th FG, Halesworth, February 1944

Robert S Johnson's third assigned aircraft, "Lucky" was used to score his third, fourth, fifth and sixth victories before being lost in the North Sea on 22 March 1944 with Dale Stream at the controls. Johnson had previously flown two C-model Thunderbolts christened Half Pint and All Hell, and had shot down his first two kills in the latter aircraft, C-5 41-6235/HV-P. Some weeks prior to "Lucky's" watery demise, Johnson had discarded the aircraft in favour of P-47D-15 42-76234/HV-P, which he logically christened "Double Lucky". This aircraft duly lived up to its nickname, as the ace is assumed to have scored all his remaining kills (bar his last two) in it, although the serial number(s) of the aircraft used for this string of victories (coded HV-P) has not been 100 per cent confirmed. Finally, now Capt Johnson flew P-47D-21 42-25512/ LM-Q Penrod & Sam to achieve his final two kills – numbers 26 and 27.

## 27

### P-47C-2 41-6271/ Rat Racer of Lt Frank McCauley, 61st FS/56th FG, Halesworth, October 1943

One of the 56th FG's early aces, 'Mac' McCauley was assigned this P-47C-2, which he named 'Rat Racer' – the words appear under the portrait of Mighty Mouse, just above the wing root. An ace who managed to score all his kills in one P-47, McCauley's aircraft shows six victory symbols, although one was later disallowed. After completing 46 missions, he left the 'Wolfpack' on 20 November 1943 and served out the war as an instructor with the 495th Fighter Training Group.

## 28

**P-47D-10 42-75207/*Rozzie Geth*/*"BOCHE BUSTER"* of Lt Fred Christensen, 62nd FS/56th FG, Halesworth, March 1944**

Although this aircraft was the first P-47 assigned to Fred Christensen, the 62nd FS's future ranking ace actually scored his first of 21.5 kills in C-2 41-6193/LM-B. However, his next 10.5 victories were all downed in this D-10, which he continued to use until the late spring of 1944. Christensen flew a further two 'razorbacks' during his 107-mission tour.

## 29

**P-47D-5 42-8476/*LITTLE DEMON* of Capt Walter Beckham, 351st FS/353rd FG, Metfield, December 1943**

Walt Beckham had *LITTLE DEMON* assigned to him at the beginning of his ETO tour, and it is assumed that he scored the majority of his total of 18 victories in it. He is not known to have been assigned any other Thunderbolt while serving with the 353rd FG, although when he was shot down by flak on 22 February 1944, he was flying D-11 42-75226.

## 30

**P-47D-11 42-75510 of Lt Col Francis Gabreski, CO of the 61st FS/56th FG, Halesworth, January 1944**

'Gabby' Gabreski used this remarkably plain D-11 to steadily build up his score during the first half of 1944, the aircraft being his third assigned Republic fighter since his arrival in the ETO in early 1943. Bearing 18 kill markings beneath its cockpit following its pilots successful double Bf 109 haul on 27 March, this P-47 was just one of several successfully flown by Gabreski during the spring of 1944.

## 31

**P-47D-10 42-75214/*POLLY* of Lt David Thwaites, 361st FS/356th FG, Martlesham Heath, March 1944**

David Thwaites was the only pilot in the 356th FG to score all his kills on the P-47 while serving with that one group. Naming both his assigned Thunderbolts (the second being P-47D-20 42-76457/QI-L) *POLLY*, Thwaites is known to have used at least three P-47s to achieve his haul of 6-0-3. Following the completion of his tour in September 1944, he returned to the USA and became an instructor.

## 32

**P-47M-1 44-21112 of Maj George Bostwick, CO of the 63rd FS/56th FG, Boxted, April 1945**

George Bostwick spread his scoring from 7 June 1944 to 7 April 1945, ending the war with eight kills. Both his P-47M-1 and an earlier P-47D-22 (42-26289/LM-Z) assigned to him whilst still with the 62nd FS were referred to as 'Ugly Duckling', although the name was not painted on either aircraft. Bostwick was the only Thunderbolt ace to shoot down an

Me 262 – he got his jet on 25 March 1945 in M-1 44-21160/UN-F. He also damaged a second Me 262 in UN-Z on 7 April .

## 33

**P-47D-22 42-26299 of Capt Cameron Hart, 63rd FS/56th FG, Boxted, December 1944**

Typical of the rather beaten-up 'razorback' Thunderbolts that some elements of the 'Wolfpack' were still flying in late 1944, Cameron Hart's aircraft shows signs of wear and tear. Although four kills adorn this fighter, its assigned pilot only scored his first victory, a probable and a damaged (all Bf 109s on 5 September 1944) in this aircraft. The personal insignia has been attributed to a similar device carried by a Panzer unit – whatever its origins, Hart liked it, and carried it over to his P-47D-28 44-19937/UN-B in which he scored four of his six kills.

## 34

**P-47D-25 42-26641 of Col David Schilling,CO of the 56th FG, Boxted, December 1944**

One of Dave Schilling's seven assigned P-47s, this fighter revealed an early 'Wolfpack' penchant for painting *Dogpatch* cartoon characters on its Thunderbolts by featuring a neat rendering of 'Hairless Joe' on its cowling – although the name of the Al Capp character was not applied. Schilling's penultimate aircraft (he was actually issued with P-47M-1 44-21125/HV-S first, but engine problems saw it ground), this D-25 was in fact used by the colonel for his 'five in a day' haul (see cover caption) on 23 December 1944, raising his final tally to 22.5-0-6.

## 35

**P-47D-21 42-25698/*Okie* of Maj Quince Brown, 84th FS/78th FG, Duxford, September 1944**

As mentioned in profile 22, Maj Brown flew another *Okie* after his original P-47D-6 had been passed on in April 1944. Pilots did not always opt to fly newer aircraft, but given the choice most did. Brown failed to score any victories in this P-47.

## 36

**P-47M-1 44-21108 of Capt Witold Lanowski, 61st FS/56th FG, Boxted, November 1944**

Witold Lanowski was one of the Polish team that joined the 'Wolfpack' in 1944, and his tally of four kills made him the second most successful pilot of this small group behind 'Mike' Gladych. The nose emblem sums up the Poles' feeling towards the enemy – a factor that while living up to the aggressive spirit of the fighter pilot, tended to colour judgement in combat. The 61st FS had most of its P-47Ms camouflaged in variations of this unconventional scheme by May 1945.

## 37

**P-47D-22 42-26044/*Silver Lady* of Maj Leslie Smith, 61st FS/56th FG, Boxted, May 1944**

Les Smith was assigned to fly a P-47 named *Silver Lady*, although it is possible this name may have also applied to earlier P-47D 42-14671. In the event, this particular aircraft was also used by a number of aces, including 'Mike' Gladych and 'Gabby' Gabreski. Smith, himself, scored seven kills, but those painted under the cockpit were not all attributable to him.

## 38

**P-47D-21 42-25512/*Penrod and Sam* of Capt Robert**

**Johnson, 62nd FS/56th FG, Boxted, April 1944**

Robert S Johnson's last P-47 was named for his groundcrew as a tribute to their outstanding work. Bob Johnson used up to four P-47s, one of which was lost whilst being flown by another pilot. This aircraft wore the ace's final score, which bettered that of World War 1 ace Eddie Rickenbacker by a single kill – at which point VIII FC chiefs said enough was enough, and Johnson returned home in triumph.

## 39

**P-47D-25 42-26628/*Rozzie Geth II*/*Miss FIre* of Capt Frederick Christensen, 62nd FS/56th FG, Boxted, July 1944**

Fred Christensen accounted for kills 14 and 15 on 27 June (Bf 109) and 5 July 1944 (Fw 190) respectively in this aircraft, although his momentous haul of six Ju 52s in a single sortie was achieved on 7 July in D-21 42-25522/LM-H

## 40

**P-47D-25 42-26413/ *"OREGONS BRITANNIA"*/*HAPPY WARRIOR* of Col Hubert Zemke, CO of the 56th FG, Boxted, June 1944**

The last Thunderbolt assigned to 'Hub' Zemke before he left the 56th to take command of the 479th FG, *"OREGONS BRITANNIA"* is one of the last known War Bond subscription aircraft to have reached the ETO. It was used by Zemke to score six kills prior to his departure, after which it was flown by Harold Comstock and other pilots to help make up the shortfall of serviceable airframes following the grounding of all P-47Ms.

## 41

**P-47M-1 44-21117/*Teddy* of Maj Michael Jackson, 62nd FS/56th FG, Boxted, January 1945**

Mike Jackson's P-47M probably shared much the same fate as other examples of the penultimate P-47 – parked on the grass at Boxted with engine cowling off and groundcrews setting about its troublesome engine. Jackson rounded out his total of eight confirmed aerial victories with a Bf 109 and an Fw 190D on 14 January 1945 flying P-47D-28 44-19780/LM-J. The extra kills marked on *Teddy's* scoreboard denote Jackson 5.5 ground victories, hence their application in white.

## 42

**P-47D-26 42-28382/ *"OLE COCK III"* of Capt Donavon Smith, 61st FS/56th FG, June 1944**

Donavon Smith's last assigned Thunderbolt was his third of the tour. He made his final combat claim on 22 February 1944 against an Fw 190, bringing his final total to 5.5. Smith ended his duty as CO of the 61st FS on 10 January 1945, which probably meant that his aircraft was taken over by one or more other pilots to fly the remaining 'Wolfpack' sorties of the war.

## FIGURE PLATES

## 1

Lt Col Dave Schilling, Deputy CO of the 56th FG at Halesworth in March 1944, is seen wearing olive drab (OD) shirt and pants, topped off with an officer's overseas cap – note the black and gold officer braid on the cap.He has a silk scarf around his neck (synonymous with fighter pilots the world over, who wore them to reduce neck chafing whilst constant-ly craning their heads to look out of the cockpit for in search of the enemy). Schilling wears Russet brown low-quarter shoes on his feet, whilst his Mae West is RAF 1941 pattern, with distinctive securing tie-tapes. Finally, the zip-closed pouch attached the right harness strap of his B-8 parachute (with AN-6510 seat pack) contains first-aid dressings.

## 2

Col 'Hub' Zemke, CO of the 56th FG at Halesworth in December 1943, wears a M-1926 officer's issue short wool overcoat over his dark OD shirt and pants. His shoes are again Russet brown low-quarter style, whilst his gloves are B-10 Russet leather. On his head, Zemke wears his prized service hat with all important soft crown ('50 mission crush' style), created by the removal of the interior stiffeners – typical AAF practice, done so as to enable a headset to worn over the hat

## 3

Lt Robert Johnson of the 61st FS/56th FG at Halesworth in October 1943 has an RAF 'C' type flying helmet on his head, fitted with standard US R-14 receivers. The latter were not a perfect fit in the rubber mounts of the British helmets, which meant that they were invariably taped into place, as can be seen here. B-7 goggles complete his headwear. Johnson's Mae West is a B-3 type, worn over a favourite A-2 leather jacket. His trousers are OD 'mustard' shade, whilst is shoes are GI service issue. Finally, Johnson's gloves are the officer-issue chamois-leather type.

## 4

Maj Gerry Johnson of the 360th FS/356th FG at Martlesham Heath in January 1944. Like his namesake in the previous artwork, he is wearing an RAF 'C' type helmet with B-7 goggles. Note the British style 'bell-shaped' jack plug in his hand, which the Americans had adapted to allow the helmet's receivers to work with their own system. The attached oxygen mask is a Type A-14. His remaining attire is identical to Bob Johnson's with the exception of his Russet brown low-quarter shoes

## 5

Capt 'Gabby' Gabreski, CO of the 61st FS/56th FG at Hor-sham St Faith in June 1943, is wearing light olive drab (shade 54) shirt, pants and 'overseas' cap, which was a combination widely chosen by ETO pilots as their woollen material made them warmer in a cold cockpit than cotton khakis. Over his A-2 jacket he has on an RAF 1941 pattern Mae West, whilst his flying boots are 1936 pattern from the same source.

## 6

Lt Col Eugene Roberts, Deputy CO of the 78th FG at Duxford in October 1943, has on officer's dark olive drab (shade 51) shirt and overseas cap, whilst his trousers are shade 54 'pinks'. Note the khaki tie tucked into his shirt as per regulations, and the silver pilot's wings pinned to his shirt above the left breast pocket. These are three inches in size, although there was a smaller two-inch size made specifically for wearing on shirts. On Roberts' left collar point is the gold/silver winged-prop device of the AAF, whilst his insignia of rank – a silver oak leaf – is pinned to the front left side of his garrison ('overseas') cap. Finally, his shoes are commercial pattern, rather than regulation Oxford-style lace-ups.

# EXTENDED RANGE

Some early 'pre-drop tank' escort missions saw Eighth Air Force P-47 groups positioning at Manston, in Kent, to top off their fuel. That way they could stretch out their range, with every few miles gained probably saving a crippled bomber or two from the unwelcome attentions of the *Jagdwaffe*. One of these missions took place on 26 June, and Lt Robert S Johnson was to remember the details for a long time afterwards. Having been previously 'chewed out' by 'Hub' Zemke and Gerry Johnson (his 'Blue Flight' leader) for breaking formation, Bob Johnson swore to stay in position on this mission, come what may.

As 'Keyworth Blue Four', Johnson experienced extreme frustration soon after heading inland over France, for he spotted enemy aircraft, called them in, and nobody else seemed to hear him. Johnson soon became frantic. The Fw 190s were boring in, and still no reaction from the rest of the Thunderbolts. While he was in the process of calling again, an Fw 190 found the range and opened fire – on Johnson's aircraft (P-47C-2 41-6235/HV-P)! Thus began a long running fight with the American almost powerless to react for his aircraft had been badly hit in that initial burst, resulting in wounds for the pilot and a jammed canopy, cutting off any chance for him to bail out. Somehow, with the Fw 190 shooting him up, the future American ace managed to set course for home.

'I am the luckiest guy on this station', Johnson later recalled. Describing the attack by the Focke-Wulfs, he said, 'They were all around me before I could make a run for it and one of them hit me from above. I heard a thud and there was a sound like the pecking of a typewriter. His machine gun bullets were making holes all over my airplane.

'I tried to dive away when something started burning the back of my head. My oxygen had become ignited. I tried to open the canopy but it

**Taken at the 78th FG's Duxford, home, this photograph shows 'Wolfpack' P-47C-2 41-6267 (which was almost certainly coded HV-V) of the 56th FG's 61st FS. It had probably been flown to the Cambridgeshire base by an experienced pilot allocated to the 78th FG for a short detachment in order to help smooth the new group's entry into combat (*IWM HU 73852*)**

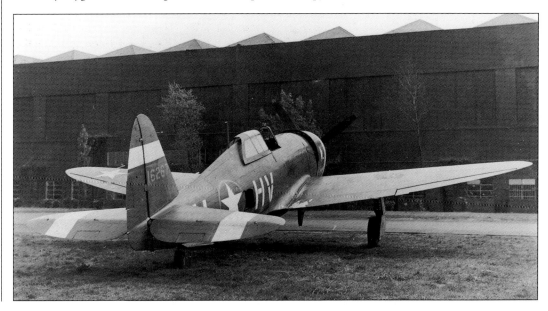

Home away from home for the fighters were the Eighth's bomber bases. This 78th FG P-47C-2 (41-6246) is seen at Ridgewell, in Essex, which was home to the B-17s of the 381st BG. As the bomber commanders came to realise that they needed all the help they could get from their 'Little Friends', fighter pilots received a warm welcome whenever they had to land at bomber bases

First USAAF fighter ace in the ETO was Capt Charles London, who scored all five of his victories in this P-47C-5 (41-6335), seen here at Ridgewell sometime between 29 June and 30 July 1943, parked amongst 381st BG B-17s. These two aircraft exemplified the early months of the Eighth's bomber offensive, for the other two key 'early players', namely the B-24 and P-38, were then still in the minority. Within a year of this photo being taken, a well known North American product had already started to overshadow the bomber protection achievements of the P-47

stuck fast. The German just kept firing and pieces of my plane would tear off as his bullets hit. Then something exploded in the cockpit and I was blinded with a shower of fluid from the hydraulic system.

'I tried another dive and the oxygen stopped burning, but I still couldn't see anything for a few minutes. When I came out of the dive, the engine was grinding badly and I throttled back to keep it from blowing. I wiped the hydraulic fluid out of my eyes, and when I looked around I found I was still at 19,000 ft. The Germans had disappeared. They had done a good job because I couldn't manoeuvre the plane, and it seemed the wings were hanging on by a couple of threads. I beat on the canopy, but it still wouldn't open. I figured I might as well relax because it didn't seem as though I had a chance in hell of getting back. I didn't feel bad. My face was bleeding and the burns on the back of my head hurt, but the lack of oxygen was making me drunk.'

Johnson was suffering from the effects of hypoxia brought on by lack of oxygen above 10,000 ft. Convinced that he was doomed, he was also certain that he could not control the aircraft. When the P-47 slipped below oxygen height the drunken effect cleared, and with the realisation that his aircraft would respond to the controls, Johnson set course for England.

'By the time I was near Dieppe I was down to 8000 ft. Off to the right I saw a blue-painted Fw 190 coming toward me. He manoeuvred for a pass and I couldn't do a thing about it except to sit there and watch him swing around on my tail for the kill. He started firing and some pieces came off my plane. Since we were both travelling at a good clip I kicked the rudder to slow down. He shot past, and when he was directly in front I let him have a few bursts. They didn't have much effect. He immediately turned around and came back. I think the Jerry knew by this time that he was fighting a cripple because he held his fire and started flying alongside.

'He stayed with me all the way over Dieppe, and it must have mystified the anti-aircraft gunners. They didn't send up any flak, which was a good break for me, because I couldn't have taken any evasive action. When we neared the Channel, the German circled my plane once or twice and then

the pilot waved. I waved back and thought he was going to let me go. But he just pulled up and took another shot at me. Then he came down and examined my plane some more. We were now below 3000 ft and evidently he didn't think I had any chance of getting home. He must have been a good-hearted Joe. Instead of finishing me off, he waggled his wings and went away.

'My engine was still grinding so I tried the stick. To my surprise the P-47 started to climb a little. I kept nursing her and she managed to struggle all the way across the Channel to England. When I came down,

I didn't have any flaps or brakes, but it was the best landing I ever made.'

This bizarre 'cat and mouse' game was not entirely unique, for such actions on the part of the Germans were occasionally reported by bomber crews, but it was rarer for fighter pilots to find themselves in such a position. After the emergency landing at Manston, Bob Johnson was advised to take a few days' rest. He did, but was back in the cockpit on 1 July.

The 26 June mission was the second most costly in terms of pilots killed that the 56th was to experience throughout the war. Of the five P-47 pilots shot down (by JG 2), four were killed, whilst a further six aircraft needed repair and Johnson's machine – well and truly shot up by the determined Fw 190 pilot from JG 26 – was deemed beyond repair.

## JULY 1943

The first day of July saw the 78th FG up for a 'Rodeo' mission which enabled future nine-kill ace (and 84th FS CO) Maj Eugene Roberts to 'get his eye in' by attacking an Fw 190. Only credited with a probable, he had to wait nearly a month before being presented with another opportunity to score his first kill on the 30th. Roberts usually flew P-47C-5 41-6330/WZ-Z *Spokane Chief*, but on the latter occasion he used C-2 41-6240/WZ-E to claim his trio of kills – his regular mount was, however, always on hand for the balance of his first tour, and he would use it

Charles London's *EL JEEPO* is seen in close up during its Ridgewell visit in June/July 1943, the fighter showing four kills beneath the cockpit rail. His striking personal badge also appeared on the starboard side in the same location. The display of four crosses means that London's Fw 190 probable on 14 May must have been claimed as a victory, for his fourth and fifth confirmed kills were not achieved until 30 July. This was not unusual, for claims were made in all good faith under wartime conditions when the exact toll taken of the Luftwaffe on any given day was next to impossible to check. After the war German loss records could be scrutinised and adjustments made to scores

The fourth fighter group to see combat in the ETO in the P-47 was the 353rd. It began operations in time to have its aircraft adorned with the red-bordered 'star and bar' national insignia introduced on 29 June 1943, although this marking only lasted until 17 September when a change was made to a dark blue outline. This alteration was due to operational considerations in the Pacific, where any red marking may have caused confusion with Japanese insignia. And although this clash could not possibly occur in the ETO/MTO, the USAAF wanted international standardisation. P-47D-2 (42-8001) of the 350th FS shows typical late summer 1943 markings, and also carries one of the vital drop tanks (a 108-gal model in this case)

This P-47D-2 was assigned to the 352nd FS/353rd FG. Photographically the 'poor relation' of VIII Fighter Command, the 353rd nevertheless produced five full P-47 aces. Note the whip, rather than mast, aerial fitted to this particular batch of Thunderbolts

to score the rest of his victories. Roberts and his aircraft often became the focus for members of the press corps visiting Duxford during the summer of 1943, reporters invariably being accompanied by a photographer. Always willing to publicise the achievements of American pilots in the ETO, the 'home press' took far a less restrictive view of censorship than their British counterparts, and freely headlined details such as the number of victories individual pilots had scored.

VIII Fighter Command headquarters tended to cast a benevolent eye on such things, for if publicity fostered a competitive spirit among the fighter pilots and created an 'ace race', so to speak, then this would hardly stifle initiative. Not everyone sought the limelight, but in others there was a desire to get their name in the papers for doing better than the next man. And nobody at HQ minded if the encouraged belief that a pilot belonged to the best group in the theatre (whichever one it happened to be) was enhanced and broadened out by words and pictures.

Newspaper stories and broadcast interviews may not generally have done much harm, but there was a downside. There is little doubt that such coverage helped the Luftwaffe build up comprehensive dossiers on all the top pilots in the Eighth, and German interrogators often scored a psychological advantage by regaling newly-captured pilots with 'classi-fied' details of their squadron, base and colleagues. Not that such a fate awaited Eugene Roberts, for he pressed on piling up his personal score until 20 October when he downed a Bf 109F/G to complete his scoring at nine kills and one probable. By then a lieutenant-colonel, and deputy CO of the 78th FG, Roberts went on to complete 89 missions with the group before taking a well-earned break in late December 1943. He would later serve a second tour in Europe flying P-51s with the 364th FG, although without adding further kills to his score.

Emulating Maj Roberts' success on the 30 July mission was fellow 84th FS pilot Capt Jack Price (flying P-47C-5 41-6333/WZ-V), who added two Fw 190s confirmed to his premier kill (again a Focke-Wulf) scored on 14 July. A member of the 78th FG since May 1942, Price had accrued considerable flying experience before actually engaging the enemy for the first time. His victim on the 14th had gone down some 20 miles north of

Abbeville, which was well known to the American pilots as the home of JG 26 – it may well have been aircraft from this *Geschwader* that met the 78th on that day. Price was flying his personal aircraft (P-47C-2 41-6270/WZ-A) at the time, although his remaining four kills were achieved in other P-47s. Crowned an ace on 26 November following a double haul in P-47D-6

42-74641/WZ-Z, Price was by then a major and had assumed command of the 84th FS from the newly-promoted Lt Col Roberts. He too survived his tour, returning to the ETO as CO of the P-51D-equipped 55th FS/20th FG in March 1945, although he failed to achieve further kills.

Throughout the war, pilots joined Eighth Air Force fighter groups either from other units or directly from the USA. On 6 July Capt Leroy Schreiber joined the 61st FS/56th FG after serving as an instructor with the training-optimised, US-based, 338th FG. He quickly found his feet in the frontline, and on the same days that Roberts and Price attained multiple kills (30 July), Schreiber 'bagged' two Bf 109s flying P-47D-1 42-7871/HV-F. Transferring to the 62nd FS in August, he had risen to the position of unit CO (and scored 12 victories, 1 probable and 6 damaged) by them time he was shot down and killed by flak whilst attacking Flensburg airfield in P-47D-21 43-25577/LM-T on 15 April 1944.

The P-47's lack of range had caused headaches for VIII Fighter Command since the aircraft's arrival in the ETO, although a solution to this problem began to reach the frontline in the mid-summer of 1943. Initially, there had not been sufficient spare production capacity available, either in the USA or England, to ensure the construction of external tanks in the numbers required in early 1943. However, this unfortunate situation had begun to improve by July 1943 – so much so that on the 28th of the month the 4th FG was able to fly 'the first belly tank show' in the the-

Whilst the P-47-trained groups like the 56th and 78th FGs (granted, the latter had been initially formed on P-38s back in the USA) made the most of their mount in combat, the formerly Spitfire-equipped 4th FG 'sweated out' a Thunderbolt replacement with more nimble handling in the shape of the P-51B. In the meantime, pilots like Maj Lee Gover, who served both as the 336th FS's Ops Officer and then briefly as its CO in late 1943, continued to make do with the Thunderbolt – in his case P-47D-6 42-74688/VF-G, christened *MISS SAN CARLOS*. Gover was just one of the many pilots who scored only ground victories (four, in his case). In some groups (the 336th FS included), pilots used the initial letter of their second name as an individual aircraft code, hence 'G' for Gover. Having finished his tour with the 336th after completing 257 combat sorties, Maj Gover was posted to the 4th FG's HQ Squadron in January 1944, where he remained until rotated home in March

One of the perks of being in the Eighth Air Force for those men stationed on RAF aerodromes blessed with good living quarters and reasonable road transport access were the regular visits made by Hollywood stars. Among those who put on popular shows were comedian Bob Hope and actress Frances Langford, who went to Duxford on 3 July 1943. Both stars were given a look over the 78th FG's aircraft, including P-47D *Vee Gail* flown by Capt Robert E Eby. The latter individual served as a combat pilot attached to Group HQ, completing one of the longest tours in the 78th FG which lasted from May 1942 to September 1944, when he became Director of Fighter Operations, Third Air Division

atre. Taking off from Debden with bulbous 200-gal tanks, the group's mission saw them providing withdrawal support for 1st Wing B-17s, rendezvousing with their charges over Emmerich. Despite the unpressurised, and not too reliable, tanks holding juts half their fuel capacity, another 100 gallons nevertheless took the P-47s to the German border – and the Luftwaffe was surprised. With their allocated bombers nowhere to be seen, the 'Eagles' took on fighters attacking other bombers and ended the the day with a tally of three Bf 109s and six Fw 190s destroyed.

At Duxford on the 30th there was an unusual air of expectancy at the 78th FG's briefing, for the P-47s flying the day's mission would carry 75-gal drop tanks for the first time. Extra fuel carried in these more reliable pressurised, but smaller, tanks meant that the group could now stay in the air for up to two hours and fifty minutes. They could fly a short distance into Germany by following a pre-planned route over Holland and, with any luck, surprise the *Jagdwaffe* as it attacked the bombers. For the 78th, the day culminated in its first real taste of action in ten missions. Well aware that the 4th had penetrated German airspace for the first time 48 hours earlier, every pilot at Duxford was eager to see how the Luftwaffe would react to a second incursion. On the board was withdrawal support for 186 B-17s sent to bomb Kassel.

Crossing the German border near Kleve, the P-47s headed for the rendezvous point over Haltern. At 1100 hours the bombers were sighted and the 78th took up station at 28,000 ft – 4000 ft above the 'big friends'.

Just before the Luftwaffe attacked, Lt Col Melvin McNickle's aircraft suddenly fell out of formation, collided with his wingman and plunged to earth. CO of the group, McNickle was extremely fortunate to survive the near headlong dive into the ground, for he had passed out when his oxygen system had failed, and was still out cold when the Dutch resistance extricated him from the wreckage of his P-47. Sadly, his wingman, James Byers, bailed out but was killed. Ex-83rd FS boss Lt Col James J Stone subsequently became the 78th's third CO in just four weeks .

The 84th FS was the first to make contact with part of a 100-strong enemy fighter force making gun and rocket attacks on the bombers. Lt Col Stone exploded a Bf 109 as did Jack Price, while Capt John Irvin (four destroyed and one damaged) shot down a further two. The day's combat casualties also included a Bf 109 that went down near Didam, in Holland, its destruction marking the first kill of future 84th FS ace Peter

Off-duty, the boyish features of leading P-47 ace Gerry Johnson might have disguised the fact that he was a highly experienced combat pilot with the famed 56th FG 'Wolfpack'. One of two aces with the surname of Johnson serving concurrently with the group in 1943/44, Gerald had scored a total of 16.5 victories (all in P-47s) prior to being shot down and captured on 27 March 1944. He had 'made ace' on 10 October 1943 in P-47C-5 41-6352/HV-T which, ironically, was not his usual mount – Johnson's assigned aircraft was P-47D-1 42-7877/HV-D

Pompetti – flying P-47C-5 41-6393 on this occasion, Pompetti had scored 5 kills and 3¹/₂ damaged by the time he was shot down and captured on 17 March 1944.

Maj Eugene Roberts made his way to the leading boxes of 'Forts' and caught an Fw 190, which he promptly shot down in flames. A second fared no better as the American opened fire on him. Finally, Roberts overhauled a Bf 109 caught just as it peeled off to attack its chosen bomber target. It never made it. With three down, Roberts became the first Eighth Air Force pilot to score a triple victory on one mission.

Bomber affiliation or good shepherd? Lt Charles Reed of the 63rd FS/56th FG eases *Princess Pat* in for a closer look at a Liberator while the bomber crew in turn take her picture. Fellow squadron pilot Capt Walker 'Bud' Mahurin had cause to rue too close an association with a Liberator, his fighter losing its tail in a collision which saw both aircraft crash, and the future ace almost lose his life before he had scored a single kill

His success was, however, overshadowed by the actions of Charles Pershing London, who became the first VIII Fighter Command ace during the course of the sortie. Sliding in behind two Focke-Wulfs, with the rest of the 83rd FS at 26,000 ft, London got a single Fw 190 before diving on a Bf 109 which exploded under the impact of his bullets. Other pilots scored victories too before being forced to break off the engagement due to rapidly dwindling fuel reserves. En route home, Quince Brown took the opportunity to strafe a train in what was believed to be the first such attack by an VIII Fighter Command pilot. He came back with gun camera film of the train's locomotive surrounded by steam to prove the point.

The exuberant Brown was nearly 'nailed' by coastal flak batteries, however, dropping so low that his propeller made contact with the North Sea and bent two tips, although the P-47 got him home. Back at Duxford, Capt London was quickly confirmed as the first ace in the ETO, his personal P-47C, 41-6335/HL-B *EL JEEPO*, having been used for all five kills.

## AUGUST 1943

As was to become standard practice, new groups to the ETO were assisted by experienced pilots on their first few missions, and on 9 August the recently-arrived 353rd FG, based at Metfield in Suffolk, was 'shown the ropes' by the 56th. No action took place on this or most other 'shakedown' missions, much to the relief of the rookie pilots. At least they had seen enemy territory, charged their guns and taken note of the weather, wondering if it was always different to that forecast by the met officer!

The 353rd flew its first official group mission on 12 August – the day future 20-kill ace Capt 'Bud' Mahurin nearly wrote himself off indulging in a little off-duty horseplay with a lone B-24. The P-47 pilot had flown some fancy aerobatics which, if nothing else, was good target practice for the Liberator gunners, and he moved up and under the bomber. Mahurin got too close, however, and propwash hit his P-47 and sucked it in under the wing. The B-24's propellers ripped at the fighter's fuselage, and Mahurin suddenly found himself diving earthwards in a tailless and totally uncontrollable P-47. He managed to bail out at 400 ft and the B-24 went on to crash-land. Mahurin was fully expecting a court martial as a result of the incident, with 'improper use of government property' being the indictment. But Zemke merely fined him $100 and chewed him out. Some would say the Liberator incident, and his first two victories on 17 August (in P-47C-2 41-6259/UN-V), proved that Mahurin had luck on his side, but he believed that all pilots needed a degree of good fortune riding with them in the cockpit. As he said to a reporter at the time;

'You've got to be lucky in this business, otherwise I wouldn't be here now. I've made too many mistakes to let myself believe that I'm good. Whenever you go up you try to do everything right; you try to think fast and remember everything you've learned. You know you're flying a good airplane and you've already proved to yourself that you're as good as, if not better than, most of the Germans you're likely to meet. But all the time you keep praying like hell that your luck doesn't run out.'

Another future P-47 ace also opened his account with a double score on 16 August, 334th FS/4th FG pilot Lt Henry 'Hank' Mills claiming two Fw 190s (out of a final score of six) in the vicinity of Paris. Like numerous other pilots, he had previously been credited with probable and damaged claims, although there was nothing quite so satisfying to a fighter pilot as a confirmed kill in line with the VIII Fighter Command rules. Aerial victories in the ETO at that time meant a great deal, as the Americans were up against pilots who were universally recognised as the Luftwaffe's best.

Lt Jim Goodson (in P-47C-5 41-6574) also claimed two Fw 190s destroyed and a third damaged over Paris on the 16th.

August 1943 marked the first anniversary of the Eighth Air Force's bold experiment in daylight bombing. And while the results so far had been fairly encouraging, there was an urgency in Washington for the bombers to hit more targets deep inside Germany. The historic long range double mission to Schweinfurt and Regensburg planned for the 17th was therefore a bold move, but the 'heavies' would be forced to fly way beyond escort fighter cover. As it transpired, the missions flown on this date showed just how costly the campaign would be if Luftwaffe fighters were left to repeatedly hit the bombers unmolested.

Despite their extra range, the P-47s could not fly as far as either of these targets, and on this occasion the enemy took maximum advantage of that fact. But the AAF fighters could 'take the heat off the "heavies"' by shooting down Fw 190s and Bf 109s well away from the bomber stream, and in this role the 56th FG did very well. Briefed to cover B-17s of the Schweinfurt force in the afternoon, the P-47s were well-positioned to take advantage of what were noted as the latest German tactics – enemy fighters were opting to fly a parallel course and overtake the bombers before wheeling round for a head-on pass from about five miles out, leaving time for the Thunderbolt pilots to position themselves. Diving in front of the bombers, they could block and break up the enemy's line-abreast run-in. Once forced to break, it was difficult for the German pilots to quickly reform in strength, resulting in large formations being chopped into smaller elements which posed less of a threat to the bombers.

This period was marked by a general assault on the bombers by twin-engined German aircraft as well as single-seaters, American fighter strength being such that the Luftwaffe could still risk sending up Bf 110 and Me 410 *Zerstörers* and Ju 88s, the crews of which had an even chance of destroying the B-17s that dominated VIII Bomber Command's efforts

Col 'Hub' Zemke is seen standing on the wing of P-47C-5 41-6330/LM-Z, which was the first Thunderbolt assigned to him as commanding officer of the 56th FG. Initially bearing a wheel insignia as a play on his nickname and the Russian phrase *"MOY TAVARISH"* ('My comrade'), Zemke had the markings removed shortly after this photograph was taken. The original print shows two iron cross markings beneath the canopy, which would date it after 13 June 1943 (the date of Zemke's first two confirmed victories) and before 17 August when he claimed his third kill. It is widely believed that all of his early successes achieved between May and August 1943 were scored in this fighter

at that time. But if they were caught by the USAAF escort, their position could become dire, for the German 'twins' were very vulnerable in a straight fight with a more manoeuvrable single-seater like a P-47.

Battling their way back to Antwerp where they would be relieved by RAF Spitfires, the P-47s scored decisively. When 61st FS pair Capt Gerald Johnson (again in 42-7877) and future 5.5-kill ace Lt Frank McCauley (flying P-47C-2 41-6271/HV-Z) fired simultaneously on a Bf 110, the result was spectacular – the fighter exploded in a huge fireball that seemed to freeze any action for a very long time. Bomber crews and fighter pilots alike (among them Bob Johnson, who had yet to score a victory) swore it was the brightest light they had ever witnessed.

Johnson had instinctively climbed as he fired, and now found himself way above the melee. He spotted a Bf 109, dived and fired, observing hits before the pilot bailed out just prior to his aircraft exploding. Johnson soon accounted for a second Bf 109, which dived into the ground and exploded after a two-second burst from his P-47's eight '.50s'.

Frank McCauley also got an Fw 190, whilst a Bf 109F fell to the guns of Lt Harold Comstock in P-47C-5 41-6320/UN-Y (his first of eventually 5.5 victories). Totally unseen by his quarry, the 63rd FS pilot was able to close to within 100 yards of his target before shearing off one of the Messerschmitt's wings with a burst of fire.

The double mission of 17 August resulted in no less than 60 B-17s being lost. Questions were asked about what went wrong by both ranking Eighth Air Force commanders and senior USAAF officers and political figures in Washington, where the seeds of the Luftwaffe's destruction began to be sown for 'harvesting' early the following year. What the USAAF generals did not readily appreciate was the cost incurred by the Luftwaffe in bringing down such a high number of bombers on one raid. Indeed, the *Jagdwaffe* had suffered increasing losses with nearly every daylight mission it tried to counter, aircraft falling to both the fierce defensive fire of the bombers as well as the growing ranks of escort fighters.

Two days after 'first Schweinfurt', Lt Jim Carter of the 61st FS/56th FG claimed a damaged Bf 109 west of Gilze-Rijen (in P-47D-2 42-7960/HV-J). His record showed that it could take an individual pilot some time to become an ace, with the almost inevitable damaged and probable claims to push back the day when five confirmed might (or might not) be the gratifying result of many hours of hard combat flying. Carter finally made ace on 4 July 1944, his ultimate total of six– all in P-47s – being confirmed on 18 November.

Pioneers in extending the P-47's range with the early 200-gal 'figure-hugging' belly tanks, the 4th FG performed the first penetration of German airspace on 28 July 1943. This photo may have been taken at the start of that very mission, as it shows the short-lived tanks on 334th FS ships, including P-47D-1 42-7924/QP-F flown by Capt Waclaw 'Mike' Sobanski. A native of Warsaw, Sobanski had fled to America in late 1939 after being wounded whilst fighting the Germans as a Polish Army infantryman. He had obtained a US passport through family connections, and after arriving in New York in the summer of 1940, he went north to Canada to join the RAF. Following the completion of his training, Sobanski was posted to the UK, where he briefly served with Nos 132 and 164 Sqns. He used his American citizenship once again in May 1943 to join the recently-formed 4th FG at Debden, and remained with the group until killed in action on D-Day. CO of the 334th FS at the time of his death, Sobanski's final tally was officially given as 2.833 aerial kills and three ground victories (see *Aircraft of the Aces 21 - Polish Aces of World War 2* for further details) (*via W Bodie*)

On 9 September the 352nd FG went operational, flying P-47Ds out of Bodney, in Norfolk. There had been the usual 'hurry up and wait' period for the first personnel to arrive, but little was possible without a full complement of aircraft. These arrived during the summer, and with future five-kill ace Col Joe Mason in command, the unit worked up to operational status, helped by ex-82nd FS (78th FG) CO Lt Col Harry Dayhuff.

Early missions for the 352nd were uneventful, and although they had not done any fighting, the pilots looked good enough to Dayhuff, who returned to Duxford after leading two 'Rodeos' on 22 September. The same quiet introduction to combat was experienced by the 355th FG at Steeple Morden, in Hertfordshire, the group flying its first full mission on 14 September – weather had delayed its combat debut by two weeks.

An Fw 190 became the first victim of ranking 353rd FG ace – and then Group Ops Officer – Maj Glenn Duncan on 23 September. Finding enemy aircraft over the French town of Nantes, Duncan's section engaged, although his kill was offset by the death of Lt George Dietz, who was shot down by enemy fighters. Duncan's great rival Capt Walter Beckham also got an Fw 190 over Nantes during the mission, this being his first confirmed kill. A member of the 351st FS, Beckham scored steadily through the remaining months of 1943 and into 1944.

Spreading the day's aerial victory honours throughout the group was always pleasing for the participating pilots, and particularly those who got nothing. They felt that maybe next time they too could do it. In this respect, future seven-kill ace Lt James Poindexter's first confirmed success (a Bf 109) was as much a victory for the 352nd FS as it was for for him.

Five 353rd FG pilots (Beckham, Duncan, Poindexter, W F Tanner and Magure) would become aces before the P-47 gave way to the P-51 in October 1944, and on 27 September one of these men, Lt William 'Mickey' Maguire of the 351st FS, shot down a Bf 109 south of Roodeschoot and damaged a second west of Emden. These were the first of five aerial victories Maguire would be credited with while the group flew the P-47, his eventual tally of seven including two on the P-51D.

'Train-busting' Quince Brown of the 78th FG also got his first victory on 27 September. Part of the 84th FS, Brown was flying his assigned P-47D-6 (42-74753/WZ-J) north-west of Emden when he 'bagged' a Bf 109. This particular Thunderbolt would be used to good effect by Brown for his next nine victories, which would take him through to late May 1944. Quince Brown would hardly have been surprised to learn that he shared his surname with other USAAF fighter pilots – but he probably would not have put the figure as high as 53, all of whom had scored one or more victories during the war!

This formation shot shows a section of P-47D-6s from the 84th FS/78th FG on a long range patrol, led by Capt Jack Price in 42-7461/WZ-Z *Feather Merchant II* – the pilot used this aircraft to gain ace status on 26 November 1943. Red outlined national insignia is in evidence on all aircraft in the picture, as are teardrop-shaped 75-gal belly tanks. These were pressurised and tended to deliver the specified amount of fuel, unlike the original bulbous tanks which were unpressurised and good for about 100 gallons only. These tanks finally made the P-47 an escort fighter to be reckoned with *(IWM HU 73849)*

# BLOODY BATTLES

Early October ushered in a particularly productive period for the 56th FG, with its Deputy CO, Maj Dave Schilling, scoring five kills in the first ten days of the month. He claimed a Bf 109 and an Fw 190 destroyed on the 2nd (in P-47C-5 41-6343/LM-W) as his first and second kills, a Bf 110 (flying P-47C-5 41-6347/LM-O) 48 hours later as his third, an Fw 190 (in P-47D-1 42-7838/LM-S) on the 8th for his fourth and another Fw 190 (using P-47D-1 42-7870/LM-R) on the 10th to 'make ace'. Future 63rd FS/56th FG ace Lt 'Bunny' Comstock also enjoyed success on the 4th, gaining his second kill when he downed a Bf 110 over Bruhl. He was flying his familiar P-47C-5 41-6326/UN-Y at the time, this particular aircraft remaining with him until year's end, by which time it was one of the last C-models still in the frontline.

The first ten days of October had also seen the 4th FG fly four 'Ramrods' into Germany, and on the mission undertaken on the 8th, Lt Duane 'Bee' Beeson of the 334th FS (in P-47D-1 42-7890/QP-B) claimed two Bf 109s (and a third example damaged) to raise his tally to six – this double haul made Beeson the group's first all-P-47 ace. That same 'Ramrod' also saw 'Eagle' Squadron veteran, and now 335th FS CO, Maj Roy Evans, 'make ace' (in P-47D-1 42-7879) with a solitary Bf 109 kill. The first of his five victories (an Fi 156) to date had been scored in a Spitfire VB on 21 November 1942, whilst his sixth, and last, was claimed in November 1944 in a 359th FG P-51D during his second combat tour.

On 14 October the Eighth Air Force returned to Schweinfurt and Regensburg and again lost 60 B-17s to defending fighters and flak. It was a difficult operation for the fighters to support, as apart from not being able to fly all the way with the 'heavies', the weather intervened. The most successful groups in terms of contact with the Luftwaffe was the 353rd, which destroyed ten aircraft, whilst the 56th claimed three – both these groups had given penetration support. Weather ruined the missions laid on by the 78th and 355th, and forced the 4th to return to Debden early.

There was relatively little fighter action during the rest of the month, the poor weather persisting with the result that a scheduled heavy bomber mission planned for 30 October was abandoned. Despite the poor conditions, 56th FG boss 'Hub' Zemke managed to further advance his score after 'making ace' on 2 October, adding a damaged and a confirmed (an Me 210 and an Fw 190 respectively) on the 18th and 20th – both near the Dutch border with Germany. After claiming his seventh victory on 5 November (again an Fw 190), Zemke temporarily bade farewell to the 56th

A wrapped up P-47C-5 (41-6345) of the 82nd FS/78th FG is seen in its Duxford revetment having its code letters MX-R painted on the cockpit cover. The aircraft was flown by Richard A Hewitt, who destroyed one Bf 109 and damaged another on 16 March 1944 (*via T Bivens*)

FG, handing it over to Col R B Landry. 'Hub' would, however, return to his 'Wolfpack' in January 1944, adding a further eight kills to his tally during his second spell as CO, which lasted until August.

October also saw VIII Fighter Command add a sixth P-47-equipped fighter group to its ranks when the 356th, based initially at Goxhill in Lincolnshire, joined the Eighth Air Force on the 15th.

## — NOVEMBER 1943 —

On 5 November future 56th FG ace Lt George Hall shot down an Me 210/410 near Enschede in P-47D-6

42-74750/UN-L. This was cause for a small celebration on Hall's part, for it was his first confirmed kill. A member of the 63rd FS, he had joined the 56th late in February 1943 and then had to wait a long while for his first victory. Hall had tasted limited success on 17 August when he claimed a Bf 109 probable in P-47D-1 42-7896/UN-H (the aircraft actually assigned to him). George Hall scored his five subsequent kills in his second allocated aircraft, P-47D-11 42-75266 UN-F.

Two of the most significant kills claimed in November fell to Capt Norman Olson of the 357th FS/355th FG, for he later went on to become the group's sole all-P-47 ace in February 1944. Having joined the 355th from the training replacement-optimised 50th FG in March 1943, Canadian-born Olson's run of successes began on 7 November when an Me 210/410 strayed into his gunsight over Amiens. Six days later he 'bagged' a Bf 109F near Zwolle. One of those pilots who was not assigned his own P-47 almost certainly because of his late transfer into the group, Olson used examples of the P-47D-2, D-5 and D-6 to score a total of six victories by 21 February – his last claims took the form of an Fw 190 shot down and a second damaged in the Lake Dummer area. These proved to be his last successes, for although Olson saw in the 355th's P-51 period, and was finally assigned his own aircraft, he was shot down and killed by flak near Celle Hofer on 8 April 1944.

56th FG pilot Walt Cook doubled his score when he downed two Fw 190s (in P-47C-2 41-6193/LM-B) near Bocholt whilst on the first sortie led by 61st FS CO 'Gabby' Gabreski on 11 November.

Ample evidence of the waxing power of VIII Bomber Command could be seen in the skies over Bre-

When Capt Gerry Johnson scored his fifth and sixth confirmed victories on 10 October 1943, the symbols that marked him out as an ace were naturally stencilled under the cockpit rim of his fighter. Having flown P-47D-1 42-7877/HV-D to get 4.5, he then switched to older P-47C-5 41-6352/HV-T, and he is presumably pictured here sat in the latter aircraft (*IWM AP 968*)

*"Lucky"* was the name aptly chosen by the 56th FG's second 'Johnson ace', Bob, for his P-47D-5, 42-8461/HV-P. Seen here at an early stage in Johnson's successful tour with the 61st and 62nd FSs, this aircraft later had two black swastikas painted the the cowling titling

men on 26 November when 405 B-17s and 103 B-24s bombed the port city's shipyards and submarine pens. The day was also the most successful to date for the fighters, all of which were up on 'Ramrods'. Take off for the 56th FG was at 1030 hours, with Dave Schilling leading. Each P-47 carried 108-gal belly tanks which were released over the Zuider Zee at 1145. The Thunderbolt pilots were greeted at the rendezvous point by the sight of bombers being attacked by wave after wave of rocket-equipped Bf 110s and Me 410s, which were charging in to fire off their projectiles under the protection of Bf 109s and Fw 190s cruising several thousand feet above the bomber stream. Having arrived first, the 62nd FS 'waded in', and in the ensuing combats the 56th claimed 15 fighters for 11 P-47s reported damaged to varying degrees.

'Bud' Mahurin as 'Red Flight' leader wasted no time in shooting down three Bf 110s and adding a fourth as a probable (the *Zerstörer* was proving to be a favourite target for Mahurin, as he had downed three on 4 October to 'make ace', and then claimed another destroyed on 3 November).

The first kill was made after Mahurin latched onto a Bf 110 which he approached from dead astern before firing at close range. The P-47's fire probably touched off one of the unfired rockets, for the enemy fighter

By 5 January 1944 Lt Bob Johnson's score stood at 11, with these kills being marked up below the cockpit of P-47D-15 42-76234/HV-P, which had been christened *"Double Lucky"* by its pilot

Walker 'Bud' Mahurin was one of the many characters who enlivened the 'Wolfpack's' war both in the air and on the ground. He achieved acedom in just three missions, flown on 17 August, 9 September and 4 October 1943. Apart from the first successful sortie, during which he flew P-47C-2 41-6259/UN-V, Mahurin scored the majority of his 19.75 kills in War Bond subscription P-47D 42-8487/UN-M *"SPIRIT OF ATLANTIC CITY, N.J."*, shown here as the ace is congratulated on the completion of another successful mission by a 63rd FS squadronmate (*IWM NYF 11561*)

The press really took to the 78th FG's Maj Eugene Roberts, as this shot of photographers taking his portrait clearly indicates. He had eight victories marked on his assigned P-47C-5 41-6630/WZ-Z, christened *Spokane Chief*, when this particular photo call took place at Duxford in late October 1943. Roberts had handed over leadership of the 84th FG to future five-kill ace Maj J C Price in late September and then assumed the position of Deputy Group CO. He would score his final kill (Bf 109F/G), again in this aircraft, on 20 October, before transferring to a desk job within VIII Fighter Command HQ – Roberts had completed 89 combat missions with the 78th FG (*IWM HU 73848*)

The 'Hub' and part of his armoury. Col Hubert Zemke led the 56th FG through its early combat months with great success, although he had a couple of narrow escapes through both enemy action and the technical problems that dogged the early-model Thunderbolts for months in 1942-43. Zemke became an ace on 2 October 1943, and like many of the top VIII Fighter Command pilots, was subsequently captured (on 30 October 1944) by the Germans after bailing out over enemy territory (*IWM EA 39048*)

shed large pieces of wing as it fell away. Repositioning himself to the rear of the bombers, Mahurin then came within a whisker of being shot down by 'friendly fire', as the gunners were blazing away at anything that looked remotely like an enemy fighter - and that included American P-47s. But this was a known hazard, and the USAAF pilots always tried to keep well out of range of the massed guns of the 'heavies'. Mahurin, watching B-17 tracer bullets passing above his canopy, instead concentrated on his second victim. The Bf 110 crew, intent on their own target, failed to take evasive action, and their fighter was soon spinning down in flames.

Breaking off, Mahurin spotted a third Bf 110 several thousand ft below and immediately dived after it. By the time they passed through 14,000 ft the American had the advantage, and his third kill of the sortie duly went down. Diving away from a P-47 was about the worst manoeuvre a German *Zerstörer* crew could attempt, for the Thunderbolt could outdive most other aircraft due to its immense bulk, and it invariably caught up with either single- or twin-engined fighters. Yet air battles in the ETO continued to see this manoeuvre used by the Germans, the attack/dive away tactic tracing its origins to early engagements with the RAF, where a power dive away often eluded pursuit. And old habits die hard . . .

The day's tally brought 'Bud' Mahurin's score to ten confirmed, making him the first Eighth Air Force double ace. Most of his kills had been achieved while flying his War Bond subscription P-47D-5 42-8487/UN-M *"SPIRIT*

The board says it all. A member of the Duxford groundcrew updates the 84th FS 'Victory Board' in October 1943, a close inspection of the entries showing Lt Peter Pompetti's 'Me 109' kill on 27 September and four of Maj Eugene Roberts' victories. The first entry is for the Fw 190 victory scored by Capt John Irvin on 16 May. Of the three squadrons that made up the 78th FG, the 84th was the least successful with 96-4-26.5 – by comparison the 82nd scored 103.5-10-39.5 and the 83rd FS 119.5-11-54 (*Bivens*)

With a haul of 12 kills, Duane 'Bee' Beeson of the 334th FS was easily the top ace of the 4th FG during its P-47 period. His success may have had something to do with the fact that he did not have to overcome the stigma attached to the Thunderbolt by veteran 'Eagle' Squadron pilots who had previously flown the Spitfire in combat. Although an RCAF recruit who briefly served with No 71 Sqn within the RAF, Beeson had failed to see any action in Spitfires prior to joining the P-47-equipped 4th FG when the 'Eagle' Squadrons were absorbed within the newly-arrived Eighth Air Force in late September 1942. Squadron, then group, gunnery officer during his time with the 4th FG, Beeson had scored 17.333 kills by the time he was shot down by flak and made a PoW on 5 April 1944. Note the 'hands off' message 'It's Beeson's' on his 'Mae West', and the battle damage to the tail of his P-47

OF ATLANTIC CITY, N.J.".

Two more victories (again both Bf 110s) made Walt Cook an ace on this mission, these kills raising his score to six. Four had been achieved while flying his assigned P-47C-5, appropriately christened *Little Cookie*. Tour expired in February 1944, Walt returned home without having added any further kills to his tally. He had flown 66 missions.

'Gabby' Gabreski also 'made ace' on this sortie, downing the almost obligatory pair of Bf 110s for the first of no less than six 'doubles' and one 'triple' he would score in the ensuing months. When 'Gabby' got back to Halesworth, his groundcrew found an unexploded 20 mm shell lodged in the P-47D-5's (42-8458/HV-F) engine compartment.

Aerial action of the kind that developed on 26 November could not have come soon enough for the 352nd FG, for they had seen no combat worthy of the name since the group's ETO debut on 9 September. Indeed, some pilots who were already flying their 27th mission started to think that it would be over before they had had a crack at the enemy!

Led by Col Joe Mason, the 352nd FG rendezvoused with the bombers as they were flying at 27,000 ft over Strucklingen at 1225 hrs. The bomber force was a mixture of B-17s and B-24s, and the fighter pilots noted that while the 'Forts' maintained a good formation, the Liberators were well strung out, making them a better target for the *Jagdflieger*.

As the 'big friends' neared Groningen the enemy struck, six Bf 109s focusing their attention on two B-24s. The German pilots soon had 'Yellow' and 'Blue Flights' of the 352nd on their tails, however, 487th FS CO

Maj John C Meyer and Lt John Bennett leading the interception. The former (flying P-47D-5 42-8529/HO-M) got the first of three Bf 109s shot down by the Bodney group that day. All in all it was a highly successful day, with VIII Fighter Command claiming a record 36-3-9.

Pilots rarely moved between groups once in the frontline, although on 29 November one of the few exceptions to the rule scored his first combat success with Bf 109 probable near Meppel. Capt Joe Bennett had arrived in the ETO with the 360th FS/356th FG in September 1943, but had duly moved to the 61st FS/56th FG on 27 November. He quickly opened his account with his new unit by claiming the probable kill as previously detailed, and went on to score five kills with the 56th FG before moving to the P-51B-equipped 336th FS/4th FG on 4 April 1944. His scoring run was abruptly stopped on 25 May, however, for he was forced to bail out over enemy territory following a collision (his second in five weeks) – he had just downed two Fw 190s, claimed a further pair as probables and damaged a fifth during this sortie, taking his tally to 8.5-4-3.

Joe Bennett's place within the 360th FS/356th FG was temporarily taken on 29 November 1943 by seasoned 56th FG ace Gerry Johnson, who was posted to Martlesham Heath to assist with the new group's introduction to combat. He subsequently showed the way in fine style by shooting down an Fw 190 and damaging a second as a temporary member of the 360th FS on 24 January 1944. He returned to the 56th shortly afterwards, becoming CO of the 63rd FS on 19 February.

On the last day of November Lt Max Juchheim joined the 83rd FS/78th FG, where he was assigned P-47D-6 42-74690/HL-J. Still flying the aircraft in 1944, he was able to score four victories in it starting on 22 February 1944 with a Bf 109 destroyed east of Eindhoven, and

P-47D-2 (42-8369) named *Frances Ann II* was part of the 'Wolfpack's' 61st FS in early 1944, although the pilot(s) who flew it has yet to be identified

Poor quality but nevertheless interesting photo (the only one extant, it seems) showing the 'Jolly Roger' pirate flag incorporating the aircraft name *HOLY JOE* on the side of Lt Joe Egan's P-47C-5 41-6584/UN-E of the 63rd FS/56th FG. He scored one victory in this aircraft (an Fw 190 on 19 August 1943) and four more while flying two different Thunderbolts (D-10 42-75069/UN-E and D-15 42-75855/UN-E), attaining ace status on 15 March 1944. He was later shot down and killed by flak in P-47D-25 42-26524 north-east of Nancy on 19 July 1944 – just two days after having been made CO of the 63rd FS

continuing up to 13 April when an Fw 190 fell to his guns over Beuchenbeuren. P-47D-22 42-26020/HL-J then became Juchheim's personal mount, and he remained with the 78th FG until forced to bail out of his Thunderbolt (42-26016/HL-A) over occupied Europe following yet another collision on 28 May 1944. His tally then stood at 9-2-2.

## DECEMBER 1943

Although later to become one of the highest scoring fighter groups in the Eighth when equipped with P-51s, the 352nd produced just one P-47 ace – Lt Virgil K Meroney. Flying with the 487th FS, Meroney claimed his first kill on 1 December 1943 when he downed a Bf 109 and shared in the destruction of an Me 210/410 south of Rheyde, flying P-47D-5 42-8473/HO-V – he would use this Thunderbolt to score all nine of his kills.

A P-47D-6 of the 351st FS/353rd FG. Relatively few photos appear to have been taken of the unit's P-47s, although the 'Slybird Group' was a hard flying and fighting outfit, pioneering ground strafing and dive-bombing techniques among its other achievements (*via Campbell*)

The 1 December air battles also drew in the 78th FG's 82nd FS, and in particular ex-4th FG pilot Lt James Wilkinson. Meeting Bf 109Gs over Eupen (in P-47D-1 42-7954/MX-L), he made no mistake about his target. It was the first of six victories Wilkinson scored with the 78th FG prior to being killed in a flying accident on 4 June 1944 in South Wales.

Ten days later it was the turn of Lt Paul Conger (in P-47D-11 42-75345/HV-T) of the 61st FS/56th FG to commence his scoring run with two Bf 110s (and a third damaged) and a Ju 88 destroyed over Langeoog Island. Although well on the way to becoming an ace, Conger would have to wait until the spring of 1944 before scoring kills' four and five.

The 11 December mission was an important one for the fighters, which had more than 600 bombers to protect. The 56th drew escort for the first two boxes of the 3rd Bomb Division 'to the limit of endurance', and the *Jagdwaffe* struck before the American armada had even made landfall over Europe. Bob Johnson and his squadronmates were at 30,000 ft above the Frisian Islands when the first bandits were called in. No attack materialised from the dozen or so fighters spotted at 35,000 ft, however, this group being sent up merely to shadow the force until they found the best down-sun position from which to attack. They soon showed their hand, as they dived into the ranks of the 62nd FS.

The *Jagdflieger* hoped that such tactics would effectively rob the bombers of their escort if they could tempt all three American squadrons to challenge this early probe. Nobody in the 56th fell for the ruse, however, with the 62nd being ordered to counter the thrust while the other squadrons stayed out of the fight and continued on course to rendezvous with the bombers as planned. Then a call came in for the 62nd to draw off four fighters, leaving twelve to 'mix it' with the Luftwaffe. It was an order that had tragic results, for Bob Johnson watched in horror as two P-47s making a turn collided. Nobody could prevent the accident which took pilots Larry Strand and Ed Kruer out of the mission.

Both men jumped and parachutes were seen. Johnson pressed on. At the rendezvous point the bombers were taking a beating, with 40+ *Zerstörers* and 60 single-seaters running in and making firing passes, or launching rockets, into the massed B-17 combat boxes. Gabreski called an attack and waded into the enemy. He said later that the appearance of the P-47s 'let all hell loose'. Johnson selected a Bf 110 and chased it as the

The legendary Francis 'Gabby' Gabreski emerged as the top US fighter ace in the ETO with 27 aerial victories. Having flown at least nine different P-47s during the course of his long combat career with VIII Fighter Command, 'Gabby's' score would have undoubtedly been higher had he not been shot down by flak on 20 July 1944 during a strafing run on Bassinheim airfield (in P-47D-25 42-26418) (*via J Lambert*)

Lt Quince Brown is seen in the cockpit of *OKIE*, which has four enemy aircraft kills and 40 fighter sweep symbols painted on its side. This particular machine was P-47D-6 42-74753/WZ-J, which Brown used to score his first ten victories, plus a 0.333 share in a Do 217. He was flying different aircraft on both occasions for his last two victories (D-5 42-8574/WZ-D and D-25 42-26567/WZ-V). After the final kill (a Bf 109) on 1 September, now Maj Brown was shot down by flak over Schleiden (in P-47D-28 44-19568/WZ-Z) five days later and murdered by an SS *Schutzstaffel* officer who was later prosecuted after the war. Sadly, Brown was one of a handful of fighter pilots in the ETO to meet such a grim fate (*IWM EA 16830*)

enemy pilot, alerted to what was going on behind him by his gunner, dived. Close behind, he was amazed that the 'twin' stayed in one piece after it recovered very low down. Flattening out into a tail chase, the German pilot kept rolling as he tried to shake the P-47, before finally Johnson pulled up, waited for the enemy aircraft to straighten up, and fired. One short burst and the Bf 110 'came apart at the seams'.

More fighter strength was added to the Eighth on 13 December when the 359th FG at East Wretham, in Norfolk, flew its first combat mission with P-47Ds. In the event, no pilots achieved acedom during the group's P-47 period, although Lt Ray S Wetmore came nearest with 4.25 kills, followed by Lt Robert J Booth with 4 – both later 'made ace' on the P-51.

Fresh from training at Luke Field, in Arizona, future ace Lt Dave Thwaites joined the 356th FG on 19 December. He was assigned to the 361st FS and allocated a P-47D, but had no chance to score any victories until early in 1944. CO of the group's 359th FS at that time was Maj Don Baccus who also later became an ace, although his score of five was only partially achieved on the Thunderbolt – he had already opened his score (in P-47D-5 42-8568/OC-T) with a Bf 109F/G kill on 29 November.

After being credited with a number of probable and damaged claims, now CO of the 353rd FG, Lt Col Glenn Duncan, reached ace status with his fifth victory (an Fw 190 over Rastede) on 20 December. On that day Capt Joe Bennett of the 61st FS opened his score (in P-47D-2 42-

Bellied-in and probably a source only of spares, Lt Col Dave Schilling's P-47D-1 42-7938/LM-S was another War Bond subscription aircraft named "HEWLETT-WOODMERE LONG ISLAND". Schilling used this Thunderbolt to down 3.5 aircraft (all Fw 190s) and damage an Me 210/410 during October/November 1943 (via Bodie)

This interestingly marked P-47D-10 42-75126/QP-F of the 334th FS/4th FG has its code letters in a non-standard grouping forward of the 'star and bar' due to the odd placement of the factory-applied national insignia. With serviceable aircraft always at a premium, this machine could not be spared from the flying schedule just to have its squadron codes applied correctly. Therefore, it remained so marked until the aircraft went into the maintenance 'shops' at Debden for routine servicing in the shops for a lengthy period. This aircraft was flown by Capt Mike Sobanski for much of its time with the 4th FG, the pilot having the name *Mike IV* painted in white just forward of the fighter's windscreen

Maj Jack Oberhansley's second P-47 was D-1 42-7883/MX-X, which he named *IRON ASS* as he had done with his first Thunderbolt, P-47C-5 41-6542/MX-W in which he scored a probable on 14 May 1943. CO of the 78th FG's 82nd FS between August 1943 and May 1944, Oberhansley had his combat record kept fully up to date on the fuselage of this aircraft, these markings becoming more elaborate as his tour progressed. For example, the mission 'brooms' painted forward of the cockpit eventually received a much more visible black background panel over the OD scheme. This aircraft was used by Oberhansley to score two victories and a probable in September and November 1943, although by the time he 'bagged' his third, fourth and fifth victories, he had received a much newer Thunderbolt (P-47D-11 42-75406/MX-Z). Promoted to lieutenant-colonel, Oberhansley scored his final kill (a Ju 88) in P-47D-28 44-19566/MX-X on the day that he was made Deputy Group CO – 28 August 1944 (*via* Bodie)

7960/HV-J) with a confirmed Bf 110 kill over Falkenburg, thus starting a run of victories that would soon make him another 'Wolfpack' ace.

## JANUARY 1944

When Lt Peter Pompetti came home (in P-47C-5 41-6393/WZ-R) from a 4 January mission, the 78th FG Intelligence section soon confirmed that he had 'made ace'. A Bf 109 downed near Coesfield, plus an Fw 190 damaged, meant that the 84th FS pilot had reached this coveted status.

The early weeks of the new year proved fruitful for other future P-47 aces too, including the new CO of the 61st FS/56th FG, Capt Jim Carter. He downed his first confirmed kill – a Bf 109 – on 11 January (the day after he was given command of the unit), returning home with evidence of a further Bf 109 damaged and a third that could only be credited as a probable. More positive success would, however, result from Carter's shooting on subsequent missions. Carter would remain at the helm of of the 61st until VE-Day, by which time he had flown 137 combat missions.

On the 14th 1st Lt Vermont Garrison (in P-47C-5 41-6573/VF-S) of the 336th FS/4th FG got his first confirmed kills when he attacked Fw 190s over Compiegne Woods. He came home to receive credits for two, to add to an Fw 190 damaged on 7 January and a percentage share in a Ju 88 hit on 16 December. On a winning streak, Garrison was an ace by 10 February, and he ultimately became the second highest-scoring 4th FG pilot (6.333 kills) on P-47s after 'Bee' Beeson (12 kills) – Hank Mills and Jim Goodson tied for third with five kills apiece.

By the beginning of 1944 some of the original pilots of the 56th FG were approaching the end of their first or second tours, and to offset any shortfall in trained pilots when these men rotated home, 'Gabby'

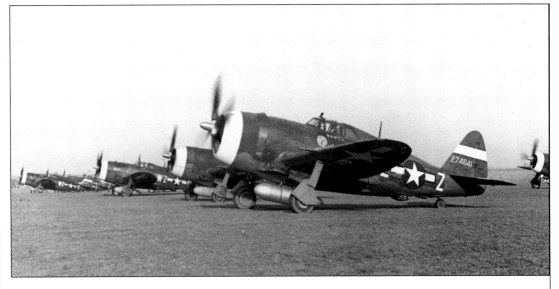

'Babies' (belly tanks) attached, the 84th FS prepares to roll out from Duxford at the start of yet another 'Ramrod' in late November or early December 1943. Nearest to the camera is P-47D-6 42-74641/WZ-Z *Feather Merchant II* of Maj Jack Price, who had used this machine to 'make ace' on 26 November when he downed an Fw 190 and a Bf 109 near Paris. Close examination of the kill markings beneath the cockpit appear to reveal 'five up' for Price (*via Bodie*)

Gabreski put forward the idea of 'recruiting' Poles serving in RAF fighter squadrons. Fluent in Polish thanks to his parentage, Gabreski had applied for an exchange posting to a 'Free Polish' unit soon after arriving in the UK, and had duly flown 13 combat missions with the RAF's No 315 Sqn between December 1942 and February 1943. Having gained valuable experience, he returned to the 56th FG, but kept in touch with the Polish friends he had made within No 315 Sqn.

By 1944, RAF fighter squadrons were encountering the Luftwaffe in ever decreasing numbers, as their Spitfire IXs had been effectively outranged by the German fighter units, which had generally pulled back inland. This move allowed the *Jagdwaffe* force to make more effective attacks on bombers, and put off clashing with the American escort fighters until the latter were at the limits of their fuel. As the bases in France and Belgium had also received plenty of attention from Allied medium bombers, the German withdrawal was also a tactically sound one.

This left many Fighter Command pilots frustrated, with the Poles in particular finding the lack of aerial activity difficult almost impossible to cope with. Knowing this, Gabreski gained authorisation from 'Hub' Zemke to encourage Polish pilots on ground tours to seek exchange postings with the USAAF, or to simply leave their desk jobs and come fly with

While the attrition rate among the Thunderbolt groups was never cripplingly high, it was nevertheless constant. 'Down in the weeds' after a combat mission is P-47C-5 41-6367, which represents a typical example of call on replacement aircraft stocks by its group while it was being repaired – always assuming that it was not so badly damaged that it was categorised a write-off

the USAAF! Amongst those to do so were 'Mike' Gladych, Tadeusz Saw-icz, Witold Lanowski, Zbigniew Janicki and Tadeusz Andersz, who all joined the 56th under a unique, and rather odd, arrangement that meant that these pilots could not be paid! This was primarily because they were told by their Polish Air Force (PAF) superiors that they would have to resign their commissions in the PAF if they chose to

Another Thunderbolt portrait taken by a bomber crew, 42-7906 was a P-47D-1 flown by the 351st FS/353rd FG. Nicknamed *Chief Wahoo*, it was flown in combat by Capt Fred LeFebre, who eventually became the squadron CO in August 1944 (*via Bodie*)

remain with the 56th FG. And while the US authorities were more than willing to use their services, the rule book could not be rewritten to accommodate men who had not been through their induction system.

Yet the Poles still wanted to get into action with the group, and the issue of money was eventually solved by the 56th FG pilots 'taking the hat round' every month to collect for their new comrades in arms. As strange as this arrangement was, it was made even more confusing by the fact that the Polish contingent continued to wear RAF rather than USAAF uniforms because that was all they had. The 56th didn't mind how they were dressed, for it was their combat experience that they were after (see *Aircraft of the Aces 21 - Polish Aces of World War 2* for further details).

The reliance placed by Gabreski's group on a handful of veteran Polish pilots reflected the fact that men arriving fresh in the UK from the USAAF's training programme not only had zero combat experience, but insufficient flying time on fighters and less than comprehensive instru-

Waiting on the line for another sortie, P-47D-2 42-8369 of the 61st FS/56th FG has not untypical stencil breaks in its three-letter codes and a repainted red outline to the national insignia. Like the majority of P-47s in the ETO, it appears to have had a relatively undistinguished career as regards victories

Demonstrating its least favoured aerial manoeuvre (climbing), a P-47D of the 62nd FS pulls away from its bomber stream

ment training. This situation continued well into 1944, and it effected instructors as well as trainee pilots. For example, Marvin Bledsoe flew a tour of operations during 1944 with the 353rd FG after completing a spell as an instructor. Upon returning home he discovered that he was one of only two pilots who had survived out of an instructor group of seven sent into action in the ETO between June and October.

On 21 January the Bottisham-based 361st FG put up its first ETO mission in the P-47D. Later famous as the 'Yellow Jackets' because of the assigned recognition colour of its P-51s, the group, like most others in the Eighth, started combat flying olive drab P-47s. Equipped with Thunderbolts for less than five months, it too failed to produce an ace before the arrival of P-51s – Maj George L Merritt, CO of the group's 375th FS, came closest with three kills.

Returning to German targets again after weeks of inclement weather, the bombers hit Hannover and Brunswick on 30 January. Strength ratios

Capt Mike Quirk banks his P-47D-11 42-75242/LM-K away from the camera, again invariably located in the waist gunner's position in an anonymous bomber. Underwing racks had yet to appear when this shot was taken in the early months of 1944, thus making visible the dissimilar sizes of the national insignia – the port wing marking had been added by groundcrews in the UK. Quirk scored 6.5 of his eventual 11 kills in this aircraft, including the all important fifth victory (a Bf 109 near Almelo) on 30 January 1944 (*via Bodie*)

An ace's mount that came to grief, P-47D-5 42-8458 led a chequered career with the 56th FG. Numbering aces like Frances Gabreski among its pilots ('Gabby' scored three victories in it, the final two on 26 November 1943 giving him ace status), this P-47 had originally been assigned to RAF-trained Flg Off Evan 'Mac' McMinn soon after he joined the 61st FS in late 1943. However, it seems that he did not use it to score any of his five kills, although an identical number of victory symbols are barely visible beneath the windscreen. McMinn was posted Missing In Action on D-Day

were 742 heavy bombers, with an escort of 635 fighters, attacked by 200 German fighters. With that superiority in numbers, the odds were firmly in favour of the USAAF, and indeed the final figures for the day reflected this. Following a number of combats, the groups came home with a tally of 45-15-31 – a rate better than ten-to-one. One of the day's final kills was a Bf 109 downed by Lt Virgil Meroney for his fifth success, making him the

Almost certainly pictured at a later date than in the previous photo, 42-8458 was surely judged a Category E write off after flipping over on landing. The date of this accident is unknown

352nd FG's first (and only) P-47 ace. His combat report read as follows;

'Leading "Crown Prince Blue Flight", I turned into twelve plus Me 109s approaching from seven o' clock at 30,000 ft and made a head on pass at the lowest one, firing a short burst from 400 yards and 10-15° deflection. I observed a few hits but did not see what became of him.

'I then made a fast 180° turn and chased a flight of four enemy aircraft. I closed on the nearest one, firing short bursts as I closed from 400 yards to 150 yards. My last burst was as he was going straight down at 10,000 ft. The right wing came off and the E/A disintegrated. I had no trouble staying with the Me 109 and could overtake him at will. I pulled up and joined some other P-47s since my flight had become separated.'

Meroney's wingman, Lt Robert I Ross, also got a Bf 109 to make it two for the 487th FS, plus a damaged. Meroney's P-47D-5 was duly decorated with a fifth iron cross beneath the cockpit, and his groundcrew enthusiastically waxed the aircraft to gain that little extra turn of speed for the next time their pilot mixed it with the Luftwaffe. This Meroney did up to 16 March, when his score stood at nine confirmed. His luck changed following the group's transition to the P-51B, however, for he was shot down by flak and made a PoW on 8 April 1944.

On 30 January a Bf 109G became Quince Brown's fifth victim, the pilot getting so close to his victim that he could clearly make out the fighter's underwing 20 mm cannon gondolas and external tank.

## FEBRUARY 1944

Ten days into February, Lt Grant Turley downed two Bf 109s in the Osnabruck area. He had joined the 82nd FS/78th FG in September 1943 and been assigned P-47D-1 42-7998/MX-N, which he promptly named 'Kitty' on one side and 'Sundown Ranch' on the other. It was subsequently used by Turley to down all his six of victories, including a double (an Fw 190 and a Bf 109) on 11 February. A pilot who was obviously a good shot, Turley made no claims for probables or aircraft damaged, all his kills being single-seat fighters. Turley's was a remarkably short career, for just over a month after scoring his first kill he was dead, shot down in combat near Barenberg, Germany, on 6 March in his personal P-47.

The 'Wolfpack' enjoyed something of a field day on 20 February when they ran across a sizeable group of Bf 110s west of Hannover. Flying in a neat 'finger four' formation, the enemy *Zerstörer* crews appeared to be quite unaware of the danger they were in. Gabreski shot down two (and damaged a third) while 61st FS pilot Lt Donavon Smith carried out what, for want of a better phase, was a 'regulation shoot-down' – shallow climbing approach, careful aiming followed by restrained bursts of fire. Gun camera film revealed that Smith was even able to select the area to fire at will. As all the Bf 110s encountered that day carried external tanks, a burst aimed at the left engine would usually pepper the tank as well. That is what happened in this instance, the aircraft falling away to starboard with the engine and tank afire to become one of two confirmed victories for Smith, who was also awarded a third Bf 110 as damaged.

Having claimed two Bf 110s on 11 December (and a half share in an Fw 190 on the same sortie), Donavon Smith 'made ace' two days later when he destroyed yet another Fw 190 to bring his final tally to 5.5-1-2.

Also scoring prolifically on the 20th was fellow 56th FG pilot Leroy Schreiber, who at last made ace with triple Bf 109 kills over Steinhuder Lake. For good measure, he damaged a Do 217 and a further Bf 109.

Twenty-four hours later it was the turn of 56th FG 'Polish flight' founder member 'Mike' Gladych to taste success. The veteran Pole had brought with him eight kills from his time with the RAF that stretched back to June 1941, and it was just this kind of experience that the 'Wolfpack' needed in its flight leader. Gladych quickly proved his worth with two Bf 109 kills on the 21st, and he followed this up with scores in the following months that took his final tally to 18-2-0.5.

Gladych, who was once summed up by Dave Schilling as 'a wild man in the air, if I ever saw one – I don't see how he lasted this long', was a worry to his fellow pilots, all of whom expected him to 'fail to return'

Guns and diamonds on a 353rd FG P-47D-15. This example, with three 108-gal 'paper' fuel tanks attached, was flown by Lt George Perpente of the 351st FS, who named the ship *FRAN* and *DOADY*. He was wingman to ranking squadron ace (and then leading ETO ace) Maj Walt Beckham when the latter was lost to flak on 22 February 1944. Perpente made a few damaged and ground claims during his tour, among the latter being a shared Fw 190 with Beckham just moments before disaster struck (*via Bodie*)

As mentioned in the previous caption, Maj Walter Beckham of the 351st FS/353rd FG became the highest scoring Eighth Air Force ace on 8 February 1944 when he downed a Bf 109 and an Fw 190 near St Hubert for his 17th and 18th confirmed victories. The only P-47 known to have been assigned to him was D-5 42-8476/YJ-X, which he christened *LITTLE DEMON*. Beckham was not flying that aircraft when he was shot down by flak on 22 February, instead being at the controls of a newer P-47D-11 (42-75226). How often he had flown that particular Thunderbolt remains something of a mystery

from virtually every mission he flew. But Gladych beat the odds, despite his overly aggressive tactics. Indeed, on one famous occasion he let the Germans do the shooting for him;

'We were over Germany escorting bombers when a fight developed fairly close to the ground. I suddenly found three Focke-Wulfs off at right angles to me and above. I tried to jump them but they kept away. I then went down on the deck among the trees. They followed me and that is exactly what I wanted. A rat race developed and they started shooting. Finally I got on the tail of one of them. He was a dead pigeon. To shoot him I had to straighten up, and one of the planes above me then put some holes in my wing. I started going home because my gas was running low, but the two remaining Focke-Wulfs started to fly in formation with me. They must have thought I was out of gas because they beckoned me to land. I motioned "OK" and kept on flying just ahead of them until we reached a German airfield.

'I knew what I'd do. I gave the field a short burst and all the ground guns opened up with everything they had. The two Germans were flying less than ten yards behind me and the anti-aircraft fire landed right among them. I didn't stay to see what happened but headed for England.'

As he crossed the coast Gladych ran out of fuel and was obliged to bail out. On the ground he was questioned by two British Army officers who were finally convinced he was Polish rather than German. Gladych's one regret was the loss of a $75,000 dollar P-47, 'the best airplane I have ever flown in combat' he said.

# MAXIMUM EFFORT

By mid-February the P-47 had reached the zenith of its frontline strength in the ETO with VIII Fighter Command (FC), eight groups (it had for a brief period in January been nine until the 358th FG joined the Ninth Air Force in place of the P-51B-equipped 357th FG, which in turn became an Eighth Air Force group) operating around 550 Thunderbolts. By comparison, the remaining fighter strength of VIII FC comprised roughly 150 P-38s and less than 50 P-51Bs. On the 22nd all the P-47 fighter groups were up, the Eighth being supported by two groups of Thunderbolts from the Ninth Air Force (358th and 365th FGs). Amongst the successful pilots on this 'maximum effort' mission was 61st FS/56th FG flight leader Capt Les Smith, who scored his first two confirmed victories after having been credited with damaged claims on two previous occasions – both Fw 190s claimed were downed over the Lippstadt area of Germany. Other pilots also scored kills including 'Gabby' Gabreski, who got a single Fw 190 in roughly the same area as Les Smith's victim had fallen. Big news of the day, however, was that the 61st FS had claimed its 100th kill, which made it the first AAF unit in the ETO to achieve three figures. Not such good news was the fact that leading VIII FC ace Walt Beckham had been downed by flak.

The loss of Beckham crowned a forgettable day for the 353rd FG, which had not started well when the B-24s they were briefed to support did not show (they had aborted due to weather), leaving the group orbiting in the designated pick up area until they latched on to three groups of B-17s. Once over Germany, the 353rd could find little sign of the Luftwaffe, so a search for enemy aircraft was initiated. CO Lt Col Glenn Duncan finally spotted aircraft on an airfield northeast of Bonn, and while he went down to attack Beckham's 351st FS maintained top cover.

Duncan's strafing run alerted local flak batteries, and as he and his

Sitting in the cockpit of his P-47D, Col James J Stone, then CO of the 78th FG, talks to newspaper correspondent Bill Hearst in early 1944. Stone had earlier gained the distinction of shooting down the first enemy aircraft claimed by the 78th FG on 14 May 1943 whilst serving as CO of of the 83rd FS. Stone commanded the squadron at that time. Although not technically an ace with five aerial kills, Stone nevertheless played an important part in ensuring the success of the P-47 as a long-range interceptor

flight pulled up, he warned the other pilots to keep low when they made their attacks. As the 351st roared across the airfield at tree top height, Beckham selected as his target a row of six Fw 190s. He 'poured on the coals' to bring his speed up to 425 mph and opened fire. As he pulled up from the pass, his aircraft (P-47D-11 42-75226) took hits and trailed flames and smoke. With his engine on fire, Beckham knew he had little chance to get away, so he opened his canopy and bailed out. He was duly welcomed by the

Germans, who thus had the leading USAAF ace in the ETO in captivity – his tally at the time stood at 18-2-4. To make matters worse, the 353rd additionally lost a further two P-47s over the airfield and a third machine earlier in the mission over Antwerp.

On a more positive note, combat over the Cologne area saw the 352nd FS/353rd FG pilot Lt James Poindexter 'make ace' by destroying two Bf 109s which he had seen arrowing in on the bombers. His fire brought spectacular results, with the first fighter exploding in front of him and the second Messerschmitt having its entire left blown wing off. Yet another 353rd P-47 went down at this stage in the sortie, however, its pilot being a member of the Ninth Air Force's P-47-equipped 366th FG on attachment to the 352nd FS to gain combat experience. Glenn Duncan got an Fw 190 for his tenth victory, while future 5.5-kill ace Lt Gordon Compton of the 351st secured his first – a Ju 88 that had just taken off from Diest Shaffen airfield. Thus, the 353rd FG experienced a not untypical victory-loss ratio of six aircraft lost for four of the enemy.

But mere figures did not reflect the experience and leadership qualities denied a group when an ace failed to return, and in that respect the result-

The sixth (more or less concurrent with the 352nd FG) fighter group to go operational with VIII FC was the 355th FG at Steeple Morden. One of the group's P-47D-2s (42-8400) from the 354th FS, coded WR-E, is shown formating with a 'heavy' on an untypically fine late winter's day in 1944

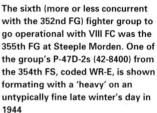

Inspecting German cannon fire damage to his P-47D in a Duxford hanger, Lt James Wilkinson of the 78th FG's 82nd FS has at least three kills marked up on his battle weary fighter, thus dating this photo at around late February/early March 1944 – he scored his fourth on 6 March 1944. Wilkinsion not only went on to become a six-kill ace (on 12 May) but also CO of his squadron. On 4 June he was killed in a flying accident near Llandovery, in South Wales, whilst still at the head of the 82nd FS

Down in the rough at Boxted, this P-47D-10 (42-75069) was assigned to Capt Joe Egan of the 56th FG's 63rd FS. This was his second assigned aircraft, and he used it to score just one kill (on 30 January 1944) en route to becoming an ace, on 15 March. No personal markings or kills are visible.

ing gap(s) that needed to be filled was considerably broader than the straightforward need for a replacement pilot(s) and aircraft. This situation was similar, but far more acute, in the *Jagdwaffe*, which was regularly losing men of vast experience in the air battles over Europe.

Although February had not been such a good month for the 353rd FG, for members of the 'Wolfpack' it had brought near-daily success. For example, on the 24th an escort mission that saw bombers flying to various German targets due to bad weather resulted in the 63rd FS's Lt John Truluck nailing a Bf 109G (in P-47D-6 42-74750/UN-L) over the Zuider Zee. This success raised his tally to five, and would later claim a further two kills by mid-March, which took his final score to 7-0-3.

On 25 February, while the 4th FG put up its first all-Mustang show in the ETO, personnel changes were being made at Halesworth. Leaving the 56th was Capt John W Vogt, who had achieved 'acedom' with the 63rd FS just three days before (in P-47D-10 42-75109/ UN-W). Transferring to the 356th FG, he was later able to score a further three kills (the last on 4 August) whilst serving as CO of the 360th FS at Martlesham Heath.

One pilot very much staying put with the 56th FG was Capt 'Mike' Gladych, who borrowed Bob Johnson's P-47 for the escort mission to the Ruhr flown by the group on 26 February. Flying number three in a four-ship flight, Gladych was suddenly nowhere to be seen. He was soon spotted by flight mates Lts Richard Mudge and Eugene Barnum some 18,000 ft below them, tailchasing a Bf 109. Diving down after him, they wondered why the Pole had not destroyed the fighter – which they swiftly did. Once back home it was discovered that Gladych had found the gun switch in his fighter inoperable, but such was his hatred of the Germans that he was determined to run the Bf 109 out of fuel (350 miles from home!), or find some other way of causing the pilot to crash.

## MARCH 1944

The first week of March saw Col Hub Zemke score his first victories in four months (he had been on leave in the USA for some of this time), downing two fighters over the Minden-Osnabruck-Dummer Lake areas on the 6th. An Fw 190 fell first, followed by a Bf 109, the 56th CO also being credited with an 0.25 per cent share of another Messerschmitt and an Focke-Wulf probable. Zemke continued to fly P-47s marked with the individual code letter 'Z', which was a 'privilege of rank' that endured for most of 1944. Zemke had flown early P-47s with his initials, but vagaries of aircraft availability meant that he also used other machines too.

The number of crosses on Lt Bob Johnson's P-47 had reached 14 by 30 January 1944, leaving the groundcrew painter with some catching up to do on the individual German aircraft type designations for each kill. These were eventually added, however, as the photo opposite clearly shows

**Probably the best known Bob Johnson shot of the war, this publicity photo was taken with the ace's score at 25 (this figure being achieved on 13 April 1944) – just one short of Eddie Rickenbacker's World War 1 total, which had been a goal that all fighter pilots assigned to the ETO had aspired to beat**

On 8 March the 56th FG's 62nd FS lost Lt Joe Icard in circumstances that were never fully established. Having become an ace two days previously by shooting down an Fw 190 in P-47D-10 42-75040/LM-I over Dummer Lake, Icard was back in that locality in the same Thunderbolt on the day he was posted Missing In Action (MIA). The loss of one ace was partly offset by the creation of another on the same mission, Capt Joe Bennett downing two Bf 109s east of Steinhuder Lake and an Fw 190 over Munstorf airfield (in P-47D-11 42-75269/HV-O). These were Joe's last victories with the 56th, as he transferred to the 4th FG a week later – where he scored three more kills flying Mustangs with the 336th FS.

Amongst those 'Wolfpack' pilots who had tasted success in late February and early March was 63rd FS ace Maj Gerry Johnson, who had claimed six kills in little more than a fortnight. He added a further two victories on the 15th, both aircraft falling near Nienburg – these kills took Johnson's tally to 16.5-1-4.5. Since returning from a short spell of combat tuition with the 356th FG, Johnson had been assigned a P-47D-11, which he apparently did not name. It was only briefly flown by him, however, as he was at the controls of P-47D-15 42-76249 (which also carried no name) when he was downed by flak on the 27th.

The various actions of the 15th had been fiercely fought, with fellow 56th FG ace Lt Fred Christensen of the 62nd FS duelling with at least six Fw 190s near Dummer Lake. In the familiar confusion of combat, the P-47 pilots opened fire on a number of enemy aircraft as they came into their gunsights, but there was little doubt about one of kills credited to Christensen (in P-47D-10 42-75207/LM-C), for the Fw 190 exploded violently under the weight of his close range fire. When the combat

'Cripes A Mighty' (partially visible in front of the cockpit) was an Australian slang expression picked up by George Preddy whilst serving with the 49th FG in northern Australia prior to his posting to the 487th FS/352nd FG in the ETO on 28 December 1942. Later one of the USAAF's top aces with 26.833 kills, Preddy flew P-47D-2s and D-5s before finding his greatest fame in the P-51B/D. Three kills are marked on this Thunderbolt, signifying his total score whilst flying the Republic fighter – each kill was achieved with a different aircraft. eventually promoted major and given command of the 328th FS in October 1944, George Preddy lost his life on Christmas Day 1944 when shot down in error by a US Army mobile flak battery near the Belgian city of Liége (*J Crow*)

This 'Wolfpack' ace quartet are made up of (from left to right) 'Hub' Zemke, Dave Schilling, 'Gabby' Gabreski and Fred Christensen, all of whom are setting an example to their fellow officers by wearing standard issue 'uniforms'! (*via Bowman*)

Although a seasoned ace with a proven track record prior to joining the 56th FG, Capt 'Mike' Gladych was not issued with his own P-47 until many months after he joined the group. One of the aircraft he used with some success was natural metal P-47D-22 42-26044 *Silver Lady*, the Pole downing a Bf 109 over Evreux on 5 July, followed by a Ju 88 near Cambrai on 12 August. Something of a favourite amongst 61st FS pilots, *Silver Lady* was also used by no less an ace than 'Gabby' Gabreski, who scored five victories with it during May-June 1944. The aircraft was actually assigned to 61st FS ace, and Operations Officer, Maj Les Smith, who shot down three aircraft with it. He became tour expired at the end of May 1944, and following his return to the USA (with six kills to his credit) the aircraft was used by numerous pilots, Gladych and Gabreski included (*via R L Ward*)

reports and gun camera film were analysed, Fred was credited with two Fw 190s destroyed and two damaged. Just 24 hours later he claimed a further pair of Fw 190s near St Dizier, raising his score to 11 and 1 shared destroyed and two damaged.

Promoted to captain at the end of March, Fred Christensen also took delivery of new D-21 42-25512/ LM-Q, which was one of the final 'razorback' D-models produced.

While all P-47Ds – either 'razorbacks' or 'bubbletops' – were externally similar, individual aircraft exhibited considerable differences under the skin, and experienced pilots would refute that any two handled exactly the same. Despite this, the leading aces generally flew a number of different P-47s in the course of a combat tour. Fred Christensen was one of just a handful of pilots fortunate enough to have his own aircraft on the line for the majority of his sorties, as many aces were obliged to fly whatever was available, and they never seemed to score kills in aircraft assigned to them. Thus, it was consequently rare for a successful pilot to score all his victories in one aircraft.

Another 56th FG ace tasting success on 16 March was Lt Stan Morrill

of the 62nd FS. Flying P-47D-11 42-75388/LM-H at low altitude, he chased an Fw 190 (again near St Dizier) until it exploded under the weight of fire from his guns. This was to be Morrill's ninth, and last, kill, for he was to die trying to save crewmen from two B-24s that had collided and crashed near Boxted on the 29th of the month – while AAF personnel and civilians were still attempting a rescue, part of the bomb load from one of the stricken Liberators exploded, causing much loss of life.

Flak claimed another ace on 17 March when Lt Peter Pompetti (in P-47D-6 42-74641/WZ-Z) fell victim to flak batteries located near Paris. He survived to become a PoW. Thunderbolt pilots were fond of calling the heavily defended areas of occupied Europe, and Germany in particular, the 'flak highway to Berlin'. They were not far off the mark, for German anti-aircraft fire was deadly at all stages of the war, and it only got worse for Allied fliers as the fight focused on the 'Fatherland' itself. But on 22 March another adversary came into the equation – weather. Diving through cloud, three Thunderbolts succumbed to turbulence and plunged into the North Sea, among them Dale Stream who was flying Bob Johnson's P-47D-5 42-8461/HV-P *"Lucky"*.

On 23 March 84th FS/78th FG pilot Quince Brown 'bagged' his tenth victory – an Fw 190 – in the vicinity of Goch. Again there was a spectacular series of explosions along the fighter's fuselage, as fire from the heavy battery of .50-in guns tore it apart. This kill was Brown's fifth in eight days.

With an outstanding record, and considerable combat experience that stretched back to the spring of 1943, Maj Gerry Johnson probably gave the mission of 27 March no more thought than any other he had flown up to that point in his tour. For him, it was uneventful in terms of enemy aircraft encountered – but Johnson would have taken on half the Luftwaffe had he known how it was to end. The truck convoy his squadron had spotted didn't look too risky – a ripe target really – and down went 'White Flight' and up came the flak. Almost simultaneously, the P-47s flown by Johnson (P-47D-15 42-76249/UN-Z) and Archie Robey were hit, the former belly landing his aircraft. Lt Robey had lowered his gear in an attempt to land and pick up Johnson, but he had to abandon his rescue when he

A firm handshake greets Francis Gabreski, back from a mission in the spring of 1944. 'Gabby's' ground-crew always kept the ace's score up to date, the elaborate flags and the identity of the German aircraft destroyed on each occasion being faithfully recorded – and carried over from aircraft to aircraft (*IWM EA 28124*)

Capt Walker 'Bud' Mahurin was invariably filmed with a smile on his face, the 63rd FS pilot enjoying great success over Europe up until he was shot down attacking a Do 217 on 27 March 1944. His philosophy was that pilots had to have luck on their side to survive, and this belief served Mahurin well. One example of this was his ability to evade capture by the Germans for nearly six weeks, living to fly and fight again in the Pacific

Taxyng accidents made a mess of aircraft and no group was exempt. The 56th's repair shops had a job on their hands when the propeller of this P-47D-15 (42-76303), with ten victories marked under the cockpit, chewed up the Mustang barely visible in the background. It was well known that the 'Wolfpack's' ground personnel didn't like the P-51 but this was taking strong feelings too far! Despite its impressive victory tally, no records exist of this machine having ever been flown by any of the 17 officially recognised aerial aces of the 56th FG's 62nd FS

found that he had no hydraulics to 'drop' the flaps due to earlier damage.

Lt Everett then tried to land, but his wingtip brushed trees as he approached and the rescue was called off. Both pilots then vacated the area together, but only Robey made England. Everett was posted MIA after he was forced to ditch in the Channel. Gerry Johnson thus became a PoW, his score having by then reached 16.5-1-4.5.

Maj Johnson was not the only 63rd FS ace to be downed on 27 March, for ranking squadron ace Capt 'Bud' Mahurin also ended the day in German-held territory after bailing out near the French town of Tours – a further two pilots were also lost to flak on the same mission, all of which combined to make this one of the blackest days of the 56th FG's war. Mahurin, having 'squirted' a Do 217 for which he received a quarter-share, was flying 'his' P-47D-5, 42-8487/UN-M (it had served him well, for most of his 19.75 kills up to late March had been scored in it).

To his credit, the rear gunner of the Dornier bomber was not cowed by the sight of a P-47 coming at him, guns blazing. He pumped rounds in Mahurin's direction and hit him, but in turn the American ace only broke off when the German bomber exploded. He then bailed out of his crippled aircraft and came down literally running as he hit the ground.

Unlike some of his colleagues, Mahurin managed to evade capture, working his way back to England by 7 May 1944. Under the prevailing regulations governing evaders, he was unable to return to combat in the ETO lest he be captured and forced to reveal the names of people who had helped him. Pilots *could* fly combat missions again, but only in other theatres, so Mahurin, who had recently been promoted to major, went out to the Pacific as CO of the P-51D-equipped 3rd Air Commando Squadron/3rd Air Commando Group.

## APRIL 1944

The new month commenced with a mission to Strasbourg on 1 April, which provoked little positive reaction from the *Jagdwaffe*. Therefore, upon their return flight home the 56th FG indulged in a little aerodrome strafing at Lille – or rather they didn't. The flight led by 61st FS CO (and 11.5-kill ace) Jim Stewart realised too late that it was a trap, having initiated the attack. The flak batteries were waiting, and the P-47 flown by Thomas Owens took hits in the fuel tanks. Stewart, screaming over the radio for Owens to bail out, flew straight into a telegraph pole which, to the amazement of watching pilots, came out of the collision in far worse shape than the Thunderbolt.

Owens failed to bail out and was killed when his P-47 rolled over and went into the ground. Stewart nursed his aircraft back to base, however, where his groundcrew discovered rather more wood in its airframe than the designers had ever intended – a piece of the pole was embedded in the wing, but Stewart had nevertheless made it back to Halesworth.

After a hectic two months of action, the 'Wolfpack' found aerial opposition hard to come by in early April. However, a bomber escort to the Husam area on 9 April gave Bob Johnson the first chance to add to his score since his trio of kills on 15 March. Left with fellow 61st FS pilot Lt Sam Hamilton to guard multiple combat boxes of Liberators against a substantial number of Fw 190s, the two P-47 pilots proceeded to charge in and disrupt the enemy formations. Watching the German pilots execute their inevitable break and dive away, Hamilton chased after them while Johnson stayed high to turn into the German top cover.

Evading multiple bounces by pairs of Fw 190s, Johnson had his work cut out when Hamilton called for help low down over the Baltic. Adding to Johnson's troubles was a frozen belly tank that refused to release. Watching a dogfight in which Hamilton gradually gained the upper hand on a determined German pilot equally bent on shooting down the P-47, Johnson lost no time in joining the party. But it was all but over before he arrived as Hamilton had succeeded in getting on the Fw 190's tail and severing a wing with a burst from his eight 'fifties'.

Just as the American opened fire a second Fw 190 had latched onto his tail, but its pilot was dissuaded from any further action as Johnson cut in. Diving and twisting, the *Jagdflieger* tried to disengage, but the P-47 ace followed each manoeuvre. Taking note of the crispness of his flying, Johnson quickly realised that his German quarry was no novice. The American finally prevailed, however, and a burst of fire finished the enemy pilot off as he tried to extricate himself from a riddled cockpit. This was Johnson's 23rd victory.

In the first successful day for what seemed a very long time, the 'Wolfpack' had other claims to total up too. One of its more successful pilots Deputy Group CO Dave Schilling (in P-47D-11 42-75388) had two Fw 190s confirmed, plus two damaged – an Fw 190 and, unusually, a Junkers

Although not a technically brilliant photo, this snap shot nevertheless shows the cockpit area of Lt Quince Brown's *OKIE* (42-74573/WZ-J) with twelve victories marked under the cockpit panel. The rows of brooms indicate the huge effort VIII FC put in to support the bomber force and decimate the Luftwaffe during the first year of P-47 operations – April 1943 to April 1944 (*Bivens*)

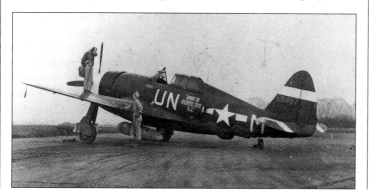

'Bud' Mahurin's P-47D-5 is about to be flown again by its regular pilot, judging by the ace's well-garbed figure on the left wing, chatting to his crewchief. Few Thunderbolt groundcrew men worked as hard as those attached to the 56th, for not only did they help sort out the technical troubles with the early P-47C and Ds, they had to do it all over again when the P-47M came along in 1945. Unlike the pilots, groundcrews did not serve tours – they remained in-theatre for the duration (*B Robertson*)

The scene hasn't changed much from the photos featuring Bob Johnson earlier in this chapter, but the aircraft flown by him has. Natural aluminium finished P-47D-21 42-5512/LM-Q *Penrod & Sam* was the ace's final mount in the ETO, and he used on his history making sortie on 8 May 1944 when he downed two German fighters to take his tally to 27 (*IWM*)

Another view of 42-5512, this time showing off the aircraft's unusual name. This combination was chosen by Johnson so as to publicise the efforts of the men on the ground (in this case crewchief Sgt J C Penrod), without whom the man in the air (Sam Johnson) would have struggled to score all of his kills. Brig Gen Jesse Auton, 65th FW CO, and Brig Gen Francis Griswold, Chief of Staff, VIII FC are seen hear being given an explanation behind the names by Johnson himself

W 34. Schilling identified this last kill as a 'Ju 234', which did not exist, so his gun camera film must have provided the confirmation that he had shot up one of the Luftwaffe's elderly single-engined courier aircraft.

Capt Paul Conger of the 61st FS/56th FG scored his fourth kill on 15 April when he shot down an Fw 190 in the Elmhorn area, although this success was more than overshadowed by the loss of yet another 'Wolfpack' ace to the ever growing flak menace. Maj Leroy Schreiber, CO of the 62nd FS, was shot down over Flensburg airfield in P-47D-21 43-25577/LM-T. A 12-kill ace, he had led the squadron since 9 February.

## MAY 1944

Re-equipment of the VIII FC groups with the P-51 gathered momentum in the spring of 1944, and the 359th FG was ready to log its first Mustang mission by the 6th. This signalled the end for pilots attempting to reach ace status on the P-47, Lt Robert Booth coming closest with four kills – he went on to 'make ace' by doubling his score with the P-51B.

Although four groups had now transitioned to the Mustang, the 56th FG remained very much a P-47 group, with pilots of the calibre of Bob Johnson continuing to take a heavy toll of the Luftwaffe in the Republic fighter. On 8 May he scored his final two kills on yet another mission to Berlin and Brunswick. His report on the engagements read as follows;

'About 30 Huns were over the bombers, their contrails snaking out in the sky. Smoke was coming from the bomber box and one was going down. I started after the Jerries and then saw an Me 109 diving at me. I rolled and fired at him, but missed. Then he squirted at me and missed. I made another turn, and he tried to outrun me, the damned fool. He went down, rolling and tuning to evade, and I hit every him half roll. When his wing came off I figured he'd had it.

'We started back up for those contrails above the bombers. I was down to about 3000 ft now, in the spotty clouds. Lt Harold Hartney, my number three man, yelled that a couple of Fw 190s were diving. He took off after them under a cloud, and I told him I'd jump him when they came out. Then he began yelling for help.

'I saw the Focke-Wulfs come out, then Hartney's Thunderbolt, and

Sgt Penfold (left), Johnson and his armourer (unknown), suitably decked out with a 'scarf' of .50-in shells, pose for an official USAAF photo

then four more Jerries chasing the Thunderbolt. I came head-on at these four. One of them was blinking at me with those .30s, and I let him have it. It got his engine and he went down smoking and blew up. The other three broke away'.

Bob Johnson's last victories (in P-47D-21 42-25512/LM-Q) first equalled, and then bettered, the score of America's ranking World War 1

ace Eddie Rickenbacker, who had downed 26 German aircraft. The breaking of the long standing record by an ETO pilot (leading American ace of all time, Richard Bong, was the first to better 26 in April 1944) all but ended Johnson's career as a fighter pilot, for the USAAF 'brass' ordered him home, effective immediately. War bond fund raising tours, talks to factory workers and interviews loomed, and Bob Johnson, who was promoted to major upon his return to America, actually took to the publicity circuit like a duck to water, and stayed with it.

With the panels removed, the right hand Browning machine guns on Johnson's P-47 are given a routine check by Sgt Penfold

# BUILD UP TO D-DAY AND BEYOND

To get five victories to mark an individual as an ace was a feat that eluded many Eighth Air Force pilots – even those who flew combat over a considerable period of time. Therefore, to make ace in a day was rightly regarded as something special, and among those who joined this select band was Lt Bob 'Shorty' Rankin of the 61st FS/56th FG. On 12 May he was one of the pilots who gave the 'Zemke Fan' the acid test, this manoeuvre being designed to cover a 180° arc of sky whilst simultaneously offering mutual protection for three formations of P-47s.

Leading 'Whippet White Flight', Rankin was keeping his eyes peeled when a formation of about 25 bandits was called in. The enemy fighters were below the Americans, some 20 miles away. Firewalling his throttle, Rankin headed in their direction, only to encounter another 25 Bf 109s at 19,000 ft, climbing to initiate an attack on the bombers.

He turned his flight into the enemy fighters, which dropped their external tanks as soon as they saw the danger boring in towards them. Manoeuvring behind one Messerschmitt, Rankin first a short burst and the Bf 109 split-essed and dived. The American followed, holding his fire as the German fighter gathered momentum and steepened its dive angle. Rankin watched its wings vibrating and began to pull his own aircraft up. The pilot had underestimated the velocity of his descent and failed to pull out, the Bf 109 crashing in a small German town north-west of Marburg.

Climbing back to altitude, Rankin spotted another Bf 109 in a shallow dive to the east. He closed rapidly on it and watched his fire pepper the fuselage and engine cowling. Throwing his canopy open, the German pilot 'hit the silk' – or tried to, as his parachute was not seen to open. Rankin then heard Zemke, as 'Fairbank Leader', call for help. Rankin headed for Zemke's position, which was over Coblenz, in southern Germany. The boss was alone and circling 30 Bf 109s, and as Rankin joined up, he went into the attack.

Covering his leader, Rankin watched Zemke shoot down a Bf 109. Pulling up, he saw more enemy fighters, so he promptly dived to latch onto the tail of a pair of Bf 109s. Spraying the left hand

P-47D-25 *Little Princess* gained some fame in 1982 when its one time pilot, Marvin Bledsoe, published *Thunderbolt*, which was a detailed account of his single tour in the ETO with the 350th FS/353rd FG. Bledsoe flew this Thunderbolt for most of his missions, which comprised primarily ground attack sorties. He duly became a ground ace in the process with 5.5 kills

machine with a short burst of fire, the American saw smoke belch out and the landing gear flop down – a sure sign of ruptured hydraulics. He switched his aim to the other Bf 109, fired and observed much the same result. Heavily smoking, the also fighter fell away with its gear extended.

Although Rankin had now downed four aircraft, he was not yet ready to quit. Making a left turn at 15,000 ft, he saw Bf 109s circling below him so he quickly latched onto a trio of fighters flying in loose formation, However, before he could open fire Rankin watched in amazement as all three pilots bailed out! He had not fired, nor had any other P-47 as far as he could see – these Bf 109s were not claimed as victories.

Two more Bf 109s ran across Rankin's sights as he climbed back to height, but the short bursts he was able to get off resulted only in damaged claims. His speed carried him past the enemy aircraft and Rankin did not pursue them for he had seen another potential target – a Bf 109 had broken out of a main gaggle and was arrowing in on Zemke's Thunderbolt. Rankin called the break as he closed on the German fighter, his fire persuading the German that chasing Zemke was futile, and as the Bf 109

D-Day was as hectic a day for the Eighth's P-47 groups, as it was for any of the tactical groups flying ground attack sorties. Fully marked and bombed up for the historic invasion is P-47D-15 *Arkansas Traveller* (the mount of Capt Dewey Newhart), which carried the name *Mud N' Mules* on the port side, with a truncated mule on the nose checkers. Newhart was serving as CO of the 350th FS when he was one of eight 353rd FG pilots shot down on 12 June during an early morning fighter-bomber attack on Dreux/Evreux which was bounced by Bf 109s. Six pilots, including Newhart, were killed during the fierce dogfight (*USAF*)

The mount of nine-victory ace Alwin Juchheim, this P-47D-6 was almost certainly 42-74690, coded HL-J (bar), which indentified it as being part of the 83rd FS/78th FG at Duxford. Juchheim obtained his first five victories in this Thunderbolt, and went on to score four more in another aircraft before being made a PoW on 28 May 1944 after a collision over enemy territory. He appears not to have decorated this particular fighter in any way – not even to the extent of applying victory symbols (*USAF*)

broke away, Rankin turned into two more Bf 109s showing hostile interest in his wingman, Lt Cleon Thomton. In his peripheral vision, Rankin saw that the Bf 109 pilot who had tried to attack Zemke had bailed out. He had downed five.

Not to be outdone, Thomton, who was on his first combat mission, shot down one of a *Rotte* of Bf 109s they had caught up with, Rankin taking the other one on. He might have had six had his ammunition not ran out just as he was positioned for a good shot.

Combat with Fw 190s not too many miles away during this mission resulted in two more confirmed kills for Capt Paul Conger, who thus joined the ace 'fraternity' within the 56th FG. In addition to the two Fw 190s definitely brought down, Conger was credited with a third Focke-Wulf damaged in the action that took place north of Marburg.

That same day also saw the 361st FG – the last P-47 unit to join the Eighth – fly its first mission equipped with Mustangs.

Twenty-four hours later the 56th FG was charged with protecting 2nd Division B-24s sent to bomb Tutow and Politz, the 'Wolfpack' dividing into 'A Group', which covered the bombers' penetration, and 'B Group', overseeing the withdrawal. Rendezvous with the Liberators took place over Heide, where the 62nd FS made contact with 40 Fw 190s which were chased. One fighter was shot down, as was a P-47 by ground fire.

Flying within 'B Group' was Lt Robert Keen of the 61st FS who, along with the rest of his unit, countered an attack on the rear of the B-24s by Fw 190s. West of Hagenow, Keen latched onto a group of fighters and downed three (plus claimed a fourth as a probable). The pilots of the first two fighters bailed out, while the third died when his Fw 190 exploded. These were Keen's first victories, and to prove that the exception can sometimes become the rule, he repeated his triple haul on 5 July. On the latter occasion the victims were Bf 109s, and the combination of the two sorties made Keen an ace while still a first lieutenant. Promoted to captain the following month, he did not enjoy any further successes.

On 22 May a double fighter escort missions resulted in victories and losses for the 'Wolfpack', the group operating alongside elements of the 356th FG. Despite the 56th becoming embroiled in a series of running battles, the latter group had little to report when it returned home, providing yet another example of the ever-changing 'fortunes of war'. The 56th adopted the 'Zemke Fan' formation over Dummer Lake, with the 61st FS heading for Bremen, the 62nd to Paderborn-Einbeck and Brunswick and the 63rd to Hanover.

The red nose band introduced in February 1944 by the 56th FG significantly brightened up the natural-metal finished 'razorback' and 'bubbletop' Thunderbolts then on strength with the group. One of those aircraft so decorated was this P-47D-28 flown by Paul Chinn of the 63rd FS. Other aircraft in the group had individualistic camouflage schemes applied from around March onwards

'Razorback' Thunderbolts survived well into the 'bubbletop era', including P-47D-21 *"HUCKLE DE BUCK"* of the 63rd FS/56th FG. The pilot(s) of this aircraft have yet to be identified. The full invasion stripes shown in this photo were worn for on a short period of time, thus dating this photo as having been taken in late June/early July 1944

Congratulations all round for Lt Col 'Gabby' Gabreski after scoring his latest kill on 5 July 1944 (a Bf 109 over Evreux) to confirm him as the leading ace in the ETO. In the background is his last Thunderbolt, P-47D-25 42-26418/HV-A, which was eventually adorned with 31 victory flags (three ground kills, which then shared equally billing with aerial claims in VIII FC) before it was lost in combat on 20 July 1944 (*IWM EA 28891*)

This day was particularly memorable for Gabreski, as he achieved his only triple haul of the war when his 12-strong 'White Flight' tangled with 15 Fw 190s spotted taking off in line abreast formation from Hoperhofen airfield. The Thunderbolt pilots – who were flying at 15,000 ft – soon sighted more fighters taking off in pairs in a mass scramble, which led Gabreski to call in the four remaining P-47s of his squadron that had been flying top cover, before diving to 3000 ft to commence the aerial battle.

'White Flight' charged in after the first eight Fw 190s, Gabreski selecting one on his first pass and setting it on fire, before turning into a second whose pilot withstood the hail of gun fire for only a short time before bailing out. As 'Red' and 'Blue' Flights attacked the remaining Focke-Wulfs, 'Gabby' observed a P-47 falling in flames, with a second smoking.

Breaking off and reforming at around 10,000 ft, the 'White Flight' pilots saw a further 25 Fw 190s a further 5000 ft below. As the P-47s dived to engage, the airfield flak opened up on them. This was obviously hazardous to German as well as American aircraft, and one of the Focke-Wulf pilots duly fired a green flare to make the gunners cease firing. The 61st FS, meanwhile, continued to attack, Gabreski shooting down his third Fw 190, while 61st FS pilots Capt James Carter and Polish volunteer Plt Off Witold Lanowski each recorded a kill apiece.

Flg Off Evan 'Mac' McMinn (also of the 61st FS) went one better by downing two Fw 190s to make him an ace. One of just a handful of flying officers to 'make ace', McMinn was yet another pilot who scored his kills in a variety of P-47Ds, his original assigned aircraft (P-47D-5 42-8458) having been written off on 1 January when it hit a 20 mm gun mounting. It had previously been damaged by flak and hit by pieces of a disintegrat-

Thunderbolts 'bought' by War Bond subscribers continued to arrive in the UK, although fewer 'bubbletop' models appear to have had names applied in this fashion. This example, P-47D-25 42-26413/UN-Z *"Oregons Britannia"*, was flown by 56th FG aces Harold Comstock and 'Hub' Zemke

Wearing the 78th FG's distinctive black and white checkerboard nose marking, this P-27D-25 (42-26551/WZ-P) was the personal mount of 84th FS CO Maj Ben Mayo, who used it to down two Fw 190s on 9 September near Giessen. Often credited with five aerial kills, Mayo's tally was downgraded to four according to both the USAF Historical Study 85 and the VIII FC's Final Assessment. Despite losing 'acedom' postwar, Mayo did at least enjoy such status during the last weeks of his combat tour (which ended with his return to the USA on 25 September), for he had also destroyed 2.5 aircraft on the ground

ing Bf 110 whilst being flown by 'Gabby' Gabreski, who scored three kills in it. McMinn was obliged to fly other P-47s to get his kills.

On 28 May Capt Max Juchheim flew his 76th mission with the 83rd FS/78th FG. Assistant Operations Officer for his unit, as well as ranking ace with nine kills, two probables and two damaged to his credit, Juchheim had been in the ETO since 30 November 1943.

The mission on this date saw bombers ranging across Germany briefed to attack a long list of oil targets and marshalling yards. Their fighter support included 208 P-47s drawn from four groups and 307 P-51s from seven. An air battle soon developed, and Juchheim began manoeuvring with his unit at 28,000 ft in preparation for an attack on an enemy formation, when his P-47D-22 (42-26016/HL-A) collided with a 353rd FG P-51. The Mustang exploded and Juchheim's Thunderbolt spun down with one wing severed, its pilot swiftly bailing out. Squadronmates dived down and circled the single parachute, trying to identify their comrade, but they had to break off at 12,000 ft when a Bf 109 appeared. The parachute was indeed carrying Juchheim, who became a PoW upon landing.

The 353rd FG's Maj Kenneth Gallup opened his score during the mission of the 28th, despatching a Bf 109 that he had caught over an airfield near Gutersloh. Formerly CO the P-47-equipped 53rd FS/36th FG, which had served in the Panama Canal Zone before eventually moving to the ETO to serve with the Ninth Air Force in March/April 1944, Ken had only been with the 353rd four days when he claimed his first kill. Promoted to CO of the 350th FS on 12 June after Capt Dewey Newhart was posted Missing in Action, Gallup had 'made ace' by 6 July and completed his scoring on 28 August (as a lieutenant-colonel) when he shot down a Fieseler Storch, shared in the destruction of a second German observation aircraft encountered in the area between the towns of Verdun and Conflan, and finished the sortie off with a half kill in a He 111. This took his final tally to nine aerial victories and one damaged.

By late May the 'Wolfpack' had received its first 'bubbletop' P-47D-25s, although these did not replace the 'razorbacks' overnight, instead being issued on a gradual, as

Many of the natural finish P-47s delivered to Duxford had a coat of green top surface paint hastily applied to make them less visible from above when the Eighth's fighter groups went over to large scale tactical operations as well as bomber escorts. In either case, camouflage was deemed to be prudent, although the group's black and white checkerboard marking was probably even more visible than 'silver' paint. This example of 'compromised camouflage' is the well photographed P-47D-25 of the 82nd FS/78th FG (via R L Ward)

required, basis. 'Hub' Zemke took his assigned 'bubbletop' Thunderbolt (42-26413/UN-Z – the first example delivered to the 61st FS) into action on 31 May, and came home with two Fw 190s destroyed, a third as a probable and a fourth damaged. He had despatched his two victims over the Gutersloh-Detmold area, and both of these and his other claims were all confirmed by his gun camera film. These successes took his tally to 12.

## JUNE 1944

One of the most pivotal months of the war got off to a bad start for the Thunderbolt community when on 4 June – two days before Operation *Overlord* – 78th FG ace Capt James Wilkinson of the 82nd FS was killed in a flying accident over South Wales. Casualties from such incidents ran into many hundreds during the war, this wasteful carnage being an unfortunate, and somewhat unavoidable, by-product of so much flying. On any given day countless numbers of aircraft were aloft performing training, courier, liaison and transport flights, not to mention routine air tests and operations. Weather often played its part in such sad losses of personnel too, and such accidents would not stop, even in peace time.

The momentous events of the 6th saw Allied fighters ranging at will over the Normandy beachheads. Ninth Air Force P-47 units were heavily committed, striking ground targets along the coast and in the immediate vicinity of the landings. Enemy fighters were not much in evidence in the face of the Allied juggernaut over the invasion beaches, although neither tactical or escort sorties by the Eighth were performed without cost. Five-victory ace Lt Evan McMinn of the 61st FS fell victim to fighters or flak (the details are uncertain) and was killed near Bernay, his aircraft (P-47D-22 42-25963) being one of five P-47s lost by VIII FC on D-Day.

Air superiority over the beaches for the vital first days of *Overlord* was maintained by hundreds of Allied fighter units, the Luftwaffe being in no position to mount anything more than a handful of token sorties, which had little effect.

Pilots of the 361st FG at Bottisham never had much chance to run up a string of victories in the P-47, although they made up for that when Mustangs arrived in May 1944. Representing the group's early period is Col Roy A Webb, CO of the 374th FS, pictured at Little Walden. He went on to score a total of eight ground victories

Twenty-four hours after D-Day, relative latecomer to the 56th FG Lt George Bostwick destroyed his first aircraft (a Bf 109) over Grandvilliers airfield in P-47D-22 42-26042/LM-G. Assigned to the 62nd FS, Bostwick had changed to P-47D-25 42-26636/LM-X by the time he scored a trio of Bf 109 kills (and a solitary damaged claim) on 4 July near Conches.

On 12 June ex-RCAF pilot Flg Off Steve Gerick of the 61st FS 'made ace', having previously achieved three confirmed kills and four damaged since the New Year. Patrolling near Evreux, his flight ran into a large group of Bf 109s and he proceeded to shoot down two Bf 109s to join the 'Wolfpack's' growing band of pilots with five or more kills – for good measure, he was also credited with having damaged a further four Messerschmitt fighters on this mission. Gerick rounded out his tour on 27 June with yet another damaged claim on a Bf 109, and a month later he transferred out of the 56th with his tally standing at 5-0-9.

Such a high number of damaged claims accruing to one pilot on a single mission is entirely understandable, for in the confusion of a sizeable air battle, both sides would tend to open fire on enemy aircraft as soon as they came across their sights. Even if hits registered, there was not always time to pursue an individual aircraft and destroy it, or to see it crash. It took a good few seconds to become fully orientated to the developing battle and to select a specific target, as other factors (particularly the amount of remaining fuel) could dictate whether or not this was possible. The sum result was that many American fighter pilots had to break off and be satisfied with only damaged claims when of course the enemy aircraft that fell out of sight sometimes failed to recover from a dive.

## JULY 1944

George Bostwick made ace on 6 July when he accounted for a Bf 109 over the Beaumont region of France in P-47D-22 42-25713/LM-M, this being his last kill for seven months. July was to be a month of intense activity for the 353rd FG, which lost just four P-47s in 29 missions. Unfortunately, amongst this small number was group CO, respected pilot and ranking ace, Col Glenn Duncan. He had scored 5.5 kills since D-Day to raise his tally to 19.5 victories, thus passing Walt Beckham's long-standing group record of 18. On 7 July Col Duncan was flying his P-47D-22 42-25971, named *Dove of Peace VII*, as part of a 45-ship penetration support mission for B-17s. Breakaway point for the fighters was Dummer Lake, and it was there that the action began.

To divert the Germans' attention away from the 'heavies', Duncan elected to strafe nearby Wesendorf airfield. He went in and peppered a He 111, but light flak quickly had his range, and as Duncan pulled up hits severed an oil line. With his engine rapidly overheating, Duncan flew west, aiming to get as far away from Germany as possible before his

Capt Fred Christensen's second assigned Thunderbolt was P-47D-25 42-26628/LM-C, which he named *Rozzie Geth II* after his girlfriend. With an accumulated scoreboard showing 21 kills, this aircraft also wore the dual name *Miss Fire* and an arresting portrait of a lady on the nose. Ranking ace of the 62nd FS by some margin, Christensen scored just two of his victories 21.5 kills in this aircraft. The individual in the cockpit is probably Christensen's crewchief, SSgt Connor

aircraft had to be put down. He didn't make it, for *Dove VII* only managed to stay airborne for another 14 minutes, by which time it had carried Duncan as far as Nienburg. He bellied in north-west of the town, and other 353rd FG pilots who were eyewitnesses to the crash landing saw Duncan throw an incendiary grenade into the cockpit and walk away from the blazing Thunderbolt. Glad though they were to see their leader alive and apparently unharmed, the pilots were nevertheless appalled at his loss to the group.

The gap left by Glenn Duncan was felt as high up as General William Kepner, commanding the Eighth's fighters. He sent the 353rd

Bob Johnson (centre) played the publicity angle for many photo sessions, although this one was hardly posed as the group was probably snapped after returning from a 'Wolfpack' combat mission. Fellow 56th FG ace Lt Joe Powers is seen on the extreme left of the line-up

a wire in which he expressed a deep regret over the day's events and despite Duncan's last call to his fellow pilots that he would be seeing them in three weeks, he would not return until April 1945. He evaded capture, walked out of Germany and spent the rest of the war with the Dutch underground organisation.

Although the 7 July had been a bad day for Glenn Duncan, for 62nd FS/56th FG ace Capt Fred Christensen it could hardly have been better, for he became the third Eighth Air Force fighter pilot to reach ace-in-a-day status. Leading his squadron on an escort mission (in P-47D-21 42-25522/LM-H), Christensen noted activity as his formation passed over an airfield at Gardelegen. Dropping down for a closer look, he saw about 35 aircraft dispersed, so he led his flight off to the east, intending to reverse and attack these ground targets. As the P-47s made their turn, the pilots saw that a dozen Ju 52s had just entered the landing pattern.

The lumbering German transports, flying in pairs, represented targets too good to pass up, and Christensen led his flight in for the kill. In his excitement he forget to drop his external tanks, but this oversight proved useful as the Thunderbolt lost more airspeed than it would otherwise have done. The slowness of the Ju 52 sometimes made it a harder target than many fighter pilots could have imagined due to the misjudgment of the relative closure speeds. Fred Christensen made no such mistake;

'I saw them peeling off to the left and making a huge orbit down the field. I entered the traffic pattern from above, went by the last Ju 52 and shot at the next one in front of me. I saw strikes on the wing and left engine but passed over him before I could see any further results. My wingman said it burned and exploded in mid-air after I passed over him.

'I lined up on the second and shot from quite close range, registering hits on both wings and fuselage. Huge flames were billowing back from the aircraft. The third Ju 52 was in a turn to the left. I fired a 15° deflection shot, noticing many strikes. Its right gas tanks were on fire when I ceased shooting. The Ju 52's pilot tried to land the aircraft on a field short of the airdrome, but the flames increased and it burned in the pasture.

'During my next attack on another Ju 52, my engine quit and I spent precious moments switching gas tanks. I went by him and dropped my tanks at the same time. I then found myself another Ju 52, took a short squirt at this aircraft and noticed a few hits. He then tried some evasive action by putting his tail in the air at a 60° angle. Given that he was only 100 ft off the ground, he couldn't pull out and crashed into the ground.

'I then lined up dead astern on the fifth (Ju 52) and waited until I was very close before firing. The hits were concentrated around the fuselage and inboard of (each) engine, where the non-seal proof tanks are located. Both wings were burning as I went by, and the aircraft peeled off to the right and dove into the ground.

'That left one aircraft right in front of the fifth machine I had just shot down, which had crashed just off the edge of the field. I pressed my attack through the flak and gave him a good burst in both wings. Flames were coming back from the outer tanks but he tried to land anyway. He did and burned in the middle of the field. In the meantime, I had to do a 180° turn to evade the fierce flak. I counted nine fires, including the one on the field. The tenth Ju 52 crashed in the town where I couldn't see him'.

In addition to Christensen's six confirmed Ju 52s (his final kills of the war, taking his tally to 21.5-0-2), Lt Billy Edens shot down three in P-47D-15 42-76363/LM-F to make him an ace and Capt Michael Jackson got one in P-47D-11 42-75237/LM-S.

A new commanding officer took over the 63rd FS on 17 July, now Maj Joe Egan (with five victories to his credit) having been with the unit since February 1943. Sadly, the new CO's tenure in this post was to last barely 48 hours, for on the 19th he was shot down and killed by the ever-deadly flak, his aircraft (P-47D-25 42-26524) falling north-east of Nancy.

Flak was easily VIII FC's deadliest foe in the last 18 months of the war, both experienced veterans and novices falling victim to the 'One more pass' syndrome – a phrase fighter pilots often called in as they dived down to work over a target that had invariably been 'woken up' by earlier strafing and/or bombing runs. It was not always an advisable course of action.

In a surprising number of cases, considering the fatal attrition suffered by the *Jagdflieger* in equally well-built aircraft, American pilots lived to rue their actions when flak shot them down, or they crashed due to some other cause. It could happen to the best, and late on 20 July the boys at Boxted had finally to give up hoping that by some miracle 61st FS CO Lt Col 'Gabby' Gabreski would return to board the transport scheduled to take him home for 30 days' leave. It was not to be for his camouflaged P-47D-25 (42-26418/HV-A), complete with scoreboard, lay broken in a cornfield a half-mile from Bassinheim airfield.

Duxford Thunderbolts were known for numerous examples of well-rendered aircraft artwork, among them the flying horse and name *Geronimo* sported by P-47C-5 41-6367/WZ-B of the 84th FS/78th FG and flown by Maj John D Irwin (*Bivens*)

The base had been spotted by Gabreski after a non-eventful escort of 4th Bomber Force 'heavies' raiding central Germany. His squadron duly strafed the airfield and then 'Yellow' and 'Blue' flights pulled off. However, there were still tempting targets to be had – a number of Bf 110s and He 111s appeared to have survived unscathed. Gabreski took his 'White Flight' down once again, and as he dropped low, he selected an He 111 and opened fire. The Heinkel immediately went up in flames and 'Gabby' decided on that one last pass. Nothing hit him, but he hit the ground, bending his prop tips and leaving his Thunderbolt staggering along, losing speed. This seemingly basic pilot error was almost certainly caused by Gabreski being caught unawares by the aircraft's excessive sink rate due to the extra fuel carried by the 'bubbletop' P-47. It was later found that pilots could easily underestimate the difference the extra fuel made to the fighter's handling, and as Gabreski's aircraft had been the first of its type delivered to the 61st FS, there had probably not been sufficient time to test its flying characteristics, especially at very low altitude.

There was nothing for it but to find a place to land – and fast. 'Gabby' found a cornfield and brought HV-A down. It tipped up but settled back, and he forced the hood off and got out. He was now on his own. Although Gabreski evaded for five days, the 28-victory ace was eventually captured.

German flak would also claim two Thunderbolt pilots from the 356th FG that day, while the 56th FG also mourned the loss of Lt Earnest, who was killed when his aircraft crashed into the Channel.

## AUGUST 1944

On 12 August 'Hub' Zemke finally bade farewell to the 56th FG and handed over the 'hot seat' to Lt Col Dave Schilling. Being given command of the 'Wolfpack' was just reward for an outstanding pilot and Zemke, who was about to take up a new assignment as CO of the Mustang-equipped 479th FG, left knowing 'his' Thunderbolts were in safe hands. Schilling's first kill as group commander came on the 28th of the month, and took his score to 14 confirmed victories and six damaged, and by 0930 he had added a 14th – a He 111 downed over the 'Siegfied Line' south of Trier. He was flying 'bubbletop' P-47D-25 42-26417 at the time, this being the first of four kills he would score in the aircraft.

Relatively few VIII FC pilots were able to score victories – or indeed have any chance to fly – the later P-47Ds fitted with the clear view canopy. This was because most had reached the end of their tours and received transfers back to the USA before their respective units received the aircraft, or the group had traded in its Thunderbolts for Mustangs. 'Razorback' models also soldiered on to the end of 1944, and it was more usual for groups to go from early P-47 models to the P-51 without ever receiving 'bubbletops'. One exception to this rule was the 78th FG at Duxford, which did not make the change over until Decem-

Looking good at Duxford, this P-47D-25 was the mount of Lt Ross Orr on 1 July 1944 when he was bounced with his bombs still attached at 16,000 ft by 30+ plus Bf 109s. The aircraft was last seen heading down in flames, but Orr bailed out to become a PoW

Quince Brown of the 84th FS/78th FG scored his last kill in this P-47D-27 (42-26567) on 1 September 1944. Five days later he attacked Vogelsand airfield in P-47D-28 44-19569/WZ-Z. What happened next was related to the 78th FG's Intelligence officer by Lt Richard L Baron, one of Brown's flight members;

'Brown called and said he was going to go over it (Vogelsand airfield) and investigate. He made a steep turn and we ended up in string formation. He went over first and I saw tracers going at him, so I hit low for the deck. I looked up and saw several strikes on his plane. He pulled up sharply as we got across and I pulled up alongside. I saw his plane shake and his canopy come off. He then bailed out at about 1200 ft. His parachute opened and I saw him land in a field. He then ran and lay down in some tall grass.'

The fact that Brown was seen to be alive and well and seemingly evading on the ground gave his colleagues back at Duxford great hope for his survival. However, they eventually learned that the P-47 ace had been captured and subsequently executed by a Schutzstaffel SS officer, who was duly tracked down and prosecuted for murder after the war (Bivens)

ber 1944. This meant that aces like Deputy Group CO Lt Col Jack Oberhansly got to use the P-47D-28 (44-19566/MX-X in this instance) in combat. The veteran pilot, who had joined the 78th FG as long ago as May 1942 and led the 82nd FS from August 1943 to May 1944, claimed his sixth, and last, victory on 28 August, his victim being a Ju 88 which crashed in the Charleroi area.

Only three Eighth Air Force groups apart from the 56th ever flew the 'bubbletop' P-47 models (from the D-25 production block onwards) in action, these being the 78th, 353rd and 356th FGs. The remaining five groups had all received P-51s as new equipment by the time the 'bubbletop' Thunderbolt made an appearance in the ETO.

## SEPTEMBER 1944

Flak caused the removal of another VIII FC ace from the order of battle on 6 September when the 84th FS's Ops Officer, Maj Quince Brown, went down west of Schleiden after attacking Vogelsand airfield in P-47D-28 44-19569/WZ-Z. Originator of the P-47 strafing attack, and the 78th FG's ranking ace with 12.333 kills, Brown was fated never to reach a PoW camp, for he was murdered by an SS officer soon after being captured.

An efficient organisation for handling prisoners, backed by a well publicised order that downed Allied fliers were to be handed over to the Luftwaffe as soon as possible, made such incidents of summary execution and murder by civilians mercifully rare, but the risks remained. And they got worse towards the end of the war when the German infrastructure began to break down in the face of the Allied advance.

German PoW cages were, by the autumn of 1944, looking increasingly like fighter pilot reunion gatherings. Another man who joined the expanding 'club' at this time was Lt Billy Edens of the 56th FG who, having scored seven aerial victories and five on the ground with the 62nd FS, was nailed by flak near Trier (in P-47D-21 42-25522) on 10 September.

Arriving back for his second tour with the 56th FG on the very day Edens went down was Maj Les Smith who, having scored six victories during his first tour with the 'Wolfpack', took over as CO of the 62nd FS. He would hold this position until 26 January 1945 when he became Deputy Group CO.

Whilst Les Smith was acclimatising himself with frontline flying once again, one of his old squadronmates, the redoubtable Capt 'Mike' Gladych, was coming to the end of an eventful tour. To mark his departure, the Pole got himself into a running fight on 21 September that carried the protagonists from east of Arnhem to north of Gorinchen, in Holland, and eventually saw a single P-47 down two Fw 190s. This double victory brought Capt Gladych's final wartime tally to 18-2-0.5, ten of the kills having been scored with the 56th FG and eight with the RAF.

# ARNHEM AND INTO GERMANY

Field Order 578 flown on 18 September 1944 would be a day the 56th FG, and other Eighth fighter groups, would long remember. The memories would not be pleasant, for all groups were ordered to fly support missions for Operation *Market Garden* – the attempt by British and Canadian forces to capture bridges over the Rhine at Arnhem, in Holland. An operation that went wrong from the start due mainly to the scattering of parachute troops up against alerted

**'Wolfpack' P-47D-28 44-19786 was flown by Lt Edward Albright of the 63rd FS**. He was killed in this aircraft on the notorious 18 September 1944 'flak busting' mission performed by the 56th FG in support of the Arnhem operation. This was easily the worst day in the 'Wolfpack's' history, as 16 P-47s were shot down and a further 12 badly damaged out of 39 that had sortied

and far stronger defences that Intelligence knew about but ignored, it began to need strong air support. This included an anti-flak effort by USAAF fighter groups, which were not the choicest of sorties to fly because to do the job effectively, pilots had to wait to be fired at in order to spot the guns to be destroyed.

Newly promoted Maj 'Bunny' Comstock, CO of the 63rd FS/56th FG, drew mission lead, although he wasn't scheduled to, and he duly led 39 P-47Ds away from Boxted at 1437, destination Turnhout, in Holland. Low cloud forced an 'on the deck' approach to be flown, and the Thunderbolts being met by intense flak. The briefing warning about not firing until fired upon was misguided, to say the least, as Allied AA units had not apparently been issued with any such restriction. They let fly and shot down one 'Wolfpack' P-47, while their Germans counterparts did far better. The problem for the American pilots was the fact that the flak was able to track them from the side – an easy enough task for experienced gun crews. Comstock's wingman was amongst those pilots shot down, although he was able to walk out and rejoin the group the following day.

When the loss figures for 18 September were released they made shocking reading. The 'Wolfpack' had lost 16 of the P-47s sortied, whilst a further 12 had suffered major battle damage. Eight pilots had bailed out or landed in Allied territory, three were wounded badly enough to be sent home, one was killed in a belly landing, another a PoW and three were MIAs.

Despite such costly failures such as Arnhem, with its unrepresentative pilot and aircraft losses, the air war was clearly going well for the Allies,

Not all Thunderbolts decorated with kill markings were necessarily flown by aces, nor did these always denote aerial victories. This P-47D-22 (42-26024/HV-O) does have kill markings barely visible on the original print, and may have been the mount of six-victory ace Capt James Carter of the 61st FS/56th FG, although his records fail to mention this aircraft specifically

This Duxford flightline shot shows the aircraft of the 82nd FS, with a kill-marked 'bubbletop' in the foreground. The 'razorback' P-47D-22 second in line is *Miss Behave* (42-26387), with the 'W' (bar) ID code denoting a duplicated letter within the squadron – note the code of the third in line 'bubbletop' (*J Crow*)

although the progress of the ground forces towards a crossing into German territory was frustratingly slow.

On 21 September Eighth Air Force headquarters reduced the 300 hours figure required for an individual pilot to complete a tour to 270 hours. The statisticians had reckoned up that the odds of a man surviving a tour at the old rate had dropped to one in one hundred, with the primary reason being the attrition exacted by ground strafing. And that push into Germany was about to experience a major setback.

## OCTOBER/NOVEMBER 1944

Having flown P-47s from Metfield until April 1944, when it moved to Raydon, in Suffolk, the 353rd FG put up its first all-Mustang mission on 2 October. One of the most dedicated of P-47 groups, the 353rd had, among its other achievements, pioneered ETO dive-bombing with single-seat fighters.

Although the fact that the Germans had managed to bring jet and rocket fighters to operational status caused extreme anxiety amongst Eighth Air Force bomber commanders, there was little they could do until the enemy showed his hand. Meanwhile, publicity about the 'jet menace', with provisional data on the salient points of the Me 163 and Me 262, was circulated to all units. The fighter pilots could not do much more than await developments and find out the hard way if the sparkling performance figures for their new adversaries were as good as Intelligence sources claimed.

On 1 November Lt Walter R Groce of the 63rd FS/56th FG found himself in a position to answer some of the questions. Eager – as were all the pilots – to put an encounter with enemy jets into his log book, Groce and a group of Mustangs attacked an Me 262 about to hit the bombers. It had been damaged (probably by fire from the P-51D flown by Lt William Gerbe of the 352nd FG), but a full deflection shot from Groce's guns did the trick. The Me 262 ran into the burst and its right side Jumo turbojet burst into flames. Groce followed the aircraft down and saw the German pilot bail out. His gun camera film so reflected the high quality of shooting, with strikes on the jet clearly visible, that Groce was awarded a half credit, as was Mustang pilot Gerbe.

That the speed and confusion of air combat as seen through a gun camera had dramatically increased with the advent of the jets was confirmed by the fact that 20th FG P-

51s (and a total of six pilots from the three groups) had also been involved in this action. After some deliberation on the part of the assessors, it was the visible evidence on film that confirmed the names of the two pilots who finally got the credit. That film was probably run more than once for other 'Wolfpack' pilots to note the salient points of the aircraft they would be up against in the coming months. Although the jet's performance had now been seen at first hand, nobody could yet answer the vital question of 'how many do they have?' with any certainty.

By 20 November the 356th FG had all but completed its conversion to Mustangs, that day recording its first P-51 mission. A further loss to the rolls of the 78th FG on 26 November was 82nd FS 'A Flight' CO, Capt Joe Hockery. Flying his assigned P-47D-28 44-19950/MX-L, he had downed two Bf 109s and hit an Fw 190 that was subsequently credited to him as a probable over the Rheine, when he tangled with more fighters and this time lost out. One of the few P-47 aces shot down by Luftwaffe fighters, seven-kill ace Hockery saw out the rest of the war as a PoW.

P-47D-28 42-28615/WZ-X was flown by Lt Robert Laho. It had a striking piece of artwork next to its name and a Spitfire-type rear view mirror – a much sought-after 'add-on' fitted to many Thunderbolts (*Bivens*)

## DECEMBER 1944

The bleak winter of 1944-45 enabled the final German army counter offensive in the West to go ahead masked by a blanket of weather that kept the Allied tactical air forces all but anchored to the ground. When news broke of the German push, it was a case of trying desperately to put all and everything in the air in an effort to prevent further enemy gains in what came to be known as the 'Battle of the Bulge'. By this late stage the 78th FG had already received its new P-51B Mustangs at Duxford, but on 19 December a 'maximum effort' Thunderbolt mission was laid on to escort 'heavies' to Trier. Forty P-47s completed the mission without sighting the Luftwaffe, with solid overcast from 10,000 ft down to a 300-ft thick ground fog prevented a concurrent attack by the fighters on Baben Heusen aerodrome, so the group strafed the section of railway running from Siegen to Giessen instead.

The word 'Flak' appears to be part of the name of this 'Wolfpack' P-47D-28, which was photographed at a time when the 56th FG was about to fall back on the earlier 'bubbletop' models (and some 'razorbacks') following delivery of the new, potent but unfortunately flawed P-47M to the last Thunderbolt group in the Eighth Air Force

Briefed to support von Runstedt's offensive, the Luftwaffe appeared (although that was not always literally true!) in considerable force, and the 78th's aircraft did later clash with enemy fighters – some 20 Fw 190s and Bf 109s. Noting that the Germans did not seem overly aggressive and ran for cloud cover, which was never very far away, the American pilots neverthe-

**61st FS CO Maj Donavon Smith probably picked up on English Cockney slang to come up with the name *'Ole Cock'* for his two aircraft, this one being the second P-47D-26 (42-28382) to be so named. Coded HV-S, it is seen at its Boxted dispersal with a pair of triple tube rocket launchers fitted under each wing, and a more passive streamer on the wingtip to alert people that the pitot head stuck out some distance from the wing leading edge – human heads did not want unexpected contact!**

less did well to shoot down seven before their adversaries disappeared into the 'soup'.

Fighting the weather more than the enemy, and having missions cancelled, enabled the 78th's pilots to both enjoy a peaceful Christmas and step up P-51 conversion training. Eventually, this left all remaining operational P-47s concentrated within the 84th FS.

Despite the weather over the new Ardennes battle front, the medium bombers and fighters went out on 26 December, 48 P-47s of the 56th FG sweeping the Malmedy and Cologne-Bonn areas, where about 20 German fighters were encountered. Maj Leslie Smith was leading the 'Wolfpack' (in P-47D-28 44-19925/LM-L) that day, and his 'Daily White Flight' dived on four Fw 190s that the P-47 pilots observed had a high cover of Bf 109s.

Having previously flown a tour with the 61st FS, during which time he had 'made ace', Les Smith had come back for a second and been given command of the 62nd. In the resulting action, he quickly despatched a Focke-Wulf, while his wingman, Lt Alfred Perry, shot down two. None of the Bf 109s came to the aid of the Focke-Wulfs, almost certainly because the 61st and 63rd FSs had positioned themselves as top cover to Smith's flight. As the 56th set course for England, any chance of a celebration in the familiar surroundings of Boxted was scotched by the weather, for the base was completely 'socked in' by fog. Consequently, some of the P-47s landed at alternative fields in England, while others turned back and put down at the first convenient base on the continent.

On 29 December the 78th operated Mustangs for the first time as 'A' and 'B' groups, with the 84th FS putting up 32 P-47s as the 'C' group. The P-51s escorted bombers while the 84th stooged around with some Ninth Air Force aircraft over Coblenz and Luxembourg, forlornly looking for the Luftwaffe. It was a similarly frustrating story the following day, with the ground controllers vectoring the P-47s around only to find friendly aircraft rather than the enemy.

The last 78th mission of 1944 saw 14 P-47s offering freelance bomber support under microwave early warning (MEW) control in return for relatively little action. However, Pat Maxwell shot down an Fw 190 for the group's 400th air combat victory of the war following a little light train strafing. He received a silver beer mug to mark the occasion.

As an interesting additional statistic of the P-47 period at Duxford, the 79th Air Service Group, which was responsible for the 78th FG's aircraft, announced that during its tour as part of the group, 227 P-47s had passed through its hands for major and minor repair and disassembly for return to depots.

## JANUARY 1945

On the day that the Luftwaffe fighter force made its last big show of strength in the West by attacking Allied airfields in Belgium and Holland, the 78th flew its last P-47 sorties from Duxford. By this time the 84th FS had just four serviceable aircraft, the remainder having been stood down or returned to depots for reissue to groups within the Ninth Air Force or the French *Armee de l'Air.*

The New Year's Day mission was to be an unusual one for the veteran P-47 unit, for the quartet of aircraft, led by Capt Wilbur Grimes, escorted the last of the Project *Aphrodite* B-17 'flying bomb' to its target. Packed with 22,000 lb of Torpex explosive, the old Fortress was well on its way to Oldenburg by the time the Thunderbolts turned for home.

This P-47M-1 was assigned to Lt Col John F Keeler, and is seen parked at Boxted. This aircraft would have been flown only sporadically during the early months of 1945 due to the lengthy engine problems which kept the penultimate Thunderbolt from reaching its full potential. These problems were finally rectified just prior to VE-Day, resulting in the M-model becoming a more familiar sight over Germany

The passing of the black and white checker-nosed Thunderbolts from Duxford meant that the 56th FG was now the sole operator of the Republic fighter in VIII FC. Waved under its collective nose from time to time was the spectre of the P-51, but the 'Wolfpack' personnel – particularly the groundcrews, who did not want to service liquid-cooled engines – managed to hold out, even when the future reliability of the P-47M (the first of which had arrived at Boxted on 3 January) looked doubtful.

The M-model was the fastest Thunderbolt of the entire series, and it also gave the fighter the kind of range the 'Wolfpack' had always needed. It could now fly 250 miles from England, stretching this figure (on internal fuel) for a range of 530 miles, which meant that with the insurance factor of bases on the continent available for emergency landings, the 56th could now cover any part of Germany. The trouble was that it took weeks to determine that the P-47M engines had not received the necessary protection from the elements before being shipped over, and reliability was consequently low.

In the meantime the group continued to fly a mix of 'razorback' and 'bubbletop' P-47Ds, during which time six-kill ace Maj Jim Carter took over leadership of the 61st FS – he would achieve no further victories, but would remain in command of the squadron until VE day.

Attrition among the Eighth Air Force Thunderbolt aces remained relatively high to the end, for although the *Jagdwaffe* failed to shoot less than a handful down, flak accounted for most of the pilots languishing in PoW camps. A few were also lost in operational accidents, including seven-kill ace Capt James Poindexter of the 352nd FS/353rd FG, who was killed in a P-51 flying accident five miles from Raydon on 3 January 1945.

Flying his assigned P-47D-28 (44-19780/LM-J) over the Rheine area on 14 January – the day the P-

Once the 78th FG became a Mustang outfit in late 1944, only the 56th FG remained P-47-equipped within VIII FC. That was the cue to extend the individualistic camouflage to denote all three squadrons, with the P-47Ms in particular being given the treatment. The 61st FS, for example, adopted a striking dark blue-black overall finish, often with red codes (*via R L Ward*)

Maj George Bostwick's P-47M-1 44-21112 sported the blue rudder of the 63rd FS and typical striking camouflage finish which tended to vary from aircraft to aircraft. CO of the squadron, Bostwick was the only 'Wolfpack' ace to tangle successfully with the Me 262, using this very aircraft

47M flew its first sorties in 56th FG colours – Maj Mike Jackson of the 62nd FS came across Bf 109s accompanied by Fw 190Ds. He attacked and shot down one of each, these final victories bringing his score to eight (including a Ju 52 he had destroyed on 7 July 1944).

On 20 January Maj Paul Conger assumed command of the 63rd FS just as the 56th FG was trying to bring the P-47M up to reliable operational status. A reflection of how demanding this was is the fact that Conger had flown his personal P-47M-1 44-21134/UN-P, named *Bernyce*, on an operation earlier in the month (the 14th) during which he had shot down a Bf 109 and damaged. Thereafter, he had reverted to aP-47D-30 (44-2045/UN-Y), as did other pilots of the group, pending the outcome of more engine trouble shooting on the P-47M.

Prior to taking over as CO of the 62nd FS on 26 January, Capt Felix 'Willy' Williamson also appears to have had little chance to fly the P-47M assigned to him. He scored no victories in it, and reverted instead to a P-47D-28 (44-19925/LM-L) in which he made 'ace in a day' on 14 January by downing four Bf 109s and an Fw 190D north of Burg. He was then issued with P-47D-30 44-20555/LM-I, which he also put to good effect by destroying a Bf 109 and an Fw 190 (plus a second Focke-Wulf damaged) on 3 February over Berlin. This haul of seven kills in the first two months of 1945 made Williamson the leading P-47 ace of 1945, and took his final score to 13-0-1. he remained in command of the 62nd FS until the end of the war.

## FEBRUARY/MARCH 1945

Capt Cameron Hart, who had joined the 56th FG's 62nd FS at the end of June 1944, also shared in his CO's success on 3 February, accompanying Capt Williamson on a free-ranging hunt for the Luftwaffe south of Berlin. Encountering over Friedersdorf airfield south-east of the embattled capital, Hart succeeded in downing two fighters for his fifth and sixth (and last) victories. Both were scored while flying P-47D-28 44-19937/UN-B. Cameron Hart was killed less than a year later when his P-47N (44-87929) crashed at Craig Field, Alabama, on 16 January 1946.

Having lost faith with his P-47M (on 26 February all 67 M-models at Boxted were grounded for more engine checks and tests), 63rd FS CO Paul Conger used P-47D-30 44-20455 for the remainder of his time with the 56th. Following on from his single kill in January, Conger also claimed a Bf 109 (plus a second Messerschmitt damaged) and an Fw 190 in the sprawling combat enjoyed by the group south east of Berlin on 3 February. These victories raised his final score to 11.5-0-4, for Conger relinquished command of the 63rd after completing his 168th combat mission on 19 March. His successor was 62nd FS ace Capt George Bostwick.

Throughout the early months of the 1945 increasing numbers of Me 262s continued to appear to harry the bombers, and although the P-51 escort groups enjoyed the lion's share of actions with the German jets, P-47s also overcame these ostensibly superior enemy aircraft on several occasions.

If Me 262s managed to climb to altitude it would usually be Mustangs that attempted to turn the German jet pilots away from their primary target, but elsewhere over the front the 'turbos' – particularly the Arado Ar 234 – could come face to face with a half dozen or so different types of Allied tactical fighter.

The second direct encounter with the jets by VIII FC P-47s came on

Close up of Bostwick's P-47M. In this case the code letters were masked off to reveal the natural metal finish beneath, the codes then being re thinly trimmed in red. Thirteen kills marked on Maj Bostwick's aircraft (denoting air and ground kills combined) have been applied with the distinctive 'frame' made by the squadron painter. These 1945 'Wolfpack' Thunderbolts had some of the most garish markings seen on USAAF fighters during the entire war

14 March, and although conventional fighters continued to appear on an irregular basis during the final weeks of the war, the time when Allied flyers would encounter them in force had passed. By March it was all but certain that the jets that had posed such a potential threat six months previously had not, and would not, materialise in significant numbers.

That the engine troubles associated with the P-47M had not been cured was reflected in an yet another Eighth Air Force grounding order on 16 March. Exasperated, high command had said that enough was enough – the 'Wolfpack's' potentially excellent Thunderbolts would remain on the ground until the engines troubles were cured. Fortuitously, it was a short time after this that the true cause of powerplant unreliablity was traced, but the 56th had still had to endure a nine day stand down until 24 March. On that day, the 'Wolfpack' flew two missions in a day, which was the first time that such a feat had been achieved in some months. Neither was productive in terms of aerial victories, however, and little was seen on the ground either.

On 25 March, things improved. Waiting about 30 minutes for the B-24s it was scheduled to escort, the 56th FG duly took up station. However, the P-47 pilots could not prevent six or seven Me 262s diving on the bombers from 18,000 ft and downing two of the high element. As the jets left the area, George Bostwick, flying P-47M-1 44-21112/UN-Z, led the 63rd FS in what appeared to be a vain pursuit. He quickly lost sight of the quarry, so instead elected to orbit Parchim airfield – the likely destination of the jets. Sure enough an Me 262 soon appeared, and Bostwick ordered Lt Edwin H Crosthwait to go after it, and the jet was duly shot down.

Maj Bostwick, having noted that Parchin was packed with 20 to 30 jets, now spotted four more in the circuit. He picked out one that looked as though it was about to land and bored in. As he did so, he saw that a second Me 262 had just broken ground, and so he duly pulled the nose of his P-47 through to get a shot at this one. Making a tight turn to avoid the Thunderbolt's fire, the jet dug in a wingtip and cartwheeled. Bostwick then picked up his original target, but could only damage it with several strikes. The downed Me 262 was credited as Bostwick's sixth aerial victory – the only occasion when a 56th FG ace added a jet to his score while flying a P-47. Crosthwait was also credited with an Me 262 confirmed.

# FINAL CLASHES

Maj George Bostwick again led the 56th on an escort to Germany on 5 April, the fighters being under strict orders to stay with the bombers which, on this occasion, were 2nd Division B-24s. But when Me 262 attacked the Liberators north of Regensburg, the P-47 pilots had no choice but to react, and one Me 262 was shot down by Capt John C Fahinger, Operations Officer of the 63rd FS, for his fourth, and last, kill of the war.

Two days later, a chase which took its American and German participants from south of Bremen to north of Hamburg ended in the last victories for George Bostwick. Again flying P-47M-1 44-21112, he led 'B group' as part of the escort 'Ramrod' sent to cover no fewer than 1200 B-17s and B-24s. For a change, the Luftwaffe rose in considerable force, and the day's various combats resulted in 64 claims by the American fighters and no less than 40 by the bomber gunners. Bostwick shot down two Bf 109s and damaged an Me 262 he found north of Hamburg, thus taking his final tally to 8-0-2 and six ground victories. Aside from his solitary success against an Me 262 on 25 March (detailed in the previous chapter), all

With the war over, the 56th FG honoured 'Hub' Zemke's contribution by painting up P-47M-1 44-21175 (a Thunderbolt sub-type he never actually had the chance to fly in combat) and displaying it along with other Allied war winning aircraft in an exhibition staged in Paris near the Eiffel Tower (*Crow*)

A close up view of the markings which adorned 'Zemke's' P-47M i Paris. After it had performed its flag-waving job, the aircraft was unceremoniously scrapped (*Crow*)

his claims had been against Bf 109s.

Against a backdrop of overwhelming American airpower, with some 1300 four-engined bombers flying into enemy airspace in clear skies, the 10 April mission was a 'maximum effort' by the 'Wolfpack'. The group sent out 62 P-47s, most if not all of them being M-models, which had been given a new lease of life thanks to engine modifications. It was to be a memorable day in terms of successful strafing attacks, for numerous pilots had a field day. A variety of aircraft were shot up by the Thunderbolt squadrons, including a Ju 88/Bf 109 *Mistel* combination which fell victim to Lt Dennis Carroll, who legitimately claimed a double ground victory.

It was whilst en route home that a solitary Me 262 was credited to Lt Walter J Sharbo who, with a good height advantage, dived on the unsuspecting Me 262 and opened fire from 600 yards. The German pilot jettisoned his canopy and the aircraft fell into Muritz Lake from an altitude of about 1500 ft. This combat, which turned out to be the last time a German jet fell to an Eighth Air Force P-47, brought the total aerial kill tally for the mission (rounding up the three half shares) to 6.5.

Another strafing spree three days later netted the 'Wolfpack' no less than 95-0-81 on the ground at Eggebeck, in Denmark. It was the group's second anniversay in-theatre, and with figures like those, it was not surprising that a number of pilots made ground 'ace' in one strike. Lt Randell Murphy of the 63rd FS actually became a double ace with ten kills, whilst squadronmate Lt Vernon Smith was credited with six.

'Bud' Mahurin and Bob Johnson during a light-hearted interview for the press. The latter pilot took these duties quite seriously, and toured America making numerous speeches to help further the war effort

Plenty of USAAF 'top brass' were interested in knowing what air combat over Europe was like, and Bob Johnson was more than happy to describe his numerous engagements. Here, he demonstrates a typical manoeuvre in even more typical fighter pilot hand language to Brig-Gen Jesse Auton, 65th Fighter Wing CO, and Brig-Gen Francis Griswold, Chief of Staff, VIII FC (*IWM*)

The pilots reported that it was like shooting 'fish in a barre' upon returning to base, their quarry being mainly Bf 110s, Ju 88s and He 111s, although most first-line single-seater fighter were also present, and they too were duly shot up as the P-47s 'buzzed' over. By the time the carnage had finally ceased, the 'Wolfpack' had surpassed the 1000 enemy aircraft destroyed mark.

The familiar menace of flak claimed a P-47 near Huhldorf on 16 April, its pilot, Capt Edward Appel of the 62nd FS being killed – he was the last Eighth Air Force P-47 pilot to be shot down during World War 2.

For what turned out to be its last mission of the war, the 56th FG put up 39 aircraft from the 62nd and 63rd FSs as 'A group', led by Maj Williamson, with the 61st contributing 18 as 'B group', led by Maj Joseph Perry. Basically performing a 'Ramrod' for B-24s, the 'Wolfpack' actually flew a freelance fighter sweep when the Liberators were recalled due to weather. Below the overcast that would have frustrated the bombardiers, the P-47s swept enemy territory from Linz to Inglestadt without finding any German aircraft. The order prohibiting ground strafing to prevent any casualties among friendly troops, just about wrapped things up for the prowling Thunderbolts. There was nothing for it but to fly back to Boxted and have the magazines unloaded. For the longest serving P-47 group in the ETO, the war was over.

## MAY 1945

Although the enemy had inflicted its final casualty on the 56th, the group nevertheless suffered yet another tragic loss on 1 May when Polish pilot Lt Albin Zychowski was killed on a routine training flight. Having joined the 'Wolfpack' later than the other Polish pilots who had transferred in during early 1944, the young Pole had nevertheless completed 32 combat missions with the 61st FS before his death, which was almost certainly the result of low-level 'buzzing'. He had apparently been one of four pilots practicing a formation peel off break when his Thunderbolt 'mushed' into the ground near Tiverton, in Devon.

As the end of the war approached, the mass wind-down of Eighth Air Force personnel and combat units included a number of aces who were sent home. One such pilot was Maj Jim Carter, who relinquished command of the 61st FS on 8 May after flying an impressive total of 137 combat missions with the 56th. His final score was 6-3-3, with all Carter's victims having been fighters, including two Bf 110s. The day Jim Carter left the 'Wolfpack' the war in Europe ended.

However, the Thunderbolt still had a handful of duties to perform, although these were more of a ceremonial than combat nature. When the Allies prepared a victory celebration in Paris, examples of all the leading US combat aircraft types were part of the display staged around the Eiffel Tower. To represent the 'Wolfpack', the P-47M-1 assigned to Lt Paul Dawson was painted up as 'Zemke's Wolfpack' with 'the Hub's' kills applied below the cockpit. The aircraft, which in common with some other P-47Ms had the deeper dorsal fin as fitted to the P-47N, also noted that the 56th had claimed over 1000 enemy aircraft during its time in the ETO.

The question of which group got the most victories – air and ground – remains a matter of conjecture to this day, with the ground kill scores in particular being impossible to accurately tally. The 'Wolfpack' was officially credited with 1006.5 victories, of which 677 were aerial kills. The group also produced 42 aces with five or more victories in aerial combat. To these were added three pilots who, under Eighth Air Force guidelines, were considered aces by adding ground successes to aerial victories, whilst a further trio of pilots claimed all their kills during strafing, without getting any in the air.

As far as the ranking aces of the Eighth were concerned, the P-47 had served the leading pilots well. It was the aircraft that many of them had cut their teeth on, and as the necessary re-equipment with Mustangs had been spread over some ten months, numerous pilots were able to score victories on both types of fighter.

For the record, the top 11 aces of the 56th were:

Francis Gabreski -        28*
Robert S Johnson -        27
David Schilling -         22.5

Lt Col Francis 'Gabby' Gabreski, top scoring ace of VIII FC, is seen in his full dress uniform after returning from his spell in a German PoW camp

Fred Christensen - 21.5
Walker Mahurin - 19**
Hubert Zemke - 18
Gerald Johnson - 16.5
Joe Powers - 14.5
Leroy Schreiber - 14
Felix Williamson - 13
Michael Quirk - 12

\* Gabreski scored a further 6.5 kills flying F-86s in Korea
\*\* Mahurin scored a further kill flying P-51Ds in the Pacific in January 1945, followed by 3.5 victories in F-86s in Korea

## FACTS AND FIGURES

A word about numbers. Of the nine – 4th, 56th, 78th, 352nd 353rd, 355th, 356th, 359th and 361st – Eighth Air Force groups equipped with the P-47 (a tenth in the shape of the 358th FG was transferred to the Ninth Air Force after just two months of service with VIII FC), only seven produced aces who scored the baseline five or more air-to-air kills with the P-47. In total, some 64 pilots qualified for 'ace status' with the Thunderbolt during their time with VIII FC, these men being distributed thus: 4th FG - 4; 56th FG - 42; 78th FG -10; 352nd FG - 1; 353rd FG - 5; 355th - 1; and 356th -1.

No pilots with the 359th or 361st FGs had the chance to become aces in their relatively short period flying the P-47 prior to switching to the P-51. This rather arbitrary breakdown is purely at the author's whim, but it

With the 28th kill added to P-47D-25 42-26418, Gabreski receives another handshake from his armourer, Cpl Joe DiFranza. This posed picture almost exactly duplicated another taken at the same time showing a member of the Eighth Air Force public relations office again pointing to the last victory flag. Understandably, records made news, and 'Gabby' received plenty of 'press' in the *Oil City Blizzard*, his local newspaper in his home town in Pennsylvania

does serve to separate the full Thunderbolt aces from the full Mustang aces, and the numerous pilots who scored with both the P-47 and P-51, as well as a handful who were also adding to their previous totals scored on the P-38 in the ETO. Further individuals who had already seen action in the Pacific before being posted to the ETO were also able to add Japanese 'meatballs' or rising sun flags to the iron crosses or swastikas they earned with the P-47 in Europe. Still other pilots had enjoyed success with the RAF. None of these have been counted for the purpose of this statistical breakdown.

It should be stressed that the scores quoted here are taken from Dr Frank Olynyk's magnificent (and hugely time saving) publications, which originate from the final written decisions of the Air Force fighter claims credits boards. After the war some downgrading of individual scores was necessary, which is why photos of P-47s showing lines of iron crosses or swastikas do not necessarily reflect the true picture if the implication is that a given pilot had more than enough kills to make him an ace. At the time claims were awarded in good faith, and an unconfirmed extra one or two was good for morale and publicity. Nobody should find fault with that.

There were of course many Eighth Air Force pilots who were quite at liberty to count themselves as aces, even if they had never seen an enemy aircraft in the air. Under an VIII FC ruling, ground kills carried legitimate credits. But it was only human nature to regard the aerial victory as more decisive and more prestigious, despite the undeniable hazard of shooting up enemy aircraft on the ground.

There is no really accurate breakdown of the type of aircraft destroyed on the ground by AAF fighter attacks, but it can be said with some certainty that during the last year of the war, the Luftwaffe left hundreds of unwanted bombers and transports littered around airfields. Eliminating these from the inventory was going to do little to effect the war effort, but five Me 262s shot up before they could take-off to intercept Allied bombers, or nightfighters destroyed during daylight strafing attacks so they could not harass RAF night bombers, was very valuable indeed.

**Back cover**
This rare colour view shows 'Gabby' Gabreski's armourers, Cpls Joe DiFranza (foreground) and John Koval, filling the left wing magazine bays of his last assigned P-47D-25 (42-26418) in which he was lost on the fateful 20 July 1944 mission. All pilots had preferences when it came to the 'mix' of ammunition to be loaded in their aircraft, and Gabreski liked a greater percentage of API (armour-piercing incendiary) rounds. (*USAF*)

# MERLIN'S REACH

By the autumn of 1943 the bomber groups of the Eighth US Army Air Force (USAAF) based in England faced a crisis. For over a year an increasing number of B-17 Fortress and B-24 Liberator groups had waged war on German industry both at home and in occupied Europe. Since the B-17's combat debut in August 1942, much destruction had been wrought by precision bombing of key industrial targets, and it was clear that the USAAF experiment of sending heavily armed bombers over Germany in daylight would not be curtailed unless drastic circumstances dictated it.

Unfortunately, the Luftwaffe's fighter force and the German flak defences were making that event a possibility. Losses of American bombers had risen to the point where, after the notorious double mission to Schweinfurt and Regensburg in October, VIIIth Bomber Command had to carefully marshall its resources. The loss figure of 60 bombers on each mission was the subject of much debate in Congress, and the US government began to question the merit of continuing the offensive if such wastage was to become the norm. For some weeks no deep penetration missions were flown from England, leading the Germans to believe that the offensive had been fatally weakened. But this was not the case – it was Europe's deteriorating weather more than any other factor that prevented the bombers penetrating Reich airspace, for there was little point in flying sorties if bombardiers could not see their targets.

While there was no doubt that the Eighth's bomber force had taken a terrible beating, most of its worthwhile targets lay in central and Eastern Germany, and to fulfil the avowed Allied policy of defeating the Third Reich before the full weight of America's might was turned against the Japanese in the Pacific, the strategic bomber force had to hit those targets. Reducing the Eighth to a short- to medium-range force would yield little.

The realisation that bombers, however heavily armed, could not battle their way alone into German airspace without heavy losses had belatedly brought P-38 Lightnings to England in 1942, primarily to act as escorts for the bombers. There was some irony in this as early plans for the 8th Air Force had envisaged the need for an escort, albeit with short-range Spitfires. The ability of RAF fighters to cover the bombers only as far as Paris was soon overtaken by events, as the Eighth quickly extended its reach to take in targets in Germany.

But the transfer of P-38 groups from England to North Africa soon after the Lockheed fighter's arrival in Europe led to few bomber missions being flown in early 1943 that were protected by anything more than short-range fighter cover. Bombers would be well protected as far as an imaginary arc drawn through the French capital on the outward leg, whilst the remnants of the force would then be picked up on the return flight and escorted for the last 200 miles or so.

With little prospect of more P-38 groups being assigned to the 8th in the immediate future, the USAAF turned to a new type, the P-47 Thunderbolt. From March and April 1943 respectively, the P-47-

Eager to get P-51s the minute the type was introduced to the ETO, the 4th FG at Debden experienced a great change of luck when Mustangs finally re-equipped the group in February 1944. Among the early exponents was Duane Beeson, seen here on the wing of his only P-51B, 43-6819, nicknamed *BEE*, in the spring of 1944

Many pilots kept pet dogs and John Godfrey's own mutt was named, appropriately, *Lucky*. Godfrey flew two P-51Bs *(H Holmes)*

equipped 4th and 56th Fighter Groups (FGs) began rebuilding the Eighth's fighter force.

While the P-47 did sterling work, there were limits as to how far it could fly even with external fuel tanks without becoming excessively heavy – as with all Republic products, the Thunderbolt was somewhat on the weighty side to start with! Nevertheless, P-47s flew their first full escort mission equipped with pressurised belly fuel tanks on 12 August 1943, and by October they were able to accompany the bombers as far as the German border, a distance from England of over 350 miles. That, however, still left a dangerous gap if the bombers' targets lay beyond Berlin. The significance of the German capital itself could hardly be overlooked, for if the fighters could reach that far, their effect on the morale of the hard-pressed bomber crews would be considerable.

Much hope was therefore pinned upon the P-38. Two groups, the 55th and 20th, were flying Lightning missions over Europe by year's end, and with its potential to reach Berlin, the big 'twin' seemed the ideal aircraft to close the 'escort gap'.

However, because of the vagaries of the European weather the P-38's fuel system and engines proved to be chronically unreliable, resulting in no end of malfunctions and poor mission effectiveness. As 1943 ended, 'all the way' escort seemed an almost unattainable goal; no other US Army fighters were readily available despite USAAF planners having considered them all, including Navy types. The only glimmer of hope was the outcome of experiments being made in England and the US to mate the Rolls-Royce Merlin engine to the airframe of the North American Aviation (NAA) P-51.

At command level VIIIth FC had a new leader from 3 August – Gen William Kepner. He refused to accept that single-engined fighters had reached the limit of their range capability in the P-47's absolute maximum of 375 miles. This figure was widely believed in USAAF and RAF circles to be unbeatable, and Kepner's predecessor, Gen Russell O'Dell Hunter, had tended to believe British doubts – after all, they had been at this game considerably longer and had given the Eighth immeasurable help right from the word go. Fortunately for B-17 and B-24 crews the RAF were, on this occasion, proved wrong.

Johnny Godfrey framed by the Debden scoreboard. Two items of personal kit visible in this portrait are the silk scarf to prevent neck chafing, and a whistle to summon help in the event of a ditching

The early Mustang groups like the 355th (who flew this P-51B from Steeple Morden in Cambridgeshire) applied only the simplest of unit markings to their aircraft. Photographed departing on another escort mission in the bloody month of March 1944, this Mustang boasts the group's distinctive white spinner and 12-in nose band. Obscured by the wing are the 'OS' squadron code letters of the 357th FS

Don Gentile, groundcrews and assorted 'top brass' discuss the way the mission went soon after the pilot's return from an escort mission over Germany in early March 1944. Gentile's personal P-51B, *Shangri-La* (43-6913), forms the backdrop for this famous photograph

The Gentile/Godfrey team helped 'sell' the leader-wingman idea to other pilots, for there was no disputing how successful it was. *Shangri-La* is seen here resting on steel planking, which makes the location somewhere other than Debden

The autumn arrival in the ETO of the 352nd and 355th FGs had enabled Kepner to reorganise his force, which then comprised ten groups. Formed into wings, and thus making the massed ranks of fighters easier to control once in the air, each group was able to make the best use of advance warning information, via radar and *Ultra* intercepts, and to ensure that a relay system provided adequate forces for all tasks, which were about to be broadened.

## ATTACK OR ESCORT?

Extremely long range was not a criteria in the original specification for the P-51. Ordered as a tactical reconnaissance type for the RAF by the British Purchasing Commission in 1940, it initially aroused little interest in USAAF circles. When it proved to offer a useful capability as a low altitude (below 10,000 ft) fighter and dive bomber, the Army placed orders, intending to deploy the new type in the attack role. As the A-36 Apache and P-51 Mustang, the NAA design went on to carve an enviable reputation as a rugged close-support fighter for the troops on the frontline during the Twelfth AAF's campaign in Tunisia and Sicily.

The Mustang story might have ended at that point, had it not been for the success of a series of test flights, beginning in October 1942, that proved the Rolls-Royce Merlin 61 engine to be capable of oustanding performance when mated to the Mustang airframe. The most important attribute of the conversion, which was immeasurably helped by the P-51's extremely efficient wing, was a hitherto undreamed of range.

Careful fuel metering of the Packard Merlin showed that it could not only run on the Mustang's full tankage of 100 octane for eight-and-a-half hours, consuming only 60 gallons an hour at a 260-mph cruise setting, but it could also provide enough power in hand for five minutes' combat. That meant that P-51s could escort bombers from the UK to the farthest point in Germany, fight off the attacking Luftwaffe, and return safely.

Unfortunately, this awesome realisation took some time to mate-rialise in the form of new aircraft. Fitting a foreign engine in a perfectly sound American design was an idea that took some explaining to certain parties. This was perfectly under-standable as the P-51's original powerplant, the Allison V-1710, was a good engine, but it was not designed for high-altitude, long-range, patrol work. Also, due to a lack of funds Allison had been unable to improve the V-1710, despite the fact that its development had begun three years earlier than the Merlin!

Widespread acknowledgement of the critical point the daylight bomber offensive had reached led to the Merlin Mustang project eventually receiving enthusiastic backing at the highest levels on both sides of the Atlantic. Among the personalities who became involved were Sir Wilfred Freeman and USAAF Commanding General, H H 'Hap' Arnold. With this kind of support behind the project there was lit-tle chance that the 'marriage would not be blessed. . .'

Development work at Rolls-Royce had produced the Merlin 65 by the end of 1942, this engine offering 600hp more than the Allison V-1710-39. Fortunately, agreement had already been reached between Rolls-Royce and the Packard company to build Merlins under licence, and by the time the XP-51B was ready for flight testing in November 1942, US engine supply was fully guaranteed. North American Aviation tooled up to build Mustangs both at their vast Inglewood plant in California – they rolled out their first P-51B in June 1943 – and in Dallas, Texas, where the first near-identical P-51C flew two months later.

Despite the Merlin Mustang being seen as the answer to the long-range escort problem, the initial P-51B group, the 354th, was still locked into the USAAF's procurement policy as a close-air support unit. Allison-engined P-51s were proving their worth in the Italian campaign, and the USAAF continued to consider the Mustang purely as a ground attack type. They viewed the 'Pioneer Mustang' group as the ideal cadre for the newly constituted tactical Ninth AAF (reformed in England on 7 September 1943) to cut their teeth on the type.

However, much behind the scenes wheeling and dealing brought a transfer of the 354th into the 8th in exchange for the 358th FG, who were equipped with Thunderbolts. This move had many long-term benefits for it not only focused the P-51B primarily as an escort fighter, but revealed the potential of the radial-engined P-47 in the ground attack role – its air-cooled Pratt & Whitney R-2800 Double Wasp powerplant was more survivable when it came to enduring light flak damage than the liquid-cooled Merlin. Both types were to serve their respective air forces well.

Gentile shows how cramped the P-51B's cockpit could become once the pilot had swathed himself in flight/survival gear

The sad wreck of *Shangri-La* which Gentile crash-landed at Debden on 13 April 1944 – just days before he was due to go home. Had it survived the accident it would undoubtedly have been shipped to the US for demonstration purposes. As it was the aircraft was good only for the scrap pile. The 4th FG commander, Lt Col Don Blakeslee, was livid when the carefully-staged press show for Gentile was abruptly terminated following the crash. Rumour has it that the wreck was bulldozed into a farmer's pond near to the Essex airfield, where it remains to this day

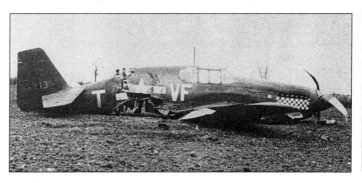

Initially, it was agreed that the 354th would operate as part of the Eighth for an indefinite period, or at least until enough Mustangs were available to re-equip its own assigned groups. To innummerable American bomber crews that change was to be a vital lifeline for the remaining 18 months of the war.

Due to the critical nature of the daylight bombing campaign in Europe in the autumn of 1943, the 354th were thrown into combat without the benefit of any stateside training on the P-51. Commanded by Col Kenneth Martin, the group had to work hard to prepare itself for the first shakedown escort mission prior to being blooded over Germany. Having flown P-39 Airacobras in the US, the 354th found the ETO a very different prospect. The first P-51Bs were shipped into Liverpool and the group began reorganising at Greenham Common, Berkshire, in early November 1943, before moving to Boxted later that month.

Few new aircraft make an entirely trouble-free operational debut, and the P-51B was no exception. European weather, which often appeared to side entirely with the Germans, contrived to plague the early Merlin Mustang missions almost as much as it had earlier done with the P-38. A long catalogue of technical faults also kept the 354th's groundcrews, and NAA's engineers, who received full reports, more than busy. Fortunately, few of these were serious enough to ground the P-51B for any length of time.

Gradually most of the bugs were eradicated, although a few were inherent in the design and could only be compensated for. Among the worst of these was the modest armament of four Browning .50 in machine guns. As a result of the P-51's slender wing profile, each pair of guns was canted over to allow the weapons to fit within the cramped confines of the flying surfaces. This arrangement resulted in the ammunition having to negotiate an acute angle as it fed off the belt tracks into the the guns' breeches. Prone to freezing in the cold, thin, air 25,000 ft over Germany, the belt feed design caused rounds to jam on the tracks, resulting in numerous stoppages. On countless occasions, pilots suddenly found they had only half their original firepower or less.

Neither did the highly-tuned Packard Merlin take kindly to the hostile conditions. Coolant leaks became almost routine 'fixes' for the Boxted groundcrews, as did fouled spark plugs and hose joints that cracked under the ultra-low temperatures. There was also a lengthy list of other minor irritations.

Nevertheless, the P-51's performance was clearly superior to any other Army fighter, and it soon

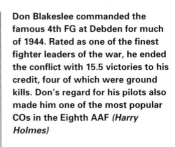

Don Blakeslee commanded the famous 4th FG at Debden for much of 1944. Rated as one of the finest fighter leaders of the war, he ended the conflict with 15.5 victories to his credit, four of which were ground kills. Don's regard for his pilots also made him one of the most popular COs in the Eighth AAF (Harry Holmes)

Everett Stewart, like other commanders, had a busy war passing on his skills to others. Stewart flew with three groups, the 4th, 352nd and the 355th

RAF slang personified on a 355th Group P-51B at Steeple Morden. Mission markers on early Eighth AAF Mustangs commonly took the form of yellow bomb stencils, this aircraft also boasting five 'brooms', which denoted successfully completed fighter sweeps

Walter Karoleski Jr of the 354th FS/355th FG made ace with a score of 5.54. Visible are salient features of the early model Mustang. Rear-view mirrors, though non-standard, were adopted by many pilots to reduce the possibility of an enemy fighter 'bouncing' them, as vision aft through the framed 'greenhouse' canopy was limited to say the least

Henry Brown was top ace of the 355th FG, with a final score of 14.20 in the air – the fifth of a kill denotes a shared victory with another pilot. His most successful day in combat was 27 September 1944 when he downed four aircraft in P-51D-5-NA 44-13305. In total, strafing victories brought his score to 28.70

made its mark. To the horror of the German *Jagdflieger,* the P-51B, which bore a marked resemblence to their own Bf 109G, also appeared the equal of not only their best aircraft, but also their most highly experienced pilots, too. Worse, the new Mustang was clearly superior to the Luftwaffe's twin-engined types, which were frequently used on bomber interception to back up the single-seaters.

One of the first pilots to demonstrate this latter point was Jim Howard of the 354th who, on 11 January 1944, despatched eight Bf 110s in short order. And he performed this remarkable feat with a gradually dwindling number of guns in his P-51B – by the time that he eventually broke off combat only a single Browning was functioning. For this feat, Howard became one of only six Army fighter pilots to be awarded the Medal of Honor in World War 2.

News of the 'hot' new Mustang spread quickly. At Debden, Lt Col Don Blakeslee, CO of the 4th FG, asked, pleaded and cajoled for his 'Eagles' to be allowed to replace their P-47s with P-51Bs. This famous group had earlier been weaned on various marks of Spitfire during their individual 'Eagle Squadron' days within the RAF and, as a result of this experience, had never felt fully confident with the immense Thunderbolt.

Blakeslee eventually got his way. As one of the most experienced fighter commanders in the ETO, he was temporarily seconded to the 354th to gain experience on the Mustang that would in turn allow his own group's combat debut to be as painless as possible. He led the first 24-ship mission on 1 December, and ten days later, following the arrival of 75-gal drop tanks, the 354th's Mustangs escorted bombers to Emden. On the 12th the target was Keil, where again the P-51Bs covered B-17s bombing the naval base and shipyards throughout the 960-mile round trip from England. Don Blakeslee led the 354th on a further four missions before returning to Debden, convinced beyond all doubt that with Mustangs, the 4th FG, which was having a lean time in terms of aerial victories, could become the scourge of the Luftwaffe.

Few P-51Bs were earmarked for other theatres at this time as the P-38 was performing well in the Pacific and the P-40 and P-47 were available in sufficient numbers to fill most other immediate requirements. Once the Merlin Mustang entered service, it was realised that the success or failure of the daylight bomber offensive in the ETO – a key element in the Allied plan to beat Germany first – rested almost entirely on having

Besides being a good all round combat aircraft, the P-51 could also endure rough handling. The Packard Merlin often protected the pilot during a hard landing, or indeed an overly low strafing pass against a ground target – this 339th FG P-51B, nicknamed *Sally*, returned from France with electricity cables snagged around its spinner! The 339th proved to particularly adept at strafing, claiming more than 100 aircraft destroyed on the ground on two separate occasions – 105 on 4 April 1945 and 118 a week later. No other group ever topped the century mark more than once

An orderly group take-off involved much work by the groundcrews, including placing the drop tanks near each aircraft ready for attachment. *Buzz Boy*, a P-51B of the 355th FG's 358th FS, will obviously fly the next sortie fitted with the tanks lying in the foreground. Its nickname came from the slang term 'buzzing', a word which summed up the strafing role of the Eighth. Indeed, pilots who indulged in this practice dubbed themselves 'Bill's Buzz Boys' after their boss, Gen Bill Kepner

enough Mustang groups in England. It was as simple as that.

As Gen Kepner said at the time, the P-51B is 'distinctly the best fighter that we are going to get over here. They are going to be the only satisfactory answer.'

## FIRST ACE

The Eighth AAF began 1944 confident that its existing fighter force would soon be boosted by new P-51 squadrons, then training in the US. Ten groups equipped with either the P-47 or the P-38 formed the backbone of the fighter force, with the 354th then the sole Mustang group. All had seen some action by the end of 1943, although the lion's share of confirmed victories had understandably fallen to the numerically superior P-47 squadrons. The first ETO ace was Charles London of Duxford's 78th FG, who achieved the magic five down on 30 July 1943. Since then, the 'ace race' had acquired a number of favourites for top honours. Maj Eugene Roberts, also of the 78th, was the second pilot to score five confirmed kills following a successful mission on 31 August.

Membership of this select band of pilots had, by the end of 1943, been expanded to include Col Hubert 'Hub' Zemke, Maj Dave Schilling, Capt Walker Muhurin, Lt Robert Johnson and Capt Gerald Johnson, all of the 56th; Walter Beckham of the 353rd; and Duane Beeson and Maj Roy Evans of the 4th. Jim Howard's victory over the Bf 110G-2s of *Zerstörergeschwader* (ZG) 76 made him the world's premier P-51 ace, and the first of many 'aces in a day' in the ETO.

During the winter months of 1943/44, the P-51B steadily proved that it had a marked superiority over the P-47 and P-38 in the escort role, although both of the latter types were subject to a lengthy programme of technical improvements. This meant that the Lightnings and Thunderbolts of early 1944 were far more capable combat aircraft than they had been only six to eight months before. The P-47, for example, could now easily cover the bombers on their return leg, and providing a separate withdrawal support force soon featured as a regular mission for the groups still equipped with the type. These sorties gave Thunderbolt pilots the chance to gain air combat victories, thus preventing the P-51 groups from stealing all the glory.

But it was the basic fact that the Mustang was the only type that could stay with the 'heavies' all the way to their targets and back that endeared it so highly to VIIIth Bomber Command. Enemy fighters still penetrated the escort screen, but now the bomber gunners, who despite their entirely circumstantial over-claiming of kills, were also

helping to gradually whittle down the pilot strength of the *Jagdwaffe*.

## ——— BIG WEEK ———

With Don Blakeslee assigned to command the 4th FG from 1 January 1944, the day when an original Eighth AAF unit would receive its first P-51Bs came that much nearer. In a determined effort to reduce German opposition in the skies over Europe, the AAF launched an all out attack on fighter production sites and airfields, giving its pilots *carte blanche* to hunt the *Jagdwaffe* across Germany and the occupied countries. Codenamed the 'Pointblank Directive', and dubbed 'Big Week' by the fighter groups, this offensive was scheduled for February.

Meanwhile, more skullduggery was being perpetrated to delay the Mustang reaching the 4th FG, or so it seemed to Don Blakeslee. A second Ninth AAF P-51 group, the 357th, had been despatched to the ETO primarily as a ground-attack wing, but once in-theatre they were quickly swapped with the P-47-equipped 358th FG, who had only recently arrived in the UK as part of the Eighth AAF. Installed at Raydon, the 357th moved to Leiston, Suffolk, and by 22 January had 15 P-51Bs on strength. At the end of that month it was announced that the Eighth AAF had finally received its first Mustang group. The 357th was infact the twelfth fighter group to be assigned to the Eighth, and they flew their first mission on 11 February.

The 4th needn't have worried for it also received Mustangs in February, and eager to put the new type through its paces, the group began pilot conversion onto type in the middle of flying 'Big Week' (20-25 February) sorties in their P-47s. With more than 50 P-51Bs on hand, the 'Eagles' were ready to fly their shakedown Mustang mission on the 26th. The weather decided otherwise, however, and the long-awaited day came on the 28th.

One hazard that an infinite number of P-51s could not overcome was Europe's notorious winter weather. Fog, mist and thick cloud often pinned aircraft to their hardstands when they should otherwise have been covering bombers. There was little point in launching on a mission if the weather prevented any hope of a rendezvous between the fighters and the 'heavies', even with the assistance of England's excellent system of radio direction. The toll of lost pilots wasted through either collision or the not inconsiderable hazard of becoming lost and running out of fuel, rose steadily during the winter months. It often happened, of course, that both bombers

After D-Day the USAAF circulated a directive indicating that full camouflage paint no longer needed to be worn by combat groups. The 357th FG preferred a top coat of green, however, and retained this modification to the standard polished metal through into 1945. This particular P-51B-10-NA was the first of four Mustangs used by the 357th's second top scoring ace, John B England, and contrary to other published works on the aces of the Eighth AAF, the aircraft actually wore the serial 42-106462 on its fin, not '463. England's most successful day in combat came on 27 November 1944 when he downed four aircraft whilst flying in a P-51D of the 362nd FS

Tactical camouflage was also widely used by the 361st FG, as perfectly illustrated here by P-51B-15 42-10692 of the 374th FS. This aircraft was the first Mustang assigned to Maj Wallace Hopkins, who finished the war with four aerial victories and four strafing kills. Unlike Hopkins' later P-51s, this machine isn't adorned with his famous sobriquet, *Ferocious Frankie*

Photographed in mid-1944 whilst still a squadron boss, Col Irwin Dregne took over command of the 357th FG on 14 January 1945. He finished the war with seven kills *(Olmsted via Bowman)*

Refuelling and an engine check for P-51B 42-106923 of the 364th FS/357th FG at Leiston, Suffolk, in July 1944. The barely readable 'nameplate' on the ground indicates the aircraft may have been nicknamed *Pistol Pete*. Few groups in Eighth AAF adorned their Mustangs with full wraparound invasion stripes as shown here, most restricting their application to the wings and fuselage beneath the 'star and bar'

and fighters took off in clear conditions, only to have the elements turn nasty en route to, or actually over, the target. In that case, the bombing would invariably lack a good concentration, leading to an inevitable return to the same target at a later date.

For the fighter pilots, more escort missions meant greater chances to rack up victories, and to perhaps achieve the minimum five kills to earn 'acedom'. Eighth AAF headquarters, whilst not exactly encouraging the cult of the fighter ace, nevertheless did little to prevent groups compiling tallies of their most successful pilots, believing that this fostered a healthy *espirit de corps* and inspired all pilots to try to emulate the high scorers.

'Acedom', however, remained an unofficial accomplishment, and provided that such enthusiasm for personal scoring did not compromise teamwork, group commanders had little choice but to concur. They did stress, however, that an escort group had to have its main task – the protection of the bombers – in mind at all times.

While this was something of a compromise in that individual pilots rightly believed that chasing away the enemy and shooting them down, even well away from the bomber stream, prevented that particular aircraft from rising to battle on a subsequent sortie, their charges could consequently remain unguarded for vital minutes. This problem was soon solved by the groups dividing their forces.

The relatively low level of activity during the closing weeks of 1943 had seen an influx of replacement bombers, so that by early 1944 Eighth AAF groups could be sent to a number of targets simultaneously. This confused and spread the defending German fighters and on occasion, gave the US escort a useful element of surprise.

On 14 January Capt Don Gentile of the 4th's 336th Squadron had shot down two Fw 190s to achieve ace status. A hazardous dogfight ensued when Gentile's P-47 was attacked by other Focke-Wulfs soon after shooting down his second kill, but he made it home. Afterwards, he viewed the experience as having been highly valuable. Having been on the receiving end of an attack by a pilot who was clearly a German *experten*, Gentile reckoned that he would find air combat that much easier in future! The law of averages had it that you couldn't always be up against the best *experten* in the *Jagdwaffe* all that often.

That said, air combat was not in any way guaranteed on every single sortie. There were days when the *Jagdwaffe* simply did not show at all, and pilots could quite easily fly a series of operations and hear about tussles with the Germans only by proxy. Overall though, January 1944 was an encouraging month for VIIIth Fighter Command, who claimed 172 enemy aircraft shot down for the loss of 65 of its own. However, bad weather had reduced the bomber offensive to only nine effective raids that same month.

## ON THE DECK

Following the avowed policy of attacking the Luftwaffe at every opportunity, VIIIth FC also introduced ace status for pilots who destroyed five or more enemy aircraft on the ground. This new concept received a mixed reception when it was announced on 8 February as ground strafing, while effective, was very hazardous. No other air force counted ground victories in this way, and it was to remain a controversial decision.

Command, however, knew that aerial kills could be elusive, particularly for average pilots. There were also periods when some units were just not in the right place at the right time, a situation that could cause a morale problem if pilots consistently failed to score on multiple missions. By encouraging ground strafing victories – and therefore aces – Bill Kepner knew that more enemy aircraft would be destroyed, which was, after all, the whole point of the exercise.

Kepner himself believed in the value of strafing, but realised that not all pilots had the skill to carry it out to maximum effect. He therefore urged group commanders to select their best crews to thoroughly learn the technicalities of ground attack work as an adjunct to regular escort operations.

By early March, VIIIth FC remained predominantly equipped with the P-47, although most groups were slated to receive Mustangs at the earliest opportunity. Standardisation of fighter and bomber types was a goal never achieved by the USAAF in England, but availability of more P-51s made the prospect of all groups flying this type much more possible than it had been in 1943. Similarly, a command preference for the B-17 over the B-24 began working through during 1944. Having all units fly one type of aircraft aided serviceability and reduced the number of spares that needed to be stocked – most parts had to be initially shipped in from the US. Establishment of base air depots in the UK, notably that at Burtonwood (county), eased reliance on the vagaries of North Atlantic convoys, and enabled many aircraft to be repaired in-theatre. New P-51s were usually shipped by sea as deck cargo on transports or escort carriers, a process that saw the aircraft 'cocooned' against the ravages of salt water and then thoroughly cleaned upon arrival in the UK.

The conversion of all groups to P-51s lay in the future and one unit, the 56th, resisted all attempts to part it from its beloved P-47s. As one of the original saviours of the Eighth, the 'Wolfpack' was allowed this indulgence. Not that 'Hub' Zemke's outfit was the only one to protest at the impending conversion. In particular the 364th and 479th FGs, which arrived in the ETO with P-38s during early 1944, howled loudly at the decision. However, most complaints were forgotten about once crews had experienced the superiority of the P-51 over the P-38 in combat.

Although not an ace in the true sense of the word, Capt Lee Eisenhart nevertheless flew a full tour of duty with the 339th FG's 505th FS from Fowlmere, in Cambridgeshire, during the height of the daylight bombing offensive in spring 1944. Looking pleased with life during a camera session at the East Anglia base, Eisenhart christened his P-51B (42-106833) *Bonny Bea* after his sweetheart back in America. He is wearing the standard summer flying rig of the day, with his parachute pack perched on the wing alongside him *(USAF)*

# NEW BLOOD

**A**s the Mustang had originally been ordered for service with the RAF, it was duly 'blooded' by the British first. Numerous tests were carried out by Rolls-Royce and the A&AEE (Aircraft & Armaments Experimental Establishment) at Boscombe Down to 'improve the breed', and a number of modifications were made to service machines. Early models fitted with the 'greenhouse' canopy came in for criticism as the high angle of the nose made ground manoeuvering quite demanding, and this was not improved by the multiple framing of the hood, which was manufactured in three sections. Other modifications were made to British aircraft, including the adoption of a new clear-view plexiglass canopy centre-section designed by a Sqn Ldr Robert Malcolm of the RAF, which virtually eliminated any visibility problems.

First tested at Boscombe Down in February 1944, and subsequently fitted to most RAF P-51Bs (Mustang IIIs), the Malcolm hood was extremely popular with pilots, and as the number of USAAF aircraft in the UK increased, there was widespread demand for it. Production in Britain remained modest, however, with many deliveries going not to the Eighth Air Force but the Ninth, who widely fitted the hood to their tactical P-51s. That left the Eighth's service depots scrambling to acquire stocks of Malcolm hoods unofficially, and although a number did work their way through to service units, and thence to operational fighter groups, there were never really enough to meet demand.

**Early P-51D-5s lacked the dorsal fin fillet, as 44-13573 of the 357th FG's 363rd FS clearly shows. Although this sub-type successfully flew numerous combat missions, fillets were sent to the UK by NAA for adoption as 'field modifications'. The dorsal appendage was designed to correct minor directional stability problems encountered with the P-51B. *Isabel III* wears two victory crosses under its windscreen (Via T R Bennett)**

In November 1943, as the Base Air Depots in the UK issued the first of a series of modifications and servicing requirements for the P-51B, NAA flew the prototype of a new Mustang model. On the 17th of that month a modified P-51B (43-12101), reconfigured as the XP-51D, made its first flight. This aircraft would eventually rectify or eliminate most of the drawbacks experienced with the early Merlin Mustangs.

## GUN POWER

In comparison with British practice, which as far as fighter armament was concerned tended to concentrate on two broad extremes of the rifle calibre (.303 in) machine gun (MG) and the shell-firing 20 mm cannon, American aircraft armament slotted admirably between the two. The

***Alice Marie II* also hailed from the 363rd FS, and was photographed in spring 1945 in one of the unit's rural-looking revetments that were specially built for the aircraft at Leiston, in Suffolk. This machine boasts a solid red rudder as applied to all 363rd FS P-51Ds in November 1944. The previous OD green scheme worn by most 357th FG Mustangs was removed in the autumn of 1944 when VIIIth FC realised that its groups were not going to France (Ethell)**

Colt-Browning .50 in MG became the standard US aircraft weapon (with all the advantages of commonality), and used in batteries of four or six in the P-51B and D respectively, it could deal effectively with virtually any adversary.

The weight of fire possible with such heavily-armed German aircraft as the Fw 190A-3 and Bf 109G, by comparison, was far higher than a battery of 'fifties', and when the Luftwaffe was able to fit the 30 mm MK 108 in their main fighter types, the long-suffering bomber crews faced one of the most devastating cannon ever used operationally. This gun was quite capable of destroying a fighter such as the P-51 with a single round if it hit the right spot.

The main drawback of such heavy calibre guns, however, was their weight, both in terms of the weapon itself and its ammunition. Similarly, only a limited amount of space was available to designers for the fitment of such large weapons, as a fighter's aerodynamics could be critically compromised by the sheer bulk of these guns. Whereas the P-51B carried a total of 1260 rounds for its quartet of MGs, the Fw 190A-3 typically carried 2520 rounds for its four 20 mm cannon and two MGs. However, despite boasting this fearsome firepower, the average German pilot using his 'main battery' of cannon on bombers consistently scored hits with only two per cent of rounds expended primarily because he fired from too far out.

Provided, therefore, that an American pilot closed with the German fighter to the average 300-400 yards, and his gunnery was up to the mark, the fact that the enemy had more firepower was not a great advantage. 'Get in close, then you can't miss', was a maxim that rarely failed.

Throughout the early months of 1944, deliveries of the P-51B to England increased, the priority being to eventually equip all the in-theatre fighter groups assigned to the Eighth Air Force, as well as and a number that were part of the new tactical Ninth Air Force. By the end of May 1944 VIIIth FC had its full complement of groups; the arrival of the 479th, the highest numbered fighter unit to be assigned, gave a

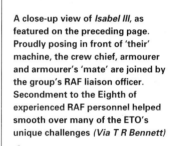

A close-up view of *Isabel III*, as featured on the preceding page. Proudly posing in front of 'their' machine, the crew chief, armourer and armourer's 'mate' are joined by the group's RAF liaison officer. Secondment to the Eighth of experienced RAF personnel helped smooth over many of the ETO's unique challenges *(Via T R Bennett)*

Lt Albert Hansen of the 339th FG strikes a pose in front of his personal P-51B, *Miss Priss* (44-13911). Like all Mustangs flying out of Fowlmere in the spring of 1944, this aircraft is adorned with high-visibility D-Day invasion stripes *(USAF)*

A pair of P-51D-5s assigned to the 4th FG's 335th FS are joined by an example from the 336th FS. All three Mustangs are equipped with the British-manufactured 108-gal 'paper' drop tanks

*Tika IV* of the 361st FG peels away from the camera-ship to give a clear view of the P-51D's lower surfaces, which despite constant attention by the groundcrew, were always streaked with oil and grime from operational flying at high altitude *(USAF)*

total of 15, plus the 354th, which would remain under its control for the time being. By then the 352nd at Bodney, the 355th at Steeple Morden, the 359th at East Wretham and the 361st at Bottisham had all switched to the P-51B. With the bomber force also strengthened, future prosecution of the air war over Europe without prohibitive losses was now a far sounder prospect than it had been just six months previously.

## RAF FIGHTER METHODS

When it came to England the Eighth Air Force 'borrowed' RAF Fighter Command techniques and procedures, with USAAF fighter groups flying operations similar in composition to those of their Allies – these early sorties thus retained their British codenames. In time, variations to these missions were introduced, with a few American appellations being added as certain types of fighter sweep were more or less unique to the Eighth Air Force. The most common sorties were codenamed *Ramrod*, *Circus*, *Jackpot* and *Rodeo*. VIIIth FC also adopted the RAF fighter pilot's standard tour of duty of 200 flight hours. Tailored to the short-range sweeps undertaken by most British units over western Europe, this yardstick had some drawbacks for the Americans as it often took four hours to complete an escort to Berlin – thus individual pilots soon became 'time-expired'.

The USAAF therefore raised the number of hours for one tour to 300, or 75 missions. Pilots could (and many duly did) volunteer for an extension, but the system meant that there was a constant rotation of fresh pilots coming into frontline squadrons. Given the choice between risking their necks further, or going home, many combat veterans naturally opted for the latter. Surprisingly perhaps, this did not work against the fighter force, but it did mean that relatively few American pilots, in common with all the Western Allied air arms, were able to achieve high air combat scores. Only ten pilots in fact shot down 20 or more enemy aircraft, and most of these did so only by flying extended tours.

Actually, there was little pressure for even the top combat pilots to stay. As the war progressed the Allies processed so many pilots through training schools in the US and the Commonwealth that there was never a shortage in the combat units. Theatre training and the regular practice of easing newcomers into the demands of the ETO by 'shakedown', shallow penetration missions on which the enemy was not expected to show in force, additionally helped make their transition as trouble-free as possible.

Not that this could ever quite quell the feeling of apprehension that a new pilot felt on his debut to combat. The ETO had an awesome reputation which preceeded it throughout the war. The Germans were the most formidable of foes, and triple ace Col Clarence 'Bud' Anderson aptly summed up how it felt to prepare for that first mission.

'My pulse was playing a Gene Krupa solo as I walked to my plane that morning and climbed into the cockpit. Once you were strapped in and sitting there, so very alone, waiting to fire up and taxy away and take-off in line, the minutes were soldiers crawling on their bellies in mud. I never was one to dwell on bad possibilities and would generally use this time to focus on the mission, thinking about what lay ahead, and preparing the way an athlete prepares for a game. But on 8 February 1944, I was a little less sophisticated about that sort of thing. I had logged 893 flying hours already, better than an hour and 20 minutes a day for two years. But only 30 hours and 45 minutes of that was in P-51s. I knew I had lots to learn. And what I was thinking about before prodding the Merlin to life was of not getting lost, not screwing up. I was more afraid of screwing up than of dying.'

Anderson's final remarks reflect the the fundamental attitude essential for any military force to operate efficiently, thus achieving an *espirit de corps* second to none. Nobody wanted to fail at his chosen contribution to the war effort, to let down his country, family and friends back home. When a man volunteered, he wanted to see the thing through. And by channelling a youthful confidence and the unquestionable excitement of flying a range of magnificent aircraft as part of the overall war effort, the US Army got its fighter pilots in abundance. For young men brought up in a machine-orientated age, the desire to fly in combat – and get paid for doing so – was an irresistable challenge.

Once assigned to one of the VIIIth FC groups a new pilot quickly realised he had joined a highly professional outfit. This special attachment to one's squadron extended to the groundcrews, who usually signed

The mount of 374th FS, 361st FG ace Wallace Hopkins was well photographed throughout mid to late 1944, usually carrying a pair of dummy 500 lb bombs, as in this case. Ordnance other than guns was used by Eighth Air Force Mustangs on an irregular, 'as required', basis, as generally there were more than enough Ninth Air Force tactical fighter bombers on hand. Hopkins shot down six aircraft during his 76-sortie tour, with this P-51D (44-13704), nicknamed *Ferocious Frankie* like his previous B-model, being his personal mount from June 1944 onwards *(USAF)*

The first of 364th FS ace Richard Peterson's P-51Ds, 44-13586 shows 14 of his 15.5 kills and, like his second Mustang (44-14868), is christened with the phrase his wife used to sign her letters. Born in Alexandra, Minnesota, Peterson scored almost all of his kills between September 1944 and April 1945 *(via J Ethell)*

Lt Col Andrew Evans Jr poses for a propaganda shot in full long-range escort kit in a P-51D of his parent unit, the 357th FG, at Leiston, in Suffolk. A seasoned combat veteran, he finished the war with six kills *(M Olmsted via M Bowman)*

up for the duration and were not subject to set tours of duty like the pilots. Unit pride was reflected in a variety of ways, including paintwork. When VIIIth FC introduced highly visible group colours for squadrons in 1944, it was for the practical purpose of aerial recognition both by fighters of the same unit and bomber crews. Additionally, the well-decorated Mustangs were in a way the equivalent of the pilots' personal transport back home, and similarities did not end there. A buffed-up automobile lasted longer, and a polished P-51 had the more practical bonus of adding a few knots of speed, which often made the difference between life and death in mortal combat over occupied Europe.

Personal embellishment of fighters was tolerated, if not officially condoned. Most commanders realised that aircraft decorated with German flags to represent victories bred a fine competitive spirit, particularly among the groundcrews who would boast that 'their' ace pilot was numbered with the best in the entire squadron or group. They would proudly show off the kills which were just as much a tribute to their hard work as the fighting spirit of the pilot in question. Congressmen and other 'top brass' who visited the bases were also impressed by such markings, although the more risque examples of aircraft art would be prudently hangared to spare anyone's blushes. War correspondents liked nothing better than to photograph and film pilots in cockpits framed by a row of swastikas, for there were few better ways to show how Americans were contributing to the war effort in Europe.

Groundcrew, rather than pilots, decorated the aircraft usually during stand-downs or maintenance periods, and on certain bases there were individuals whose artistic talents were so much in demand that they were employed on an almost full-time basis dealing with requests. A more practical use of paint, outside of tactical markings, was to apply the names – the pilot, crew chief and armourer – of those associated with a particular machine on a daily basis.

Evans Jr commanded the 362nd FS from late 1944 onwards, his own personal P-51D (44-64851) being christened *Little Sweetie 4*. As can be clearly seen, its pilot's combined scoreboard of air and ground kills is proudly displayed beneath the cockpit. The 357th FG was the first P-51 outfit assigned to the Eighth, and it duly scored more aerial kills than any other Mustang unit in the ETO – its 609 victories placed it second overall only to the 56th's Thunderbolt squadrons, who claimed 674 *(M Olmsted via Bowman)*

When VIIIth FC began adding ground strafing to the fighter groups' repertoire, there were some unexpected challenges; the Luftwaffe had long since pulled the bulk of its fighter force back into Germany to stay largely outside the range of the P-47, whilst conversely strengthening flak defences to deal with bombers over occupied France. Also, it was one thing for the command to draw up a plan to strafe German airfields, but quite another to locate them all; RAF maps were used to plot those that were known, but group commanders stressed that pilots would have to be prepared to find, and possibly to fight, their way home individually after attacking them. Navigation over hostile territory, with a sea crossing before landfall in England, was quite a challenge, and an aspect of combat that had not been over-stressed in training.

It also took time to perfect the technique of ground strafing if parked aircraft, installations and vehicles were to be destroyed, rather than merely receiving a few repairable holes. This was not an easily acquired skill as most groups had been trained to perform high altitude flying, not ground attack. And while all German airfields were defended by AA installations, at that stage of the war the most forward ones were not exactly crammed with fighters.

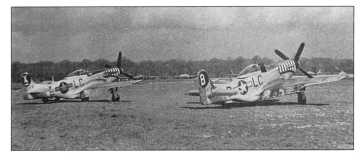

Therefore, pilots duly found themselves taking a steadily rising toll of bombers, transports and liaison aircraft, not the all important fighters; it was true that Kepner's idea was to deny the Luftwaffe aircraft of any kind, but a lack of quality interceptor targets on the ground meant that the P-51 groups now performing bomber escort missions were still opposed by strong enemy fighter formations. However, the Mustang's range meant that pilots were now quite capable of taking on the *Jagdwaffe* 'in its own back yard', as some of the early missions were to show.

A number of German fighters were definitely being destroyed on the ground, although again it wasn't realised that the enemy would continue to produce aircraft at an ever-increasing rate, irrespective of the bombs dropped on industrial plants. Of equal, if not greater importance was that the Allied pilots occasionally got amongst German training aircraft and shot the hapless *Jagdflieger* of tomorrow down with ease.

As time went by an extremely accurate picture of Luftwaffe airfield util-

One of the first units assigned to VIIIth FC back in August 1943, the 20th FG had persevered with the P-38 right through until the arrival of P-51Cs in July 1944. These 77th FS Mustangs were photographed on the dispersal at the eastern end of their base at Kingscliffe, in Northamptonshire, soon after the group picked up P-51Ds in the late summer of 1944 *(Ethell)*

Fine formation flying for the camera by a quartet of 362nd FS, 357th FG Mustangs led by Capt Harvey Mace at the controls of *Sweet Helen*, alias 44-13558/G4-B. The second P-51 in the line up (nicknamed *Wee Willy*) wears four kill markings

CHAPTER TWO

isation was built up, but as with any highly mobile force, the Germans could switch bases rapidly, and a constant watch had to be maintained by photo reconnaissance. It was in this area too that *Ultra* intercepts were so valuable to Eighth AAF commanders, for German unit movements inevitably created a considerable degree of radio traffic before and during the transfer. With this intelligence in hand it became relatively easy for the Allies to plot where units were stationed, and which aircraft they flew.

Strafing soon began taking its toll on the Mustang force though, fighters often being downed by only a few well-placed rounds, particulaly if the Merlin's coolant system was hit. Capt Duane Beeson, an early P-51B ace with the 4th FG's 336th FS, was hit by flak and shot down on 5 April during a strafing run across an aerodrome west of Brandenburg – he spent the rest of the war as a POW.

## GENTILE FAREWELL

Another major loss for the Eighth barely a week later was Capt Don Gentile, although he was not claimed by the Germans, rather the US rotational system for pilots. April 13 1944 was a day of mixed emotions for both Gentile and his CO, Lt Col Don Blakeslee. The former had won the first 'Ace Race' by beating the legendary Eddie Rickenbacker's Great War score of 26 kills (6 of Gentile's 27.83 victories were strafing kills, however), and a huge throng of local and US media representatives gathered at Debden to meet the Eighth's then leading ace following his last sortie.

Upon his return to the Essex base, Gentile buzzed the field in time-honoured fashion, the well-decorated *Shangri-La* 'pouring on the coals' and giving the assembled crowd a real thrill. But Gentile's last low pass was a little too low, and the red-nosed Mustang scraped the ground with its radiator as it shot past the press. Fighting for control, Gentile managed to belly land the P-51B and walk away virtually unscathed – the aircraft, however, was totalled. Blakeslee had earlier said that if anyone in his group wrote off an aircraft through mis-adventure they would be immediately transferred home. Time-expired in any case, Gentile was duly despatched back to America.

Two days later, a full-scale *Jackpot* mission netted a record bag for VIIIth FC. Fifty-eight victories were claimed (18 in the air and 40

The 353rd FG at Raydon, in Suffolk, flew yellow and black chequer-nosed P-51Ds in combat from November 1944, the unit having been previously equipped with P-47s. *Stasia II* (44-15587) was part of the 352nd FS and was regularly flown by Capt A R Rosatone

Lt Leroy Pletz brings *Donna-Mite* (44-11624) of the 353rd FG's 352nd FS home to Raydon in early 1945. His mount is a relatively rare Dallas-built P-51K, fitted with the none-too-successful Aeroproducts propeller in place of the Hamilton-Standard device found on most Mustangs. The new prop was built primarily because Hamilton-Standard could not keep up with demand, and although it incorporated several new innovations, it suffered from excessive blade imbalance

George Vanden Heuval, a 5.5 victory ace with the 361st FG, flew P-51D *Mary Mine* with the 376th FS. This photograph was taken in March 1945 at a very muddy Chievres when the group transferred to Belgium for a spell of duty under Ninth Air Force control

Aircraft damage from flak (as here) and all other causes was methodically photographed by the USAAF for accounting purposes during the war. This picture shows the tail of P-51D 44-142541 of the 364th FG, which got home on 24 October 1944 despite reduced rudder control. Markings on the trim tab are believed to have denoted a P-51 of a flight leader *(USAF)*

on the ground) as fighters hit airfields in France and the Low Countries.

Bomber escort was resumed on 18 April, a day that took the 4th to Berlin. Nobody ever thought of the 'Big B' as a milk run, and on this sortie the Luftwaffe showed just why. Maj George Carpenter, a 335th FS ace with 11.3 kills already to his credit, waded into a mixed force of Bf 109s and Fw 190s. He quickly despatched two fighters before being badly hit by a well-handled Bf 109G, several cannon strikes wrecking his engine. Carpenter rapidly lost height in his smoking Mustang, and although he managed to shake off his initial assailant, the American was soon finished off by a lone Fw 190 – he 'took to the silk' just as the Merlin was on the point of bursting into flames. The 4th also lost Lt Lloyd Henry and ace Capt Vic France on the this sortie, the latter being killed when he hit the ground whilst attacking Fw 190s in the circuit at Genthin airfield.

But the following day the 4th's fortunes changed marginally for the better. Sharing bomber escort duties to Kassel with the 352nd, 355th and 357th FGs, the 'Eagles' downed five – this score was equalled by the 357th, whilst the 355th came home with three, as did the Bodney outfit. Two of the 352nd's kills were claimed by the Group's eventual third ranking ace, 1st Lt John Thornell. One major loss during this mission, however, was that of 4th FG double-ace Capt Charles Anderson, who had been shot down in the melée of combat that had included a good few rounds aimed in error at Mustangs by the B-17 gunners.

The 357th FG, whose pilots became 'top dogs' amongst the Eighth's Mustang groups in terms of aerial victories, had a good 24 April. Shepherding the bombers during the 'target support' phase of the operation, the 355th and 375th (the former also building an enviable reputation for its prowess in ground strafing) destroyed 42 enemy fighters between them. The Luftwafe's folly of sending twin-engined aircraft after the bombers was dramatically highlighted when seven were shot down by the 357th. This was yet another occasion when the enemy persisted in peforming their split-S and power dive manoeuvre in order to escape from the P-51s, but which often led directly to their demise due to the latter's speed advantage. American pilots easily kept apace with the fleeing enemy, picking them off at will as soon as they levelled out of their dives literally feet above the ground.

At this height the P-51B could usually overhaul either of the German single-seaters, often with terminal results. By simply out-flying their opponents, Allied pilots drove their quarry literally into the ground. At zero feet there was no margin for error, with all sorts of obstacles to avoid, and the *Jagdflieger*, who were by now showing distinct signs of inexperience, often failed to see trees, rising ground or buildings in their path.

Following an enemy aircraft down and away from the bombers could,

205

however, give Allied pilots problems of their own, as the rest of the formation would simply disappear when, intent on the chase, the charging fighters would shoot off in pursuit of the enemy. Often a rejoin could be affected, although numerous pilots simply high-tailed it home alone.

In combat great store was put on the leader-wingman team, and the aces would be the first to acknowledge that mutual support was vital to scoring kills, as without a 'second pair of eyes', pilots, no matter how good they were, risked being bounced by marauding Fw 190s or Bf 109s.

A solitary kill adorns the canopy bar of P-51D 44-13777 *Rough and Ready* of the 357th FS, 355th FG at Steeple Morden, in Cambridgeshire. This aircraft was flown by a number of different pilots within the squadron from late 1944 *(H Holmes)*

The old 'one-two' punch was practised to great effect throughout the Eighth's tenure in the UK, with one of the first such fighter teams to come to the public's attention consisting of Don Gentile and John Godfrey.

The former was honest enough to express a feeling held by most pilots fresh to the ETO – that by being sent to tackle the *Jagdwaffe*, they were being pitted against 'supermen' who knew all the angles when it came to air combat. Although Gentile soon learnt that this was not totally true, few pilots denegrated the enemy once he had been met in combat.

Godfrey, commenting on Gentile's technique, said, 'It's his aggressiveness. He's got a split-second jump on any other fighter I ever saw. Your ordinary good flier sees a flock of Huns below him – and he counts them. Gentile sees a flock and he's after them in the same instant. He'll hit the one he can get to quickest. Reflexes, I guess. When it comes to the pinch, he's got a little something extra.'

An effective fighter escort relied on a reasonably integral formation to be flown by the bombers, who in turn relied on a good assembly over

The 355th started flying P-51s from Steeple Morden in March 1944, having earlier cut their teeth on the P-47. Duran M Vickery Jr flew 44-14910, christened *Bama Bound*, this machine also wearing the name of his future wife *Ann-Anita*. As with most decorated P-51s, these terms of endearment were carried on the port nose region of his Mustang *(Vickery)*

John F Tulloch Jr flew this strikingly-marked P-51D, nicknamed *JAKE THE SNAKE*, with the 358th FS, 355 FG from Steeple Morden in the spring of 1945. It bears not only his personal insignia, but also four kill markings on the canopy bar, and like many pilots of the time, Tulloch Jr has fitted two external rear-vision mirrors to the canopy rail of his Mustang

England. When this went awry, the fighters had the devil's own job to protect hundreds of B-17s or B-24s strung out across miles of sky. Such a shambolic assembly happened on the 29 April Berlin mission, which was compounded by a navigational error that saw the bombers spaced out as much as 40 miles away from their briefed position.

This total chaos resulted in 17 Fortresses being lost in-bound to the target due to the spread out bomber stream, whilst a further 38 B-17s and 25 B-24s were shot down as a result of the *Jagdwaffe*'s attention over and around the German capital itself. Powerless to intervene in this carnage, US fighters downed a mere 14 aircraft in a series of small-scale actions.

By going all out for the Luftwaffe in April the groups had netted positive results – an estimated 825 aircraft had been shot down, with a further 493 destroyed in on the ground. P-51Bs had claimed three-quarters of the victories, but this effort had cost 163 aircraft, including 67 Mustangs. Although it was expected that strafing kills would be achieved at a higher cost, April's figures showed that three P-51s had been lost per 100 sorties against airfields, and just one for every 100 escort missions flown.

Most significantly, the Luftwaffe had lost 489 pilots in April, with only 396 replacements joining the frontline *Gruppen*. The American offensive had also prompted the denuding of other fronts to boost Reich defence, a situation that would only get worse in the coming months.

As the year progressed, and the D-Day landings drew ever nearer, fighters of the Eighth participated in a wholesale laying waste of tactical targets in France. Whilst all this was taking place, more groups were converting to the P-51B, among them the 339th FG at Fowlmere, and they soon went on the offensive over Europe. Many of these missions went unchallenged, as the *Jagdwaffe* was marshalling its force for the defence against the bombers. For example, on 8 May an enormous air battle developed over Brunswick and Berlin, that day's dual bomber targets, and over 200 German fighters were observed.

Over Dutch territory the *Jagdflieger* made head-on passes at the 'heavies', but the 359th shot down 11 of them. Upon reaching the target areas, the 352nd made contact with about 150 fighters just as they rendezvoused with the bomber force. There was a heavy undercast over Germany that day which tended to favour the Luftwaffe, and the P-51s chased a number of enemy fighters into cloud, only to quckly lose contact with their foe. Lt Col John Meyer, CO of the 352nd's 487th FS, and one of the Eighth's most successful pilots, experienced this frustration before sighting a plum target – a section of Fw 190s still carrying their centreline tanks. Meyer, and his wingman, Capt Hamilton, joined up and bounced them, the former quickly despatching a Fw 190.

However, as Meyer climbed away, he spotted several fighters lining up astern of Hamilton. He quickly pushed the nose of his P-51B down and closed on the tail-end fighter, whose pilot duly bailed out without Meyer firing a single shot! Gaining altitude once again, Meyer and Hamilton were joined by the 328th FS's ranking ace, John Thornell, who arrived just in time to engage a gaggle of Bf 109s.

The fighetrs dived away from the P-51s through a hole in the clouds, pursuued by a stream of .50 calibre bullets from Thornell's guns. One of the Bf 109s blew up, whilst the other pair broke wildly, with Thornell and Meyer on their tails – both were swiftly shot down. This same mission also saw Lt Carl Luksic of the 352nd FG become the Eighth's first 'ace in a day'

John Tulloch Jr poses with his highly imaginative personal emblem of a Messerschmitt-strangling serpent name JAKE! He flew 44-14163 exclusively throughout his tour from Steeple Morden. This marvellous album snap shot also provides excellent detail of the standard fighter pilot rig in the last year of the war

On 13 May the 355th FG got amongst the Me 410s of ZG 26, inflicting heavy casualties. Lt Col Gerald Dix, and his wingman, watched two of the enemy fighters collide before shooting down a further pair – the group ended the day with six Me 410s to its credit. The 357th also tangled with the twin-engined fighters and claimed three.

In the run up to D-Day many groups were temporarily assigned to full-time strafing duties, performing *Chattanooga* strikes against German and French locomotives. The 339th, however, continued to undertake escort work, and on one sortie in May 1944 came across a formation of 17 enemy aircraft. The Group downed 13 in several minutes, with Lt Chris 'Bull' Handleman of the 505th FS putting himself in the record books by becoming the first teenage ace in the Eighth Air Force – he was just 19.

On 24 May the 4th's Lt Ralph 'Kidd' Hofer, one of the more colourful characters in the group, shot down two more enemy aircraft for his 13th and 14th kills to date. Two days later the Eighth's last assigned fighter group flew its first mission with the P-38, VIIIth FC thereby achieving one of its primary goals of having all 15 groups in combat before D-Day.

Oil was now a priority target for the bomber force, and these missions became notorious for the hot reception Allied crews could expect both from flak and fighters. Politz, the target on 29 May, was among the worst. Flying escort on this mission was the 359th FG, who took on some 40 Fw 190s, and among the victors that day was the Group's ranking ace, Lt Ray Wetmore of the 370th FS. Also satisfied with the day's hunting were pilots of the 361st FG. Nicknamed the 'Yellow Jackets', they had repeatedly tackled dozens of single and twin-engined fighters that had attempted to charge through the Liberator formations – they ended the sortie with 12 kills.

Remarkably few aces of the Eighth were killed in combat, but there were exceptions. On 30 May a huge force was out over a variety of

German targets, and the 357th did particularly well, claiming 17 enemy fighters in a swirling air battle that ranged from 30,000 ft down to tree-top level as the *Jagdwaffe* made their attacking runs and dived away.

However, among the US casualties was Capt Fletcher Adams, one of the Group's first aces whose score then stood at 9.5 kills. Heading home, Adams' flight of four combat-weary P-51s was bounced out of the sun by a *schwarme* of Bf 109Gs, and he was fatally hit on their first pass. Despite losing their formation leader, the remaining Mustang pilots reacted quickly and downed all four of their antagonists.

An extremely youthful looking 2nd Lt Arthur C Cundy of the 352nd FS, 353rd FG uses fighter pilot 'hand talk' to tell how it was to his fellow aviators in a beautifully posed propaganda shot taken in late 1944. Cundy's final score was six kills, and they were all shot down with this aircraft, P-51D 44-15092/SX-B. The location for this squadron portrait was Eye, in Suffolk, home to the B-17s of the 490th BG. The actual reason for this seemingly high-spirited visit by the 352nd FS to the bomber base remains unknown

Col Glenn Duncan with the P-51D he flew only briefly upon his return to the helm of the 353rd FG in April 1945, following a long spell with the Dutch Resistance! All his 19.50 kills were achieved in P-47s prior to him being shot down on 1 July 1944., The Mustang he flew whilst serving as group commander in April/May 1945 was 44-73060/LH-X. The badge on the nose of his aircraft was a personal decoration, not one based on a squadron insignia – his previous P-47s had also worn it

# A WILDER PONY

**G**en Dwight D Eisenhower's pre-D-Day message to the troops that the 'Planes overhead will be ours' was no empty boast. By the time 6 June dawned, the Allied air forces had indeed made the coast of France so dangerous for the *Jagdwaffe* that the Supreme Commander could confidently predict that little interference would come from that quarter.

The air umbrella for *Operation Overlord* was indeed overwhelming, and the Eighth's fighter force formed an integral part of the detailed plan worked out to ensure that Allied fighters would be over the fleet in continual relays as the troops stormed the Normandy beaches. As they did so, P-38s, chosen because their silhouette was amongst the most distinctive in the Allied air arsenal and therefore the least likely to be fired on by trigger-happy naval gunners, began the fighter patrols. Over the actual invasion area there was little for them to do, and many pilots felt more than a little frustrated to say the least, particularly when news of the wholesale carnage of US troops on *Omaha* and *Utah* beaches was relayed back to VIIIth FC bases in England.

The Luftwaffe did eventually put in an appearance in small numbers during the afternoon of 6 June, with the 4th FG shooting down an Fw 190 after a hairy incident over an aerodrome flak trap, and the 355th later ran into ten very surprised Ju 87s. Led by Lt Col Gerald Dix, the group dived down onto the Stukas, whose panic-struck crews hastily sought the sanctuary of any flat ground in the vicinity and attempted to land. Eight were quickly destroyed by the P-51 pilots, who then resumed their patrol.

Stukas also stumbled across the 357th FG later that day, and another seven were shot down, elements of the 339th putting in an opportune

An impromptu ceremony around appropriately named and decorated 505th FS P-51D, 44-15315, to honour a favoured WAC. The lady in question cut the ribbon around the 339th FG Mustang's nose, before accepting a bouquet from the assembled air- and groundcrews on an overcast day in the autumn of 1944. Unfortunately we don't know who she was, who flew this P-51, or what ID letter it wore, aside from the 505th's standard '5Q' combination *(USAF)*

Some groups 'made up the numbers' on missions by flying mixed P-51B and D formations, particularly during the transitionary phase between models during the 'D-Day summer' of 1944. Exhibiting all three major derivatives of the Merlin Mustang in one formation, these P-51s are again 339th FG machines, although this time they hail from the 503rd FS

appearance during the same interception and claiming two for their trouble. Part of the reason for the Luftwaffe's desultory reaction in Normandy was the widely-held belief (particularly by Hitler) that the invasion would really take place in the Pas de Calais. Only gradually was it confirmed that this was indeed the main invasion force, and not a diversion on the part of the Allies. Once this was realised, German air activity gradually began to increase, although the Luftwaffe was never in a position to prevent the troops getting off the beaches. Ground attack missions made up the lion's share of the sorties performed by the US fighter groups on D-Day, and there were inevitable losses to flak – in a total of 1873 sorties flown by VIIIth FC, 26 enemy aircraft were claimed for 26 fighters downed.

By 8 June the Luftwaffe had moved fighters into French airfields in range of the invasion forces. A number of air battles that day saw upwards of 100 enemy fighters facing many times that number of Allied aircraft of all types. The 339th scored heavily, claiming 11 out of a total of 31.

Lt Archie Tower of the 505th FS was leading an early-morning dive-bombng mission when one of the pilots in his section spotted a gaggle of Fw 190s above them. Tower immediately engaged them and picked off the first fighter with a 60-degree deflection shot. It was still pretty dark and the American pilots, having scattered the Fw 190s, went down to low-level to investigate lights on an enemy airfield. Greeted by a heavy flak barrage, Tower and his wingman hit the deck and high-tailed it for home, but not before they shared in the destruction of a Do 217 bomber.

By June 1944, four groups – the 4th, 339th, 352nd and 361st – had taken delivery of the first P-51Ds to equip the Eighth. These groups initially flew a handful of missions with mixed formations consisting of both models, although the P-51Bs were soon replaced when more D-models arrived. By July six groups – the 20th, 55th, 355th, 357th, 359th and

One of the last groups in the Eighth to transition onto the P-51, the 55th FG were also amongst the most colourful of Mustang operators. The 343rd FS, in particular, came up with this slick way to combine tactical camouflage and the natural metal finish then coming into vogue. For a time, all squadron aircraft sported 'half and half' paintwork, trimmed with the group's prancing mustang insignia on either the fin or rudder. *Miss Marilyn II* was the regular mount of Robert Welch, a six-victory ace who scored four of his kills during the fall of 1944. He had yet to open his account, however, when this photograph was taken by a squadron mate as they cruised over the parched farmland of Essex during a training flight from their Wormingford base in August 1944

364th – had the P-51D. It would be another three months, however, before the 479th became the next group to make the change-over in September, with the 353rd in October, the 356th in November and the 78th in December. The last three groups did not recieve the P-51B but went straight from the P-47 to the P-51D.

D-Day, and all the missions flown in its immediate wake, were handled by the P-51B, along with P-47s and P-38s, and all of them proved more than capable of clearing a path for the advancing ground troops. As the Allies attempted to secure their foothold in France, so more and more ground attack sorties were requested, thus increasing the number of strafing missions flown by each group. Luckily, more than enough Mustangs and pilots were available to cope with the demand, and units began regularly flying formations split into 'A' and 'B' flights to handle both the strafing and bomber escort tasks on the same sortie, although the latter remained the primary role of the P-51 groups.

Transition to the Mustang was not always trouble free, particularly for those pilots hwo had grown used to the larger and heavier P-38. The 55th FG made the switch without too many traumas, helped by the VIIIth FC policy of seconding an experienced theatre commander to smooth the process. Nevertheless, the torqueless P-38 was a complete contrast to the the P-51, and unfamiliarity with the latter's external tanks, and its inherently unstable flight characteristics with them full soon after take-off, nearly spelled disaster for some pilots, as observed by Maj Ed Giller.

'Our first combat mission as a squadron flying P-51s with full internal and external tanks was a bit of a mess. On climbing out from the base in full squadron formation at 800 ft, the unit in front of us had just pulled up into the lower cloud deck at 1000 ft, when out of the bottom of the cloud came a spinning P-51. By some miracle the pilot dropped his wing tanks and success-

**Although photographed at roughly the same time as squadron mate Welch's P-51D, Ed Giller's *The Millie G* (one of four he flew!) exhibits subtle differences in unit markings, like the barely discernible prancing horse on the rudder, and the thicker borderline between the OD and natural metal. This machine became quite famous years after the war when a profile artist working for a highly respected British aviation journal depicted its camouflaged area as having been painted bright red! It was, of course, OD, the dark shade serving to obliterate the P-51D's serial number, 44-14985. Visible beneath the canopy bar are two small victory crosses (Giller)**

**Stern view of *The Millie G* during one of the many PR flights flown by Ed Giller for official purposes in the late summer of 1944. Why this particular P-51 was chosen for these sorties is unknown, but it could perhaps have had something to do with its overall pristine condition**

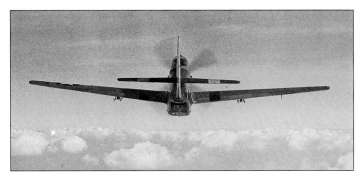

In common with several other groups, the 55th did not always repaint the tail serial numbers when squadron colours were applied. *Cherry*, flown by R Gibbs of the 343rd FS, was credited with downing five enemy aircraft. Its rudder is a solid shade of yellow, the unit's traditional colour, and like *Lady Val* below, it bears no trace of the once stylish OD rear fuselage common amongst 343rd FS Mustangs only a few months before. This photograph was taken in the winter of 1945

One of the four original P-38 Lightning groups within the Eighth, the 55th FG received Mustangs in July 1944. *Lady Val* was part of the much photographed 343rd FS, and it wears the familiar prancing stallion as an additional identification marking. The shade of yellow used on the rudder appears to be much darker than that worn by *Cherry* (see above), however, and the OD anti-glare panel has also been extended around the cockpit itself

fully pulled out of his dive at about 50 ft – his Mustang was left with a permanently bent fuselage, and in a weak radio voice he announced that he was aborting. I'll never know how he made the recovery.'

The 55th nevertheless carried on, although some of the pilots had been shaken by the incident. At 25,000 ft a tight 360-degree turn was called and at least half a dozen pilots spun out. All of them had the presence of mind to jettison their tanks, and each recovered some distance below. It was just as well that the ex-P-38 pilots came to realise one of the foibles of the P-51D early on.

## FROM ENGLAND TO RUSSIA

On 26 June 1944 the Eighth laid on the first of the *Frantic* missions, which was for all intents and purposes a *Ramrod Shuttle*, with its final destination being Russia. An edgy Don Blakeslee took the lead of this first flight, his cockpit stuffed full of maps. He was fully aware at the start of this very important mission how big a responsibility rested on his broad shoulders. Aside from the 45 P-51s of his own group, Blakeslee also had a further 16 from the 352nd to help fly 'shotgun' for the three wings of Fortresses that the fighters would accompany non-stop to the Russia. He could not afford to waste fuel in combat over Germany, and was grateful that the *Jagdwaffe* all but passed up this mighty armada as it ran into its target of Ruhland. The Mustangs traded shots with a mere handful of enemy fighters, but did not chase after the fleeing Germans as they would have normally done – two enemy fighters were shot down nevertheless.

Blakeslee ploughed on. 'Kidd' Hofer, ever the individualist, flagrantly disobeyed his CO's orders and chased a fighter to the deck; he failed to rejoin. With 580 miles covered, the pilots were jubilant to see Piryatin below them, and they all landed without incident. They would be the

213

guests of the Russians for four day before returning home, via Italy. As it transpired, they would be escorting far fewer B-17s than they'd come with as the enemy carried out a very accurate night strike on their base at Poltava, destroying 43 'heavies'. Fortunately, the fighters' temporary home at nearby Piryatin was not touched.

On 26 June Blakeslee led a Penetration Target Withdrawal Support from Russia to Drohobycz, in Poland, and the fighters then headed south for Lucera, in Italy. Hofer, who had single-handedly navigated his aircraft to Kiev only to find he had been posted as MIA, now rejoined the flock, but a problem with his P-51B kept him, and three other 4th FG pilots in his flight, on Russian soil for a time.

Bidding farewell to their charges over the coast of Yugoslavia, the main formation of fighters peeled off to fly across the Adriatic and land at Lesina, Madna and San Severo. There they were hosted by members of the 325th FG, the famed 'Checkertails' of the Fifteenth Air Force, who were also equipped with Mustangs. The four P-51s that had had to turn back into Russia now attempted to join the party, but only one made it to Sicily, where he crash-landed on the beach – the other two landed at the sprawling Italian mainland airfield at Foggia. That only left the 'Kidd' who, true to form, ignored orders, went after a gaggle of Bf 109s and then ran low on fuel near his destination. Luckily for him he was intercepted by Spitfires and guided safely to Malta. The next day he flew onto Foggia, via Catania, just in time to rejoin his group for their next sortie.

Blakeslee had organised a com-

*Dolly* was part of the 505th FS, 339th FG, the P-51 also wearing the name *Happy IV* in a small black rectangle below the port exhaust stubs. It was the personal mount of the Group's last wartime CO, Lt Col William C Clark, who assumed command of the 339th on 14 April 1945. This P-51D ended the war wearing 11 kills beneath its cockpit, all but one of which denoted a strafing victory. In fact Clark was credited with no less than six kills in one sortie two days after taking the helm. This tranquil scene was photographed during the Easter service at Fowlmere in 1945

Robert Buttke, a two-tour veteran of the 55th FG, scored 5.5 kills flying 44-15025, christened *Lovenia (Ethell)*

bined fighter sweep from Italy, in company with the 352nd and 325th FGs, to the Budapest area, where they found around 80 Bf 109s. The P-51s had stirred up a hornet's nest, and a series of vicious combats followed which resulted in four 4th FG aircraft being rapidly shot down. Deacon Hively, one of the Group's leading aces, was wounded early on in the dogfight, but still destroyed three fighters, whilst his wingman, Grover Siems, was jumped and hit by a burst of fire that straddled his cockpit. He too sutained painful wounds, but was able to shoot a Bf 109 off Hively's tail. It was, however, the end of the 'Deacon's' war, as he was soon rotated home. Of the quartet from the 4th who were shot down, two became PoWs and two were killed – the seemingly indestructable Hofer was one of the latter, crashing fatally at Mostar, in Yugoslavia. The 4th would never be the same again without the antics of the 'Kidd' from Missouri.

Whilst the P-51D could do most things outstandingly well, one feature that NAA had not considered was its ability to perform as an impromptu frontline rescue aircraft. Due to its generous cockpit space, it could accommodate two men in an emergency marginally better than the P-51B, and on more than one occasion a pilot was eternally grateful for this unexpected bonus. It was still a tight squeeze, however, and not a recommended practice, despite the fact that pilots were successfully rescued.

A black and white 'piano keyboard' nose marking was chosen for the 20th FG's Mustangs. Photographed at Kingscliffe relaxing between sorties in the autumn of 1944 is third ranking ace of the Group, Harley L Brown, who joined the 55th FS upon his arrival in the ETO in August 1944. At that time, the 20th FG was just transitioning from P-51Cs to Ds, and Brown soon came to grips with the type. Returning home in March 1945 having scored six kills, his most successful sortie was flown on 2 November 1944 when he claimed two Fw 190s and a single Bf 109

One such rescue was performed in Germany on 18 August when 355th FG ace Lt Royce Priest heard a plaintive R/T transmission.

'My plane's been hit by flak. I'm gonna belly it in.'

It was Capt Bert Marshall Jr, a fellow ace from the 355th. Priest acted quickly.

'Land in a road, coach. I'll land and pick you up.'

Howls of protest came over the R/T. Such action could mean two P-51s lost to the group. But Priest was adamant. Marshall failed to find a road and his P-51D was now lying in a field. The earth looked too soft to take-off in a heavily laden Mustang, so Priest picked a field of corn stubble about three quarters of a mile off. He side-slipped his big fighter in, cutting the throttle just above stalling speed. Coming to a stop with room to spare, Priest hauled his P-51 around and taxied it back along the path he had earlier made when he landed – he had now made for himself a temporary runway. Marshall, meanwhile, was setting a less than Olympic pace towards his rescuer.

'It was tough going. I wasn't in shape for that kind of stuff. I got pooped out. Every now and then I had to slow down to a fast walk. And I got kind of mad because I remembered that I only had two American cigarettes, and I didn't like the idea of sticking around in France with only two American cigarettes.'

Priest obligingly eased the Mustang across the rough and Marshall clambered aboard, accompanied by a stream of profanities which only

When viewed from the starboard side many P-51s looked very 'government issue', this being because personal markings were most commonly painted on the port side from which, in true equestrian tradition, the pilot climbed aboard. This 'dorsal finless' Mustang was amongst the first batch of P-51Ds supplied to the 4th FG soon after D-Day. Its 'QP-F' code denotes that it belonged to the 334th FS at Debden

ended when Priest stood up in his cockpit, threw his parachute out and said 'Get in!'. He then sat in Marshall's lap, 'gunned' the engine and taxied back to his home-made runway. The overweight P-51 eventually unstuck and barely cleared a haystack at the end of the field. Back at Steeple Morden, the tower was informed that there were two pilots aboard the aircraft, and clearance was given for a straight in approach and landing. A routine recovery ensued, and two very happy pilots duly climbed out of the cockpit.

## SIGHTING THE GUNS

An optical sight was fitted to the P-51B and early D-models, this device incorporating lenses and reflectors that put a 'bull's eye' ring and dot on a slanted glass panel set above the sight housing, and in front of the bullet-proof glass windscreen that was a reassuring 12 inches thick. Fine manufacturing tolerances ensured that the pilot wasn't hampered by distortion whilst using the device. Behind and to the right of the sight glass was an iron ring with a centre dot. This dot was aligned with a thin metal rod, topped by a round 'bead', set forward of the windshield on the cowling. If the pilot was unable to use the new sight for any reason, the old 'ring and bead' still gave him a chance of hitting his quarry.

During the autumn of 1944 the P-51D was cleared to use the new K-14 lead-computing gunsight. This revolutionary piece of equipment automatically displayed the correct angle of deflection required to hit a moving target, and was thus the answer to many a pilot's prayer. Deflection shooting was a skill many found difficult to master, irrespective of the aircraft they were flying, or the air force in which they flew.

The only alternative to the good deflection shot was to get

Herb Rutland of the 356th FG's 360th FS is adorned with all the personal equipment a USAAF pilot needed to survive an ETO tour in fighters in the bloody winter of 1944/45. Immediately below his gloved hand can be seen the glass reflector pane of the 'Ace Making' K-14 gun sight. Also, note how weathered the painted canopy rail is following its use as a 'lean to' for pilots climbing in and out of the cockpit (H Rutland)

Winning an enviable reputation as dedicted bomber escorts, the pilots of the 356th FG consequently produced fewer aces than most groups – only six in fact. However, they did boast the most elaborate markings within VIIIth FC! In this marvellous shot taken from a B-17 at the beginning of a sortie, a trio of 360th FS P-51Ds come in close for a good look at the bomber *(H Rutland)*

'Buzzing the field' was a popular pastime when pilots had something to celebrate. Officially frowned upon, it was often viewed with a 'blind eye', particularly if a popular boss came back to visit his old unit. Here, five-kill ace Col Don Baccus in the right-hand P-51D returns to visit Martlesham Heath, in Suffolk, and 'his' 356th FG in May 1945 after being posted to command the 359th FG at East Wretham *(H Rutland)*

in very close, and this method of attack brought with it its own problems, not the least of which was the danger of debris flying back from the target as soon as the pursuing pilot opened fire. Also, stricken fighters often suddenly exploded violently if hit in the fuel tank.

Deflection shooting didn't entirely eliminate such hazards, but it significantly reduced them, and the K-14 (widely known as 'the ace-maker' sight in the Eighth) was eventually issued to all P-51 groups. A light touch was required to use it effectively, with the pilot having to resort to the 'ring and bead' if his target rapidly reversed direction, as such violent manoeuvring could easily cause the K-14's tempramental gyros to 'tumble' as the pilot tried to follow his quarry.

Lt William Beyer of the 361st FG's 376th FS was one who reaped the rewards of the K-14 early on during a mission to Kassel on 27 September. About 40 enemy fighters broke through the escort and headed for the bombers. Flying above a group of eight Fw 190s, Beyer and his wingman quickly lined one up and closed to 1000 yards. The P-51s fired at long-range and chased the *Jagdflieger* as he shed his canopy and plunged into cloud. Making a tight 360-degree turn, Beyer, who followed the Fw 190 into the overcast intent on delivering the killer blow, was suddenly surprised when he spotted a German pilot in a parachute.

Another Fw 190 was soon picked up, and it began to split-S and perform a number of tight turns – this was the Focke-Wulf pilot's trump card as few fighters could match the Fw 190 in a turning fight. However, Beyer had not read that particular flight manual, and he stayed glued to the German's tail. In attempting a climb, the enemy lost his advan-

217

Parked on PSP (Pierced Steel Planking) matting, *Ain't Misbehavin* hailed from the 357th FG's 362nd FS. It wears two small kill markings just below the anti-dazzle panel, and was photographed at its Leiston base between sorties in November 1944. Parked across the dispersal from 'G4-M' is an overall OD P-51D, one of the last camouflaged Mustangs then still flying with the Group *(M Olmsted)*

Major Leonard 'Kit' Carson was the premier ace of the 357th FG, scoring 18.50 kills in a single tour with the 362nd FS. P-51K 44-11622, christened *Nooky Booky IV*, was hs penultimate Mustang, and it carried his full kill tally, including 3.50 strafing victories, on the port side. An advocate of the close-in attack, Carson achieved most of his kills in the final six months of the war, including five in one sortie on 27 November 1944

tage, and as Beyer's fire hit his machine, he promptly bailed out. A third Fw 190 was soon destroyed as Beyer continued his one-man war, but number four appeared to be a liitle more experienced than his colleagues, and he tried desperately to shake of the P-51 snapping at his heels. His desperate manoeuvring even including dropping his flaps and wheels and waiting for the Mustang to overshoot. Beyer had seen that trick before, however, and duly followed suit before letting rip with his guns. The Fw 190 shuddered violently, and the pilot quickly abandoned his mortally wounded fighter as more .50 calibre bullets found their target.

Diving for the deck was a fifth Fw 190, and Beyer quickly gave chase. This time he was being led into power lines by the fleeing German. The Mustang went over them while the Focke-Wulf opted to go under. Now enjoying a height advantage, Beyer made no mistake, and the fifth enemy aircraft spiralled into the ground and exploded. Beyer was an ace-in-a-day.

Meanwhile, over at Leiston the 357th FG's pilots were quietly compiling a scoring record that would see them finish top of the list for aerial victories in the P-51. However, unlike other bases, the small Suffolk strip appeared not to rate too highly with war correspondents of the time, and neither 'Bud' Anderson or Chuck Yeager can ever remember seeing a single one. As Anderson put it,

'No war correspondents ever dropped by our base, to my knowledge. Neither did Bob Hope or any of the Hollywood roadshows. F373 (Leiston) was out of the way, off by itself, not big or different enough among the 130-odd bases in England to rate special attention. I did a radio interview one time in London about becoming an ace, but I never did hear how it came out, and seldom saw clippings from the papers back home. I'd been vaguely aware that when you did or said anything special they would send word home. I'd shoot down an airplane and Mom and Dad would hear about it over the radio and read about it in the papers. Our PRO was always taking your picture and typing up press releases, mailing what the wire services couldn't use to each man's hometown. We were vaguely aware of all that, but it wasn't until I returned home that I realised how busy people had been turning us into heroes.'

By the autumn of 1944 the American pilots were observing at first-hand the deterioration of the Luftwaffe's pilot training programme. There was no shortage of

A very young Lt Preston Easley poses in front of 'his' P-51D, *The Virginia Squire*. Assigned to the 360th FS, Easley was not alone within the 356th FG in having an elaborate personal badge painted on the nose of his Mustang *(H Rutland)*

Lt Henry Roe's *'Miss Pam'* in the red trim of the 78th FG's 82nd FS. The yellow fin tip may have been an additional flight identification marking applied at squadron level. As with all 78th FG Mustangs, this machine has a half black/half white propeller spinner

courage shown by their adversaries, but the basic skill level of the new *Jagdflieger* was beginning to wane in the face of the ever-burgeoning daylight bomber onslaught. The quality of the fighter escorts had in nine short months improved out of all recognition, and the majority of American pilots went into battle confident that their equipment was the best that could be supplied, that in the P-51D they were flying one of the best fighters in the world, and that when they got home there was ample fuel for their next sortie. It was also unlikely that their airfield would have been in any way disturbed by the attentions of the enemy during their absence. Few of these advantages were now available to the Germans.

That the quality of the Luftwaffe's pilots had plunged was manifested in fighters stumbling about unsure of what to do in combat, blindly following their leaders. They were all too often easy victims for escort fighters. Combat reports noted that the Germans appeared not even to remember the cardinal rule for survival in combat of jettisoning tanks before engaging the enemy. Multiple claims on one mission were further evidence of the problems facing the *Jagdwaffe*, which now often made only a weak reposte to the USAAF, and on some missions wasn't seen at all. Nobody could yet afford to be complacent, however.

# THE COLOUR PLATES

This 18-page colour section profiles some of the most famous aircraft of the aces flown within the Eighth AAF, plus many lesser known examples never before illustrated. The artworks have all been specially commissioned for this volume, and profile artists Chris Davey, John Weal and Iain Wyllie, plus figure artist Mike Chappell, have gone to great pains to portray both the aircraft and the pilots as accurately as possible, following much in-depth research.

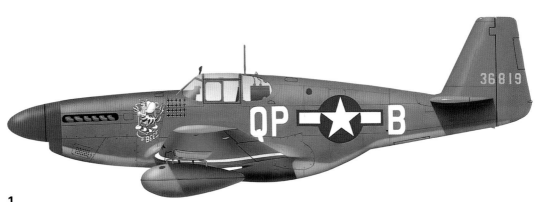

**1**
P-51B-5-NA 43-6819 *BEE*, flown by Captain Duane W Beeson, Officer Commanding 334th Fighter Squadron, 4th Fighter Group, April 1944

**2**
P-51B-15-NA 42-106924 *Salem Representative*, flown by Flight Officer Ralph 'Kidd' Hofer, 334th Fighter Squadron, 4th Fighter Group, May 1944

**3**
P-51B-5NA 43-6636 *ILL WIND*, flown by 1st Lieutenant Nicholas 'Cowboy' Megura, 334th Fighter Squadron, 4th Fighter Group, April 1944

**4**
P-51D-25-NA 44-73108 *Red Dog XII*, flown by Major Louis 'Red Dog' Norley, Officer Commanding
334th Fighter Squadron, 4th Fighter Group, April 1945

**5**
P-51B-10-NA 43-7172 *Thunder Bird*, flown by 1st Lieutenant Ted Lines, 335th Fighter Squadron,
4th Fighter Group, April 1944

**6**
P-51D-20-NA 44-72308 *RIDGE RUNNER III*, flown by Major Pierce 'Mac' McKennon, Officer Commanding
335th Fighter Squadron, 4th Fighter Group, Spring 1945

**7**
P-51B-5-NA 43-6913 *Shangri-La*, flown by Captain Don Gentile, 336th Fighter Squadron,
4th Fighter Group, March 1944

**8**
P-51D-20-NA 44-64153 (unnamed), flown by Major Fred Glover, Officer Commanding 336th Fighter Squadron, 4th Fighter Group, April 1945

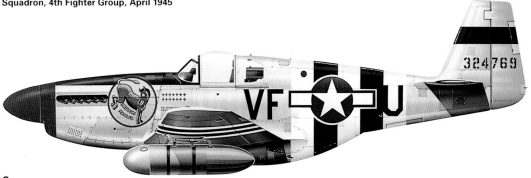

**9**
P-51B-15-NA 43-24769 *MISSOURI MAULER*, flown by Captain Willard 'Millie' Millikan, 336th Fighter Squadron, 4th Fighter Group, May 1944

**10**
P-51D-5-NT 44-11161 *June Nite*, flown by 1st Lieutenant Ernest Fiebelkorn, 77th Fighter Squadron, 20th Fighter Group, November 1944

**11**
P-51D-5-NA 44-13761 *HAPPY JACK'S GO BUGGY*, flown by Captain Jack Ilfrey, 79th Fighter Squadron, 20th Fighter Group, September 1944

**12**
P-51D-10-NA 44-14223 *KATYDID*, flown by Lieutenant Colonel Elwyn Righetti, Officer Commanding 338th
Fighter Squadron, 55th Fighter Group, early 1945

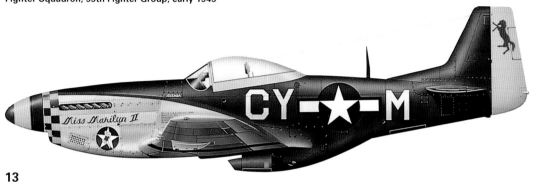

**13**
P-51D-5-NA 44-13837 *Miss Marilyn II*, flown by 1st Lieutenant E Robert Welch, 343rd Fighter Squadron,
55th Fighter Group, October/November 1944

**14**
P-51D-20-NA 44-72218 *Big Beautiful Doll*, flown by Colonel John Landers, Officer Commanding
78th Fighter Group, 1945

**15**
P-51D-5-NA 44-13808 *Yi-Yi*, flown by 1st Lieutenant Francis Gerard, 503rd Fighter Squadron,
339th Fighter Group, October 1944

**16**
P-51B-15-NA 2106872 *PATTY ANN II*, flown by 1st Lieutenant John F Thornell Jr, 328th Fighter Squadron,
352nd Fighter Group, July 1944

**17**
P-51D-15-NA 44-14906 *CRIPES A'MIGHTY*, flown by Major George Preddy, Officer Commanding
328th Fighter Squadron, 352nd Fighter Group, Christmas Day 1944

**18**
P-51B-5-NA 43-6704 *HELL-ER-BUST*, flown by 1st Lieutenant Edwin Heller, 486th Fighter Squadron,
352nd Fighter Group, September 1944

**19**
P-51D-10-NA 44-14812 *Slender, Tender & TALL*, flown by Major William Halton, Officer Commanding
487th Fighter Squadron, 352nd Fighter Group, April 1945

**20**
P-51D-10-NA 44-14151 *PETIE 2ND*, flown by Lieutenant Colonel John Meyer, Officer Commanding 487th Fighter Squadron, 352nd Fighter Group, August 1944

**21**
P-51C-1-NT 42-103320 *(Little Ann)*, flown by 1st Lieutenant Glennon Moran, 487th Fighter Squadron, 352nd Fighter Group, September 1944

**22**
P-51B-10-NA 42-106449 *Princess ELIZABETH*, flown by 1st Lieutenant William Whisner, 487th Fighter Squadron, 352nd Fighter Group, May 1944

**23**
P-51D-10-NA 44-14237 *Moonbeam McSWINE*, flown by Captain William Whisner, 487th Fighter Squadron, 352nd Fighter Group, February 1945

**24**
P-51D-20-NA 44-72374 *BETTY-E*, flown by Lieutenant Colonel Wayne Blickenstaff, 350th Fighter Squadron, 353rd Fighter Group, March 1945

**25**
P-51D-25-NA 44-73060 *Dove of Peace*, flown by Colonel Glenn E Duncan, Officer Commanding 353rd Fighter Group, April 1945

**27**
P-51D-15-NA 44-15625 *MAN O'WAR*, flown by Colonel Clairborne Kinnard Jr, Officer Commanding 355th Fighter Group, early 1945

**28**
P-51D-25-NA 44-73144 *Man O'War*, flown by Colonel Clairborne Kinnard Jr, Officer Commanding 355th Fighter Group, April/May 1945

**26**
P-51D-15-NA 44-15092 *ALABAMA RAMMER JAMMER*, flown by 2nd Lieutenant Arthur C Cundy, 352nd
Fighter Squadron, 353rd Fighter Group, October 1944

**29**
P-51B-10-NA 42-106448 *THE HUN HUNTER/TEXAS*, flown by 2nd Lietenant Henry Brown, 354th Fighter
Squadron, 355th Fighter Group, April 1944

**30**
P-51D-5-NA 44-13305 *THE HUN HUNTER/TEXAS*, flown by 1st Lieutenant Henry Brown, 354th Fighter
Squadron, 355th Fighter Group, late summer, 1944

**31**
P-51D-15-NA 44-15255 *DOWN FOR DOUBLE*, flown by Lt Colonel Gordon Graham, 354th Fighter Squadron,
355th Fighter Group, March/April 1945

**32**
P-51B-15-NA 42-106950 *The Iowa Beaut*, flown by Robert E Hulberman (rank unknown), 354th Fighter
Squadron, 355th Fighter Group, June/July 1944

**33**
P-51D-5-NA 44-13677 *MISS STEVE*, flown by 1st Lieutenant William Cullerton, 357th Fighter Squadron,
355th Fighter Group, post-November 1944

**34**
P-51B-5-NA 43-6928 *OLE II*, flown by 1st Lieutenant William Hovde, 358th Fighter Squadron,
355th Fighter Group, March/April 1944

**35**
P-51D-25-NA 44-73108 *OLE V*, flown by Major William Hovde, Officer Commanding 358th Fighter Squadron,
355th Fighter Group, December 1944

**36**
P-51D-15-N 44-15152 *JERSEY JERK*, flown by Major Don Strait, Officer Commanding 361st Fighter Squadron,
356th Fighter Group, December 1944/January 1945

**37**
P-51B-15-NA 43-24824 *OLD CROW*, flown by Captain Clarence 'Bud' Anderson, 362nd Fighter Squadron,
357th Fighter Group, May 1944

**38**
P-51D-10-NA 44-14450 *OLD CROW*, flown by Captain Clarence 'Bud' Anderson, 362nd Fighter Squadron,
357th Fighter Group, late 1944

**39**
P-51K-5-NT 44-11622 *Nooky Booky IV*, flown by Captain Leonard 'Kit' Carson, 362nd Fighter Squadron,
357th Fighter Group, Christmas Day 1944

**40**
P-51B-10-NA 42-106462 *U'VE HAD IT!*, flown by Captain John England, 362nd Fighter Squadron,
357th Fighter Group, early Fall 1944

**41**
P-51D-10-NA 44-14709 *MISSOURI ARMADA*, flown by Major John England, Officer Commanding
362nd Fighter Squadron, 357th Fighter Group, December 1944

**42**
P-51D-25-NA 44-72199 (unnamed), flown by Captain Charles Weaver, 362nd Fighter Squadron,
357th Fighter Group, April 1945

**43**
P-51B-5-NA 43-6933 *SPEEDBALL ALICE*, flown by 1st Lieutenant Don Bochkay, 363rd Fighter Squadron,
357th Fighter Group, April 1944

**44**
P-51D-20-NA 44-72244 (winged Ace of Clubs badge), flown by Captain Don Bochkay, 363rd Fighter Squadron,
357th Fighter Group, February/March 1945

**45**
P-51D-20-NA 44-63621 *LITTLE SHRIMP*, flown by Captain Robert Foy, 363rd Fighter Squadron,
357th Fighter Group, January 1945

**46**
P-51D-15-NA 44-14888 *GLAMOROUS GLEN III*, flown by Captain Charles 'Chuck' Yeager, 363rd Fighter
Squadron, 357th Fighter Group, November 1944

**47**
P-51B-5-NA 43-6935 *Hurry Home Honey*, flown by Captain Richard Peterson, 364th Fighter Squadron,
357th Fighter Group, May/June 1944

**48**
P-51D-5-NA 44-13586 *Hurry Home Honey*, flown by Captain Richard Peterson, 364th Fighter Squadron,
357th Fighter Group, October 1944

**49**
P-51D-20-NA 44-72164 *THE SHILLELAGH*, flown by Lieutenant Colonel John Storch, Officer Commanding
364th Fighter Squadron, 357th Fighter Group, early 1945

**50**
P-51D-5-NA 44-13606 *LOUISIANA HEAT WAVE*, flown by 1st Lieutenant Claude Crenshaw,
369th Fighter Squadron, 359th Fighter Group, November 1944

**51**
P-51D-10-NA 44-14733 *Daddy's Girl*, flown by Captain Ray Wetmore, 370th Fighter Squadron,
359th Fighter Group, early 1945

**52**
P-51D-5-NA 44-13704 *Ferocious Frankie*, flown by Major Wallace Hopkins, 374th Fighter Squadron,
361st Fighter Group, Summer 1944

**53**
P-51D-10-NA 44-14164 *DETROIT Miss*, flown by 1st Lieutenant Urban Drew, 375th Fighter Squadron, 361st Fighter Group, October 1944

**54**
P-51D-15-NA 44-15076 *Betty Lee III*, flown by 2nd Lieutenant William T Kemp, 375th Fighter Squadron, 361st Fighter Group, September 1944

**55**
P-51D-25-NA 44-72719 *Constance*, flown by Major George Ceuleers, 383rd Fighter Squadron, 364th Fighter Group, late 1944

**56**
P-51D-5-NT 44-11243 *Betty Jo IV*, flown by Major Samuel Wicker, 383rd Fighter Squadron, 364th Fighter Group, December 1944

**57**
P-51D-20-NA 44-63263 *PENNY 4*, flown by Colonel John Lowell, Acting Officer Commanding,
364th Fighter Group, November/December 1944

**58**
P-51D-25-NA 44-73045 *Lucky Lady VII*, flown by Captain Ernest 'Ernie' Bankey,
364th Fighter Group, early 1945

**59**
P-51D-30-NT 44-11674 *BOOMERANG JR*, flown by Lieutenant Colonel Arthur 'Art' Jeffrey, 434th Fighter
Squadron, 479th Fighter Group, March 1945

**60**
P-51D-25-NA 44-72922 *SCAT VI*, flown by Major Robin Olds, 434th Fighter Squadron,
479th Fighter Group, February/March 1945

1. Captain Leonard K 'Kit' Carson of the 362nd/357th FG, circa November 1944

2. An AAF Captain wearing the latest 1945-style Eighth Air Force fighter pilot combat clothing

3. Captain Don Gentile in dress uniform, circa March 1944, just prior to him returning to the USA

4. Major Pierce McKennon of the 335th FS, 4th FG, at Debden, circa March 1945

5. Colonel Don Blakeslee, Commanding Officer of the the 4th FG at Debden, circa June 1944

6. 1st Lieutenant in the standard Eighth Air Force dress uniform of late 1944

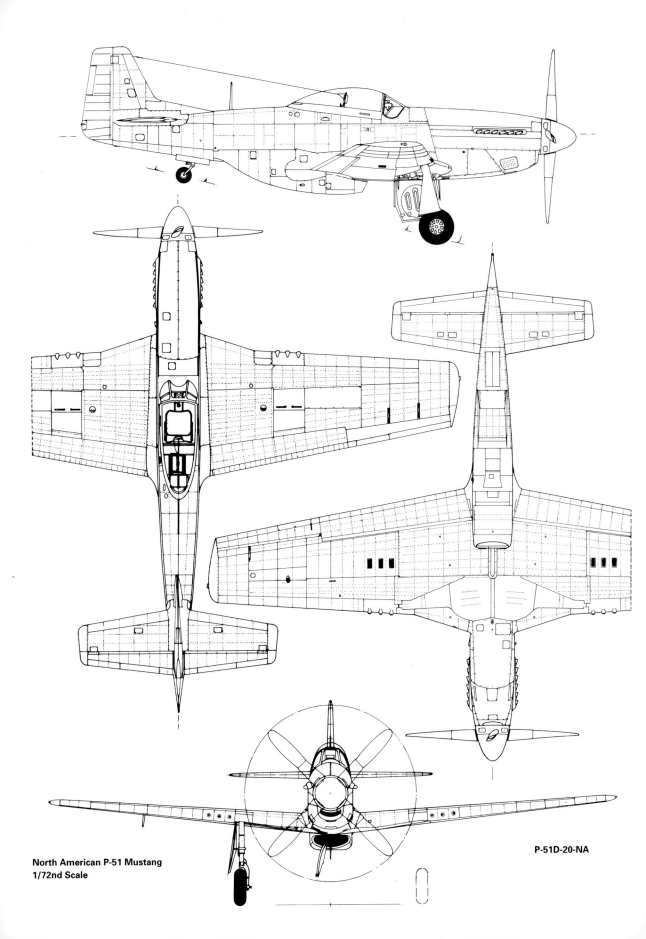

**North American P-51 Mustang**
**1/72nd Scale**

P-51D-20-NA

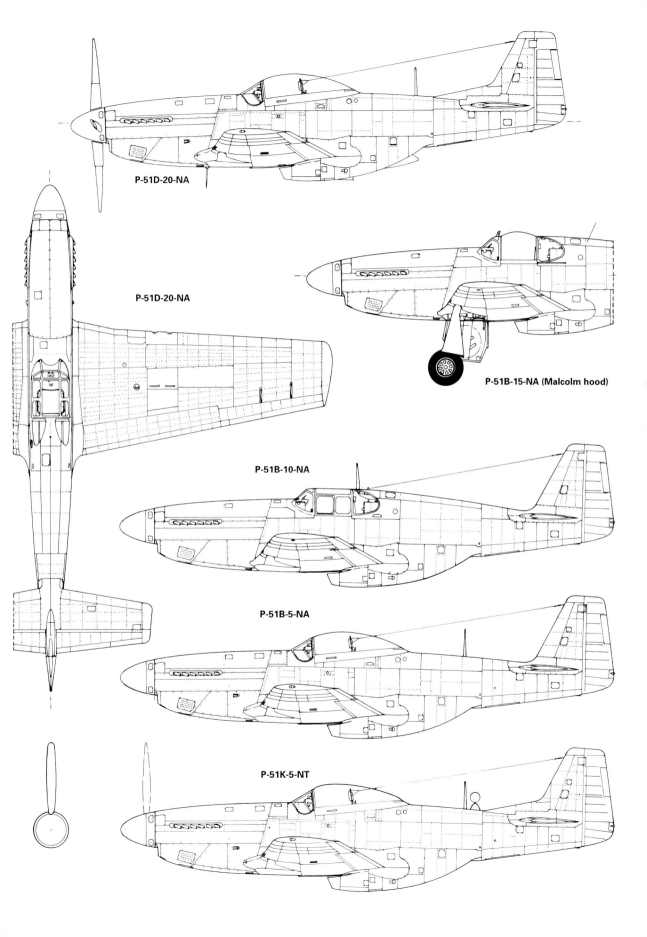

P-51D-20-NA

P-51D-20-NA

P-51B-15-NA (Malcolm hood)

P-51B-10-NA

P-51B-5-NA

P-51K-5-NT

# COLOUR PLATES

## I

**P-51B-5-NA 43-6819 *BEE*, flown by Captain Duane W Beeson, Officer Commanding 334th Fighter Squadron, 4th Fighter Group, April 1944**

The first Mustangs to reach the Eighth Air Force were painted in overall olive drab (OD), with neutral grey undersurfaces. The colours blended gradually into one another through the use of a slight overspray. Recognition stripes in white were initially applied across the wings, tailplane, fin and around the nose. Duane Beeson was Don Gentile's rival in the Eighth Air Force's first 'Ace Race' aiming to beat Great War ace Eddie Rickenbacker's record of 26 enemy aircraft downed, but he was shot down and captured on 5 April 1944, when his score had reached 22.08, including 17.3 air-to-air kills, 5.3 of which were scored in the Mustang.

## 2

**P-51B-15-NA 42-106924 *Salem Representative*, flown by Flight Officer Ralph 'Kidd' Hofer, 334th Fighter Squadron, 4th Fighter Group, May 1944**

A rebellious maverick who habitually flew in a blue and orange college football shirt, the 'Kidd' began his flying career in the RCAF, transferring to the USAAF in June 1943. The *Salem Representative* was Hofer's third P-51B, assigned to him in April 1944 – his first two aircraft had been lost while being flown by other pilots. The aircraft had drab upper surfaces, with a very high demarcation on the fuselage, and a red band across the fin in the same position as the discontinued recognition marking. Black recognition stripes were retained underwing and under the tailplane. An ace even before promotion from Flight Officer to Lieutenant, Hofer was killed in action over Yugoslavia on 2 July 1944, shot down by a Bf 109. He was credited with 15 enemy aircraft in the air, and destroyed another 15 on the ground, prior to his death.

## 3

**P-51B-5NA 43-6636 *ILL WIND*, flown by 1st Lieutenant Nicholas 'Cowboy' Megura, 334th Fighter Squadron, 4th Fighter Group, April 1944**

The factory camouflaged P-51B *Ill Wind* flown by Nicholas 'the Cowboy' Megura, who amassed a total of 11.83 air-to-air kills, with another 3.75 by strafing. Megura (by then a Captain) crash-landed in Sweden after being hit in the glycol tank in error by a P-38 on 22 May 1944. He was prohibited from re-entering combat after his repatriation due to the rules of his previous internment. On most early camouflaged (and natural metal) Mustangs the specified white nose recognition band gave way to Group colours (red for the 'Eagles' of the 4th FG, for example) while the tailfin stripe was deleted because it broke up the distinctive outline of the Mustang's tail. White stripes were retained on the wings and tailplane, however (black on natural metal aircraft).

## 4

**P-51D-25-NA 44-73108 *Red Dog XII*, flown by Major Louis 'Red Dog' Norley, Officer Commanding 334th Fighter Squadron, 4th Fighter Group, April 1945**

During December 1944 the 12-inch red nose band used by the 4th FG was extended aft to 24 inches on the upper decking, curving down and aft towards the wingroot. Aircraft had already started to gain more colour from October 1944

onwards, when squadron coloured fin bands or trim tabs were replaced by coloured rudders, with red for the 334th FS, white for the 335th FS and blue for the 336th FS. Two-digit squadron identification codes were applied to most Eighth Air Force Mustangs ahead of the star and bar, with an individual letter aft or on the tailfin. Although a deadly serious professional in the air, Norley was known as something of a prankster on the ground, and a fanatic for red-dog poker, which provided his nickname. He amassed 10.3 aerial victories, scoring nine of them in the P-51.

## 5

**P-51B-10-NA 43-7172 *Thunder Bird*, flown by 1st Lieutenant Ted Lines, 335th Fighter Squadron, 4th Fighter Group, April 1944**

Ted Lines, from Mesa, Arizona, decorated his Mustangs with appropriate Indian-style artwork and bestowed the name *Thunder Bird* on them. With ten officially recorded aerial victories and another three credited by the Group, but not recognised by the Victory Credits Board, Lines was a little-publicised member of the 4th FG. This P-51B was eventually replaced by similarly named, similarly marked P-51D 44-13555 (WD-D). Reflecting the Mustang's multi-role capability, *Thunder Bird* is seen here toting bombs underwing, and wears full black recognition stripes on wings and tail.

## 6

**P-51D-20-NA 44-72308 *RIDGE RUNNER III*, flown by Major Pierce 'Mac' McKennon, Officer Commanding 335th Fighter Squadron, 4th Fighter Group, Spring 1945**

A talented pianist and music student from the University of Arkansas, McKennon initially showed little aptitude for flying, being washed out of USAAF training. Undeterred, he joined the RCAF and eventually reached a Spitfire squadron based in Britain, before finally transferring to the USAAF in November 1942. Shot down twice, McKennon avoided capture the first time, and was smuggled out by the French Resistance. His second period in enemy territory was of much briefer duration, since one of his pilots landed and flew his squadron commander back to Debden on his lap! McKennon amassed 11 aerial victories, seven of them in the P-51, with a further 9.68 strafing kills. His final Mustang, shown here, carried an Arkansas razorback on the nose, rushing past two parachutes! The black-edged white rudder denoted the 335th FS.

## 7

**P-51B-5-NA 43-6913 *Shangri-La*, flown by Captain Don Gentile, 336th Fighter Squadron, 4th Fighter Group, March 1944**

Winner of the 'Ace Race' to reach Rickenbacker's 26 kills (racking up 21.83 aerial and six ground victories by April 1944), Gentile's personal kill list, and Gen Eisenhower's remark that the youngster from Ohio was a 'one-man air force', obscure his contribution as a team-player, whose unselfish partnership with wingman John T Godfrey proved mutually beneficial. Rejected for pilot training by the USAAC, Gentile followed the example of many of his compatriots and enlisted with the RCAF, scoring his first kill (and receiving a British DFC) as a member of No 133 'Eagle' Sqn flying Spitfires in support of the Dieppe landings. Gentile transferred to the USAAF with his squadron in

September 1942, achieving 2 Spitfire and 4.33 P-47 kills before converting to the P-51 and scoring a further 15.5. The beautifully decorated *Shangri-La* broke its back when Gentile hit the runway during a low-level pass after completing his last operational mission on 13 April 1944. He later flew a silver P-51D with similar markings during a fund-raising drive in the USA.

## 8
**P-51D-20-NA 44-64153 (unnamed), flown by Major Fred Glover, Officer Commanding 336th Fighter Squadron, 4th Fighter Group, April 1945**
A former pro-baseball player with the *St Louis Cardinals*, Fred Glover was another ace rejected out of hand by the USAAF, trained by the RCAF, and later transferred back to the service that had spurned him. Glover did not join the 4th FG until 1944, and flew only the Mustang, gaining 10.3 aerial and 12.5 strafing victories. His airborne kills included an Me 163 Komet, which made the fatal error of slowing down for its firing pass on a USAAF bomber formation. Glover flew a succession of Mustangs, this one being the last. The anti-dazzle panel was painted in the 336th Sqn's adopted blue, as was the canopy frame (these denoting his status as CO) and of course the rudder.

## 9
**P-51B-15-NA 43-24769 *MISSOURI MAULER*, flown by Captain Willard 'Millie' Millikan, 336th Fighter Squadron, 4th Fighter Group, May 1944**
After having a stipulated $350 of dental work carried out, Willard Millikan was allowed to join the USAAC, but was washed out of training for an 'inherent lack of flying ability'. Even in the RCAF, which he subsequently joined, Millikan showed little promise and was advised to become a ferry pilot. Despite a reputation for emphasising protection of the bombers, and supporting other members of his flight (rather than chasing after enemy fighters hell-for-leather), Millikan quickly became an ace, eventually amassing 13 aerial victories, ten of them while flying the P-51. Millikan's war ended on 30 May 1944 when his wingman collided with him after being hit by flak. Both pilots bailed out to become PoWs, Millikan subsequently escaping, but not in time to return to operations. Leading the F-84 equipped 121st Fighter Squadron of the DCANG, Millikan's post-war Air Guard service included taking his unit to Korea.

## 10
**P-51D-5-NT 44-11161 *June Nite*, flown by 1st Lieutenant Ernest Fiebelkorn, 77th Fighter Squadron, 20th Fighter Group, November 1944**
At 6ft 4in and 16 stone, Ernest Fiebelkorn must have found the Mustang's cockpit a trifle cramped. Nevertheless, flying this Dallas-built P-51D and others, including 44-14823/LC-F *Miss Miami*, he became the 20th Fighter Group's top-scorer with 9.5 kills. He was a slow starter, though, not opening his account until 2 November 1944 when he downed three aircraft. That same month also saw the addition of seven black and six white nose stripes behind the 20th FG marking.

## 11
**P-51D-5-NA 44-13761 *HAPPY JACK'S GO BUGGY*, flown by Captain Jack Ilfrey, 79th Fighter Squadron, 20th Fighter Group, September 1944**

In naming his P-51, Jack Ilfrey repeated the sobriquet he'd applied to his P-38 Lightnings, flown with the 1st and 20th Fighter Groups. All of his eight kills were scored on the Lightning. The 20th Fighter Group's constituent squadrons eschewed the use of coloured rudders, instead repeating the aircraft's individual letter in a triangle (55th FS), circle (77th FS) or square (79th FS). Like many 79th FS P-51s, Ilfrey's Mustang had its serial number overpainted.

## 12
**P-51D-1O-NA 44-14223 *KATYDID*, flown by Lieutenant Colonel Elwyn Righetti, 338th Fighter Squadron, 55th Fighter Group, early 1945**
In addition to 7.5 aerial victories, Elwyn Righetti amassed a score of 27 ground victories — the highest individual score in the Eighth. He was promoted to full Colonel in command of the 55th Fighter Group from February 1945, but was lost on 17 April following a successful belly-landing, after being hit by ground fire, on an airfield he had earlier been strafing. Righetti had destroyed nine enemy aircraft during this mission alone, and soon after being captured near *KATYDID*, was killed by a furious mob of German 'civilians'. The 55th introduced coloured rudders from October (green for the 338th FS, yellow for the 343rd FS and, from December, red for the 38th FS). Righetti's kill markings were applied in the form of broken Swastikas.

## 13
**P-51D-5-NA 44-13837 *Miss Marilyn II*, flown by 1st Lieutenant E Robert Welch, 343rd Fighter Squadron, 55th Fighter Group, October/November 1944**
Bob Welch scored six air-to-air kills, most of them during the heavy fighting of Autumn 1944, with a further 12 strafing credits. His 343rd Fighter Squadron P-51D was typical of the unit's aircraft, with the lower part of the nose in natural metal, but with the rear fuselage, fin and upper surfaces in dark green. The red prancing horse insignia began to appear in late 1944, and a narrow two-inch band (in the squadron colour) was applied behind the green and yellow chequers from about November.

## 14
**P-51D-20-NA 44-72218 *Big Beautiful Doll*, flown by Colonel John Landers, Officer Commanding 78th Fighter Group, 1945**
Scoring six victories in the Pacific with the 49th FG whilst flying P-40s, Landers was posted to a succession of Eighth Air Force fighter units, flying a series of P-38s and P-51s, all of which were named *Big Beautiful Doll*. From the 38th FS of the 55th FG (scoring four kills in P-38s and flying Mustang 44-13823/CG-O) he was promoted to command the 357th FG (flying another *Doll*) between 11 October and 2 December 1944, before moving to Duxford to take command of the 78th FG. After the war he commanded the 361st FG. Appropriately enough, the Imperial War Museum at Duxford painted its P-51D in the colours worn by Landers' Mustang, although the aircraft is presently displayed at their Lambeth headquarters, rather than at their Cambridgeshire airfield. He scored 14.5 victories, 8.5 of them while serving with the Eighth (4.5 in Mustangs), amassing a further 20 ground victories, including eight during one mission!

## 15

**P-51D-5-NA 44-13808 *Yi-Yi*, flown by 1st Lieutenant Francis Gerard, 503rd Fighter Squadron, 339th Fighter Group, October 1944**

Francis Gerard's Mustang shows the markings of the 339th FG to advantage, though two-inch coloured nose bands and coloured rudders (red for the 503rd FS, green for the 504th and yellow for the 505th) were added from early 1945. The 339th trained as a dive bomber unit before re-equipping with P-39s and converting to the fighter role. They were thrown in at the deep end, receiving Mustangs only after their arrival in England. The 339th FG began operations with P-51 Bs on 30 April 1944, and in its one year of operations claimed 239.5 air-to-air and 440.5 ground victories, an Eighth Air Force record. Gerard himself scored eight aerial victories, the last as a Captain in March 1945.

## 16

**P-51B-15-NA 42-106872 *PATTY ANN II*, flown by 1st Lieutenant John F Thornell Jr, 328th Fighter Squadron, 352nd Fighter Group, July 1944**

Finishing the war as the Group's third ranking ace, and top-scorer of the 328th Fighter Squadron, Thornell opened his account with 4.25 P-47 victories. He in fact led the Group's scoring league table until his return to the USA in June 1944, giving Preddy and Meyer the opportunity to overtake him! When he left the squadron in July 1944 he was the first of the unit's pilots to reach 300 operational hours, and had amassed 17.25 aerial victories (13 while flying P-51s) and two ground victories. His Malcolm-hooded aircraft is seen here with the later extended blue nose markings and a coloured rudder tab.

## 17

**P-51D-15-NA 44-14906 *CRIPES A'MIGHTY*, flown by Major George Preddy, Officer Commanding 328th Fighter Squadron, 352nd Fighter Group, Christmas Day 1944**

George Preddy's last assigned aircraft was this P-51D, flown after his return from R&R to take command of the 328th Fighter Squadron, and it carries the squadron's standard red rudder and canopy rail name tag. A stylised barber's pole was painted on the right hand side of the cowling, reflecting the part-time 'career' of his crew chief! His previous aircraft, flown while serving with the Groups 487th FS, included P-51D *CRIPES A 'MIGHTY* 3RD (44-13321/HO-P) and P-51B *CRIPES A'MIGHTY* 2ND (42-106451/HO-P), as well as the original *CRIPES A'MIGHTY*, a P-47-RE in which Preddy scored his first three victories. The style of lettering used for Preddy's personal markings varied enormously on all four aircraft. With 26.83 air-to-air kills, 23.83 of them scored while flying Mustangs (and three strafing victories), Preddy was the top-scoring P-51 pilot of the war, although if air and ground kills are counted his old rival John Meyer (who could add 13 strafing kills to his 24 aerial victories) took the title.

## 18

**P-51B-5-NA 43-6704 *HELL-ER-BUST*, flown by 1st Lieutenant Edwin Heller, 486th Fighter Squadron, 352nd Fighter Group, September 1944**

Factory-applied camouflage was abandoned in January 1944, primarily to save cost and time in the factories, but it also resulted in both a minor weight saving and improved performance through reduced drag. Aircraft delivered after February 1944 arrived in-theatre in natural metal, but camouflaged uppersurfaces were reintroduced from May 1944 for those units expected to serve overseas after the invasion. Such camouflage used British paint, and was applied at unit or depot level. Towards the end of 1944 such camouflaging was abandoned, and many aircraft were stripped back to a metal finish. Several 352nd Group pilots were reluctant to give up their drab-painted P-5IBs, one, Lt Sheldon Heyer, reportedly being jokingly threatened with court martial before he would accept a trade-in! Edwin Heller's P-51B, wearing 11 victory markings, is fitted with a sliding, blown, Malcolm hood, which gave much improved visibility and which would have made *HELL-ER-BUST* a particularly desirable mount. Heller scored 5.5 air-to-air victories, but 16.5 ground kills swelled his final tally to 22!

## 19

**P-51D-10-NA 44-14812 *Slender, Tender & TALL* flown by Major William Halton, Officer Commanding 487th Fighter Squadron, 352nd Fighter Group, April 1945**

Replacing John Meyer as commander of the 487th Fighter Squadron in November 1944, William Halton had already scored one victory while flying P-47s (and P-5IBs) with the 328th FS, before replacing George Preddy as Operations Officer of the 487th. He then scored another kill in his new P-51D, which he continued to fly as squadron commander, raising his victory tally to 11.5.

## 20

**P-5ID-10-NA 44-14151 *PETIE 2ND*, flown by Lieutenant Colonel John Meyer, Officer Commanding 487th Fighter Squadron, 352nd Fighter Group, August 1944**

After flying Iceland-based P-40s on fruitless convoy patrols, and scoring three victories while flying the P-47, John Meyer got into his stride once strapped into a Mustang from the 352nd Fighter Group. His first aircraft (P-51B 42-106471) was named *Lambie II* and then *PETIE*, and it was in this machine that he racked up the majority of his kills. The P-51D illustrated did not look like this for long, since Meyer thought the name in white and victory markings in yellow looked too bland, so he ordered Sgt Sam Perry to brighten them up, in order to 'scare the hell out of the damned Germans'. *PETIE 2ND* was overpainted with bright orange stripes, and the kill markings were changed to orange! *PETIE 2ND* was Meyer's mount for only two victories, and he scored more in another P-51D (44-15041) *PETIE 3RD*. He continued to fly and score after being reassigned as Deputy Group Commander in November 1944. Meyer claimed two MiG-15 kills while flying with the 4th FIW in Korea, before retiring as a General in 1974.

## 21

**P-51C-1-NT 42-103320 (*Little Ann*), flown by 1st Lieutenant Glennon Moran, 487th Fighter Squadron, 352nd Fighter Group, September 1944**

Glen Moran's combat record was impressive. Credited with 13 air-to-air victories, he scored these during a relatively short period of time, notching up a tally more rapidly than his more famous squadron mates Meyer and Preddy. He scored most of his victories in this machine, which replaced his original aircraft (P-51B 42-6912/HO-M) after an April 1944 landing accident. It was a Dallas-built P-51C-1-NT, and is seen here with underwing fuel tanks and D-Day recognition stripes.

## 22

**P-51B-10-NA 42-106449 *Princess ELIZABETH*, flown by 1st Lieutenant William Whisner, 487th Fighter Squadron, 352nd Fighter Group, May 1944**

William Whisner's first Mustang was this P-51B. From late April 1944 the 352nd Fighter Group's blue nose marking was extended aft from being a 12-inch band to slope aft and upwards to cover the exhaust stubs, and squadron rudder colours (blue for the 487th FS, red for the 328th and yellow for the 486th) were introduced from November 1944. Whisner's P-51B retained the standard early Mustang canopy, which greatly restricted visibility. He ended the war a Captain, with 15.5 aerial and three ground victories.

## 23

**P-51D-10-NA 44-14237 *Moonbeam McSWINE*, flown by Captain William Whisner, 487th Fighter Squadron, 352nd Fighter Group, February 1945**

William T Whisner scored his first victories, whilst flying as George Preddy's wingman when the 352nd still flew P-47s, four more while flying other Mustangs during the remainder of his first combat tour, and the rest in this aircraft. *Moonbeam McSWINE* was equipped with a K-14 gunsight, which reportedly made deflection shooting much easier, as Whisner's second-tour total of 10.5 victories testifies. Whisner went on to become the 51st Fighter Interceptor Wing's first jet ace in Korea, and also served in Vietnam, albeit not as a combat pilot.

## 24

**P-5ID-20-NA 44-72374 *BETTY-E*, flown by Lieutenant Colonel Wayne Blickenstaff, 350th Fighter Squadron, 353rd Fighter Group, March 1945**

Wayne Blickenstaff scored four of his ten aerial victories on 27 November 1944, and four more on 24 March 1945. His aircraft wears the extended chequers and coloured rudder adopted in November 1944, and the aircraft's code letters are outlined thinly in yellow. While the 350th FS used yellow as its squadron colour, the 352nd used black, while the 351st left their rudders silver. The 353rd FG accounted for 330.5 enemy aircraft in air combat and 414 on the ground, losing 137 fighters in return.

## 25

**P-51D-25-NA 44-73060 *Dove of Peace*, flown by Colonel Glenn E Duncan, Officer Commanding 353rd Fighter Group, April 1945**

Glenn Duncan's period at the helm of the 353rd was interrupted on 7 July 1944 when he was shot down in his P-47 over Holland. After successfully belly-landing the 'Jug', Duncan evaded capture and worked with the Dutch Resistance until the allied advance through the Low Countries allowed him to return to his unit. Returning to his command on 22 April 1945, Duncan was assigned this P-51D, which took over the same *Dove of Peace* nickname as his P-47 had carried. All of Duncan's 19 victories were scored in the Thunderbolt.

## 26

**P-51D-15-NA 44-15092 *ALABAMA RAMMER JAMMER*, flown by 2nd Lieutenant Arthur C Cundy, 352nd Fighter Squadron, 353rd Fighter Group, October 1944**

Arthur Cundy's *ALABAMA RAMMER JAMMER*, wearing typical early 350th FG markings as they appeared shortly after the P-51 entered service with the Group on 2 October 1944. Whereas most camouflaged aircraft lost the white recognition stripes painted on their tailfins, the similar black stripes painted on natural metal Mustangs tended to be retained. The nose chequers were extended aft during November 1944, to avoid confusion with the black and white chequered Mustangs of the 55th FG. Squadron rudder colours were introduced at the same time, and coloured outlines were added to the identity code letters. One of Cundy's six kills is marked below the windscreen.

## 27

**P-51D-I5-NA 44-15625 *MAN O'WAR*, flown by Colonel Clairborne Kinnard, Officer Commanding 355th Fighter Group, early 1945**

Clairborne Kinnard Jr returned to the 355th Fighter Group as commander in late February 1945, after a three-month spell in command of the 4th Fighter Group, where he flew a P-51D (44-14292/QP-A) also named *Man O'War*. His first mount with the 355th was initially unnamed, however, and wore the red rudder and nose band associated with the 354th FS, but soon picked up the *Man O'War* name in a red lightning flash. This aircraft was fitted with distinctive twin mirrors on the canopy arch. All eight of Kinnard's aerial victories were achieved in the Mustang.

## 28

**P-51D-25-NA 44-73144 *Man O'War*, flown by Colonel Clairborne Kinnard, Officer Commanding 355th Fighter Group, April/May 1945**

To distinguish his aircraft as that of the Group Commander, Kinnard had no rudder colours on his last *Man O'War*, and used an all white nose, with no red outline. This aircraft carries the distinctive cylindrical external fuel tanks which were made from laminated paper to save weight, and thus also avoid the use of strategic materials. These would only last a few hours once filled with fuel, as the volatile fluid began to attack the paper and glue after a period of time. They had to be jettisoned before landing for flight safety reasons.

## 29

**P-51B-I0-NA 42-106448 *THE HUN HUNTER/TEXAS*, flown by 2nd Lieutenant Henry Brown, 354th Fighter Squadron, 355th Fighter Group, April 1944**

Henry Brown's first Mustang, named *THE HUN HUNTER/ TEXAS* was a P-51B delivered in the standard camouflage of olive drab and neutral grey, with white recognition bands. Brown applied his kill markings in a red stripe, which expanded to become a large panel, with several rows of crosses. When D-Day stripes were applied, they encircled the entire rear fuselage, with star-and-bar and squadron codes superimposed.

## 30

**P-51D-5-NA 44-13305 *THE HUN HUNTER/TEXAS*, flown by 1st Lieutenant Henry Brown, 354th Fighter Squadron, 355th Fighter Group, late summer, 1944**

Brown's second *HUN HUNTER* was a P-51D delivered in natural metal finish, but with RAF dark green top surfaces having been added in the run up to D-Day. Top scorer within the 355th FG having achieved 14.2 aerial and 14.5 ground victories, Henry Brown (by then a Captain) became a PoW after being shot down by flak on 3 October 1944. Coloured nose bands and rudders had not been added to the Mustangs of the 355th FG at this early stage of the war.

## 31

**P-51D-15-NA 44-15255 *DOWN FOR DOUBLE*, flown by Lieutenant Colonel Gordon Graham, 354th Fighter Squadron, 355th Fighter Group, March/April 1945**
A white letter 'C' was applied to many 355th Fighter Group Mustangs flown by command pilots, including this aircraft, assigned to the newly promoted Lt Col Gordon Graham, a 7 aerial/9.5 ground victory ace who scored all of his kills while flying the Mustang. From late 1944 355th Fighter Group HQ aircraft also had white nose bands extended aft below the exhausts, with the painted area edged in red. The 355th Fighter Group was the leading Eighth Air Force air-to-ground victory scoring fighter unit, with 502 ground kills — it also achieved 365.5 aerial victories, thus making it the third most successful destroyer of enemy aircraft in the air.

## 32

**P-51B-15-NA 42-106950 *The Iowa Beaut*, flown by Robert E Hulberman (rank unknown) 354th Fighter Squadron, 355th Fighter Group, June/July 1944**
Although not assigned to him, ace Frederick Haviland flew *The Iowa Beaut* on a number of occasions, and scored several of his nine aerial and six ground victories in the aircraft. Despite the impressive tally of victory markings, no trace of Hulberman himself, whose name appears on the nose, can be found in listings of Eighth Air Force air or ground aces. Two-tone disruptive camouflage, almost certainly using two very similar RAF paint colours, has been applied to a natural metal aircraft, necessitating the application of white recognition stripes above and below the wings and tail in place of the normal black ones.

## 33

**P-51D-5-NA 44-13677 *MISS STEVE*, flown by 1st Lieutenant William Cullerton, 357th Fighter Squadron, 355th Fighter Group, post-November 1944**
1st Lt William J Cullerton claimed five air-to-air and 15 air-to-ground victories, ranking him 29th among Eighth Air Force aces under the system in force in Europe at the time, where no distinction was drawn between air and ground kills. The Eighth Air Force was out-of-step with other units, and official recognition of ground kills was withdrawn postwar. Cullerton's P-51D carried a blue rudder and a 12-inch blue nose band, markings adopted by the 357th FS after November 1944. Several other 357th FS Mustangs carried the same 'Licking Dragon' motif on their noses.

## 34

**P-51B-5-NA 43-6928 *OLE II*, flown by 1st Lieutenant William Hovde, 358th Fighter Squadron, 355th Fighter Group, March/April 1944**
William Hovde's *OLE II* in regulation finish, with factory applied olive drab upper surfaces, neutral grey undersides and white recognition stripes around the wings, nose, tailplane and across the fin, seen shortly after the 355th Fighter Group began conversion from the P-47 to the Mustang. The fin stripe was soon deleted because it was felt

to be counter-productive, breaking up the distinctive shape of the Mustang's tail, and most Groups overpainted the nose stripe and spinner in individual colours.

## 35

**P-51D-25-NA 44-73108 *OLE V*, Major William Hovde, Officer Commanding 358th Fighter Squadron, 355th Fighter Group, December 1944**
Several of Hovde's later Mustangs (including *OLE V* and *OLE IV*) carried the same legend in cyrillic script, originally applied during a 'shuttle-bombing' escort mission. This translates as Major Vazh Hovde, the name of Hovde's father, who was of Russian extraction. Hovde ended the war with 10.5 aerial and two strafing victories. The aircraft has a yellow nose band and rudder, the identifying marks used by the 358th Fighter Squadron after November 1944.

## 36

**P-51D-15-NA 44-15152 *JERSEY JERK*, flown by Major Don Strait, Officer Commanding 361st Fighter Squadron, 356th Fighter Group, December 1944/January 1945**
Squadron colours were not adopted by the 356th FG until December 1944, when coloured rudders (yellow for the 359th FS, red for the 360th FS and blue for the 361st) were introduced, followed by coloured spinners from February 1945. Not equipped with P-51s until November 1944, the 356th FG was the 'hard luck' group of the Eighth, with a higher loss-to-kill ratio than any other fighter unit, claiming 201 aerial and 75.5 ground victories for the loss of 122 aircraft. Don Strait's 13.5 air-to-air kills included 10.5 in the Mustang, the last being a trio of Fieseler Storchs! Strait was not credited with any air-to-ground victories.

## 37

**P-51B-15-NA 43-24824 *OLD CROW*, flown by Captain Clarence 'Bud' Anderson, 362nd Fighter Squadron, 357th Fighter Group, May 1944**
Formed at Tonopah, Nevada, the 357th Fighter Group was the first P-51-equipped unit in the Eighth Air Force, beginning combat operations in February 1944. Its aircraft were among the most colourful, with red and yellow nose chequers and a variety of individual names and nose art. The 357th scored a higher number of air-to-air kills than any other unit in the Eighth, accounting for about a quarter of the Mustang aces in the Eighth, and coming second only to the 354th FG in the number of aces it produced. This P-51B wears the original olive drab camouflage, with invasion stripes around the fuselage and wings and the Group's red and yellow striped spinner and chequered nose band.

## 38

**P-51D-10-NA 44-14450 *OLD CROW*, flown by Captain Clarence 'Bud' Anderson, 362nd Fighter Squadron, 357th Fighter Group, late 1944**
Initially flown by Anderson in drab and neutral grey, by December 1944 *OLD CROW* had been stripped to a bare metal finish, and had picked up a red rudder (the identifying colour of the 362nd FS), though it retained invasion stripes. Clarence Anderson ended the war with 16.25 aerial victories, plus a single strafing kill. Staying in the USAF, he served as a test pilot for many years before flying F-105s in action over Vietnam.

## 39

**P-51K-5-NT 44-11622** *Nooky Booky IV*, **flown by Captain Leonard 'Kit' Carson, 362nd Fighter Squadron, 357th Fighter Group, Christmas Day 1944**

Top-scorer of the 357th Fighter Group with 18.5 aerial victories (plus 3.5 more by strafing) was Leonard Carson. He chalked up the bulk of his score during the final six months of the war, many of his victims falling to the guns of this, his fourth Mustang, a Dallas-built P-51K. From November 1944 the 357th Fighter Group adopted coloured rudders for its constituent squadrons (red for the 363rd FS, yellow for the 364th and no colour for the 362nd). Until December 1944 most of the unit's aircraft were camouflaged.

## 40

**P-51B-10-NA 42-106462** *U'VE HAD IT!*, **flown by Captain John England, 362nd Fighter Squadron, 357th Fighter Group, early Fall 1944**

The first of four P-51s flown by the 362nd Fighter Squadron's John England, typical of natural metal P-51 Bs given a hasty coat of camouflage on the top surfaces in anticipation of service from continental forward airfields. In fact, the extraordinary range and endurance of the Mustang, the continuing importance of the US daylight bombing offensive and the availability of other fighter types for close support and tactical work made such basing unnecessary. His squadron was among the first to receive Berger G-3 anti-g suits (after initial trials by the 339th Fighter Group), and replace its Mk II and Mk VIII reflector sights with the new K-14 gyro gunsight, a combination which England used to devastating effect.

## 41

**P-51D-10-NA 44-14709** *MISSOURI ARMADA*, **flown by Major John England, Officer Commanding 362nd Fighter Squadron, 3S7th Fighter Group, December 1944**

In December 1944 England's *MISSOURI ARMADA* was still painted in the original Eighth Air Force olive drab and neutral grey camouflage, and, as an aircraft from the 362nd Fighter Squadron, lacked a coloured rudder. England scored his final victory (of 17.5 air-to-air kills) on 14 January 1945, and finished his tour soon afterwards. Staying in the USAF post-war England was killed in a flying accident on 17 November 1954 at Toul-Rosiere.

## 42

**P-51D-25-NA: 44-72199 (unnamed), flown by Captain Charles E Weaver, 362nd Fighter Squadron, 357th Fighter Group, April 1945**

Bedecked with 11 victory symbols, representing eight aerial and three strafing kills, Captain Charles E Weaver's P-51D also sported a massive and beautifully executed reclining nude. The practise of the 362nd Fighter Squadron of not using coloured rudders made their aircraft the least striking of the 357th Fighter Group, but many of the unit's pilots compensated for this by applying gaudy nose art. The 357th was the first with P-51s, and scored more air-to-air victories (609.5) than any other Mustang-equipped Group, although its relative lack of strafing success (106) put it behind the 352nd and 355th FGs overall.

## 43

**P-5IB-5-NA 43-6933** *SPEEDBALL ALICE*, **flown by 1st**

**Lieutenant Don Bochkay, 363rd Fighter Squadron, 357th Fighter Group, April 1944**

The Mustangs of the 357th originally flew without distinctive unit insignia, apart from their two-letter unit codes and individual aircraft letters. The white nose bands and spinners were soon replaced by red and yellow chequers, however. Don Bochkay frequently flew as part of a flight of four aircraft, that comprised Jim Browning (a seven-victory ace killed in action on 9 February 1945), Chuck Yeager (11.5 victories), Clarence Anderson (16.25 victories) and Bochkay himself.

## 44

**P-51D-20-NA 44-72244 (winged Ace of Clubs badge), flown by Captain Don Bochkay, 363rd Fighter Squadron, 357th Fighter Group, February/March 1945**

Major (from March 1945) Don Bochkay planned and led a number of successful missions against German jet bases during the closing weeks of the war, downing two Me 262s himself to bring his score to 13.83 aerial victories. His last three aircraft were all unnamed P-5lDs, but all carried his large 'winged Ace' insignia on their engine cowlings. Bochkay was not credited with any air-to-ground victories.

## 45

**P-51D-20-NA 44-63621** *LITTLE SHRIMP*, **flown by Captain Robert Foy, 363rd Fighter Squadron, 357th Fighter Group, January 1945**

One of Robert Foy's first aircraft was a drab-painted P-51D named *Reluctant Rebel* (44-13712/B6-V), but this later illustrated aircraft is better known, and was flown by the pilot for most of his 15 aerial and 3 ground victories. Foy enjoyed something of a charmed life, being plucked out of the Channel twice, and even managing to fly home after hitting a tree during a low flypast of a downed foe. Foy ended the war as a Major.

## 46

**P-51D-15-NA 44-14888** *GLAMOROUS GLEN III*, **flown by Captain Charles 'Chuck' Yeager, 363rd Fighter Squadron, 357th Fighter Group, November 1944**

Chuck Yeager's blend of cockiness and fearlessness served him as well in his career as a fighter pilot as it later did as a test pilot. Yeager ended the war with 11.5 aerial victories, including two Me 262 jets. On the other side of the ledger, Yeager was himself shot down by an Fw 190, but evaded capture and eventually returned to the UK, via Spain, with the help of the French Resistance. This P-51D was the third of Yeager's Mustangs, all named after his sweetheart. The red rudder (applied to the unit's aircraft from November 1944) denotes the 363rd Fighter Squadron.

## 47

**P-51B-5-NA 43-6935** *Hurry Home Honey*, **flown by Captain Richard Peterson, 364th Fighter Squadron, 357th Fighter Group, May/June 1944**

*Hurry Home Honey* was a P-51B flown by Captain Richard Peterson of the 364th Fighter Squadron. Invasion stripes encircle the entire rear fuselage, marring the effectiveness of the camouflage and necessitating the application of a black outline to those code letters applied over the white paint. One of the 357th Fighter Group's original pilots, Peterson notched up a tally of 15.5 air-to-air and 3.5 air-to-ground kills.

## 48

**P-51D-5-NA 44-13586 *Hurry Home Honey*, flown by Captain Richard Peterson, 364th Fighter Squadron, 357th Fighter Group, October 1944**

Peterson was assigned at least two P-51Ds, both of which he named *Hurry Home Honey*, inspired by the way his wife concluded her letters to him. This aircraft has green top surfaces extended to the vertical fin, while his other similarly marked D was overall natural metal, and had the yellow rudder of the 364th Fighter Squadron. Peterson was a slow starter, scoring most of his victories during the last nine months of the war.

## 49

**P-51D-20-NA 44-72164 *THE SHILLELAGH*, flown by Lt Colonel John Storch, Officer Commanding 364th Fighter Squadron, 357th Fighter Group, early 1945**

From November 1944, the 357th Fighter Group allocated rudder colours to two of its squadrons, yellow for the 364th and red for the 363rd, aircraft of the 362nd retaining natural metal. The abandonment of camouflage did not signify that the skies over Germany were safe, however, since there were still a handful of highly experienced Luftwaffe *experten* flying, and in the wrong hands aircraft like the Fw 190D and the jet-powered Me 262 could still give a P-51 pilot a very hard time. Storch claimed 10.5 aerial and 1.5 ground victories. One can only wonder if Storch knew what a 'Shillelagh' was, since a simple club was painted on the nose of his aircraft, whereas the real Irish weapon has a sloping, hammer-like head! Storch began his first tour as a Captain, being promoted to Major in May 1944.

## 50

**P-51D-5-NA 44-13606 *LOUISIANA HEAT WAVE*, flown by 1st Lieutenant Claude Crenshaw, 369th Fighter Squadron, 359th Fighter Group, November 1944**

Crenshaw's finest moment came on 21 November 1944, when he was credited with downing four Fw190s. This achievement was even more impressive when one considers that only three of Crenshaw's guns were working, and the manoeuvring nature of the engagement had forced him to fire at deflection angles of up to 90+ degrees! No less than 14 Mustangs were lost that day, and many bombers were also downed by a Luftwaffe that was far from beaten. The 359th Fighter Group initially used a green spinner and 12-inch green fuselage band as its marking, adding squadron rudder colours in November 1944. The 369th Fighter Squadron used red rudders, the 368th yellow and the 370th blue. Crenshaw gained seven air-to-air victories, and three strafing kills.

## 51

**P-51D-10-NA 44-14733 *Daddy's Girl*, flown by Captain Ray Wetmore, 370th Fighter Squadron, 359th Fighter Group, early 1945**

The 359th Fighter Group extended its green nose band aft in late 1944, curving down over the exhaust stubs and under the wing leading edge. Ray Wetmore's *Daddy's Girl* has this later style green nose and blue rudder of the 370th Fighter Squadron. With 21.25 victories, 16 of them scored in Mustangs (plus 2.33 strafing kills), Wetmore was the top-scorer of the 359th. For his final kill, he shot down the fourth and last Me 163 Komet to fall to the guns of Eighth Air Force

Mustangs. Wetmore continued in the USAF postwar, only to die when his F-84 crashed on 14 February 1951.

## 52

**P-51D-5-NA 44-13704 *Ferocious Frankie*, flown by Major Wallace Hopkins, 374th Fighter Squadron, 361st Fighter Group, Summer 1944**

Wallace Hopkins flew a succession of aircraft named *Ferocious Frankie*. His natural metal invasion-striped B was 42-106655, and this was replaced by the aircraft illustrated. The group marking of a 12-inch yellow nose band and spinner was extended aft from about August 1944, following the style of the 352nd FG's blue nose. Rudder colours were added from November 1944, with red for the 374th FS, blue for the 375th and yellow for the 376th. Prior to this some aircraft carried coloured trim tabs. Hopkins, with his eight confirmed victories evenly split between air and ground, eventually rose to become a Lieutenant Colonel and the Deputy Commander of the Group.

## 53

**P-51D-10-NA 44-14164 *DETROIT Miss*, flown by 1st Lieutenant Urban Drew, 375th Fighter Squadron, 361st Fighter Group, October 1944**

A former instructor, Urban Drew scored six air-to-air victories and a solitary strafing kill in his one and only combat tour with the 361st, including two Me 262s downed in a single mission. This unique feat earned Drew a much belated Air Force Cross (in lieu of the discontinued Distinguished Service Cross), awarded on 12 May 1983! His second tour was in the Pacific with the 414th FG. Before rudders were painted in squadron colours some aircraft featured small patches of colour on the fin tip, wingtips and canopy rail. Drew's aircraft wore 374th FS colours.

## 54

**P-51D-15-NA 44-15076 *Betty Lee III*, flown by 2nd Lieutenant William T Kemp, 375th Fighter Squadron, 361st Fighter Group, September 1944**

Kemp scored a total of six air-to-air victories with the 361st Fighter Group, all of them while flying the P-51D. He also won a Distinguished Service Cross in July 1944 for his defence of the bombers he was escorting, closing to within 15 yards of an Fw 190 to down it after three of his guns jammed! His first aircraft, *Betty Lee II*, also carried the name *Marie*, but by the autumn of 1944 Kemp was flying this aircraft, *Betty Lee III*.

## 55

**P-51D-25-NA 44-72719 *Constance*, flown by Major George Ceuleers, 383rd Fighter Squadron, 364th Fighter Group, Late 1944**

*Constance* was flown by the top-scoring ace of the 364th Fighter Group, Major (later Lieutenant Colonel) George Ceuleers. He scored two of his 10.5 confirmed kills (all air-to-air) in his P-38 (*Connie & Butcher*), which carried the same squadron codes as this Mustang. The 364th eventually adopted a blue-and-white striped nose band and white spinner as its unit insignia, but squadron colours were not used. Instead the 383rd FS applied the individual aircraft code letter in a black circle on the fin, the 384th in a black square and the 385th in a black triangle.

## 56

**P-51D-5-NT 44-11243 *Betty Jo IV*, flown by Major Samuel Wicker, 383rd Fighter Squadron, 364th Fighter Group, December 1944**

This Dallas-built P-51D was the mount of Major Samuel Wicker, who scored four air-to-air victories in the Mustang during December 1944, adding these to his three victories notched up as a Captain when flying the P-38 with the same squadron. Wicker was not credited with any air-to-ground victories.

## 57

**P-51D-20-NA 44-63263 *PENNY 4*, flown by Colonel John Lowell, Acting officer commanding, 364th Fighter Group, November/December 1944**

*PENNY 4* was flown by John Lowell, whose tally of 7.5 aerial victories included 4.5 in the Mustang. He racked up a further nine air-to-ground victories. As Group Commander, Lowell bagged the individual aircraft letter 'L' for himself, and flew an aircraft from the 384th Fighter Squadron.

## 58

**P-51D-25-NA 44-73045 *Lucky Lady VII*, flown by Captain Ernest 'Ernie' Bankey, 364th Fighter Group, early 1945**

Continuing to fly the same aircraft assigned to him as a member of the 385th Fighter Squadron, Bankey held an appointment within the 364th Fighter Group staff from December 1944, but nevertheless managed to increase his score from two to 9.5! On 27 December 1944 Bankey was able to make the astonishing radio call, 'I've got 50 Jerries cornered over Bonn!' – he then proceeded to rapidly shoot down four of them in the ensuing melée, and share another with his wingman. Bankey also added eight air-to-ground credits to his 9.5 air-to-air kills.

## 59

**P-51D-30-NT 44-11674 *BOOMERANG JR.*, flown by Lieutenant Colonel Arthur 'Art' Jeffrey, 434th Fighter Squadron, 479th Fighter Group, March 1945**

The 479th Fighter Group did not convert from P-38s to P-51s until September 1944, and as a result, the Group scored less air-to-air victories (155) than any other, although it also lost significantly fewer of its own aircraft (69) and pilots! This Dallas-built P-51D was the mount of Lieutenant Colonel Arthur Jeffrey, who scored 10 of his 14 kills (all air-to-air) in the Mustang, most as a Major. This total included the Eighth Air Force's first victory over the Messerschmitt Me 163 Komet on 29 July 1944.

## 60

**P-51D-25-NA 44-72922 *SCAT VI*, flown by Major Robin Olds, 434th Fighter Squadron, 479th Fighter Group, February/March 1945**

Robin Olds scored nine aerial victories in the P-38, making him the top Eighth Air Force Lightning ace, and another four in the P-51. His 11 strafing victories took his combined total to 24, placing him the 17th in the Eighth Air Force's ace listing. This P-51D was the last of a series of consecutively numbered SCATs, and is typical of 479th FG Mustangs in having no Group nose colours, instead using only a red rudder (and a red oil cooler intake lip) to signify the 434th Fighter Squadron. Olds led the Eighth TFW's 'Wolfpack' during the Vietnam war, flying F-4C Phantoms IIs, and added four MiG kills to his wartime total. His individual tally of kills was less important than his inspirational leadership of the Wing in this later conflict.

## FIGURE PLATES

### 1

Captain Leonard K 'Kit' Carson of the 357th Fighter Group in full 1944 flying kit. The fur-collared B-15 jacket was popular with fighter pilots, and usually worn over a regulation olive drab shirt and khaki tie. Both American and RAF-pattern goggles and flying helmets were commonly used. The standard B-5 seat parachute harness is shown over A-4 coverall trousers, along with an oxygen mask and R/T leads, plus an inflatable B-4 'Mae West' lifejacket, crucial for North Sea crossings.

### 2

An AAF Captain wearing the latest 1945-style Eighth Air Force fighter pilot kit. A B-4 'Mae West' lifejacket is worn over an A-2 leather jacket and silk scarf to prevent neck chafing, with the abdomen and legs swathed in a Berger-type G-3 anti-G-suit to prevent unconsciousness in high-speed combat. The optional sidearm is a Colt .45-cal automatic, and GI canvas shoes are worn here.

### 3

Captain Don Gentile in dress uniform, circa spring 1944. Along with AAF insignia, Gentile was entitled to wear RAF 'wings' over the right breast pocket of his A-1 uniform jacket, which bore captain's 'bars' on the shoulder tabs. An Eighth AAF patch was worn on the left shoulder only, and medal ribbons were sewn below the AAF wings. Slacks, or 'pinks', were worn with standard issue GI shoes.

### 4

Major Pierce McKennon of the 4th FG's 335th FS in A-4 flying coveralls which are largely devoid of insignia, apart from the Eighth AF shoulder patch (also worn at the trouser waistband). Tucked into the intermediate B-15 jacket, with fur-trimmed collar, is the universal silk scarf to prevent neck chafing. The trousers had pockets for maps, whilst the A-6A winter flying boots were of AAF pattern. An all-important ditching whistle is worn on a neck lanyard.

### 5

Colonel Don Blakeslee of the 4th FG shown immediately after a mission, wearing an A-2 leather flying jacket, AAF officers' OD slacks and GI shoes and socks. The AAF C-type flying helmet with integral R/T earphones is worn with tinted double-lens goggles and the much sought-after RAF-issue silk flying gloves. A rank badge is worn on the shoulder of the flying jacket.

### 6

This 1st Lieutenant wears the standard AAF issue OD 'M1944' 'Ike jacket', with pilot's wings on the right breast over medal ribbon bars. An Eighth AF patch was worn on the left shoulder only, and the 'overseas cap', piped around the turn-up in AAF orange, has a single silver (metal) bar of rank, while the sleeve badge is fabric. An AAF tie and OD wool shirt and trousers are also worn, as are standard GI shoes.

# OUTCLASSED

Air combat over Europe in mid-1944 brought American pilots into contact with what amounted to a new age of flying, and one that would very rapidly render their superb aircraft obsolete. Fortunately for the Allies, German scientists were only able to provide a taste of the vast effort that had gone into bringing this next generation of aircraft up to operational status.

German jet and rocket development had been under close Allied scrutiny for many months before the first aircraft powered by these revolutionary engines were met in combat by the Eighth Air Force. There was considerable speculation – and no little apprehension – as to how these potentially lethal new weapons would be deployed. Pilots noting the existence of jets and rockets were closely questioned at debriefing so that accurate intelligence reports could be circulated to all units, particularly the fighter groups.

The purpose of these reports was to devise new tactics for the fighter force, but in reality little could be done in this area – if the P-51 could not catch the jets then pilots could hardly shoot them down. It was very much a situation of wait and see, however unpalatable this appeared.

On 28 July 1944 the 359th FG had drawn escort duty for a bomber force heading for Merseburg. As the Mustangs approached the target area, Col Avelin P Tacon Jr heard a call from one of his pilots. Two condensation trails were heading for the bomber stream, betraying the presence of fast aircraft – very fast. He reefed his P-51 into a 180-degree turn and his flight attempted to cut off the jets. They had little chance. The Me 262s shot away, one diving for the ground, the other climbing up into the sun – there was nothing a piston-engined fighter could do to catch them

Gen Kepner, digesting this and similar sighting reports, advised his groups that '. . . probably the first thing seen will be heavy, dense contrails high up at 30,000ft and above, approaching the rear of the bombers. Jet aircraft can especially be expected in the Leipzig and Munich area. . .'

Kepner and all his group commanders realised that the kind of challenge that now confronted his pilots was unlike any other. In maximum level speed alone the P-51 was outclassed, and if the Germans managed to form multiple *Gruppen*

The final group assigned to VIIIth FC was the 479th. This formation consists of three 434th FS P-51Ds, the lead Mustang (44-14395) being christened *The ONLY Genevieve*, whilst alongside it is *The YAKIMA Chief* (44-14523). Pilots of the P-51s were Bob Kline and Harold Stott respectively

The 479th was based at Wattisham, in Suffolk, throughout its time in the ETO. Originally a P-38 group, it was not, however, the last to receive P-51s as it converted to D-models in September 1944, ahead of both the 78th and the 353rd FGs. This Mustang, nicknamed *The Impatient Virgin*, is also a 434th FS machine

equipped with jets, the slow bombers would be decimated.

In the ensuing weeks the 'jet menace' loomed ever larger. On 5 August Messerschmitt Me 163 Komets attacked a formation of P-51s protecting bombers, and shot down three of them at close range. However, the 359th FG evened the score a little only days later.

Watching out for enemy aircraft over Leipzig on 16 August, Lt Col John B Murphy saw the bombers being attacked by an Me 163. As he turned and made after it, the tiny rocket aircraft appeared to cut its

throttle and pounce on a straggling B-17. To save the hapless Fortress, Murphy firewalled his own throttles, which resulted in his airspeed indicator nudging the 400-mph mark. He steadily closed on the Me 163 which, in the meantime, had overshot its intended victim and flattened out at medium altitude. Murphy closed right in and fired. Strikes were observed on the enemy machine's vertical tail and fuselage as the American banked away to kill speed. His wingman, Lt Cyril Jones, fired from slightly below as the enemy pilot executed a split-S and dived. Jones kept after him but hit the jetwash and momentarily blacked out. The Komet pilot quickly took advantage of this and raced away out of range.

But the sortie was not over as Murphy had spotted another jet 5000 ft below him. He dived, cut inside the Me 163's turning circle, and scored hits on the fuselage. There was an explosion and suddenly the rear of the fuselage broke away – there would be no doubt about this kill.

Further skirmishes between Mustangs and Komets took place through to October, after which time Allied aircrews were thankfully able to report that the jet threat was not materialising as fast as had been earlier feared. It soon became clear that the Me 163 had limited endurance, and

A detailed close-up of the nose art of Harold Stott's *The YAKIMA Chief*, plus of course the pilot himself. Although the 479th had the shortest of combat records in the ETO, its pilots neverthelss achieved a few notable first and lasts, like claiming the first Me 163 destroyed (this distinction fell to ranking ace Capt Art Jeffrey on 29 July 1944), and downing the last German aircraft shot down by the Eighth in World War 2 (Lt Hilton Thompson achieved this feat on 25 April 1945 when he despatched an Arado Ar 234 'Blitz' bomber near Salzburg, in Austria)

356th FG pilot Herb Rutland's immaculate late-build P-51D on the PSP in April 1945 at Martlesham Heath – the steel sheets had been laid down due to the heavy spring showers in East Anglia that year

although highly manoeuvrable, it appeared to be capable of little more than an 'all or nothing' full power climb, leaving its pilot with only seconds of attack time up his sleeve, before he was obliged to dive away.

## COMBATING THE ME 262

The Me 262 was in a completely different class though. A sleek twin-engined jet capable of superb acceleration, it appeared to be the main threat. However, on 7 October, Lt Urban Drew of the 361st FG's 375th FS showed that the P-51 was still capable of 'taking the ring' with the jet and emerging victorious if cleverly flown. Drew surprised two Me 262s taking off from Achmer aerodrome, and using his speed and altitude to full advantage, quickly shot both jets down. This was indeed gratifying news, for if the Mustang pilots could use their aircrafts' excellent piston-engined performance to obtain a good tactical position before the enemy jets had a chance to build up speed, the theat might still be contained.

That Drew's double Me 262 kill was no fluke was shown by none other than top P-47 exponent, 'Hub' Zemke, that same day. Formerly of the 56th FG, the 'Hub' had only recently forsaken his favourite Thunderbolt for the cockpit of a Mustang, following his posting to command the 479th FG. In the process of helping his Group transition from the P-38 to the P-51D, he and his wingman, Lt Norman Benolt, attacked what they took to be a Bf 109. Good strikes were observed and the enemy aircraft shed a wing and crashed – it was not until the two pilots' combat film was developed back at their Wattisham base that an Me 262 was clearly revealed.

While it was realised soon enough how formidable an opponent the Me 262 could be to conventional fighters, the German pilots tried everything they knew to avoid the escorts and shoot down only the all-important bombers. However, there were usually so many American fighters present that this was all but

A trio of 356th FG P-51Ds from the 360th FS cruise in formation over East Anglia during the spring of 1945. This gritty group had a particularly hard war, being the final P-47 outfit to transition to the P-51 (the 56th FG never made the swap from Thunderbolt to Mustang). Due to its total devotion to escorting the bombers, the 356th scored the least number of kills in VIIIth FC, and suffered the worst ratio of losses to victories – 276.5 enemy aircraft destroyed for the loss of 122 P-47s and P-51s *(H Rutland)*

Arguably the most famous series of aircraft flown within the 359th FG were those nicknamed *Daddy's Girl*. They were all piloted by the group's leading ace, Ray Wetmore, his sobriquet adorning P-47D 42-75058, P-51B 42-106894 and finally P-51D 44-14733. The young Californian flew no less than 142 missions between 1943 and 45, scoring 21.25 aerial victories and 2.33 strafing kills *(Ethell)*

impossible. This situation left the *Jagdfleiger* with little choice but to blast their way through to the bombers, and on 1 November the 20th FG had one of its number shot down in flames by a diving Me 262 intent on stopping a formation of B-17s. Beginning his attack from 38,000 ft, the enemy pilot appeared to have broken off his run after destroying a solitary P-51D. However, he then turned back towards the bombers, and dozens of Mustangs and Thunderbolts the attempted cut him off.

Lt Dick Flowers of the 20th and Lt Gerbe of the 352nd fired at him first, then a 56th FG P-47 joined the fray. Three other pilots tried their luck before the Me 262's right engine flamed out and the pilot decide to 'hit the silk'. Gerbe and Lt Groce, the 56th FG pilot, shared the kill.

'Bud' Anderson had a couple of skrmishes with the German jets.

'I might have shot down the first one I saw, but I was so excited at seeing a jet that I butchered the chance. We hadn't joined up with the

The legendary triple ace Clarence 'Bud' Anderson's second *Old Crow* (P-51D-10-NA 44-14450), posed against a Christmas backdrop at Leiston during the festive season in 1944/45. Only a matter of weeks before, this Mustang had still worn its OD and grey scheme so favoured by the 357th FG, and Anderson in particular – at least the 110-gal 'paper' tank still wears matt grey paint! The Group were also one of the last outfits to remove the 'D-Day stripes' from their P-51s. A native of Newcastle, California, Anderson successfully completed two tours with the 362nd FS, flying 116 sorties and scoring 16.25 aerial kills whilst in the ETO *(Anderson)*

bombers yet – this (attack by the jets) might have been a ploy to get us to drop our tanks early – who knows? But I looked down and saw a 262 flying right-to-left across our course, straight and level, a few thousand feet under us. I knew the 262 was much faster but I had enough altitude to build up some speed and was thinking that if I peeled off and down right now, staying upside down so I could keep him in view, falling at just the right angle to come out behind him (coming out ahead of him could prove mighty embarrassing), I might just get off a burst before he could run off and vanish.

'To get rid of your drop tanks, first you routinely turn the switch to internal fuel in order to avoid interrupting the flow of gas to the engine. But I'm excited now. I'm thinking, "Drop 'em and GO!" I hit the release without switching my tanks, roll over into my dive – and the engine quits cold!

'I figure it out almost instantly, switch my tanks and restart the engine. The prop runs away, just like always, until finally it catches and settles back down. All this wastes time, and I'm cursing my own stupidity. But in spite of it all, he's still down there and I'm still in position, falling like a brick and thinking I can still pull this off. I put the pipper dead on him and maybe, if I fire right now, I might hit him. But I'd have to be lucky. I'm at maximum range, going like hell and I think I'm overtaking him. I tell myself to be patient, and that in a couple of seconds I'll have a good shot. And then the 262 disappeared! He was really moving and in an eyeblink that jet just shrank up and vanished behind my gunsight's bull's-eye of light.'

The time-honoured maxim 'he who has height controls the battle' was never truer than when VIIIth FC met the jets. But the Germans still had a useful force of conventional fighters which might or might not be tempted into combat – at that stage of the game it was hard to anticipate just what the Americans might be faced with. To make the enemy's reaction more certain, they could always pull a ruse, as Anderson explains.

'On 27 November, we tried some new tactics. It was technically speaking a strafing raid. But we used that as a ruse, hoping to draw out their fighters. The Mustangs of the 353rd Group arranged themselves in bomber formation and our planes flew the standard zig-zag escort pattern

Joe Thury was the scourge of the Luftwaffe in April 1945. For example, as part of the 339th's 504th FS, he led two strafing attacks that month that resulted in the group claiming no less than 200 aircraft destroyed in total! Thury's score was 26.5 confirmed, all but one of these being ground kills. After the second sortie, *Pauline*, alias 44-14656 of the 504th FS, had to be junked due to it being flak damaged and over-stressed

Lt Philip Petitt and *Princess Pat* of the 505th FS, 339th FG *(Ethell)*

**Damaged by flak during a strafing mission over Germany on 15 January 1945, *DANA KAY* nevertheless carried her pilot safely back to his base at Honington, in Suffolk. Assigned to the 364th FG's 383rd FS, the lightly damaged P-51D is having its unused ammunition removed from the magazines by squadron armourers prior to it being moved to the unit's hangars *(USAF)***

**Rolling out at Honington, the furthest of these 383rd FS, 364th FG P-51Ds was the mount of George Cueleers, the Group's leading ace with 10.5 kills. He was a veteran of 103 missions, and this shot was taken only weeks after Cueleers' unit had converted from P-38s to P-51s in late July 1944, hence the fact that only three kills are marked below its cockpit – he scored two victories whilst flying P-38s *(Ethell)***

above them. The idea was to fool the German radar and scramble the interceptors. It worked almost too well. They threw themselves at us 100 miles southwest of Berlin, north of Leipzig. The enemy pilots must have had coronaries when they discovered what they were attacking – not B-17s, but more than 100 fighters spoiling for trouble. Our pulses jumped, too, when we saw the hornet's nest we'd stirred up, for they came, not by the dozens, or scores, but in insect-like clouds we called "gaggles". For whatever reason, they decided to hit this raid with every airplane they had.

'It was the biggest concentration of enemy airplanes I had ever seen! They came in two clusters of 80 to 100 planes each. I'd seen 100 all together before, but here were two groups that big, mostly Focke-Wulfs. They were coming at us almost head-on, at 11 o'clock; we turned into them as they passed us and all hell broke loose.

'I fell on a straggler who broke smartly and ran for the deck. Letting him go, I turned and went back where the fighting was, with wingmen Ray Wolf close beside me. I picked out a 190 ahead at about 31,000 feet, closed to within 250 yards before he knew what was happening, and hammered him with a burst that made flashes all over the fuselage. When he didn't do anything, I followed up with another, and he rolled over slowly, too slowly, and fell into a spin. The pilot must have been dead. I turned

away, looking for targets. There were airplanes darting all over the sky.'

'Bud' Anderson, and the rest of the 357th FG's pilots, had a field day. 'Kit' Carson got five, Chuck Yeager claimed four and Anderson three – these later 'went into the records as two and a probable'. The group had put up 49 P-51s and came home with a score of 31 enemy fighters destroyed, which at that time was a record, for the loss of a single P-51.

## NEW SUITS

By the autumn of 1944, G-suits had been developed for pilots, and the 339th and 357th were amongst the groups which combat-tested them. They were filled with either water or air, and were designed to prevent black-outs during high speed manoeuvres, as 'Bud' Anderson recounts.

'The Mustangs, generally speaking, could take harder turns than the people who flew them. Long before the wings flew off, the pilots would simply lose consciousness. The blood drained from his head by centrifugal force, measured in Gs. Five Gs and you might "gray out" but be able to function. Six or so and you could "black out" and lose consciousness. The form-fitting suits simply inflated as the airplane pulled Gs, hugging you, and preventing your blood from running from your brain all at once.

'They were strictly experimental, which was why we had two different

P-51D *Milly* of the 360th FS, 356th Group, was flown by Don F Jones in the last months of the war. As with many Mustangs of the period, the pilot has had nose art applied to his machine in the photographic-reproduction style popular at the time *(H Rutland)*

Robert Garlich flew *Luscious Jr* with the 355 FG's 357th FS from Steeple Morden. He arrived in the ETO in the second half of 1944, and finished the war as an Eighth AF ace with 6.50 ground kills. Of the Group's three squadrons, the 357th was probably the least publicised as they boasted none of the outfit's major aces *(Garlich)*

Duran Vickery Jr poses for a quick photograph for 'the folks back home', before strapping into *Ann-Anita/Bama Bound* and heading out on a patrol over the Low Countires during the spring of 1945. Assigned to the 355th's 354th FS, Vickery Jr claimed four strafing kills whilst in the ETO, three of which have been sprayed up on the canopy bar of 44-14910 *(D Vickery Jr)*

Lee Mendenhall oversees routine maintenance work on his 354th FS, 355th FG P-51D, christened *Texas Terror IV* (44-13571) at Steeple Morden during the summer of 1944. The SCR-695 radio transmitter receiver (and its associated SCR-522 device) was crucial to the effectiveness of the P-51 as an escort fighter. Therefore, at the first hint of trouble the groundcrews would whip off the canopy and give the kit a thorough going over

kinds. The water suits were like overalls. The crew chief filled them up at the top with a funnel and pitcher (as I recall, it took several pitchers) and when the mission was done you would sit on the wing, open two little drains at your ankles and the water would simply empty in two silver streams. The problem with the water suits was that they were cold, and I only wore one a couple of times. We tried filling them with warm water, but at six miles up they cooled quickly. The air suits, attached to a G-sensitive valve, drew air through a line that ran from the pressure side of the engine's vacuum pump. These suits wrapped around your abdomen, thighs and calves in three sections that looked like a cowboy's chaps, and they inflated automatically. These worked much better.

'With the G suits, we could fly a little harder, turn a little bit tighter. We could pull maybe one extra G now, which gave us an edge. There was no resistence to wearing them as we understood what they meant right away: wearing one was the same as making the airplane better.'

At the edge of a new era of flight, the American fighter pilots could have done with a fully pressurised cockpit to prevent the very painful condition that divers know as the 'bends'. Flying at 40,000 ft-plus with nothing more than an oxygen mask, the nitrogen in the human bloodstream could congeal in the joints, causing intense pain. One cure used in 1944 was to pre-breathe 100 per cent oxygen before the mission to purge the bloodstream of nitrogen. It was a condition that did not affect all pilots the same way, as some found that constant exposure to high altitudes acclimatised their bodies.

Often, more fundamental problems tended to manifest themselves at this altitude. Sometimes the P-51's demisters decided to pack up and the pilot suddenly found himself sitting there blind, looking at an opaque white wall. The guns too were adversely affected by high altitudes, particularly if their heaters malfunctioned.

# MISSION COMPLETED

After its last brief fling on New Year's Day 1945 during *Operation Bödenplatte*, the *Jagdwaffe* was never again to appear in such force on a single mission. VIIIth FC, the RAF and other Army Air Force formations, not to mention the Red Air Force in the east, had the enemy totally surrounded. Gradually the separate fighting fronts contracted to squeeze the remaining life out of the Third Reich. The last months of the war saw VIIIth Bomber Command continuing to pound Germany targets from the west while the Fifteenth Air Force flew from its southern Italian airfields to hit Austria and eastern Europe.

Escort duties occupied the Eighth's Mustang force throughout the period, there now being frequent sorties which were merely routine outings for the pilots, with little sign of the enemy fighter force. Yet *Bödenplatte* had shown that the Germans were quite capable of surprising the Allies, and the pilots realised they were overflying what amounted to a hotbed of technological genius, however battered airfields, factories, railyards and seaports might appear to be from an altitude of 30,000 ft.

Vast numbers of buildings, any one of which could have housed a small production line for a secret weapon, were never bombed, and even with the gift of hindsight, it is impractical to imagine that all these targets could have been destroyed in any case with the technology then

available. Strategic bombers could only concentrate on the main urban centres and recognised tactical targets as briefed, and while the medium bombers and fighters did what they could to destroy many smaller targets, a significant number had to remain untouched as they appeared to be seemingly innocuous and totally unconnected with the war effort.

The Germans also went underground in order to continue the production of fighters and rockets, as well as an amazing array of advanced weapons. Camouflaging of airfields, utilisation of road sections as runways and an elaborate system of dispersing fighter strips in wood and heathland enabled Luftwaffe interceptors to keep flying, and oblige the Allied fighter force to remain alert. A vast industrial effort managed to ensure that there would be fighters for pilots to fly, and by a near-miracle, enough fuel to power them. Supplies of oil and high octane petroleum

**Arguably one of the most famous pilots to serve in the USAAF during the war, Col John Landers was also amongst the most experienced. He was an ace in both the Pacific and European theatres (one of only a handful of pilots to achieve the double), where he saw action in all the major combat types. Landers sobriquet, *Big Beautiful Doll*, and his impressive scoreboard, adorned almost a dozen airframes during his career, but reached its zenith with P-51D-20-NA 44-72218, which he flew from December 1944 until war's end whilst CO of the 78th FG**

A little bent, and some distance from its home base of Duxford, this crestfallen 83rd FS, 78th FG P-51D was photographed at an isolated Soviet strip dripping bodily fluids after one of the many Shuttle missions in early 1945. Judging by the damage to the wheel nearest the camera, *Lottie* may have experienced a ground loop on landing (*USAF*)

Lt Warren Blodgett of the 84th FS, 78th FG, flying *'LITTLE CHIC'* (44-72099), formates with Capt James Farmer in 44-15731, nicknamed *Mischievous Nell*. The kill markings on the former's canopy bar denote ground strafing victories (*Ethell*)

were ever dwindling, and this was one of the major factors (compounded by a severe pilot shortage) that crippled the Luftwaffe's jet force, thus easing Allied fears of mid-1944 that these advanced fighters would gain the ascendancy over Germany.

## LAST KILLS

The Luftwaffe's dire position by 1945 was also the cause for serious concern on English fighter bases – how could new pilots hope to score victories with the enemy keeping his head down? The only chance a pilot had of destroying an enemy aircraft, let alone becoming an ace, was by claiming ground kills. Even that was becoming difficult, or so the scuttlebutt said. VIIIth FC was in the exasperating situation of having more than enough eager pilots, but few targets left for them to shoot at.

This was a period when groups of fighters, ranging freely across the length and breadth of Germany, could turn up little that was worth the ammunition expenditure. But some groups seemed to be able to find the Luftwaffe in its hides. One such outfit was Joe Thury's 339th FG who, on a number of occasions in April 1945, came back with evidence of multiple strafing passes and widespread destruction.

Pilots also noted grimly that as Germany's territory contracted so the available number of flak batteries rose; both large calibre guns and the small and deadly multi-barrel mobile type that frequently guarded airfields, and could put up withering sheets of fire in the path of low

257

flying fighters, proliferated. These weapons began to surround any worthwhile target in substantial numbers.

Not that air-to-air combat had entirely given way to victories on the ground. The 359th FG at East Wretham, in Norfolk, were another of those units who rarely hit the headlines, but that fact hardly detered the pilots of the green-nosed

P-51s from carving their own niche within VIIIth FC. The Group's leading ace, Ray S Wetmore, emerged as one of the foremost exponents of the P-51 in the ETO, scoring 16 of his 21.25 aerial victories in the Mustang.

Wetmore served two combat tours which enabled him to witness the last gasps of the Luftwaffe's once mighty fighter force. That the enemy could still make things more than a little uncomfortable for the Americans had been amply demonstrated on 27 November when Wetmore and his wingman, Lt Robert York, became embroiled in a seemingly one-sided dogfight – the odds were 50 to one! The former quickly called in help when two further gaggles of fighters numbering roughly 100 aircraft each were sighted north of Munster. Unfortunately, the rest of his flight had aborted due to engine trouble with one of the P-51s, and Wetmore and York found themselves stalking the massive force alone. When the enemy saw the size of the opposition, the hunters became the hunted. 'We had to attack in self-defence', Wetmore said later.

With little choice remaining, the P-51s waded into the fighters and Wetmore and York quickly reduced the odds by one a piece. A good burst with 20 degrees deflection brought Wetmore's second kill. He then turned into the attack of another Bf 109, and the pair twisted and turned as the respective pilots strove for the upper hand. It finally fell to the American, and he shot off all his remaining ammunition, where-upon his foe bailed out. Defenceless now, Wetmore spent the next ten minutes bluffing out attacks by more fighters, before extricating himself from the melée.

He followed up this success with another big score on Valentine's Day 1945. Vectored by ground control onto enemy fighters in the vicinity of an aerodrome west of Dummer Lake, he sighted four Fw 190s flying in trail below him. The 359th ace dived and shot down the last Focke-Wulf in line. Firing at a second, Wetmore saw the pilot attempt to

Lt Charles Oldfield was shot down while strafing a Luftwaffe airfield near the German border with Holland in this very aircraft (44-63555) on 25 February 1945. He then successfully evaded the enemy and arrived back at Duxford courtesy of the Dutch resistence on 5 April. Oldfield rejoined the 84th FS and flew several more patrols over Germany before VE-Day (Ethell)

Kitted out for a long-range Shuttle mission to Russia, pilots of the 364th FG pose in front of BATAVIA BLITZ in March 1945

The code 'N2' and a circled individual aircraft letter signified the 383rd FS of the 364th FG, based at Honington. Although the only frontline combat unit at the large Suffolk base, the Group was always surrounded by assorted B-17s from the 3rd Bomb Division as the airfield was home to the 1st Strategic Air Depot, who specialised in repairing and overhauling the big four-engined Boeing bomber. This close relationship with elements of VIIIth Bomber Command could explain why the 364th was one of only two groups (the 20th was the other outfit) to adopt bomber-style tail markings for its individual squadrons

break and dive, but he had no altitude and snap rolled into the ground.

Shooting down a third Fw 190, Wetmore called in his wingman to take out the last enemy machine. Shots were exchanged before a fogged windscreen ruined the pilot's aim, and Wetmore finished him off. Reforming, he and his wingman climbed up to attack another pair of Fw 190s and as they made their pass another P-51 joined the fray. The newcomer and Wetmore opened fire simultaneously, and both Germans bailed out – the 359th's leading ace was credited with four downed and one shared.

His last kill of the war occured on 15 March, just over a month before the 359th's final mission. The Mustangs were again operating around Berlin when Wetmore, leading a flight, spotted two Me 163s orbiting around Wittenberg. Closing to 300 yards, he watched in awe as one of the fighters zoom climbed. He followed the Komet as well as he could, and at 20,000 ft its engined flamed out. The Me 163 executed a split-S and dive, with Wetmore's P-51 stuck to its tail. The ASI spun and with 600 mph indicated, Wetmore opened fire at 200 yards. Throwing his machine into a right bank, the German took several telling hits. More strikes then chopped away half the left wing and the pilot jumped out.

Ray Wetmore was the leading Eighth Air Force pilot of 1945, but others were continuing to build their scores too in the last months of the war, including Donald J Strait of the 356th FG. Having flown one tour with the group during its P-47 period, Strait was posted back to his old group in the autumn of 1944, thus giving him the chance to fly both the P-51, and possibly increase his score. He had been credited with three kills while flying the Thunderbolt.

Strait's first opportunity to re-aquaint himself with aerial combat came on 26 November whilst he was leading the 361st FS in the vicinity of Osnabruck. Over 40 Bf 109s appeared, hell bent on attacking the bombers his Group was escorting that day. The P-51 pilots punched off their drop tanks and bounced the enemy fighters. Soon after engaging the first gaggle, Strait saw the German top cover some 1500 ft above. Climbing up to deal with this threat, he closed on a lone Bf 109 and scored many hits on it from about 350 yards, sending it down trailing smoke. A new wingman joined Strait as he looked out for more enemy aircraft at 13,000 ft. The two Mustangs latched onto another Bf 109, which characteristically dived. Strait's shots hit home, but the *Jagdflieger* sought a turning match in order to secure his escape. His wingman scored more hits, then Strait finished the damaged fighter off with a well-aimed burst from 250 yards away.

With two victories on 5 December, Don Strait found more air combat on Christmas Day. In action again with Bf 109s, he had a nasty moment when his first victim of the day deposited oil and coolant all over his windscreen. Skidding away, Strait almost rammed his foe, whose propeller had stopped. He flew past the *Jagdflieger* just as he belly-landed in a field.

Strait watched his wingman fire on a second Bf 109, but the Mustang pilot had apparently not seen another enemy fighter pursuing him. Urgently calling for his colleague to break, Strait could not prevent the German from scoring hits on the turning P-51. Quickly onto the enemy's tail, Strait was still hampered by the film of coolant on his windscreen and could not see well enough to shoot. Sensing his chance, the Bf 109 pilot snap rolled away and the Mustangs called it a day.

Another pilot who did well on the P-51 was Robin Olds of the 479th. Destined to make more of a name for himself over 20 years later as an F-4 Phantom II pilot in the Vietnam conflict, Olds flew the P-38 well enough to become the Eighth's leading ace on the type (nine kills), before the group switched to the P-51 in September. His first Mustang victory came on 6 October 1944, and he went on to claim three more kills in the P-51D before VE-Day, an achievement helped immeasurably by his ability at deflection shooting in conjunction with the K-14 gunsight.

Having knocked down an Fw 190 with a no-deflection burst on 6 October, Olds did not score again until 9 February 1945 when, taking care to get the Bf 109 square in the K-14 and allowing a small degree of deflection, he let the sight computer do the rest. He was some distance away from the target at 450 yards when he opened fire, and was therefore very surprised when this first burst hit the enemy aircraft. Twice more Olds ranged in the Bf 109, and again hits were seen, the third burst being enough to send the German down. Similar results were obtained on another Bf 109 and an Fw 190 on 19 March. Approaching his first kill, Olds mortally hit it with a 50-degree deflection burst, whilst the second

Possibly one of the most famous publicity shots ever taken by Eighth AF war photographers, this mixed formation of 375th FS, 361st FG Mustangs was seen up from Bottisham, in Essex, just weeks after D-Day on 11 July 1944 – during the previous two months the Group had been heavily invovled in *Chattanooga* sorties, and had claimed no less than 23 locomotives destroyed in France. Sadness surrounds this stunning shot, as the pilot leading the four-ship in *LOU IV*, Group CO, Col Tom Christian, was shot down and killed on 12 August 1944 in this very machine. On a more positive note, the second P-51D in the formation was being guest flown on this occasion by the Group's third-ranking ace, 1st Lt Urban Drew, who usually piloted P-51D 44-14164, nicknamed *DETROIT Miss* – he finished his ETO tour with six aerial kills, including two Me 262s on the same sortie. Alongside him is Lt Bruce Rowlett in his personal Mustang, *Sky Bouncer*, whilst occupying the number four slot in soon to be retired P-51B 42-106811 is Lt Francis Glanker

(the Fw 190) tried barrel-rolling its way out of Olds' fire, but to no avail.

On 7 April his group was part of an escort for B-24s attacking Duneberg. Rapidly moving contrails below the bomber stream betrayed the presence of jets, and Olds' flight immediately performed a split-S and plunged down on the Me 262s. This time the Germans used their speed to maximum advantage, and Olds' solitary burst was fired more as a token gesture at

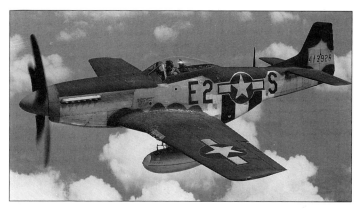

A close-up of 44-13926, taken during the same photo-shoot as featured on the opposite page, shows the crudely sprayed appliction of OD paint hastily added to 375th FS P-51s when VIIIth FC thought it was going to have to forward deploy fighters to France soon after D-Day. 44-13926 was almost brand new when this shot was taken from a 91st BG B-17. Later assigned to Lt Abe Rosenberger, the P-51 was written-off in a crash soon after on 9 August 1944 whilst being flown by a Lt Don Dellinger, who was killed

the 'tail-end Charlie' out of sheer frustration. Better results were, however, obtained nearer to the bombers, where Olds found Bf 109s hacking at the Liberators. He chased one through a formation of B-24s, holding fire lest he hit one. Emerging out the other side, Olds unleashed more bursts until the enemy bailed out.

Among the 4th FG pilots at Debden who returned for a second bout with the *Jagdwaffe* was Louis 'Red Dog' Norley. Back in the saddle of a P-51, this time a D-model, he set about improving on his previous score of 8.33 from the first tour. Now a flight leader with the 335th FS, Norley nailed two Fw 190s during operations in support of *Operation Market Garden* over Arnhem in September 1944, as well as an Me 163 over Merseberg on 2 November, to complete his scoring with the 335th. He was then promoted to CO of the 4th FG's 334th FS in January 1945. Flying in that capacity on 19 March, he was leading A Flight as they cleared the skies ahead of the bombers. Nothing much was seen on the outward leg, but on the return 'Red Dog' got a Bf 109 in his sights and soon sent it down.

On 17 April, Norley, who remained 334th commander until war's end, scored his last kill, an Fw 190D. Cutting off the enemy's approach to the bombers, Norley

Capt Charles 'Chuck' Yeager named all his P-51s after his future wife, Glennis. This is number three (44-14888), coded 'B6-Y', and it was clinically used by the legendary 363rd FS flight commander to down a considerable chunk of his 11.5 aerial victories over Christmas 1944/45. It was photographed parked on the PSP at Leiston soon after a snow squall had blown through the Suffolk base – one of many during the last bitter winter of the war *(USAF via Yeager)*

fired at his quarry from over 600 yards away in the hope of scaring him off as he knew he would never hit the Focke-Wulf from that distance. He then stopped firing as his chase was taking him and his target dangerously close to the bombers. Then, to Norley's horror, the Fw 190 carried on and crashed headlong into a B-17. Both immediately went down, the Mustang pilot convinced that the German must have been killed by his long-range burst, as the latter hadn't fired a single round as he closed on the Fortress.

While the 4th had always had healthy competition with the 56th for leadership in terms of combined air and ground kills, the 'Eagles' hated conceding the lead to the Thunderbolt outfit. By 16 April they were looking for a target that would put them ahead. Flying A and B groups, with

Norley leading the latter, the 4th found targets on German airfields and came home with a score of 105 destroyed. Norley's contribution was four strafed to destruction on Gablingen aerodrome, making his final wartime total 11.3 aerial kills and five destroyed on the ground.

### TOP ACES

Among the 4th's most successful pilots was Pierce W 'Mac' McKennon, an individual who had initially endured the not unusual experience of being told by the USAAF that he lacked inherent fly-

ing ability. Washed out, McKennon was undeterred and promptly shipped out to Canada. There, the RCAF's training syllabus was much more realistic in its appreciation of ability, and McKennon was eventaully posted to the UK and assigned to a Spitfire squadron. He saw no action, however, and transferred to the USAAF in November 1942. Posted to the 4th, McKennon quickly showed how little talent he had by becoming one of the group's first P-47 aces! P-51 kills followed, and by the time he went home at the end of his first tour, he had 10.5 kills in the air to his credit.

He returned to Debden on 18 August 1944 and soon set about boost-ing his score. Things didn't turn out too well for him, however, and on 28 August he was shot down. Evading the Germans, McKennon spent nearly a month with the French resistance, before returning to England in September. On Christmas Day 1944 he shared a Bf 109 with another pilot but thereafter all his subsequent victories were ground kills. Then, on 18 March the Neubrandenburg airfield flak claimed McKennon. He safely bailed out and Lt George Green headed in to pick him up. With 'Mac' on his lap, Green flew back to Debden. Being twice shot down whilst strafing didn't deter McKennon from further low-level sorties, and he finished the war with a score of 20.68, 11 of them aerial kills.

Like 'Bud' Anderson, John England of the 357th owed part of his air combat success to both the K-14 gunsight and the G-suit. One particular kill, he reckoned, would not have happened had it not been for the fact that he was wearing such a suit. On 13 September, England was leading 'Dollar Squadron' (the 362nd FS) at 8000 ft when he spotted a Bf 109 in a dive – it was soon overhauled as England closed to 800 yards distance at an altitude of 3000 ft. Seeing that his quarry was heading for an airfield, England wound his P-51 up to 400 mph and turned tightly to close the range to 500 yards. With the K-14 'locked-on', England fired, observing strikes on the Bf 109's engine and cockpit before it crashed – he went on to down two more Bf 109s on that mission. England's score continued to rise until he was rotated back to the US with his total at 17.5.

Without a doubt Leonard K 'Kit' Carson found the air war in Europe, as opposed to the Pacific, much more to his taste. On the point of head-ing for the Far East with a P-39 outfit, he instead joined the 357th FG. His first victory was on 8 April 1944, and his chosen technique for success

Yeager thought extremely highly of his groundcrew, who had to turn his Mustang around between sorties in some of the worst weather ever recorded in East Anglia in the first months of 1945. Ever conscious of their well being, he has ventured out here to 'shoot the breeze' with his crew chief and armourer as they take a break from tending to *GLAMOUROUS GLEN III* in February 1945 *(USAF via Yeager)*

was to bore in close to his victim, rather than rely on deflection shooting. This method brought with it serious risks, but in Carson's case, it never failed. And like other pilots in the group, he too ran 'Clobber College', the 357th's combat school, for a time, passing on his unique skills.

'There were no tactical geniuses around to spread the gospel on how to stay alive in a dogfight with the Luftwaffe when we arrived in England in December 1943. Our training in the States had never envisaged seven-hour missions at 30,000 ft in weather where unfamiliarity with instrument flying would kill you faster than the enemy could.'

This 4th FG P-51D, nicknamed *Rebel*, was photographed during a visit to RAF Digby, in Lincolnshire, in the summer of 1944. It was later renamed *Betty Jane II* and credited with three kills

When he addressed newcomers, he pulled few punches about how things were in the ETO, and how their first missions would see them flying as wingmen to the more senior pilots.

'We always start on the basis of two-ship element. It will be evident in a matter of seconds whether its going to be a one-on-one scrap or not; your leader will know it and so will you. If the enemy is that thick you'll be able to pick your own target, but clear yourself to the rear before you do. If you're threatened from the rear, call your leader by name and tell him you're leaving him. He'll help you if he can.

'Don't freeze and don't panic. If you're jumped, remember in the P-51 you've got (other than the Spitfire) the best defensive fighter in the business. Reef it in with full power and manoeuvring flaps or shove the stick right into the instrument panel – do anything you can to break his line of sight on you. Once you've done that, he can't lay a glove on you. I would recommend in your first encounter or two that you do not attempt any flat-out, gut-wrenching dogfights. You may have to, but if the choice is yours, don't do it. Get the feel of it first, size up the enemy and note the patterns they run in the attack. Stick to your leader – you'll live longer. You'll be busy enough as it is.

'Don't fret because you think you're in an isolated position as a wingman. We have a lot of wingmen in this group who are aces. This is an alien sky and a hostile environment, so get used to it a little before you take on the hard ones.'

He was equally straight about the weather. 'Two out of three days that you fly, you're going to have to fight it. There's lots of rain, snow, ice and poor visibility and its as big a problem as the enemy. Its not as hard as it sounds as the P-51 is a good weather airplane with gyro instruments. Forget the needle-and-ball routine of cadet training. The P-51's primary flight instruments are

When hostilities ceased, low flying restrictions were quickly reintroduced in England to discourage pilots, who were eagerly awaiting transfers home, from indulging in a little 'buzzing' to relieve the boredom. Individual aircraft codes were quickly applied in large black letters under the wings so that any bystanders on the ground who witnessed such high spirits could accurately report their sightings to the relevant authorities. This P-51D wears the letters 'PI-B' under each wing, thus denoting that it belonged to the 352nd's 360th FS, and was usually flown by Lt James Charlton *(H Rutland)*

boxed with yellow tape for emphasis; get familiar with using the artificial horizon and the gyro compass. With a little practice you can fly this airplane down to a frog's hair on instruments. Anyone who has a casual attitude towards flying in this climate is going to wind up wearing an 8000-lb alumimium coffin at the bottom of the North Sea. If you lose visual contact with the man ahead when climbing through clouds, go on instruments instantly. Trust your gyros – they work very well.

'Weather over here compels you to do a lot of low altitude navigation in poor visibility. Sometimes visibility is bad at high altitude, too. If you're separated, remember those two course headings. If you're at Berlin, the course home is 270 degrees. If you're over Munich its 310 degrees. So, your mission today puts you somewhere in between. OK. Steer a meridian course home on 290 degrees. Britain is 600 miles long – you can't miss it! The squall lines and thunderstorms we get over here in the spring and summer are violent – stay out of them. Either go around or over them.

'Get to know the coastline of England as this will be your biggest aid to zeroing in on home base. I refer of course to the east coast, say from Dover round to Yarmouth. While you're at it, pinpoint the RAF emergency strips at Manston and Woodbridge. They're not only landmarks but great places to land in a pinch.'

On gunnery, 'Both the RAF and we have found that the common problem of new pilots in combat is to underestimate the range of targets by a factor of two. When new pilots think they're shooting at 200 yards, its actually closer to 400. Don't try for the big deflection shot, that is 30 degrees and up. You'll miss at least four times out of five. Get dead astern and drive in to 200 yards or less, right on down to 50 yards. Deflection shooting isn't the whole story; if you close up to 200 yards and fire a couple of one-second bursts, you'll nail him. Your .50 calibre slugs have steel cores. We don't use tracer as it gives a false sense of distance and direction, but when the steel cores hit home, they strike sparks which appear as winking lights so you'll know you're scoring.'

When the guns fired in the P-51, the velocity loss was less than one mile per hour. All pilots felt was the vibration of the guns firing.

Finally, Carson imparted these words of advice, 'Think strategic

Herb Rutland's aircraft, also pictured postwar at Martlesham Heath, wore the code 'PI-R' beneath its wings. The stylish scroll on the canopy bar that denoted the pilot's name on each machine was a feature applied to the 360th FS's P-51s towards the end of the war. Herb Rutland shipped back to America with the rest of his Group in October/November 1945 (H Rutland)

A more than familiar sight on a seven-hour mission! The instrument panel of the P-51D was functional, and few pilots complained about any lack of visibility through that great perspex dome

No photograph in this volume better sums up the sheer might of VIIIth FC in last year of the war than this remarkable shot taken on Thursday, June 7, 1945 during a victory open day held at the 78th FG's Duxford home. Each of the three rows of Mustangs was comprised of a single squadron, with the 83rd FS filling the middle rank. A close study of the latter unit's aircraft reveals that they are in fact Dallas-built P-51Ks, unlike the aircraft of the remaining two lines, which are standard D-models. Behind P-51K 44-11563 is 'F-HL', which wears five small swastikas and a large green clover leaf motif below its cockpit. Like the 356th FG, the 78th also shipped back to the USA in November 1945

escort; get in the habit of thinking about five and six and even seven-hour missions. Dress for the missions as if you were going to walk out of Germany. Make sure you have a good pair of boots. Above all, make sure you have a good foam rubber pad to sit on; that goddamn dinghy pack is like a slab of granite and it will ruin you. Regarding the fatigue problem on long missions – five hours and up is where it gets you in the legs and fanny. When you fly six and seven hour missions, the groundcrew will probably have to lift you out of the cockpit.'

That the new blood of the 357th learned the curriculum set at 'Clobber College' well is in no doubt – the group had the highest scoring victory rate for the last year of the war, and boasted no less than 46 aces. Carson ended up with 18.5 kills to place him 11th in the overall Eighth Air Force ace listing.

Fellow 357th ace Chuck Yeager reckons that approximately one in twenty-five missions had to be aborted because of the weather, and that it was flight rather than group commanders who had the most effect on the performance of a unit in the ETO. His acknowledgement of the part played by the groundcrews included this comment,

'Many of our P-51s flew 50 straight missions without an abort and my crew chief got a bronze star medal for his work. Regarding the fighters themselves, I flew the P-47, P-38, Bf 109 Fw 190, Spitfire and several other lesser known types, and the P-51D was by far the best war machine; the Mustang would do for eight hours what the 'Spit' would do for 45 minutes!

'The P-51D solved all the problems we had experienced with the B-model, and the only bad flight characteristic (of both) came about when the fuselage tank was full. This wasn't exactly dangerous, but one had to be careful when turning. We were also glad to see the back of the P-51B with its four guns and bad ammunition feed.'

Another pilot who was to win lasting fame (as arguably the most famous American test pilot of all time) after the shooting had stopped, Chuck Yeager finished the war with 11.5 aerial victories.

# THE 'BLUE-NOSERS'

**O**f all the Eighth Air Force's illustrious fighter groups, the 352nd did better than most in the air combat stakes, coming fourth in the overall group listings with an impressive 519 confirmed kills. Among other 'claims to fame', the group turned in the second highest number of aerial kills in one day – 38 on 2 November 1944 – and its 487th FS was the only squadron in VIIIth FC to win a Distinguished Unit Citatation. Subsequently, the total from 2 November was adjusted to 25, but this in no way downgraded a truly meritorious display of flying.

Formed at Mitchell Field, Long Island, in October 1942, the 352nd consisted of three units, two of which – the 486th and 487th – were originally the much older 21st and 34th Sqns respectively. The third was the 328th, a brand new outfit that stood up at the same time as the Group.

On 9 March 1943 the group moved to Farmingdale Army Air Field, adjacent to the Republic Aviation plant, and began training on the P-47. It moved to Westover in May and thence to Camp Kilmer, New Jersey, on receipt of overseas movement orders – group personnel actually embarked in the liner *Queen Elizabeth* for a fast trans-Atlantic crossing.

The 352nd was assigned to VIIIth FC on 6 July 1943, and assembled at Bodney, in Norfolk, two days later under the command of Col Joseph L Mason, who had lead the group since May. Its initial combat aircraft was the Thunderbolt, examples from the P-47D-5 to D-16 (razorback) production blocks being flown for the first nine months of operations.

The 352nd flew its first escort mission on 9 September 1943, and was heavily engaged with the Luftwaffe right from the start. These sorties often took them to just inside the German border, the limit of the P-47's range. The fifth group to be assigned to VIIIth FC, the 352nd became part of the 67th Fighter Wing in October 1943, under whose control it was to remain, apart from a short break in the winter of 1944-45, until the end of the war. The group received P-51Bs in April 1944, followed by a few P-51Ds in June. Both models looked resplendent in the dark blue group colour from which it was to take its nickname.

In common with all other Eighth Air Force fighter groups, the 352nd's success in combat carried a

Capt Ralph Hamilton of the 487th FS was not at all pleased when invasion stripes were applied to his P-51B in May 1944 – he stormed around the dispersal at Bodney demanding to know who had vandalised his formerly pristine *Frances B TOO*. Ironically, on D-Day itself George Preddy actually flew this aircraft over the Normandy beaches!

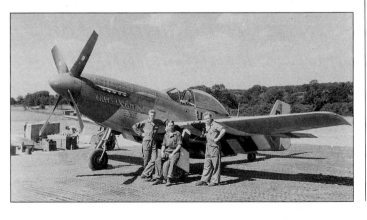

George Preddy's *CRIPES A' MIGHTY 3RD*, pictured in the dispersal at Bodney with its faithful groundcrew. On 6 August 1944 this machine had been used by Preddy to despatch a record six Bf 109s over Brandenburg – this shot was taken only a matter of days latter during a large press visit to Bodney to meet the Eighth's newest 'ace in a day'

Another of the shots taken on the same press day shows armorers of the 487th busily toiling away under the afternoon sun, replenishing the six .50 calibre Brownings fitted in the wings of Preddy's P-51D – throughout his combat career, Preddy never once suffered a malfunction with his guns. The squadron artist had been kept busy adding new crosses to *CRIPES A' MIGHTY 3RD*'s uniquely placed scoreboard prior to the press descending on the small Norfolk base – the fruits of their labour are clearly visible in this shot

Preddy was on his way to becoming the top overall ace of the ETO when he was shot down by US anti-aircraft fire on Christmas Day 1944. His liking for English colloquialisms stretched to him naming four out of the five P-47s and P-51s he flew with his favourite saying of them all!

price – on 8 April the then leading ace with nine kills, Capt Virgil Merony, was shot down and made a PoW, but on the 24th, Edwin Heller more than evened up this loss by destroying seven enemy aircraft (both in the air and on the ground) to become an ace.

## BLOODY MAY

May 1944 was hardly a memorable month for the group for among the pilots lost was Capt Frank Cutler of the 486th FS (8.5 victories), who was killed during the first Berlin mission on the 13th. Carl Luksic, who then had 15.2 victories to his credit (8.5 of which were aerial kills), was shot down on the 24th to become a PoW, and on 28 May Capt Woodrow Anderson (with 13.5 victories, most of which were strafing kills) was lost after his parchute failed to open. Better results were obtained by the group at the end of the month, however.

Lt Glennon T Moran scored three victories during the 352nd's P-47 period and went on to knock down ten more enemy aircraft with the Mustang. He had a great day on 29 May when the 487th FS's bomber escort ranged far into eastern Germany. Over Gustrow around 40 enemy fighters appeared to attack the bombers, and Moran chased an Fw 190 down from 22,000 to 3000 ft before his fire made an impression. The German half-rolled and went in from a altitude of about 1000 ft.

On the climb-back to height, Moran and his wingman, Lt Jule Conard, saw many fighters above. They nevertheless climbed up to attack, and one Bf 109, who had broken off from the dogfight, carelessly strayed across Moran's nose and was quickly shot down. Both he and Conard then destroyed a Bf 109 bent on strafing an American airmen in a parachute.

A series of dogfights kept the blue-nosed Mustangs busy on 30 May, and the group came home with 14.5 victories. Moran's contribution was two downed and one damaged, again with Conard as wingman. Moran's total put him level with the unit's leading ace at that time, Virgil Merony.

The months of April and May 1944 were also highly satisfying for George Preddy, who had made a slow start to his victory tally with the P-47. The switch to the P-51 brought rapid results, and boosted his score to 11.33 during that period. Escorting bombers to Magdeburg on 20 June, Preddy shot down an Fw 190 and shared an Me 410 with Lt James Woods.

On 21 June the 352nd accompanied the 4th to Russia for the second of the shuttles, following in the footsteps of Mustang units from the Fifteenth Air Force who had escorted the bombers from Italy. On 7 July Capt Orville Goodman led the 486th FS so well that the pilots came home to report 11 enemy aircraft downed without loss.

Among the pilots who rotated home at this time after a successful tour with the 352nd was John Thornell. On an escort mission on 21 June, Thornell completed his tour by setting a small record when he became the first pilot in the group to reach 300 operational hours. He had also scored 17.25 aerial victories since his debut on 14 September 1943.

On 18 July the group claimed 21 kills, four of them falling to George Preddy, whose eye was now well and truly tuned to the tricks of the enemy, and on 6 August he set a record – six down on one mission. Preddy was leading 'White Flight' at the time as part of the group escort to the Brandenburg area. They ran into 30-plus enemy fighters as they stalked the bombers at 27,000 ft, and concentrating on their four-engined targets, the Bf 109 pilots maintained formation, seemingly oblivious to the P-51s gradually whittling down their number. No less than five Bf 109s (undoubtedly flown by combat

A formidable partnership – Preddy and his armourer, Sgt M G Kuhaneck. In this no doubt staged picture, the ace and the 'ace maker' ham it up for the press. Preddy enjoyed being able to share his success with those who had helped him achieve it. Quite what the sergeant was pointing out to his boss over 50 years ago has been lost over the ensuing decades

Amongst the lesser known pilots of the 352nd FG was 11.5-victory ace Major William Halton. A seasoned campaigner who had earlier flown both P-47s and P-51Bs with the 487th FS, Halton took over the squadron when John Meyer was promoted to Deputy Group Commander in November 1944. His personal P-51D-10-NA was nicknamed *Slender, Tender & TALL*, and was photographed here at a misty Asche airfield in Belgium in February 1944 during the Group's brief sojourn to the less than sunny Continent

**Having dispensed with his 75-gal 'teardrop' tanks to give him optimum manoeuvrability at low-level, Lt Karl Dittmer taxies out in *DOPEY OKIE* at Asche to commence yet another short-range patrol over the slowly advancing Allied frontline in mid-January 1945. Part of the much-vaunted 487th FS, Dittmer had claimed a solitary kill up to this point in his career in the ETO**

novices) fell to Preddy's marksmanship. Diving to 7000 ft after one pilot who actually attempted to break away, he soon despatched it earthward to claim his six kill in a row. Added to a further six scored by other 352nd pilots, this day was a truly memorable one, particularly for Preddy, who had run his total up to 27.83. Of these, 22 and the shared fraction had been in the air. George's comment when asked about his feat became a classic of under-statement: 'I just kept shooting and they just kept falling.'

Preddy commanded the 328th when the squadron went hunting on 2 November. A gaggle of Bf 109s was ripped apart, with no less than 25 Axis fighters being lost – this meant that the Group had achieved a scoring rate of more than one every 60 seconds as the intercept had been completed in less than 20 minutes. Capt Don Bryan led the squadron's score with five, and ace Capt Henry Miklajyck added two more to his score of 5.5 before he himself was shot down and killed in this whirlwind action.

Blue-nosed Mustangs were again at the *Jagdwaffe*'s throat on 21 November, a day that recorded another huge air battle, composed this time of 50-plus Focke-Wulfs. The unit's 'B' Group routed the enemy formation southeast of Leipzig, Capt Whisner claiming six and a probable (adjusted later to five and a probable) and Lt Col John Meyer three. The former's flight from the 487th FS had been covering bombers pounding the synthetic oil refineries at Merseburg when 50-plus Bf 109s were seen to attack the formation. Diving to 29,000 ft, the Mustangs pounced on the Messerschmitts' covering group, which was composed of Fw 190s. Whisner heard John Meyer (group lead) direct him to attack a pair of stragglers at the rear of the formation. He destroyed both in quick succession before boring in on three more.

Whisner quickly despatched one of these, and then closed in to 200 yards and destroyed his fourth enemy fighter for the day. Then he ranged in on another pair of Fw 190s and made short work of both. Whisner then dived and shot a further Focke-Wulf off a Mustang's tail. Unfortunately not all of these victories could be confirmed, although Whisner was awarded a respectable five destroyed plus two probables – and a DSC.

## MOVE TO BELGIUM

In an effort to break the deadlock caused primarily by the appalling winter weather of 1944-45, and the unexpected German panzer thrust through the Ardennes 'bulge', the 352nd and 361st FGs were detached to the continent. Based at Y-29, alias Asche, in Belgium, from 23 December, the 'Blue-Nosers' faced a Christmas with little chance of a stand-down from duty. On Christmas Eve, Preddy indulged in a game of craps and scooped the pot to net $1000. Never a spend-thrift, he intended to invest his winnings in war bonds.

Then came one of the Eighth's blackest days, made all the more sadder because it was not the enemy who downed George Preddy, but American anti-aircraft fire. As had been routine for some time, Preddy had led his 328th FS on a low-level patrol over the battlefront and downed two ground-hugging Fw 190s. He was in the process of chasing several others over the snow-covered forests when the aircraft broke out over an open field. Unfortunately for Preddy, a battle-weary US anti-aircraft unit let fly at the second group of fighters with a deadly quad .50 calibre machine gun mounting as they shot over their position, fatally wounding the American ace, whose P-51 ploughed into the snowy field at speed.

It was just the kind of incident that many pilots had learned to be wary of – often during a strafing run it was not the leading aircraft the gunners shot down but the ones following. Gun crews had very little time to react as they had to range in their weapons in order to have a chance of hitting fast, low flying, aircraft. This they did as the first enemy aircraft flew over, ready for the next flight. In Preddy's case the US gunners had been warned of enemy aircraft in their vicinity, and when the fighters appeared they assumed them to be hostile. They missed the Fw 190s completely, but hit Preddy's machine. Only a few rounds were fired before the mistake was realised, but by then it was far too late for the Eighth's top ace.

Two days later, the 352nd waded into another mass of German fighters in the vicinity of Bonn, and again the outcome was loaded heavily in the Group's favour. To Maj Bill Halton's triple score was added another 19 shared among the other pilots. More action was still to come though.

It was a prudent move by John Meyer to get his 487th FS airborne from Asche early on New Year's Day 1945. A man who earned a fine reputation for 'thinking like a German', Meyer had a hunch that the Luftwaffe just might gamble on 1 January as a good day to catch the Allied airfields napping – he felt the enemy would believe a New Year's Eve hangover might have caused the pilots to lay in that morning. Meyer postponed the 487th's party by one day – it proved to be a wise decision. The P-51s barely had air under their wheels before all hell broke loose. Racing across the field were a mass of Fw 190s, part of a force of 800 fighters briefed to attack Allied airfields in Belgium. They were ambushed over Asche.

The 352nd's pilots found themselves pressing their firing buttons

*BONNY* was a P-51K flown by Lt Gordon Cartee during the last months of the war. A relatively unknown pilot, Cartee was actually John Preddy's wingman throughout his time as CO of the 328th FS. Nicknamed *Steph-N-Jane* on the port side of its nose, 44-11560, was photographed at Bodney in early May 1945, accompanied by its two dedicated groundcrewmen

John Preddy's great rival within the 352nd FG was John Meyer, who ironically hailed from the same squadron – the 487th FS. Both pilots scored heavily throughout the second half of 1944, and unlike Preddy, Meyer chose to mark his kills up with swastikas, rather than the nore conventional crosses. Unfortunately, the latter soon realised that his burgeoning scoreboard was barely visible from a distance, particularly in the air, so he ordered the 'squadron artist' to repaint the yellow kill markings with a heavy black shadow – that way his German foes might see them better!

Devoid of any kill markings whatsoever, P-51D 44-13557 was in fact the last of four Mustangs flown by William Halton during his two tours with the 352nd FG. This machine was photographed at Bodney in late May 1945

almost before they had retracted their landing gear, the targets were that close. In a whirling series of dogfights, Bill Whisner shot down four, as did Capt Sanford Moats; Meyer himself knocked down two for his 23rd and 24th victories. Whisner had his aircraft hit by an Fw 190, this being the one and only time that an enemy aircraft had ever touched him. With his P-51 holed in both wings, the oil tank and left aileron, Whisner proceeded to line up a Fw 190 and shoot it down. The unique circumstances of the combat, and the superb reaction by the 487th, brought them a Distinguished Unit Citation for a battle that became known as the 'Legend of Y-29'. It was the only occasion when a unit based in northwest Europe received this award, and Meyer's foresight and leadership was recognised with a DSC. Whisner was also decorated, an Oak Leaf Cluster being added to the DSC awarded on 21 November. In total the group were credited with 23 aircraft shot down and one damaged on 1 January.

Having mounted an operation that was little short of a disaster of its own making, the Luftwaffe was hardly able to support von Runstedt's bold bid to break the Allied ring of steel, and by mid-January he was forced to retreat. The 352nd followed. A base move to Chievres saw the Mustangs seeking out whatever targets they could find over the next few weeks, but the enemy rarely showed, at least in large numbers.

On 14 March Don Bryan found some action in the vicinity of Remagen, where the last intact bridge across the Rhine became a focus of frantic Allied attempts to take and hold it while the Germans did their upmost to destroy it. Escorting A-26 Invaders over the area, Bryan and his comrades came upon German fighters protecting an Arado 234 jet bomber about to attack the bridge. Bryan dropped his tanks and closed on the bomber, but could not catch it – it had at least a 50-mph advantage. The Ar 234 made an abortive attack and then made a run for safety – unwittingly, as it transpired, towards a group of 56th FG P-47s. Realising that the enemy would soon see these aircraft and most likely turn eastwards to avoid them, Bryan positioned his Mustang to spring a trap. It worked. The Arado pilot turned as anticipated and Bryan firewalled his throttle. At 250 yards range his fire knocked out the jet's right engine, whereupon the pilot put it into a series of shallow diving turns and short pull-ups. Bryan hammered the bomber again and the left engine went out. Emitting white smoke, the Arado rolled over onto its back and plunged straight into the ground. This victory brought Bryan's score to 13.34, the second highest for the 328th FS.

# BODNEY REVISITED

It was back to Bodney for the 487th on 13 April, their stint in Belgium having been more than eventful. The group had, by this stage, enjoyed a new CO for over seven months, Col James D Mayden having taken over from Col Joe Mason in November 1944.

Capt Ray Littge of the 487th FS played an important part in two of the group's final missions on which they encountered the enemy, leading section attacks on German airfields. On 16 April the group claimed 39-0-27, and the following day significantly bettered this with 66-0-24. Littge was credited with nine destroyed and five damaged on the two strafing runs. During the latter strike on Prattling aerodrome, Littge's aircraft came under fire from flak batteries. Shrapnel punctured the engine reservoir tank, causing all the aircraft's oil to be lost, as well as severing the manifold pressure lines and shooting off a foot-and-a-half of its left wing. Seven passes were made over the field, Littge destroying two highly valauble Me 262s in the process. These strafing attacks earned him a DSC, and raised his score to 23.5 (10.5 aerial kills).

Now the end was clearly in sight – Germany had been all but overrun by the time the 352nd flew its last ETO mission on 3 May. When the final figures for enemy aircraft downed in Europe were compiled, George Preddy and John Meyer topped the list of pilots who had scored the majority of their kills on the P-51. Preddy's tally stood at 23.83 out of 26.83 in Mustangs, and Meyer 21 out of 24. John England emerged as number five, with all of his 17.5 victories having been achieved whilst flying the P-51. Ten pilots had been awarded the DSC while serving with 352nd. Like most other VIIIth FC groups, the 352nd shipped out of Bodney, bound for the USA, in November 1945.

Lt Lothar Fieg flew *Katydid* with the 328th FS during the second half of 1944. Like several other units within VIIIth FC, this squadron used the small trim tab on the rudder as an appropriate place to display individual flight markings, which usually took the form of coloured bars. By coincidence, the 55th FG also had a P-51D christened *KATYDID*, which was flown by the Eighth's leading ground attack ace, Lt Col Elwyn Righetti

*Little Stinker* carried an appropriate skunk painting under the forward exhausts, and was flown by Lt Leonard Gremaux. The 'PZ' codes denote an aircraft of the 486th FS, perhaps the least known of the Group's trio of squadrons. Their relative anonymity no doubt stems from the fact that they failed to produce a single high-ranking ace within the 352nd FG

# APPENDICES

## P-38 LIGHTNING ACES OF WORLD WAR 2 IN EUROPE AND THE MEDITERRANEAN

### Twelfth Air Force

| Name | Group | Aerial Victories |
| --- | --- | --- |
| William J Sloan | 82nd | 12 |
| Frank D Hurlbut | 82nd | 9 |
| Louis E Curdes | 82nd | 8 (9) |
| Claude R Kinsey | 82nd | 7 |
| Ward A Kuentzel | 82nd | 7 |
| Lawrence P Liebers | 82nd | 7 |
| Meldrum L Sears | 1st | 7 |
| Herbert E Ross | 14th | 7 |
| Harley C Vaughn | 82nd | 7 |
| Edward T Waters | 82nd | 7 |
| Richard A Campbell | 14th | 6 |
| Ray Crawford | 82nd | 6 |
| James W Griffiss | 1st | 6 |
| William J Schildt | 82nd | 6 |
| Thomas A White | 82nd | 6 |
| Charles J Zubarik | 82nd | 6* |
| Jack M Ilfrey | 1st | 6** (8) |
| Paul R Cochran | 82nd | 5 |
| Rodney W Fisher | 1st | 5 |
| Harry T Hanna | 14th | 5 |
| Daniel Kennedy | 1st | 5 |
| John A Mackay | 1st | 5 |
| T H McArthur | 82nd | 5 |
| Ernest K Osher | 82nd | 5 |
| Joel A Owens | 1st | 5 |
| Newell O Roberts | 1st | 5 |
| Gerald L Rounds | 82nd | 5 |
| Virgil H Smith | 14th | 5** |
| Sidney W Weatherford | 14th | 5. |
| Darrell G Welch | 1st | 5 |
| Lee V Wiseman | 1st | 5 |
| John L. Wolford | 1st | 5 |

### Fifteenth Air Force

| Name | Group | Aerial Victories |
| --- | --- | --- |
| Michael Brezas | 14th | 12 |
| William L Leverette | 14th | 11 |
| Walter J Carroll | 82nd | 8 |
| Thomas E Maloney | 1st | 8 |
| Phillip E Tovrea | 1st | 8 |
| Charles E Adams | 82nd | 6 |
| James D Holloway | 82nd | 6 |
| Donald D Kienholz | 1st | 6 |
| Armour C Miller | 1st | 6 |
| Leslie E Anderson | 82nd | 5 |
| Louis Benne | 14th | 5 |
| Herbert B Hatch | 1st | 5 |
| Warren L Jones | 14th | 5 |
| Carroll S Knott | 14th | 5 |
| Franklin C Lathrope | 1st | 5 |
| Richard J Lee | 1st | 5 |
| Marlow J Leikness | 14th | 5 |
| Jack Lenox | 14th | 5 |
| John W McGuyrt | 14th | 5 |
| Everett Miller | 1st | 5 |
| Robert K Seidman | 14th | 5 |
| Oliver B Taylor | 14th | 5 |
| Herman W Visscher | 82nd | 5 |
| Paul H Wilkins | 14th | 5 |
| Max J Wright | 14th | 5 |

() Final score in brackets

\* Zubarik had two extra victories not officially recognised

\*\* Final scores altered after Twelfth Air Force changed shared victory policy

# Eighth and Ninth Air Forces

| Name | Group | Aerial Victories |
|---|---|---|
| Jack M Ilfrey | 20th | 8 (scored 6 with Twelfth AF) |
| James M Morris | 20th | 7.33 |
| Lawrence E Blumer | 367th | 6 |
| Lindol F Graham | 20th | 5.5 |
| Gerald Brown | 55th | 5 |
| Robert L Buttke | 55th | 5 (+1 with P-51D) |
| Clarence O Johnson | 479th | 5 (4 with 82nd FG, +2 with P-51D) |
| Lenton F Kirkland | 474th | 5 |
| Joseph E Miller | 474th | 5 ( 4 with 14th FG) |
| Robert C Milliken | 474th | 5 |
| Robin Olds | 479th | 5 (+8 with P-51D and +4 with F-4C with 8th TFW during Vietnam War) |

## Victory lists of ETO/MTO P-38 aces with 7+ kills

### William J Sloan

| | |
|---|---|
| 7/1/43 | 1 Bf109 |
| 30/1/43 | 1 Bf109 |
| 2/2/43 | 1 Bf109/1 Do 217 |
| 15/2/43 | 1 Bf109 |
| 20/5/43 | 1 Ju 88/1 MC 200 |
| 18/6/43 | 1 MC 200 |
| 5/7/43 | 1 Re 2001/1 Bf 109 |
| 10/7/43 | 1 MC 202 |

### Michael Brezas

| | |
|---|---|
| 8/7/44 | 1 Bf 109 |
| 14/7/44 | 2 Bf 110/1 Fw 190 |
| 19/7/44 | 1 Fw 190 |
| 20/7/44 | 1 Bf 109 |
| 22/7/44 | 2 Fw 190 |
| 7/8/44 | 2 Bf 109 |
| 25/8/44 | 2 Fw 190 |
| 22/7/43 | 1 Bf 109 |

### William L Leverette

| | |
|---|---|
| 9/10/43 | 7 Ju 87 |
| 14/12/43 | 1 Bf 109 |
| 24/2/44 | 1 Bf 110 |
| 18/3/44 | 1 Bf 109 |
| 12/4/44 | 1 Bf 110 |
| 2/9/43 | 1 Bf 109 |

### Frank D Hurlbut

| | |
|---|---|
| 11/5/43 | 1 Ju 52/3m |
| 20/5/43 | 1 Fw 190 |
| 24/5/43 | 1 MC 202 |
| 10/7/43 | 3 Fw 190 |
| 7/8/43 | 1 Fw 190 |

### Walter J Carroll

| | |
|---|---|
| 10/6/44 | 1 Bf 109 |
| 24/6/44 | 1 Bf 109 |
| 4/7/44 | 1 Ju 52/3m |
| 7/7/44 | 1 Bf 109 |
| 8/7/44 | 3 Me 410 |
| 26/7/44 | 1 Fw 190 |

### Louis E Curdes

| | |
|---|---|
| 29/4/43 | 3 Bf 109 |
| 19/5/43 | 2 Bf 109 |
| 24/6/43 | 1 MC 202 |
| 27/8/43 | 2 Bf 109 |

### Thomas E Maloney

| | |
|---|---|
| 28/3/44 | 1 Bf 109 |
| 23/4/44 | 2 Bf 110 |
| 28/5/44 | 1 Do 217 |
| 31/5/44 | 1 Bf 109 |
| 18/7/44 | 1 Fw 190 |
| 15/8/44 | 2 Bf 109 |

### Philip E Tovrea

| | |
|---|---|
| 31/5/44 | 1 Bf 109 |
| 10/6/44 | 1 Bf 109 |
| 16/6/44 | 2 Bf 109 |
| 2/7/44 | 1 Fw 190 |
| 18/7/44 | 2 Fw 190/1 Bf 109 |

### James M Morris

| | |
|---|---|
| 5/2/44 | .333 He 111 |
| 8/2/44 | 2 Bf 109/2 Fw 190 |
| 11/2/44 | 1 Bf 109 |
| 24/2/44 | 1 Bf 110 |
| 7/7/44 | 1 Me 410 |
| 5/4/43 | 2 Ju 52/3m |

### Claude R Kinsey

| | |
|---|---|
| 29/1/43 | 1 Bf 109 |
| 30/1/43 | 1 Bf 109 |
| 17/2/43 | 1 Cant Z 506 |
| 23/2/43 | 1 Cant Z 506 |
| 15/3/43 | 1 Bf 109 |

### Ward A Kuentzel

| | |
|---|---|
| 20/3/43 | 1 Bf 109 |
| 20/5/43 | 1 Bf 109 |
| 18/6/43 | 1 MC 202 |
| 28/6/43 | 1 MC 202 |
| 10/7/43 | 1 Fw 190/1 Ju 88 |
| 22/7/43 | 1 Bf 109 |

### Lawrence P Liebers

| | |
|---|---|
| 14/5/43 | 1 MC 202 |
| 21/5/43 | 1 MC 202 |
| 18/6/43 | 2 MC 202/1 MC 205 |
| 10/7/43 | 1 Fw 190 |
| 20/8/43 | 1 Fw 190 |

### Herbert E Ross

| | |
|---|---|
| 9/5/43 | 1 MC 202 |
| 18/7/43 | 2 Ju 52 |
| 25/8/43 | 1 MC 202 |
| 26/8/43 | 1 Bf 109 |
| 29/8/43 | 1 Bf 109 |
| 6/9/43 | 1 Fw 190 |

### Meldrum L Sears

| | |
|---|---|
| 1/1/43 | 1 Ju 52 |
| 12/1/43 | 1 Fi 156 |
| 10/4/43 | 4 Ju 52 |
| 12/4/43 | 1 Bf 109 |

### Harley C Vaughan

| | |
|---|---|
| 15/1/43 | 1 Bf 109 |
| 30/1/43 | 1 Fw 190 |
| 12/3/43 | 1 Cant Z 1007 |
| 20/3/43 | 1 Ju 88 |
| 17/4/43 | 1 Ju 88 |
| 23/4/43 | 1 Cant Z 501 |
| 14 /5/43 | 1 MC 202 |

### Edward T Waters

| | |
|---|---|
| 12/3/43 | 1 Cant Z 1007 |
| 17/4/43 | 1 Fiat BR 20 |
| 20/5/43 | 1 Bf 109 |
| 18/6/43 | 1 Bf 109 |
| 28/6/43 | 1 MC 202 |
| 30/6/43 | 1 Fw 190 |
| 10/7/43 | 1 Bf 109 |

### Jack M Ilfrey

| | |
|---|---|
| 29/11/42 | .5 Bf 110 |
| 2/12/42 | 2 Bf 109 |
| 26/12/42 | 2 Fw 190 |
| 3/3/43 | 1 Bf 109 |
| 8/3/43 | .5 Bf 109 |
| 24/5/44 | 2 Bf 109 (scored with Eighth Air Force) |

# THE APPENDICES

## OPERATIONAL DEBUT DATES FOR VIIIth FIGHTER COMMAND GROUPS

| | | | | | |
|---|---|---|---|---|---|
| **4th** | **(1)** 10 Mar 43 – P-47; *(P-51B from 25 Feb 44)* | **352nd** | **(5)** 9 Sept 43 – P-47; *(P-51B from 8 Apr 44)* | **357th** | **(13)** 11 Feb 44 – first *Eighth AF P-51 Group* |
| **20th** | **(11)** 28 Dec 43 – P-38; *(P-51B from 20 July 44)* | **353rd** | **(4)** 12 Aug 43 – P-47; *(P-51D from 2 Oct 44)* | **359th** | **(10)** 13 Dec 43 – P-47; *(P-51B from 5 May 44)* |
| **55th** | **(8)** 15 Oct 43 – P-38; *(P-51D from 19 Jul 44)* | **354th** | **(9)** 1 Dec 43 – *First P-51 unit in ETO (this unit was always technically part of the Ninth Air Force)* | **361st** | **(12)** 21 Jan 44 – P-47; *(P-51B from 12 May 44)* |
| **56th** | **(2)** 3 Apr 43 – P-47; *throughout combat ops* | | | **364th** | **(14)** 3 Mar 44 – P-38; *(P-51D from 28 Jul 44)* |
| **78th** | **(3)** 13 Apr 43 – P-47; *(P-51D from 29 Dec 44)* | **355th** | **(6)** 14 Sept 43 – P-47; *(P-51B from 9 Mar 44)* | **479th** | **(16)** 26 May 44 – P-38; *(P-51D from 13 Sept 44)* |
| **339th** | **(15)** 30 Apr 44 – P-51D; *throughout combat ops* | **356th** | **(7)** 15 Oct 43 – P-47; *(P-51D from 20 Nov 44)* | | |

On 1 Jan 1944 VIIIth FC had the 4th, 56th, 78th, 352nd, 353rd, 355th, 356th and 359th FGs (eight groups) operating with P-47s, and (two), the 20th and 55th FGs, with P-38s. By 6 June 1944, VIIIth FC had the 4th, 339th, 352nd, 355th, 357th, 359th and 361st FGs (seven groups) with P-51s, and the 20th, 55th, 364th and 479th (FGs) with P-38s (four groups), plus the 56th, 78th, 353rd and 356th FGs with P-47s (four groups).

## —— MUSTANG GROUPS, AND THEIR SQUADRONS, OF THE EIGHTH ——

**4th Fighter Group**
334th Fighter Squadron
335th Fighter Squadron
336th Fighter Squadron

**20th Fighter Group**
55th Fighter Squadron
77th Fighter Squadron
79th Fighter Squadron

**55th Fighter Group**
38th Fighter Squadron
338th Fighter Squadron
343rd Fighter Squadron

**78th Fighter Group**
82nd Fighter Squadron
83rd Fighter Squadron
84th Fighter Squadron

**339th Fighter Group**
503rd Fighter Squadron
504th Fighter Squadron
505th Fighter Squadron

**352nd Fighter Group**
328th Fighter Squadron
486th Fighter Squadron
487th Fighter Squadron

**353rd Fighter Group**
350th Fighter Squadron
351st Fighter Squadron
352nd Fighter Squadron

**355th Fighter Group**
354th Fighter Squadron
357th Fighter Squadron
358th Fighter Squadron

**356th Fighter Group**
359th Fighter Squadron
360th Fighter Squadron
361st Fighter Squadron

**357th Fighter Group**
362nd Fighter Squadron
363rd Fighter Squadron
364th Fighter Squadron

**359th Fighter Group**
365th Fighter Squadron
366th Fighter Squadron
367th Fighter Squadron

**361st Fighter Group**
374th Fighter Squadron
375th Fighter Squadron
376th Fighter Squadron

**364th Fighter Group**
383rd Fighter Squadron
384th Fighter Squadron
385th Fighter Squadron

**479th Fighter Group**
434th Fighter Squadron
435th Fighter Squadron
436th Fighter Squadron

# TOP ACES OF THE EIGHTH—GROUP BY GROUP

| Name | score | personal aircraft (P-51s only) |
|---|---|---|

## 4th Fighter Group

| Name | score | personal aircraft (P-51s only) |
|---|---|---|
| Gentile, Don | 19.83 | P-51B 43-6913/VF-T<br>*Shangri-La* |
| Beeson, Duane | 17.33 | P-51B 43-6819/QP-B<br>*BEE* |
| Godfrey John | 16.3 | P-51B 43-6765/VF-P<br>P-51B 42-106730/VF-P<br>*Reggie's Reply*<br>P-51D 44-13412/VF-F |
| Hofer, Ralph | 15 | P-51B 42-106924/QP-L<br>*Salem Representive* |
| Goodson, James | 15 | P-51B 43-13848/VF-B<br>P-51B 43-6895/VF-B<br>P-51D 44-13303/VF-B |
| Carpenter, George | 13.2 | P-51B 43-6575/WD-I<br>*Virginia*<br>P-51B 42-106675/WD-I |
| Millikan, Willard | 13 | P-51B 43-24769/VF-U<br>*Missouri Mauler*<br>P-51B 43-6997/VF-U |
| Hively, Howard | 12 | P-51B 43-6898/QP-J<br>*The Deacon*<br>P-51D 44-15347/QP-J |
| McKennon, Pierce | 12 | P-51B 42-106911/WD-A<br>*Yippi Joe*<br>P-51B 43-6896/WD-A<br>P-51D 44-14221/WD-A<br>*RIDGE RUNNER II*<br>P-51D 44-14570/WD-A<br>*RIDGE RUNNER*<br>P-51D 44-63166/WD-A<br>P-51D 44-72308/WD-A<br>*RIDGE RUNNER III* |
| Megura, Nicholas | 11.84 | P-51B 43-6636 /QP-N<br>*Ill Wind*<br>P-51B 43-7158 /QP-F |
| Blakeslee, Don | 11.50 | P-51B 43-6437/WD-C<br>P-51B 42-106726/WD-C<br>P-51D 44-13779/WD-C |
| Clark Jr, James | 11.5 | P-51B 42-106650/QP-W<br>P-51B 43-6726/QP-W<br>P-51B 43-6560/QP-W<br>P-51D 44-13372/QP-W |
| Norley, Louis | 11.3 | P-51B 43-12416/VF-O<br>P-51B 43-6666/VF-O<br>P-51B 43-6802/VF-O<br>P-51D 44-15028/WD-O<br>P-51D 44-15350/VF-? |

| Name | score | personal aircraft (P-51s only) |
|---|---|---|
| Anderson, Charles | 10.5 | P-51D 44-72196/QP-O<br>P-51D 44-73108/QP-O<br>*Red Dog XII*<br>P-51B 43-6972/VF-N<br>*Paul*<br>P-51B 43-7181/WD-L |
| Glover, Fred | 10.3 | P-51B 43-12214/VF-C<br>*Rebel Queen*<br>P-51D 44-14787/VF-B<br>P-51D 44-64153/VF-B |
| Lines, Ted | 10 | P-51B 43-7172/WD-H<br>*Thunder Bird*<br>P-51D 44-13555/WD-D<br>*Thunder Bird* |
| Woods, Sidney | 10 | P-51D 44-72251/QP-A |

## 20th Fighter Group

| Name | score | personal aircraft (P-51s only) |
|---|---|---|
| Fiebelkorn, Ernest | 9.5 | P-51D 44-11161/LC-N<br>*June Nite*<br>P-51D 44-14823/LC-F<br>*Miss Miami* |
| Morris, James | 7.3 | (P-38 only) |
| Brown, Harley | 6 | P-51D 44-13779 /KI-N<br>P-51D 44-11250 /KI-A<br>*Be Good/Brownies'*<br>*Ballroom* |
| Lindol, Graham | 5.5 | (P-38 only) |
| Ilfrey, Jack | 8* | P-51D 44-13761/MC-O<br>*HAPPY JACK'S GO*<br>*BUGGY* |
| McKeon Joseph | 6* | P-51D 44-13992 /LC-C<br>*Regina Coeli III* |
| Price, Jack | 5* | P-51D 44-14693/LC-G<br>*Feather Merchant 5th* |

*\* Victories primarily scored with other units*

## 55th Fighter Group

| Name | score | personal aircraft (P-51s only) |
|---|---|---|
| Lewis, William | 8 | P-51D 44-13907/CY-S<br>P-51D 44-14907/CY-S |
| Cramer, Darrell | 7.5 | P-51D 44-14121/CL-Z<br>*Mick #5* |
| Righetti, Elwyn | 7.5 | P-51D 44-14223/CL-M<br>*KATYDID*<br>P-51D 44-72227/CL-M<br>*KATYDID* |

| Name | score | personal aircraft (P-51s only) |
|---|---|---|
| Landers, John | 14.5* | P-51D 44-13823/CG-O |
| | | *Big Beautiful Doll* |
| | | P-51D 44-72218/WZ-I |
| | | *Big Beautiful Doll* |
| | | P-51D 44-   /B6-? |
| | | *Big Beautiful Doll* |
| | | P-51D 44-72218/E2-I |
| | | *Big Beautiful Doll* |

\* Victories scored primarily with other units

## 78th Fighter Group

| Name | score | personal aircraft (P-51s only) |
|---|---|---|
| Brown, Quince | 12.34 | (P-47D only) |
| Jucheim, Aldwin | 10 | (P-47D only) |
| Roberts Jr, Eugene | 9 | P-51D 44-15061/5E-O |
| | | *Jimmie the First* |

## 339th Fighter Group

| Name | score | personal aircraft (P-51s only) |
|---|---|---|
| Bryan Jr, William | 8.5 | P-51D 44-13601/D7-J |
| | | P-51D 44-15074/D7-J |
| | | *Big Noise* |
| Gerard, Francis | 8 | P-51D 44-13808 /D7-U |
| | | *Yi Yi* |
| | | P-51D 44-150003/D7-U |
| Schafer Jr, Dale | 8 | P-51D 44-14671/D7-C |
| | | P-51D 44-72147/D7-C |

## 352nd Fighter Group

| Name | score | personal aircraft (P-51s only) |
|---|---|---|
| Preddy, George | 25.83 | P-51B 42-106451/HO-P |
| | | *CRIPES A'MIGHTY 2ND* |
| | | P-51D 44-13321 /HO-P |
| | | *CRIPES A' MIGHTY 3RD* |
| | | P-51D 44-14906 /PE-P |
| | | *CRIPES A' MIGHTY* |
| Meyer, John | 24 | P-51B 42-106471/HO-M |
| | | *Lambie II* |
| | | P-51D 44-14151 /HO-M |
| | | *PETIE 2ND* |
| | | P-51D 44-15041 /HO-M |
| | | *PETIE 3RD* |
| Thornell, John | 17.25 | P-51B 42-106872/PE-T |
| | | *PATTY ANN II* |
| Whisner, William | 16 | P-51B 42-106449/HO-W |
| | | *Princess ELIZABETH* |
| | | P-51D 44-14237 /HO-W |
| | | *Moonbeam McSWINE* |
| Bryan, Donald | 13.34 | P-51B 423-6894 /PE-B |
| | | *Little One II* |
| | | P-51D 44-14061 /PE-B |
| | | *Little One III* |

| Name | score | personal aircraft (P-51s only) |
|---|---|---|
| Moran, Glennon | 13 | P-51B 42-6912 /HO-M |
| | | P-51C 42-103320 /HO-M |
| | | *Little Ann* |
| | | P-51D 44-13320 /HO-M |
| Halton, William | 11.5 | P-51B 42-106717 /PE-T |
| | | *Slender, Tender and TALL* |
| | | P-51D 44-13966 /PE-T |
| | | *Slender, Tender and TALL* |
| | | P-51D 44-14812 /HO-T |
| | | *Slender, Tender and TALL* |
| | | P-51D 44-13557 / HO-T |
| | | *Slender, Tender and TALL* |
| Littge, Raymond | 10.5 | P-51C 42-103320/HO-M |
| | | *Pluribus Unum* |
| | | P-51D 44-13320 /HO-M |
| | | *Silver Dollar* |
| | | P-51D 44-72216 /HO-M |
| | | *Helen* |

## 353rd Fighter Group

| Name | score | personal aircraft (P-51s only) |
|---|---|---|
| Duncan Glenn | 19 | P-51D 44-73060 /LH-X |
| | | *Dove of Peace VIII* |
| | | (P-47D only) |
| Beckham, Walter | 18 | (P-47D only) |
| Blickenstaff, Wayne | 10 | P-51D 44-72374 /LH-U |
| | | *BETTY-E* |

## 355th Fighter Group

| Name | score | personal aircraft (P-51s only) |
|---|---|---|
| Brown, Henry | 17.2 | P-51B 42-106448/WR-Z |
| | | *Hun Hunter/Texas* |
| | | P-51D 44-13305 /WR-Z |
| | | *Hun Hunter/Texas* |
| Hovde, William | 10.5 | P-51B 43-6928 /YF-I |
| | | *OLE-II,* |
| | | P-51D 44-13531 /YF-I |
| | | *OLE-III,* |
| | | P-51D 44-   /YF-I |
| | | *OLE-IV,* |
| | | P-51D 44-73108 /YF-I |
| | | *OLE-V* |
| Havilland Jr, Fred | 9 | P-51D 44-14405/OS-H |
| | | *Barbara* |
| Elder, John | 8 | P-51B 42-106732/OS-R |
| | | *Moon* |
| | | P-51D 44-63633 /OS-R |
| | | *Moon* |
| Kinnard Jr, Clairborne | 8 | P-51B 43-6431 /WR-A |
| | | *Man O'War* |
| | | P-51D 44-15625 /WR-A |
| | | *MAN O'WAR* |

| Name | score | personal aircraft (P-51s only) |
|---|---|---|
| | | P-51D 44-73144 /WR-A |
| | | *Man O' War* |
| | | P-51D 44-14292 /QP-A |
| | | *Man O' War* |

## 356th Fighter Group

| Name | score | personal aircraft (P-51s only) |
|---|---|---|
| Strait, Don | 13.5 | P-51D 44-15152 /QI-T |
| | | *JERSEY JERK* |
| Scheible, Wilbur | 6 | P-51D 44-76457 /QI-Z |
| | | (44-10583) |
| Thwaites, David | 6 | (P-47D only) |

## 357th Fighter Group

| Name | score | personal aircraft (P-51s only) |
|---|---|---|
| Carson, Leonard | 18.5 | P-51D 44-13316 /G4-C |
| | | *Nooky Booky II* |
| | | P-51K 44-11622 /G4-C |
| | | *Nooky Booky IV* |
| England, John | 17.5 | P-51B 42-106462 /G4-H |
| | | *U'VE HAD IT!* |
| | | P-51D 44-13735 /G4-H |
| | | *U'VE HAD IT!* |
| | | P-51D 44-14709 /G4-H |
| | | *MISSOURI ARMADA* |
| Foy, Robert | 17 | P-51D 44-13712 /B6-V |
| | | *Reluctant Rebel* |
| | | P-51D 44-63621 /B6-V |
| | | *LITTLE SHRIMP* |
| Anderson, Clarence | 16.5 | P-51B 43-24824 /B6-S |
| | | *OLD CROW* |
| | | P-51D 44-14450 /B6-S |
| | | *OLD CROW* |
| Peterson, Richard | 15.5 | P-51B 43-6935 /C5-T |
| | | *Hurry Home Honey* |
| | | P-51D 44-13586 /C5-T |
| | | *Hurry Home Honey* |
| | | P-51D 44-14868 /C5-T |
| | | *Hurry Home Honey* |
| Bochkay, Don | 14.84 | P-51B 43-6933 /B6-F |
| | | *SPEEDBALL ALICE* |
| | | P-51D 44-15422 /B6-F |
| | | P-51D 44-72244 /B6-F |
| Kirla, John | 11.5 | P-51D 44-14624 /G4-H |
| | | *Spook* |
| | | P-51D 44-72180 /G4-H |
| | | *Spook* |
| Yeager, Charles | 11.5 | P-51B 43-74650 /B6-Y |
| | | *GLAMOROUS GLEN* |
| | | P-51D 44-13897 /B6-Y |
| | | *GLAMOROUS GLEN II* |
| | | P-51D 44-14888 /B6-Y |
| | | *GLAMOROUS GLEN III* |

| Name | score | personal aircraft (P-51s only) |
|---|---|---|
| Storch, John | 10.5 | P-51D 44-13546 /C5-R |
| | | *THE SHILLELAGH* |
| | | P-51D 44-72164 /C5-R |
| | | *THE SHILLELAGH* |
| Broadhead, Joseph | 10 | P-51B 43-12227 /G4-V |
| | | *Baby Mike* |
| | | P-51D 44-14798 /G4-V |
| | | *Master Mike* |

## 359th Fighter Group

| Name | score | personal aircraft (P-51s only) |
|---|---|---|
| Wetmore, Ray | 21.25 | P-51B 42-106894 /CS-P |
| | | P-51D 44-14733 /CS-L |
| | | *Daddy's Girl* |
| Doersch, George | 10.5 | P-51B 43-24810 /CS-J |
| | | P-51D 44-72067 /CV-R |
| Booth, Robert | 8 | P-51B 43-6757 /IV-F; |
| | | P-51D 43-7199 /IV-F |
| Crenshaw, Claude | 7 | P-51B 42-106689 /IV-S |
| | | P-51D 44-13606 /IV-I |
| | | *LOUISIANA HEAT WAVE* |
| | | P-51D 44-15016 /IV-I |
| | | *HEATWAVE* |

## 361st Fighter Group

| Name | score | personal aircraft (P-51s only) |
|---|---|---|
| Spencer, Dale | 9.5 | P-51B 43-24808 /E9-D |
| | | P-51D 44-14217 /E9-D |
| Beyer, William | 9 | P-51D 44-14144 /E9-N |
| Drew, Urban | 6 | P-51D 44-14164 /E2-D |
| | | *DETROIT Miss* |
| Hopkins, Wallace | 6 | P-51B 42-106655 /B7-H |
| | | *Ferocious Frankie* |
| | | P-51D 44-13704 /B7-H |
| | | *Ferocious Frankie* |
| Kemp, William | 6 | P-51C 42-103749 /E2-X |
| | | *Betty Lee/Marie* |
| | | P-51D 44-14270 /E2-X |
| | | *Betty Lee II* |
| | | P-51D 44-15076 /E2-X |
| | | *Betty Lee III* |

## 364th Fighter Group

| Name | score | personal aircraft (P-51s only) |
|---|---|---|
| Cueleers, George | 10.5 | P-51D 44-13971 /N2-D |
| | | P-51D 44-15020 /N2-D |
| | | P-51D 44-72719 /N2-D |
| | | *Constance* |
| Bankey Jr, Ernest | 9.5 | P-51D 44-15019 /5E-B |
| | | P-51D 44-73045 /5E-B |
| | | *Lucky Lady VII* |

| Name | score | personal aircraft (P-51s only) |
|------|-------|-------------------------------|
| Fowle, James | 8 | P-51D 44-13829 /5Y-J<br>*Terrie Claire*<br>P-51D 44-14184 /5Y-Q<br>*Terrie Claire III* |

## 479th Fighter Group

| Name | score | personal aircraft (P-51s only) |
|------|-------|-------------------------------|
| Jeffrey, Arthur | 14 | P-51D 44-14423 /L2-O<br>*BOOMERANG JR.*<br>P-51D 44-11674 /L2-O<br>*BOOMERANG JR.* |
| Olds, Robin | 13 | P-51D 44-  /L2-W<br>*SCAT IV*<br>P-51D 44-14426/L2-W<br>*SCAT V*<br>P-51D 44-72922/L2-W<br>*SCAT VI*<br>P-51D 44-72922/L2-W<br>*SCAT VII* |
| Gleason, George | 12 | P-51D 44-14740/L2-H<br>*Hot Toddy* |
| Candelaria, Richard | 6 | P-51K 44-1175/J2-K<br>*My Pride and Joy* |

# RATIO OF KILLS TO LOSSES GROUP BY GROUP

**Eighth AF Fighter Groups – aerial kill ratio to losses (all types of fighters flown)**

| Ranking | Group | Kills | Losses |
|---------|-------|-------|--------|
| 1 | 56th | 674 | 128 |
| 2 | 357th | 609 | 128 |
| 3 | 4th | 583 | 241 |
| 4 | 352nd | 519 | 118 |
| 5 | 355th | 365 | 175 |
| 6 | 78th | 338 | 167 |
| 7 | 353rd | 330 | 137 |
| 8 | 55th | 316 | 181 |
| 9 | 364th | 256 | 134 |
| 10 | 359th | 253 | 106 |
| 11 | 339th | 239 | 97 |
| 12 | 361st | 226 | 81 |
| 13 | 20th | 212 | 132 |
| 14 | 356th | 201 | 122 |
| 15 | 479th | 155 | 69 |
| **Totals:** | | **5276\*** | **2016** |

\*2.75 enemy aircraft destroyed for every fighter lost

---

# SPECIFICATIONS

### P-51B Mustang
*Type:* single-seat, long-range escort fighter
*Armament:* four Colt-Browning M2 .50 in machine guns with total capacity of 1260 rounds; capable of carrying a single 500-lb bomb under each wing for ground attack missions
*Powerplant:* one Rolls-Royce (Packard) Merlin liquid-cooled V-1650-7 engine developing 1330 hp for take-off
*Dimensions:* span 37 ft; length 32 ft 3 in; height 12 ft 2 in
*Weights:* max loaded 11,800 lbs; empty 7010 lbs
*Performance:* max speed 440 mph; cruising speed 362 mph: service ceiling 41,800 ft; range 880 miles (with 2 x 75-gal drop tanks)

### P-51D Mustang
*Type:* single-seat, long-range escort fighter
*Armament:* six Colt-Browning M2 .50-in machine guns with total capacity of 1000 rounds; external stores up to 1000 lbs of bombs or 6 x High Velocity Aerial Rockets (HVARs)
*Powerplant:* one Rolls-Royce (Packard) Merlin liquid-cooled V-1650-7 engine developing 1490 hp for take-off
*Dimensions:* span 37 ft; length 32 ft 3 in; height 12 ft 2 in
*Weights:* max loaded 12,100 lbs; empty 7635 lbs
*Performance:* max speed 437 mph; cruising speed 362 mph; service ceiling 30,000 ft; range 1000 miles with 2 x 110-gal drop tanks

# INDEX

References to illustrations are shown in **bold**. Colour plates and Figure plates are prefixed 'pl.' and 'fig. pl.', with page numbers and caption locators in brackets.